FOURTH EDITION

HUMAN RESOURCES MANAGEMENT FOR EFFECTIVE SCHOOLS

JOHN T. SEYFARTH

Virginia Commonwealth University

Boston   New York   San Francisco
Mexico City   Montreal   Toronto   London   Madrid   Munich   Paris
Hong Kong   Singapore   Tokyo   Cape Town   Sydney

Executive Editor: *Arnis E. Burvikovs*
Editorial Assistant: *Megan Smallidge*
Marketing Manager: *Tara Whorf*
Editorial-Production Service: *Chestnut Hill Enterprises, Inc.*
Manufacturing Buyer: *Andrew Turso*
Cover Administrator: *Kristina Mose-Libon*
Electronic Composition: *Omegatype Typography, Inc.*

For related titles and support materials, visit our online catalog at www.ablongman.com.

Between the time Website information is gathered and then published, some sites may have closed. Also, the transcription of URLs can result in typographical errors. The publisher would appreciate being notified of any problems with URLs so that they may be corrected in subsequent editions.

Library of Congress Cataloging-in-Publication Data

Seyfarth, John T.
    Human resources management for effective schools / John T. Seyfarth. — 4th ed.
      p. cm.
    Includes bibliographical references and index.
    ISBN 0-205-41276-9 (alk. paper)
    1. School personnel management—United States.   2. School management and
organization—United States.   I. Title.

    LB2831.5.S46 2005
    371.2'01'0973—dc22

2004013031

Printed in the United States of America
10 9 8 7 6 5 4 3   09 08 07 06 05

To Susie and Chuck

CONTENTS

CHAPTER THREE

Preparing for Personnel Selection   31

CHAPTER FOUR

Obtaining Information and Evaluating Applicants   46

CHAPTER FIVE

Selecting Administrative and Support Personnel   68

CHAPTER SIX

Motivation of Personnel   93

CHAPTER SEVEN

Induction   113

CHAPTER EIGHT

Professional Development for Educational Personnel   130

CHAPTER NINE

Evaluating Employee Performance   153

CHAPTER TEN

Compensation and Rewards   176

CHAPTER THIRTEEN

Collective Bargaining in Schools   234

PREFACE

Human resources management is an essential administrative function in all types of human services organizations; the tasks carried out by the personnel in these units, when performed properly, help organizations to accomplish their mission. A school district's success in attracting, selecting, and retaining good teachers determines whether it will be able to improve student achievement and prepare young people to lead responsible and productive lives as adults.

Effective human resources management requires staff members who understand the importance of their assignment and who are aware of the connection between what they do and how much and how well students learn. These staff members must understand the processes involved in administering a human resources program and be prepared to search for and adopt practices that work well in their districts.

Increasingly, governments are mandating accountability in schools and applying sanctions to the schools that fail to meet the standards established by policymakers. Human resources administrators thus operate in settings in which standards are high and the price of failing to meet the standards is costly. Thorough and comprehensive preparation is necessary in order for these administrators to perform their jobs successfully. This book is written for the purpose of helping to accomplish that result.

Since the publication of the third edition of *Human Resources Management for Effective Schools,* a number of new developments have helped to emphasize again the crucial role of human resources management in schools. The most far-reaching of these changes is the passage of No Child Left Behind, the controversial legislation that brought new language to discussions about human resources management, including such phrases as "highly qualified" and "adequate yearly progress," and introduced sanctions for schools in which students fail to register learning gains. It is not yet clear what impact this legislation will have on school practice, but it promises to be extensive. No Child Left Behind is discussed in several chapters in this fourth edition.

Among other new developments since the third edition appeared are court decisions favoring employees who have brought legal action under the Fair Labor Standards Act claiming they are owed backpay for overtime work. In some cases these decisions have meant that employers must pay large lump sum settlements for work performed over a number of years. The potential impact of this trend on school districts is considerable. This development is reported in Chapter 10.

Chapter 4 has been reorganized to provide new information on the use of data on personal motivation for teacher selection. People choose jobs that promise to allow them to find expression for internal motivations such as the desire to be creative, exercise influence, or perform a socially significant service. Research has shown that information on internal motivators can help improve the accuracy of predictions about which applicants will be effective teachers. The chapter suggests questions that can be used by interviewers to identify an applicant's motivators.

A new feature of Chapter 9 is a glossary of evaluation terms that helps clarify the distinction among such terms as *assessment, appraisal, rubric, rating,* and *scale*. The need for more precise and accurate measures of teacher performance has been obvious for some time, and the development of a more precise vocabulary is a first step toward reaching that goal.

The Online Resources section at the end of each chapter has been expanded to include many more of the Internet sites that provide information of value in human resources management. Also, chapter references have been updated in the fourth edition, and new suggested activities have been introduced throughout the book. Six new case studies are also included in this edition.

Supplemental material for this text is available online at the Allyn and Bacon website: www.ablongman.com/edleadership. This site provides links to many useful sites, chapter objectives, test questions, and activities.

ACKNOWLEDGMENTS

I am indebted to the students, colleagues, and practitioners whose experiences and insights I have drawn on in writing this book. I wish also to thank my reviewers, whose comments and suggestions helped to make this a better book: Michael Cunningham, Marshall University; Ann Hassenpflug, University of Akron; David Husley, University of West Georgia; Gayla H. Lawson, University of Houston, Victoria; and Rosa Weaver, Northern Kentucky University.

John T. Seyfarth
Richmond, Virginia

CHAPTER ONE

HUMAN RESOURCES MANAGEMENT AND EFFECTIVE SCHOOLS

This book is about managing people in schools. Its objective is to make prospective and practicing school administrators aware of the wide range of activities covered by the term *human resources management* and to present the best of current practice in personnel work. Effective personnel practices are prerequisite to bringing about improved student learning, and all decisions relating to selection, placement, evaluation, development, promotion, and termination of employees should be made with that outcome in mind.

School administrators whose responsibilities include any aspect of human resources management will be interested in this book. All of the activities of personnel department staff members involve personnel management, and many of the duties of principals and assistant principals also fall under that heading. When a principal interviews an applicant for a secretarial position, plans a professional development program for faculty, or evaluates a counselor's performance, he or she is engaging in human resources management. The importance of the principal's role in human resources decision making is increasing as school districts move toward wider implementation of site-based management and decentralization of responsibility for some personnel decisions to the school level.

Most personnel decisions have either a direct or indirect impact on the quality of instruction. When a decision is made to employ a teacher, counselor, or aide, when a new personnel evaluation procedure is implemented, or when a compensation plan is adopted, there are likely to be implications for the quality of instruction. The potential impact of personnel decisions on instruction should be taken into account at the time these decisions are made. Our knowledge of teaching and learning is not yet extensive enough that we can always predict with a high degree of confidence what effects such decisions will have. However, as a result of advances in research on teaching, we are able to make these decisions now with much more confidence than was possible even a few years ago.

PLAN OF THE CHAPTER

This chapter reviews the efforts made to improve American schools over the past twenty-five years and includes a discussion of No Child Left Behind, the far-reaching and controversial federal law that created stringent new accountability requirements for school personnel. Chapter One also presents a model of student learning that shows how human resources functions contribute to student growth and learning. This chapter also discusses organizational effectiveness and shows how our views of effective schools change over time. All of the chapters in the book include a list of online references, and all chapters except this one feature Suggested Activities.

This book rests on three assumptions. The first assumption is that identifying applicants who will be effective teachers requires considerable knowledge and skill. Those who say "I know a good teacher when I see one," imply that choosing good teachers is easy, but the fact is that predicting which applicants will be successful in the classroom requires a good deal of knowledge and skill, and even some luck.

The second assumption is that individuals who are average or even below-average performers in their first few years in the classroom can develop over time into effective and caring teachers. Why is this so? In part, it is the result of their determination to do a better job, but it is also due to the support they receive from other teachers and administrators with whom they work.

The third assumption is that identifying good prospects for teaching assignments is not enough in itself to ensure an effective instructional program. Principals and other teachers must work together to produce conditions in schools that promote teacher efficacy and student learning.

HUMAN RESOURCES MANAGERS

All school administrators are, in a sense, human resource managers, because their work involves supervising employees. The tasks performed by these administrators are vital to achieving improved learning results in schools. These tasks include identifying and recruiting qualified candidates, diagnosing and helping to correct performance problems, improving employee knowledge and skill, and retaining competent employees (Chambers, 2001). If these functions are not performed in a timely and highly effective manner, it will be impossible to achieve the district's goals for student achievement.

When a school district lacks administrators who can perform the human resources management functions in a timely and effective manner, a number of undesirable results ensue. The quality of classroom instruction varies randomly, with some students being exposed to well-qualified and effective teachers while others are taught by individuals who lack critical skills. Innovation becomes problematic because instructional staff members are not helped to master new content or implement new methods or adopt new technologies. Staff morale suffers, and employee turnover increases. Higher turnover means that higher costs are incurred in finding replacements for the employees who leave. To avoid these kinds of problems, district-level administrators must make a commitment to develop administrators with superb human resources management skills. This must be a high priority for districts that are committed to improving student achievement.

All of the functions involved in human resources management should make a contribution, either directly or indirectly, to student learning. If any function is not currently helping to enhance student knowledge, it should be redesigned in such a way that it will do so.

The key to student academic achievement is the teacher. Good teachers help students learn while they are in their classrooms, but the beneficial effects of good teaching continue after the students have moved on. Researchers have found that children who were taught by a good third-grade teacher continued to show above-average achievement gains in the fourth and fifth grades. The beneficial effects from repeated exposure to effective teachers are compounded. Students who have three strong teachers in a row attain achievement test scores that are 50 percentile points greater on average than the scores of students who are taught by three ineffective teachers in a row (Loeb, 2001). Thus, it is important that school systems set a goal of placing an effective teacher in every classroom, but to ensure that students learn they must do more than simply hire competent personnel. School districts must also ensure that the culture and working conditions in schools support and facilitate teachers' work.

MODEL OF STUDENT LEARNING

Figure 1.1 depicts a model of student learning showing how the human resources management functions contribute to student achievement. The heart of the model is the link between teacher behavior, student effort, and student learning. Two human resources management functions (performance evaluation and professional development) act directly to influence teachers' behavior in the classroom. Through professional development teachers learn new methods of teaching and become familiar with new material and technologies. Evaluation provides feedback that helps teachers improve their performance.

Ideally, these activities occur within a work environment that reflects a mission and culture that are characterized by administrative support and by the availability of adequate compensation and rewards, high-quality induction programs, and the use of appropriate conflict-management strategies. When these elements are in place and operating effectively, an environment is created that facilitates teachers' work and enhances student learning.

The search for ways to improve student performance began in earnest in the early 1980s, after the National Commission on Excellence in Education (1983) warned that poor-quality schools were a threat to the nation's security. That warning prompted actions by the federal government and the various states to improve

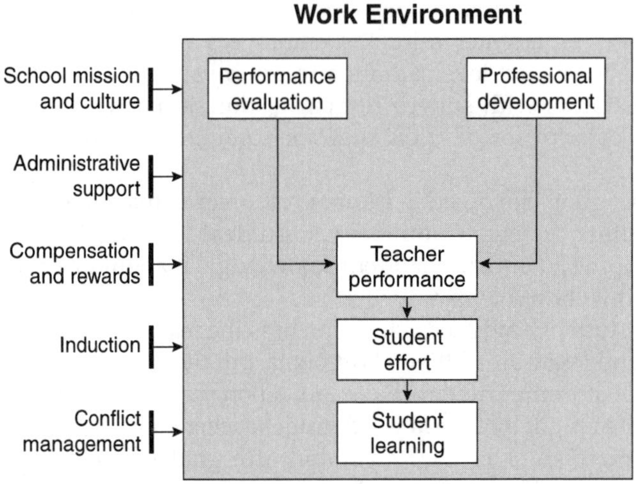

Work Environment

School mission and culture → | Performance evaluation | | Professional development |

Administrative support →

Compensation and rewards → | Teacher performance |

Induction → | Student effort |

Conflict management → | Student learning |

FIGURE 1.1   **Relationship of Human Resources Functions to Student Learning**

the quality of instruction in American schools. A number of states established standards for student achievement and began requiring standardized tests in core subject areas to track students' progress toward achievement of the new standards. The states also instituted tougher regulations over teacher certification, adopted revised procedures for teacher evaluation, and reduced class sizes in the early grades and in critical subjects such as English. Recent research indicates that these efforts have begun to pay off.

According to data from the National Assessment of Educational Progress (NAEP), student scores in mathematics rose between 2000 and 2003, with 31 percent of fourth-grade students and 27 percent of eighth graders reaching the "proficient" level of performance in 2003, up from the 22 percent of fourth graders and 25 percent of eighth graders who scored at that level three years earlier. In reading, 24 percent of fourth graders attained the proficient level in 2003, the same percentage as 2002. Twenty-nine percent of eighth graders were proficient in reading in 2003, down from 30 percent one year earlier.

The initial analysis of these data suggested that providing additional instructional resources to teachers had contributed to the improvement in test scores and that implementing even modest increases in support for schools serving children from low-income families also helped. Reductions in class size, especially in prekindergarten and the early grades, were also associated with improved student performance (Grissmer, Flanagan, Kawata, & Williamson, 2000; Manzo & Galley, 2003; Smith, Molnar, & Zahorik, 2003).

Smaller classes and more funding for instructional materials both contribute to teachers' feelings of efficacy, which may account, at least in part, for the observed improvements. The researchers found that providing additional instructional materials to teachers or hiring more teachers in order to reduce class size had a more beneficial effect on achievement than increasing teachers' salaries (Grissmer, et al., 2000).

According to some researchers, teachers' salaries have no relationship to student achievement. Hanushek (2001, p. 175) stated "there is virtually no relationship between teacher salaries and student achievement." However, there is agreement that the quality of teachers in low-income and inner-city schools is below that in some suburban localities (Lankford, Loeb, & Wyckoff, 2002). These discrepancies in quality can be addressed by adjusting salaries to compensate for the competitive disadvantages in teacher recruitment experienced by schools with low student achievement.

Our knowledge of ways of allocating resources optimally for the improvement of student learning is very limited. We do not know, for example, whether funds devoted to purchasing instructional materials result in a one-time-only boost to student achievement or if those benefits are ongoing and cumulative. Neither do we know whether the gains to student achievement from the purchase of instructional materials are subject-specific.

Policymakers and administrators need to know more about how to combine resources to achieve synergy. Are additional instructional materials alone a better investment in student learning than providing professional development programs for teachers? Or, if some combination of new materials and training is ideal, what percentage of the total expenditures should go to each? Also, it would be helpful to know which teachers (beginning, mid-career, or experienced) are most likely to benefit from professional development opportunities. There are logical arguments to be made for each level, but little empirical evidence to support any of these arguments.

As state-sponsored experiments with new approaches to school improvement have continued, a picture has emerged of ideal practices that should be part of school reform. Thompson (2003) depicted what he called a high-performance school system with eight features that have been shown to contribute to increasing student achievement. The eight are described in the paragraphs that follow.

Standards-based. Challenging standards define what students should know and be able to do at each level.

Clear mission. The high-performance system adopts as its mission to enable all students to meet challenging standards and develops policies and procedures for managing budgets and human resources that contribute to that goal.

School climate. Schools and district offices maintain nurturing, supportive, respectful relationships with students, parents, and others.

Assessment. High-performance districts assess school performance and use the results to provide prompt and targeted assistance to schools that need help.

Professional development. Ongoing, high-quality professional development opportunities designed to help achieve the district mission are provided for all employees in these districts.

Resources. Resources, including personnel, funds, time, and material, are distributed in such a way as to support powerful instructional practices in all schools.

Data collection. Schools are seeking assistance in analyzing, organizing, and interpreting data for the purpose of making program improvements (Lafee, 2002). This process is referred to as data-driven decision making and is defined as the process of selecting, gathering, and analyzing data to identify instructional or student achievement problems and acting on those findings (Streifer, 2002).

Communications. High-performance districts communicate frequently with patrons and other internal and external stakeholders to keep them abreast of the schools' performance and to invite their participation in decisions about school programs.

NO CHILD LEFT BEHIND

Congress borrowed many ideas that states had pioneered when it reauthorized the Elementary and Secondary Education Act of 2002, better known as No Child Left Behind (NCLB). The model of accountability embodied in that legislation uses student outcomes as a measure of teacher performance and organizational adaptability, features public reporting of school performance, and focuses on schools rather than districts or states as the basic unit of accountability (O'Day, 2002). Under NCLB, average test scores are used to determine whether schools are making Adequate Yearly Progress (AYP) in raising student achievement. Schools that fail to make AYP on their state's achievement tests will be identified as needing improvement, even if they do not receive federal funds. Scores on the requisite tests will be reported by ethnic and racial classifications, special education status, and by English proficiency; unless all groups show progress, the school can be classified as needing improvement (Renter & Hamilton, 2003).

NCLB provides that Title I schools that do not make AYP for two consecutive years must allow students who choose to do so to transfer to another public school or public charter school in the same district that is not classified as needing improvement. After three years of failing to make AYP, a Title I school must offer supplemental educational services to low-income students after school, during the summer, or on weekends (Renter & Hamilton, 2003).

NCLB also requires that every classroom have a "highly qualified" teacher; the definition of *highly qualified* in the legislation refers to holding a college degree and full teacher certification, along with evidence that the teacher knows the subject he or she teaches. Knowing one's subject does not require a degree in the subject, since passing a state-approved test is also acceptable. The states are free to add additional requirements to the definition of "highly qualified," although it is unlikely many will choose to do so because increasing the requirements will make it more difficult to attract teachers, especially in shortage areas (Walsh, 2003).

NCLB has been the subject of much criticism because of its reliance on standardized tests as the sole indicators of student performance and, hence, of school success. One of the most frequent complaints about the use of standardized tests for accountability purposes is that this use leads to an overemphasis on raising test scores and results in a narrowed curriculum. Koretz (2002) had that charge, among others, in mind when he wrote that

> overly simplistic reliance on achievement tests in accountability systems can produce perverse incentives and seriously inflated estimates of gains in student performance (p. 753).

The "perverse incentives" Koretz (2002) refers to include the temptation for teachers to "teach to the test," which can have the effect of producing impressive-appearing gains in test scores even though students' actual understanding of the domain of knowledge on which they were tested has improved little. When teachers teach to the test, they spend a disproportionate amount of time on tested content and neglect other subject matter. Indeed, Koretz cited research from Kentucky showing that fourth-grade teachers in that state, whose students were tested on science, spent more time teaching that subject and less time teaching mathematics, whereas in the fifth grade, where students were tested on mathematics and not science, the opposite effect occurred.

Critics of the use of standardized test results for accountability charge that, in addition to narrowing the curriculum, the practice diverts time from instruction to allow time to prepare students to take the tests and creates dilemmas for teachers arising from feelings of incompetence, anger, and, in some cases, guilt (Leithwood, 2001).

The use of test scores as the sole indicator of school performance is also criticized for neglecting a wide range of other types of student knowledge, skills, and dispositions that are equal in value to the skills measured by standardized tests. Some educators have expressed concern that the attention to accountability and reliance on student achievement data in assessing schools' performance is forcing schools to neglect other equally important student outcomes, including the socioemotional aspects of children's development (Allen, 2003).

Sirotnik (2002) noted that parents "demand . . . that future citizens develop intellectually well beyond 'the basics' " and identified some of the performances that are neglected by the accountability system mandated by NCLB.

> A responsible accountability system will include many forms of assessment that tap directly into the actual performances that students are expected to demonstrate, [including] reading, writing, speaking, problem solving, experimenting, inquiring, creating, persisting, deliberating, [and] collaborating . . . (p. 666).

School Decentralization

The warning by the National Commission on Excellence in Education (1983) that poor-quality schools were a threat to the nation's security prompted efforts by the policymakers to change the highly centralized structure of school districts in order to permit more involvement by principals and teachers in decisions about instruction. Decentralization and school-based management were two of the structural reforms that were adopted in an effort to improve the quality of instruction.

Two types of decentralization were tried. Horizontal decentralization occurs when authority is distributed more widely within the district office. Assistant superintendents, supervisors, coordinators, and other specialists assume increased responsibility for specific decisions. Rather than confer only with the director of instruction when considering instructional changes, a principal might also meet with several content specialists. In vertical decentralization, authority is moved downward, so that decisions that previously were made at the top of the ladder are delegated to individuals holding positions at middle and even lower levels of the organizational structure. School-based management is an example of vertical decentralization (Brown, 1991).

The assumption behind vertical decentralization is that staff members in the schools understand students' problems and needs and are in a better position to make correct decisions about the use of resources than district staff members. Decentralization frees educators at the school site to take initiative to create effective responses to the educational needs of students (Martin, 1993). Administrators become facilitators, and other staff members' roles are expanded to include policy making and governance (Milstein, 1993).

Decentralization is not easily accomplished, and it entails costs as well as benefits. It requires district-level staff members to change the way they view their roles and it requires them to adopt a service orientation. Such a change is likely to be resisted, since many who are affected by decentralization struggled to attain their positions and are unwilling to surrender their authority and influence easily (Wissler & Ortiz, 1988).

Advocates of downward decentralization argue that administrators should delegate decisions about instructional methods and procedures to teachers since "no one knows better how to do a job than the person who does it." However, that statement is only true when workers are well informed about the relative advantages and disadvantages of alternative ways of performing a job. For that reason, redesigning jobs to permit jobholders to make decisions about work methods should be accompanied by staff development programs to prepare individuals to exercise that responsibility wisely (Lawler & Mohrman, 1991).

For all of the potential problems, there is general agreement that vertical decentralization can help reduce the bureaucratic control that many feel intensifies the problems of the schools. That has led to the introduction of school-based management, an arrangement that entails delegating authority over certain decisions to teachers and administrators in the schools.

School-Based Management

Almost one-fourth of school districts responding to a nationwide survey in 1989 reported they had adopted school-based management (SBM), and an additional one-fourth were considering doing so (Prasch, 1990). A more recent National Education Association (1991) survey showed that about 30 percent of local association presidents who responded reported that the districts in which they worked had some form of SBM.

School-based management constitutes a significant departure from the bureaucratized, centralized system of school governance that emerged during the Progressive Era in the United States (Snauwaert, 1993). For the first seven decades of the twentieth century, schools and school districts were consolidated into fewer and fewer units. The number of school districts dropped from 128,000 in 1932 to 15,000 in 1990, and the number of public elementary schools fell from 233,000 in 1932 to 44,000 in 1991 (*Historical Statistics,* 1975; McDowell, 1993).

The move toward fewer and larger districts and schools was undertaken primarily for reasons of efficiency, and although the residents of many communities were unhappy to see their schools closed, they agreed to the restructuring because of promised benefits for students. Many students had to travel great distances to school after consolidation took place, but the schools they attended were larger and better equipped, the teachers were better trained, and programs were more comprehensive than those in the schools they left.

However, consolidation had disadvantages as well as advantages. It increased the influence of educational bureaucracies, encouraged lack of responsiveness, and hampered accountability. School-based management has been proposed as a remedy for the dysfunctional features of centralized school bureaucracies. It is promoted as a way of increasing flexibility, accountability, and productivity in schools (Brown, 1991). One superintendent described SBM as goal driven, needs responsive, results oriented, and teamwork/group operationalized (Prasch, 1990).

Under SBM, decisions that have traditionally been made by district office administrators are delegated to school councils or committees. Part of the appeal of SBM is the belief that it restores the essential mission of schools—instruction of students—to the center of educators' attention and it conveys a philosophy that all other activities of the district exist to support that mission (Prasch, 1990).

Features of SBM. Among the defining features of SBM plans are site-based budgeting to allow alternative uses of resources; governance committees composed of teachers, parents, and community members; increased autonomy in choice of staffing configurations and selection of personnel; power to modify the school's curriculum to serve specific needs of students; a process for obtaining waivers of local or state regulations; and an expectation for an annual report on progress and school improvement (Cawelti, 1989). Not all plans incorporate all of these features, but a school must have some of them in order to be considered an SBM school.

Districts differ in the types of services they choose to decentralize. Some districts delegate decisions about particular parts of the budget but not about personnel or curriculum; some decentralize certain aspects of the curriculum; and others decentralize other decision areas. Other services are usually handled centrally. Purchasing is normally centralized, but teachers are encouraged to participate in decisions about the types of instructional materials and equipment to be purchased. Some experts recommend centralizing payroll, legal services, transportation, and food services (Prasch, 1990).

Site-based management frequently involves decentralization of the services provided by instructional coordinators and subject specialists. These individuals may be called on to provide help with staff development and training or to assist teachers with instructional or management problems. In some cases, schools that use these services pay a fee for them (Brown, 1991).

Advantages of SBM.   A number of advantages and disadvantages of SBM have been identified. The claimed advantages include better programs for students; full use of human resources; higher-quality decisions; increased staff professionalism, satisfaction, loyalty, and commitment; development of staff leadership skills; clear organizational goals; improved communication; support for staff creativity and innovation; greater public confidence; enhanced fiscal accountability; and higher student achievement (David, 1989; Prasch, 1990).

Benefits from site-based decision making cited by respondents to the National Education Association (1991) survey were increased involvement of employees in decisions and improved coordination of programs and activities within schools. One local president cited as a benefit the fact that all participants come to meetings as equals. Others indicated that trust among teachers, parents, and administrators had risen, lines of communication had opened, and morale had improved. "Because more people have access to the decision-making apparatus, there is more room for new initiatives and addressing problems," according to one association president (National Education Association, 1991, p. 17).

An advantage of SBM that is mentioned more often than any other is increased flexibility in use of resources. In Cincinnati, instructional leadership teams in 14 elementary schools decided to eliminate the position of librarian and hire an additional teacher instead. An assistant superintendent in the district noted that schools are legally required to have teachers but that decisions about hiring other support staff are made by each school (www.slj.com/article/news/19991018_6625.asp).

Disadvantages of SBM.   Disadvantages of SBM mentioned most frequently include increased workloads for teachers and administrators, less efficiency, diluted benefits of specialization, uneven school performance, greater need for staff development, possible confusion about new roles and responsibilities, and coordination difficulties (Prasch, 1990).

A common complaint about SBM is that the planning process is highly time consuming, particularly during the first year of implementation (Brown, 1991). As a result, some teachers choose not to participate. They believe that the amount of time devoted to the tasks associated with site-based decision-making projects lessens their instructional effectiveness (National Education Association, 1991; Chapman, 1990).

ORGANIZATIONAL EFFECTIVENESS

A persistent dilemma for organizations is managing the factors that influence performance in such a way that employees are able to make progress toward attaining the organization's goals. Performance is influenced by three factors: employee knowledge and ability, employee motivation, and the environment of the workplace. When those factors are satisfactory—that is, when employees have the knowledge and ability to perform their jobs and are motivated to do their jobs well, and when the work environment facilitates employees' efforts—then superior results are likely to be achieved and the organization will be regarded as effective (Rowan, 1996). Many characteristics and outcomes have been used as indicators of organizational effectiveness, including productivity, efficiency, profit, accidents, employee absenteeism, turnover, job satisfaction, and evaluations by external entities (Campbell, 1977). Ratings of the effectiveness of schools are usually based on efficiency, equality, quality, or, more recently, accountability (Glasman, 1986).

Taxpayers' organizations and political leaders demand efficiency in use of resources; civil rights groups and parents argue for equality; and parents and employers who hire the schools' graduates seek quality. The insistence by political leaders on greater accountability for schools came about as a result of their perception that, although appropriations for schools had continued to rise, student performance remained flat or fell. These leaders began to demand a quid pro quo agreement that the schools would produce increased student achievement in return for additional revenues for the schools. NCLB was a direct outgrowth of this demand for accountability.

Efficiency as a Goal

Efficiency was the dominant theme in school administration during the early years of the twentieth century, when the new profession of educational administration was charged with the task of preparing the schools to accommodate a flood of students from immigrant families. Pressed by rapidly rising enrollments and limited resources, administrators turned to the corporate world to find ways to accomplish the task they had been assigned. From industry they borrowed the spirit, if not the methods, of scientific management. Efficiency continued to be emphasized in schools until the emergence of the human relations movement helped to achieve balance in the schools during the 1930s.

Equality as a Goal

The emphasis on equality came into prominence with the U.S. Supreme Court's decision ruling that segregated schools violated the constitutional rights of minorities (*Brown* v. *Board of Education,* 1954, 1955). Interest in equality of educational opportunity broadened during the 1970s to include not only racial minorities and females but also students with mental and physical disabilities. The Education for

All Handicapped Children Act mandated far-reaching changes in programs serving people with disabilities; it also required expansion of services and added safeguards to protect procedural rights of students.

Quality as a Goal

Quality of school programs is an issue that has received periodic attention from citizens and legislators, often in connection with national crises. The National Commission on Excellence in Education (1983) aroused the nation's concern when it declared that the United States was threatened by a rising tide of mediocrity as a result of the deteriorating quality of education. The Commission's report was one of many such studies that appeared about that time and that sounded similar themes.

These concerns led to an energetic effort to identify teaching techniques that would result in reliable increases in student achievement through research. The idea was to discover the techniques that successful teachers had figured out on their own and that other teachers could adopt and that would result in steady gains in student achievement. This body of research was known as process-product research, and it was aimed at identifying teaching strategies that consistently produced increased student achievement without regard to the content being taught or the ages of the students.

The term *direct instruction* is the name given to the model of instruction that emerged from the process-product research. Direct instruction consists of a series of teacher-directed activities, beginning with review, followed by presentation, guided practice, feedback, and independent practice (Rosenshine & Meister, 1995).

Although process-product research enhanced our understanding of some of the factors that contribute to student achievement and disproved the claim that schools made no difference and that student achievement was solely attributable to students' IQ and family factors, it nevertheless left many questions unanswered. Most of the research was carried out in urban elementary schools, and it was not clear if similar results would have been obtained had the studies had been conducted in rural areas or in middle or high schools.

Concerns also arose about uncritical acceptance of the findings of the process-product studies. Most of the studies relied on correlational statistics, which show whether two variables are related in some systematic way. For example, a correlation might show whether reducing class size is associated with increased student achievement (a negative correlation) or if lengthening the school day is accompanied by higher achievement (a positive correlation). The problem with this approach is that correlations cannot be used to establish cause and effect. Does reducing class size actually produce increased achievement, or does some unnamed intervening factor lead to the learning gain? Correlational studies cannot answer such questions.

Some critics charged that the definition of *effectiveness* used in the process-product research was too narrow. Typically, process-product studies compared the behavior of teachers whose students attained above-average learning gains with those of teachers whose students had lower or no gains. Learning gains were measured by test scores, while other important outcomes such as good citizenship and demonstrated leadership were ignored.

The hope that process-product research would lead to a prescription for school improvement was not realized. Although the studies identified certain teaching behaviors that had an effect on student learning, the research did not make clear the conditions under which those behaviors were most likely to produce positive results, nor did they show administrators how to help teachers acquire those behaviors. The research was incomplete in that respect.

Accountability

Many educators acknowledge that the public has a right to expect schools to be accountable, and they agree that schools have often failed to be as open and responsive as they could have been. Being accountable means that the public is given access to information about how each school is performing and, when a school is performing poorly, action is taken to identify and correct the causes of poor performance (Raywid, 2002). Accountability legislation enacted by the various states and by Congress in NCLB prescribes that schools will be evaluated on how well students perform on tests that measure their knowledge of prescribed outcomes. What is new is not the use of tests to measure students' knowledge; that practice has been common for many years. What is different is the use of these tests to rank schools and determine penalties for the schools in which students are not making adequate progress.

SUMMARY

Human resources management has a direct impact on schools' instructional effectiveness by decisions about recruitment, selection, induction, evaluation, and development of instructional staff members. The effectiveness of schools is determined by student achievement, following learning standards developed by the states, as measured by standardized tests. Process-product research led to extensive reforms in teaching practices in schools. Later, state-developed achievement standards were introduced and attention focused on ways of decentralizing decision making and involving more people at the school level in decisions that affect student learning. *School-based management* is the term used for the practice of allowing teachers, administrators, and parents to make certain decisions about allocation of human and material resources.

ONLINE RESOURCES

American Association of School Administrators
(www.aasa.org/issues_and_insights/technology/s)

This website has resources for districts seeking to learn more about data-driven decision making.

Center on Education Policy
(www.cepdc.org/pubs/nclb_full_report_jan2003/nclb_full_report_jan2003.pdf)

The Center issued a report on the findings from the first year of the implementation of No Child Left Behind legislation. The report is titled *From the Capital to the Classroom: State and Federal Efforts to Implement the No Child Left Behind Act* and is available at this site.

Education Trust (www.edtrust.org/main/main/DTM.asp)

Education Trust, a school reform advocacy and research group, found more than 4,700 schools with high minority or high poverty enrollments that did not use selective admissions policies yet performed well in math or reading. These schools help debunk the myth that high poverty or high minority schools cannot meet high achievement goals. This site provides more information about the high-performance schools.

National Assessment of Educational Progress (NAEP) (www.nces.ed.gov)

Scores on NAEP tests by state and demographic classification are available at this website.

National Association of Elementary School Principals (www.naesp.org)

Click on Data-Based Decision Making for information on collecting and using data to improve school performance.

National Center for Research on Evaluation, Standards and Student Testing (CRESST) (www.cse.ucla.edu)

This site contains information on the development and use of evaluation and testing techniques that can be used to improve school performance.

REFERENCES

Allen, R. (2003, November). Building school culture in an age of accountability. *ASCD Education Update, 45,* 1, 3, 7–8.

Brown v. Board of Education of Topeka, 347 U.S. 483 (1954).

Brown v. Board of Education of Topeka, 349 U.S. 294 (1955).

Brown, D. (1991). *Decentralization: The administrator's guidebook to school district change.* Newbury Park, CA: Sage.

Campbell, J. (1977). On the nature of organizational effectiveness. In P. Goodman and J. Pennings (Eds.), *New perspectives on organizational effectiveness* (pp. 13–55). San Francisco: Jossey-Bass.

Cawelti, G. (1989, May). Key elements of site-based management. *Educational Leadership, 46,* 46.

Chambers, H. E. (2001). *Finding, hiring, and keeping peak performers.* Cambridge, MA: Perseus.

Chapman, J. (1990). School-based decision making and management: Implications for school personnel. In J. Chapman (Ed.), *School-based decision-making and management* (pp. 221–244). London: Falmer.

David, J. (1989, May). Synthesis of research on school-based management. *Educational Leadership, 46,* 45–47, 50–53.

Grissmer, D., Flanagan, A., Kawata, J., & Williamson, S. (2000). *Improving student achievement.* Santa Monica, CA: Rand.

Hanushek, E. A. (2001). The truth about teacher salaries and student achievement. In W. M. Evers, L. T. Izumi, and P. A. Riley (Eds.), *School reform: The critical issues* (pp. 174–176). Stanford, CA: Hoover Institution Press.

Hill, P. W. (2002). What principals need to know about teaching and learning. In Marc S. Tucker and Judy B. Codding (Eds.), *The princi-*

pal challenge (pp. 43–75). San Francisco: Jossey-Bass.

Historical statistics of the United States: Colonial times to 1970. (1975). Washington, DC: U.S. Department of Commerce, Bureau of the Census.

Koretz, D. M. (2002, Fall). Limitations in the use of achievement tests as measures of educators' productivity. *Journal of Human Resources, 37,* 752–777.

Lafee, S. (2002, December). Data-driven districts. *School Administrator, 59*(11), 6–7, 9–10, 12, 14–15.

Lankford, H., Loeb, S., & Wyckoff, J. (2002, Spring). Teacher sorting and the plight of urban schools: A descriptive analysis. *Educational Evaluation and Policy Analysis, 24*(1), 37–62.

Lawler, E., & Mohrman, S. (1991). High-involvement management. In R. Steers and L. Porter (Eds.), *Motivation and work behavior* (5th ed., pp. 468–477). New York: McGraw-Hill.

Leithwood, K. (2001). School leadership and educational accountability: Toward a distributed perspective. In T. J. Kowalski and G. Perreault (Eds.), *21st century challenges for school administrators* (pp. 11–25). Lanham, MD: Scarecrow Press.

Loeb, S. (2001). Teacher quality: Its enhancement and potential for improving pupil achievement. In David H. Monk and Herbert J. Walberg (Eds.), *Improving educational productivity* (pp. 99–114.) Greenwich, CT: Information Age.

Manzo, K. K., & Galley, M. (2003, November 19). Math climbs, reading flat on '03 NAEP. *Education Week,* pp. 1, 18.

Martin, L. (1993). *Total quality management in human service organizations.* Newbury Park, CA: Sage.

McDowell, L. (1993). *Public elementary and secondary schools and agencies in the United States and outlying areas: School year 1991–92.* Washington, DC: U.S. Department of Education, National Center for Education Statistics.

Milstein, M. (1993). *Restructuring schools: Doing it right.* Newbury Park, CA: Corwin.

National Commission on Excellence in Education. (1983). *A nation at risk: The imperative for educational reform.* Washington, DC: U.S. Government Printing Office.

National Education Association. (1991). *Site-based decision making: The 1990 NEA census of local associations.* Washington, DC: Author.

O'Day, J. A. (2002, Fall). Complexity, accountability, and school improvement. *Harvard Educational Review, 72,* 293–329.

Prasch, J. (1990). *How to organize for school-based management.* Alexandria, VA: Association for Supervision and Curriculum Development.

Raywid, M. A. (2002, February). Accountability: What's worth measuring? *Phi Delta Kappan, 83,* 433–436.

Renter, D. S., & Hamilton, M. (2003, May). First signs of the new accountability. *Principal Leadership, 3,* 10–12.

Rosenshine, B., & Meister, C. (1995). Direct instruction. In L. Anderson (Ed.), *International encyclopedia of teaching and teacher education* (2nd ed., pp. 143–149). Tarrytown, NY: Pergamon.

Rowan, B. (1996). Standards as incentives for instructional reform. In S. Fuhrman and J. O'Day (Eds.), *Rewards and reform: Creating educational incentives that work* (pp. 195–225). San Francisco: Jossey-Bass.

Sirotnik, K. A. (2002, May). Promoting responsible accountability in schools and education. *Phi Delta Kappan, 83,* 662–673.

Smith, P., Molnar, A., & Zahorik, J. (2003, September). Class-size reduction: A fresh look at the data. *Educational Leadership, 61,* 72–74.

Streifer, Philip A. (2002). *Using data to make better educational decisions.* Lanham, MD: Scarecrow Press.

Thompson, S. (2003). A high-performance school system. In F. M. Duffy, *Courage, passion, and vision* (pp. 101–112). Lanham, MD: Scarecrow Press.

Walsh, K. (2003, June 4). A blessing in disguise. *Education Week,* pp. 28, 30.

Wideen, M., Mayer-Smith, J., & Moon, B. (1996). Knowledge, teacher development and change. In I. Goodson and A. Hargreaves (Eds.), *Teachers' professional lives* (pp. 187–204). London: Falmer.

Wissler, D., & Ortiz, F. (1988). *The superintendent's leadership in school reform.* New York: Falmer.

CHAPTER TWO

PLANNING FOR STAFFING NEEDS

Planning represents an effort to anticipate and shape the future. The process of planning involves identifying a desired future state, assessing conditions and trends that may influence the organization's ability to achieve that state, and developing strategies to reach the goal. Few organizations are successful for very long without planning.

This chapter addresses several issues related to planning in schools. Evidence suggests that schools will continue to be at a competitive disadvantage vis-à-vis other employers in seeking to attract and retain well-qualified personnel (Pounder, 1987). For that reason, it is important to anticipate staff needs and to plan carefully to recruit, select, and retain employees with the qualifications to help the district achieve its goals.

PLAN OF THE CHAPTER

This chapter deals covers the following topics: (1) strategic planning for schools, (2) selecting strategic goals, and (3) determining staff needs.

STRATEGIC PLANNING

The process of strategic planning begins with the preparation of a district mission statement, a declaration of the district's commitment to certain academic, social, and health outcomes for students and teachers (Sybouts, 1992). Personnel in each school in the district then compose a school mission statement, reflecting the values of the district mission and integrating unique elements of the school's context, programs, and purpose. The school mission statement acknowledges standards for student achievement established by the district or state. Mission statements are not necessarily limited to lists of outcomes; they may also identify qualities of the school's culture that are valued by staff members and suggest preferred forms of interaction among teachers, students, and parents. Exhibit 2.1 shows examples of three school mission statements.

EXHIBIT 2.1
MODEL SCHOOL MISSION STATEMENTS

MAPLE GROVE (WISCONSIN) ELEMENTARY SCHOOL
Staff, students, and parents of the Maple Grove community will work cooperatively to create a safe and positive environment where learning is valued and differences are accepted. We have a firm commitment to provide all children with meaningful learning opportunities. These opportunities will develop personal integrity, a substantial knowledge base, a productive work ethic, and the capacity and self-motivation for lifelong learning.

PERALTA ELEMENTARY SCHOOL, LOS LUNAS, NEW MEXICO
Faculty and staff of Peralta Elementary School are in the business of delivering quality education in the form of instruction, guidance, and support for all children served by the school. The effectiveness of such a delivery system will be evidenced by increases in attendance, achievement, and parental and family involvement, and a decrease in the frequency of school-related problems.

SOUTHWEST MIDDLE SCHOOL, ORLANDO, FLORIDA
The mission of Southwest Middle School is to provide a safe and stimulating learning environment, which will promote academic excellence, lifelong learning, a positive self-image, a feeling of belonging, responsibility, and community involvement.

The school mission statement should be prominently displayed in the entryway and at other strategic locations throughout the building, including classrooms, and on the school's website. Posting the mission statement prominently helps to keep it in the forefront of people's thinking and encourages them to find ways of achieving the goals identified in the statement.

Mission statements can serve a useful purpose, helping teachers, administrators, and students to focus their efforts and attention on the valued outcomes highlighted in the statement. However, if the process of developing the mission statement has revealed differences among members of the school community regarding priority goals, there is value in clarifying the meanings of the terms used in the mission statement because many of the words we use may carry more than one meaning. One way to clarify meanings and work toward a consensus is by carrying out a *mission scan* (Castallo, 2001).

In performing a mission scan, members of the school community discuss the mission statement and examine various interpretations of the phrasing. This process can lead to discovery of the differences in interpretation of terms such as *safe environment, lifelong learning, diversity,* and *academic excellence.* These discussions allow participants to explore the various meanings attributed to these terms and to work toward adoption of a language that everyone understands and accepts.

Consider a phrase such as "safe environment." Some participants may believe that the phrase refers to a school building that is free of physical hazards, whereas for others it may bring to mind the provision of crossing guards on nearby streets. Still others may believe that the phrase refers to the absence of threats to students and teachers from armed students or intruders (Castallo, 2001).

When a group has clarified the meanings they wish to assign to terms in the mission statement, the hard work of bringing the mission to fruition begins. A technique used to initiate this process is called *visioning* (Conzemius & O'Neill, 2001). Visioning involves mentally constructing images of what the future might be like if the goals identified in the mission statement are achieved. The process is similar to a technique used by athletes preparing to perform. Baseball players in the on-deck circle rehearse their swing, and gymnasts and divers act out their routines in pantomime while waiting to perform. By mentally picturing a flawless performance, these athletes strive to perfect the execution of their routines. An organization can use visioning to encourage members to construct mental images of how the organization might change as a result of achieving the goals specified in the mission statement.

The principal of a school who conducts a visioning activity might ask teachers to imagine what their classrooms would look like, what students would be able to do, what topics would be discussed in faculty meetings, and what would transpire in parent conferences when the goals envisioned in the mission statement are realized. The principal might also ask teachers to envision student artwork that might be displayed in hallways, to describe what honors and awards students might win, and to explain how teachers might collaborate to improve school programs. Imagining what the future will be like and describing it to those with whom one works is the first step toward bringing the desired future state into being.

Visioning also serves another purpose. It enables individuals to imagine a different situation from the one in which they find themselves at the moment and encourages them to begin to consider the actions they might take to make the vision reality. By capturing a mental image of a future that is different from the present, members of the community become aware of the actions needed in order to bring that future into being. Thus, visioning is a valuable tool to prepare a school faculty to begin the change process.

Critical Issues Analysis

Strategic planning operates on two assumptions—that the future evolves from the present and that it will be different from the present (Hatten & Hatten, 1988). Planners use a process called *environmental assessment* to identify trends that are evident in the external environment that have implications for the organization's ability to accomplish its mission. One technique used to produce an environmental assessment is critical issues analysis. *Critical issues analysis* begins with planners identifying potential critical issues and submitting each one to a test. The test involves three questions (Wilkinson, 1986)*:

1. Will the issue affect the performance of the organization?
2. Will it require allocation of organizational resources?
3. Can the organization reasonably expect to control or exert significant influence on the impact the issue has on the organization's performance?

If the answer to all three questions is *yes*, then the issue is a critical one. Consider these examples of issues the faculty of a school engaged in developing a strategic plan might assess:

1. A nearby school has failed to make adequate yearly progress for three consecutive years, and students in that school will be given an option to transfer to another school in the district, including yours.

2. The superintendent of the district has proposed providing laptop computers for all students and requiring teachers to develop computer-based instruction in mathematics and science beginning in the coming school year.

3. A native of France is a very successful foreign language teacher in your school but does not hold a permanent teaching certificate and therefore may be released for failing to meet the requirement of NCLB that all teachers be "highly qualified."

4. After increasing for three years, mathematics scores in your school dipped slightly this year; English and history scores were unchanged from the previous year.

Wilkinson's (1986) test questions will be applied to these four problems to determine those that qualify as critical issues.

Testing Issues

Question 1. Which issues will affect the performance of the school? All of the issues have the potential to affect the performance of the school. An influx of students from the nearby school will change the demographic profile of your school and may increase social and racial tensions. Requiring computer-based instruction in mathematics and science could result in either learning gains or losses depending on how prepared teachers are to adopt the new instructional approach. Losing a

*Various citations from Wilkinson (1986) on pages 19–22 are reprinted with permission. G. Wilkinson, "Strategic Planning in the Voluntary Sector," in J. Gardner, R. Rachlin, & H. Sweeny (Eds.), *Handbook of Strategic Planning* (New York: Wiley, 1986), copyright © 1986. Reprinted by permission of John Wiley & Sons, Inc.

native-speaking foreign language teacher is always regrettable, and if it is not possible to replace the departing teacher with one who is equally well-prepared, it is likely that the foreign language students' performance will be affected. The drop in mathematics scores and the lack of gains in English and history are all signs of a performance problem that could easily worsen if corrective action is not taken soon.

Question 2. Which issues will require reallocation of resources? Additional resources should be forthcoming if a number of students transfer from the nearby school, which will minimize the need to reallocate resources; however, some space that is currently used for offices and storage may have to be converted to classrooms. If many of the students who transfer need remedial assistance, then some reallocation of personnel and material resources may be called for. Presumably the computer initiative will include additional resources for professional development and purchase of computers, but the school may need to reallocate resources to purchase computer software. No reallocation of resources should be needed for the French teacher because the school will retain the position. On the issue of lagging mathematics scores, some reallocation of resources may be needed, depending on the cause of the drop in scores. Tutoring assistance for students who are falling behind and additional professional development activities for mathematics teachers are two possible approaches to the problem, and both will require reallocation.

Question 3. On which issues can the school expect to have an impact? Your school will have no influence on whether students in the nearby school decide to transfer to your school but can have an impact on the response that is made if a number of students request such a transfer. If the decision has been made to move to a computer-based curriculum, then your impact will be limited to details of the implementation. You may be able to persuade district officials to delay removing the French teacher if you can present a plan by which she can obtain certification in a reasonable amount of time. The faculty in your school can certainly have an impact on students' performance on prescribed tests.

Using Wilkinson's (1986) test, two issues (transfer of students from the nearby school and addressing the drop in mathematics test scores) qualify as critical items because all three questions are answered in the affirmative for these issues.

Futures Wheel

To help assess the probable impact of critical issues, planners prepare a futures wheel for each critical issue. An advantage of the futures wheel is that it helps planners trace the impact of an event two, three, or even four stages beyond the immediate results.

Figure 2.1 shows an example of a futures wheel illustrating how transfers of students from a nearby school will affect the school program. One possible result is that classes will have more students or that space presently devoted to storage or offices will be converted to classrooms. Another outcome that can be expected is the need to welcome new students and redevelop a spirit of unity and cohesiveness within the student body. If new teachers are assigned to the school, there will also be a need to welcome them and offer an induction program for them.

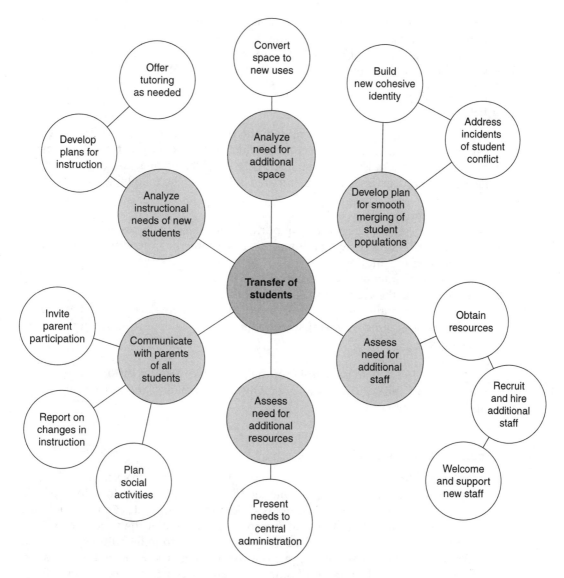

FIGURE 2.1   Futures Wheel Illustrating Effects of Student Transfers

Ranking Issues

When the futures wheel has been completed, participating planners discuss the range of opportunities and threats posed by each issue under examination and rank them on three dimensions: probability, impact, and imminence. Probability and impact are rated on 10-point scales. For *probability,* a rating of 1 indicates that the rater believes the event is highly improbable, whereas a rating of 10 reflects a judgment that it is highly probable. For *impact,* 1 indicates negligible impact, whereas 10 indicates a judgment of major structural change. For *imminence*, a 3-point scale is used, with judges rating how soon a development is predicted to occur. Rating choices are near term (up to one year), medium term (next three years), and long term (next five years) (Wilkinson, 1986).

Issue Brief

When the ratings have been compiled, the planners identify issues that are perceived as being most likely to occur and which will have the greatest impact on the organization. These issues are then subjected to detailed analysis. For each of the issues analyzed, an issue brief is prepared containing the following information:

1. Title and definition of the issue
2. Identification of threats and opportunities related to the issue
3. Identification of driving influences—environmental forces that give the issue momentum and force
4. Potential outcomes of alternative scenarios
5. Impact on the organization of each of the scenarios
6. Planning challenges—a set of "need to" statements setting out the overall actions required of the organization to maximize opportunities or minimize threats

An example of an issue brief for the problem of issuing laptop computers to students and introducing new interactive mathematics and science curricula appears in Exhibit 2.2.

Selecting Strategic Goals

At this point the team working on the strategic plan is ready to select a small number of strategic goals that will become the focus of employees' efforts for a period of one to five years. The strategic goals should reflect the district and school mission statement and should take into account the results of the visioning process described earlier and draw on the information contained in the futures wheel and issue briefs. Choosing strategic goals is a challenging task because it requires setting aside some goals in favor of others that are judged to be more critical. To be successful, the strategic plan must recognize that resources of time, energy, and money are limited and must be devoted to a limited number of important but attainable outcomes. The most common error in developing strategic plans is striving to accomplish too much.

Once the strategic goals have been selected, consideration must be given to developing interim targets that will serve as markers for progress on the way to achieving each of the goals. For example, if a school adopts the strategic goal of having every child able to read at grade level within four years, an interim target might be to increase the percentage of third-grade children reading at grade level from 72 percent to 80 percent during the first year of the plan and from 80 percent

EXHIBIT 2.2

SAMPLE ISSUE BRIEF

    I. Title

       Providing laptop computers to students and adopting computer-based instruction in mathematics and science

   II. Challenges and opportunities

       Challenges: Securing teachers' support for the new program and preparing them to adopt a computer-based instructional approach; preparing students to care for and use computers responsibly; informing parents about the new program and obtaining their support; minimizing the amount of learning loss as a result of the conversion to the new approach.

       Opportunity: Teachers and students gain access to a large volume of online instructional materials; students and teachers increase their technological sophistication; stage is set for introduction of computer-based instruction in other subjects; individualized assistance is available for students who have difficulty with content.

  III. Driving forces

       Demand for increased productivity; demand for improved student achievement; advantages gained by increasing access to online resources.

  IV. Prospects

       Worst case: Lack of teacher enthusiasm for new approach dooms it to failure and student achievement lags.

       Best case: Teachers embrace the new approach and students' interest and achievement both improve.

to 88 percent during the second year, and so on. Interim targets make the task of reaching the strategic goal more manageable by breaking the work into subtasks. The thought of raising the reading proficiency of all the children to grade level is intimidating at first, but achieving small, steady gains each year over a four-year period appears doable.

DETERMINING STAFF NEEDS

Enrollment projections enable administrators to anticipate future enrollments and recruit and hire teachers and other personnel needed to staff the schools, but enrollment projections are only as useful as they are accurate. Underestimating enrollments may mean that class sizes will have to be increased or more teachers hired; overestimating results in more teachers being hired than are needed. Accurately estimating future enrollments requires a good bit of skill as well as luck. The longer the range of a prediction, the greater the possibility for error.

Long-term predictions on school enrollments in the United States made in the early 1960s proved to be far from accurate because those who made them used assumptions that turned out to be faulty. Planners assumed that the birthrate would continue unchanged for the foreseeable future. They failed to anticipate the advancements in birth control that made family planning easier and more practical. As a result, the birthrate dropped and so did school enrollments. Enrollment projections are only as accurate as the assumptions on which they are based.

The U.S. Department of Education projects total school enrollments of about 54.5 million students in 2005, dropping slightly to 54.2 million in 2009. The Department reported that 3.05 million teachers were employed in public and private elementary and secondary schools in 1997 (2.65 million in public schools) and projected that the total number of teachers would increase slightly to 3.17 million by 2009, of whom 2.77 million are expected to be working in public schools (National Center for Education Statistics, 1999).

Colleges and universities graduate more teachers than are actually needed in some subject areas and too few in others. Because not all graduates who prepare to teach actually enter the profession, data on the number of people who graduate from teacher preparation programs are not an accurate guide to teacher supplies. Recent research has shown that only about six out of ten graduates of teacher preparation programs actually take jobs in the field, and, of those who do enter teaching, between one-third and one-half leave the profession within the first five years (National Governors Association, 1999), although there is debate about how many of those who resign actually transfer to teaching positions in other districts or eventually return to the classroom after a break (Wayne, 2000).

The greatest shortages of teachers are found in special education, mathematics, science, and English as a Second Language. Foreign language teachers and teachers of vocational subjects are also in short supply in some localities. To determine how many new teachers must be hired in a district, it is necessary to know how many students can be expected, what teacher–student ratio is to be used, and how many currently employed teachers will return. Once that information is available, plans can be drawn up for hiring teachers, if new hires are required. To determine how many teachers are expecting to return to their jobs, most school districts survey teachers early in the spring using a form on which teachers indicate whether they plan to return to their jobs the following year. Those who are not planning to return are asked whether they are retiring, requesting a leave-of-absence, or applying for a transfer to a different school in the district (Marczely & Marczely, 2002).

Cohort Survival Method

The method that is used most often to predict future enrollments is called the *cohort survival method*. The word *cohort* originally referred to a division of soldiers in the Roman army. It has since come to mean any group of people who begin a venture together. People who were born in the same year or who were initiated into a college fraternity at the same time are examples of cohorts. For purposes of predicting school enrollments, we consider a cohort to be any group of students who start school together. A cohort may lose members when individuals move away or drop out of school, or gain members when students transfer into a school.

The cohort survival method is based on the assumption that the future will be like the past. For the short term, that is usually a safe assumption. Drastic changes in population do not normally occur within the space of a year or two, nor do people's habits change quickly. However, in school districts near military bases or in communities with industries that are sensitive to economic fluctuations, relatively large variations in enrollment can occur with no advance warning.

The cohort survival method is most accurate in districts in which school enrollments are relatively stable or in which enrollment trends are consistent. The method is less accurate in predicting enrollments for districts with fluctuating enrollments (Alspaugh, 1981). The accuracy of any prediction diminishes as the distance from the predicted event increases. Predicting enrollments one year in advance is more accurate than predicting enrollments 5 or 10 years ahead. There are two reasons for loss of accuracy over time. Unforeseen events can affect school enrollments, and errors in predicting near-term enrollments compound over time, creating ever-larger distortions.

Persons who calculate enrollment projections for school districts try to limit error to less than 1 percent of actual enrollments. A 1 percent error rate means that for a projection of 1,000 students, the actual enrollment will fall between 990 and 1,010, and that for a projection of 10,000 students, the actual enrollment will fall between 9,900 and 10,100. For small errors, districts are usually able to accommodate the difference by increasing (or decreasing) class sizes slightly or hiring an additional teacher or two. However, larger errors have more significant repercussions.

If enrollments exceed the projection by just 100 students, a district may have to employ several additional teachers and locate space for that many more classes. If projections call for more students than actually enroll, the district may be responsible for paying salaries for some teachers who are not needed.

Most districts that use cohort survival analysis prepare separate projections for each school and then combine them to obtain a district total. Since most districts now maintain automated enrollment data, it is fairly simple to carry out the necessary calculations at the district office. The results are usually reviewed by principals, who are sometimes aware of impending events, such as a plant closing or construction of a new subdivision, that will affect their schools' enrollments. With this information, adjustments are made and the final predictions prepared. Projecting an accurate district total is somewhat easier than predicting correct enrollments for individual schools since district enrollments are generally more stable.

Projecting First-Grade Enrollment

In preparing enrollment projections for kindergarten, data on the number of births five years earlier are used. In the example shown in Table 2.1, projections over a five-year period in a district with increasing enrollments are averaged to obtain the mean enrollment ratio. In actual practice, enrollment figures for ten years or even

**TABLE 2.1   Developing Kindergarten Enrollment Projections
for a District with Increasing Enrollments**

1 BIRTH YEAR	2 LIVE BIRTHS	3 STARTING YEAR	4 ENROLLMENT	5 ENROLLMENT RATIO
1993	2073	1999	2019	.9740
1994	2097	2000	2044	.9747
1995	2105	2001	2069	.9829
1996	2118	2002	2093	.9882
1997	2121	2003	2136	1.0071
1998	2206	2004		

Step 1: Divide the enrollment (col. 4) by the number of live births
five years earlier (col. 2) to obtain the enrollment ratio (col. 5). The
enrollment ratio for 2000 is 2044/2097 = .9747. A ratio greater than
1.00 means that the number of kindergarten students exceeded the
number of births five years earlier.

Step 2: Add the enrollment ratios and divide by 5
(.9740 + .9747 + .9829 + .9882 + 1.0071 = 4.9269; 4.9269/5 = .9854).
This is the mean enrollment ratio.

Step 3: Multiply the number of live births five years earlier by the
mean enrollment ratio to obtain the projected enrollment for the
2004 school year (.9854 ↔ 2206 = 2174).

more are used in the calculations. Using more years produces more reliable estimates (Schellenberg & Stephens, 1987).

Retention Ratios

To project enrollments for grades 2 through 12, a retention ratio is calculated by
dividing each year's enrollment at a given grade level by the previous year's
enrollment at the next lower grade level. This procedure is repeated for each of five
years prior to the current year. A mean retention ratio is obtained, and the mean is
multiplied by the current year's enrollment in the next lower grade level to obtain
the enrollment projection for the upcoming year. This procedure is illustrated in
Table 2.2, using hypothetical data to project enrollments in grade 7 for a district
with decreasing enrollments. When projected enrollments are obtained for all
grades, they are added to the kindergarten projections to obtain the projected districtwide total enrollment.

When enrollment trends are evident, allowance should be made by adjusting
the projection either up or down. If the enrollment ratio has increased each year for
the previous five years, there is a good chance that it will continue to increase
(although perhaps at a declining rate), and using the average for the previous five

TABLE 2.2   Developing Seventh-Grade Enrollment Projections for a District with Decreasing Enrollments

1 YEAR	2 6TH-GRADE ENROLLMENT	3 YEAR	4 7TH-GRADE ENROLLMENT	5 RETENTION RATIO
1998	2964	1999	2847	.9605
1999	2496	2000	2391	.9579
2000	2473	2001	2378	.9616
2001	2280	2002	2132	.9351
2002	2144	2003	2117	.9874
2003	2057	2004		

Step 1: Divide the seventh-grade enrollment by the previous year's sixth-grade enrollment to obtain the retention ratio (col. 5) for a given year. The retention ratio for 1999 is 2847/2964=.9605.

Step 2: Find the sum of the five retention ratios and divide by 5 (.9605 + .9579 + .9616 + .9351 + .9874 = 4.8025; 4.8025/5 = .9605). This is the mean retention ratio.

Step 3: Multiply the number of students enrolled in grade 6 in 2003–2004 by the mean retention ratio to obtain the projected number of seventh-grade students for 2001 (2057 ↔ .9605 = 1976).

years will underestimate the enrollment. On the other hand, if the trend shows a decline over a five-year period, the enrollment ratio is likely to overestimate enrollments. Depending on the direction and magnitude of the trend, an adjustment of the final enrollment figure may be needed.

Most administrators prefer to underestimate rather than to overestimate enrollments because the potential cost to the district is smaller in the case of underestimates. Enrollments that exceed projections slightly can often be accommodated by increasing class sizes, but once a teacher has been hired there is no way that the money for his or her salary and benefits can be recaptured (unless a contingency clause has been included in the contract).

A sizable one-time increase or decrease in the retention ratio affects the mean ratio and may bias enrollment estimates. For example, in Table 2.2 the ratio for 2002 (.9351) is lower than the other figures and is probably an aberration. When it is used to calculate the mean retention ratio, the obtained figure will be likely to underestimate actual enrollments. When this happens, an adjustment can be made to correct the estimate.

Determining Staff Allocations

School systems rely on enrollment projections to determine how staff resources will be allocated. Teachers, aides, counselors, librarians, and assistant principals are assigned on the basis of the number of students expected to enroll in each school. If the enrollment projections indicate that a school will have an increase in enrollment, a decision must be made whether additional staff are needed and, if so, in which positions or grade levels. Schools that lose students may have to give up positions.

Information about resignations and retirements are taken into account, and a determination is made on the number of employees who must be employed, transferred, or laid off. If additional staff members are needed, action is taken to initiate interviews with qualified applicants.

In recent years, school districts have begun to look at other factors in addition to enrollment in deciding how to allocate personnel. One plan is to award points to a school based on the types of students with particular needs. Schools might receive 1 point per student, with additional points for each child on free lunch, each child with a disability, or each child who is gifted. Some districts grant additional faculty resources for schools with high mobility.

Staffing arrangements in site-managed schools are generally determined by the principal and teachers of the school, who have the option of reconfiguring staff to better meet the needs of the students. The faculty in a school might decide, for example, to hire fewer teachers and more aides or to do without an assistant principal in order to gain an additional teacher or several aides. Such a system provides a way to allocate staff that is equitable, and it lets each building control the configuration of staff to meet its needs.

SUMMARY

Planning is an effort to anticipate and prepare for the future by mobilizing an organization's resources to attain a desirable future state. In strategic planning, a school identifies its goals and develops strategies for attaining them. Strategic planners carry out a critical issues analysis by identifying forces that are expected to affect the school's operation, require allocation of resources, or that can be influenced by the school. Following analysis and discussion, selected issues are chosen for further study and a brief is prepared for each issue.

One of the important tasks in human resources planning is projecting staff needs. This involves projecting enrollments and determining the number of personnel needed to staff the schools. Procedures are set in motion to recruit and select additional staff or, if enrollments are dropping, to reduce staff size.

The cohort survival method is the most widely used technique for projecting enrollments. This method is most accurate when school enrollments are stable or trends are consistent; it is least accurate when enrollments fluctuate.

SUGGESTED ACTIVITIES

1. Draw a futures wheel for a problem faced by a school with which you are familiar. Choose a problem that is likely to occur and that will have an impact on the school.

2. Write an issues brief for the problem you identified in Question 1.

3. Prepare a futures wheel illustrating possible effects of implementing the accountability features contained in No Child Left Behind.

4. Examine the mission statements shown in Exhibit 2.1 and write definitions for key terms from each of the statements. Then compare your definitions with those of one or two other people and carry out a mission scan by discussing the differences in your definitions.

ONLINE RESOURCES

National Center for Education Statistics
(www.ed.gov/offices/OSFAP/Students/repayment/teachers/tsa.html)

This site lists critical areas of shortage in teacher supplies by state.

The following websites are resources for districts seeking teachers and contain recommendations for actions that districts can take to increase their applicant pool.

National Commission on Mathematics and Science Teaching for the 21st Century
(www.ed.gov/americacounts/glenn)

This site, which contains the report of a citizen's panel headed by former Senator John Glenn, recommends ways of increasing the nation's supply of teachers of mathematics and science. Among other ideas, the panel recommended summer institutes, more financial aid, and better pay for teachers.

National Teacher Recruiting Clearinghouse (www.recruitingteachers.org)

The Clearinghouse brings individuals seeking teaching jobs and districts attempting to locate qualified applicants together. It provides links to departments of education and advice to districts on websites for recruiting and retaining teachers.

Teacher Advancement Program (www.mff.org/tap/tap.taf)

The Teacher Advancement Program, sponsored by the Milken Family Foundation, employs a comprehensive and systemic strategy for addressing recruitment, training, induction, professional development, compensation, performance evaluation, and career advancement.

Teach for America (www.teachforamerica.org/flash_movie.html)

Teach for America is a corps of recent college graduates with academic majors who commit two years to teach in underresourced urban and rural public schools.

REFERENCES

Alspaugh, J. (1981, Summer). Accuracy of school enrollment projections based upon previous enrollments. *Educational Research Quarterly, 6,* 61–67.

Castallo, R. T. (2001). *Focused leadership: How to improve student achievement.* Lanham, MD: Scarecrow Press.

Conzemius, A., & O'Neill, J. (2001). *Building shared responsibility for student learning.* Alexandria, VA: Association for Supervision and Curriculum Development.

Hatten, K., & Hatten, M. (1988). *Effective strategic management: Analysis and action.* Englewood Cliffs, NJ: Prentice-Hall.

Marczely, B. & Marczely, D. W. (2002). *Human resource and contract management in the public school.* Lanham, MD: Scarecrow Press.

National Center for Education Statistics. (1999). *Projections of education statistics to 2009.* Washington, DC: U.S. Department of Education.

National Governors Association. (1999). *Teacher supply and demand: Is there a shortage?* [On-line.] Available: www.na.org/pubs/issueBriefs/2000/000125Teachers.asp

Pounder, D. (1987). The challenge for school leaders: Attracting and retaining good teachers. In W. Greenfield (Ed.), *Instructional leadership: Concepts, issues, and controversies* (pp. 287–301). Boston: Allyn and Bacon.

Schellenberg, S., & Stephens, C. (1987). *Enrollment projection: Variations on a theme.* Paper presented at the annual meeting of the American Educational Research Association, Washington, DC.

Sybouts, W. (1992). *Planning in school administration: A handbook.* New York: Greenwood.

Wayne, A. J. (2000, September). Teacher supply and demand: Surprises from primary research. *Education Policy Analysis Archives, 18*(47). [On-line.] Available: (*epaa.asu.edu/epaa/v8n47.html*).

Wilkinson, G. (1986). Strategic planning in the voluntary sector. In J. Gardner, R. Rachlin, and H. Sweeny (Eds.), *Handbook of strategic planning* (25.1–25.23). New York: Wiley.

CHAPTER THREE

PREPARING FOR PERSONNEL SELECTION

Selecting school personnel involves matching applicants' qualifications to selection criteria. To the extent that a good match is achieved, employees will be successful in their work. However, when an applicant is placed in a position that does not fit his or her qualifications, the individual will experience frustration and will not do high-quality work.

PLAN OF THE CHAPTER

This chapter presents a model of the selection process and explains how selection criteria are developed and applied to identify qualified applicants for vacant positions. Chapter 4 examines how information about applicants is obtained and evaluated. The following topics will be discussed in this chapter: (1) a model of the selection process, (2) identifying selection criteria, (3) job-specific selection criteria for teaching, (4) selecting personnel for other positions, and (5) teacher shortages.

A MODEL OF THE SELECTION PROCESS

The selection process has four objectives: (1) to ensure that individuals selected to work for an organization possess the knowledge, skills, and abilities to perform their jobs effectively; (2) to help individuals make informed decisions about whether to accept an offer of employment; (3) to create a sense of commitment to the organization on the part of new employees; and (4) to commit the organization to provide the support necessary for newly hired employees to succeed. A sound selection process results in hiring employees who possess the knowledge, skills, and abilities needed in the job for which they are hired and who are committed to the organization (Lawler, 1992).

To achieve the first objective, the employer identifies criteria related to successful performance on a job. Job-specific criteria are the knowledge, skills, and abilities that are integral to success in a specific position. Nonjob-specific criteria are characteristics that contribute to success in many different jobs. Knowledge of and ability to apply the principles of physical conditioning are examples of job-specific criteria for an athletic coach, just as ability to use a power saw is a job-specific criterion for a carpenter.

Nonjob-specific criteria are attributes that contribute to successful performance in many jobs. Examples of nonjob-specific criteria are the ability to express ideas clearly, regular attendance on the job, avoidance of alcohol and drug abuse, a positive attitude toward the job, and willingness to work cooperatively with other employees.

By assessing indicators of the selection criteria, an employer rates applicants for the position and hires the person whose qualifications best match the selection criteria. An example of an indicator of knowledge of the principles of physical conditioning is successful completion of a course on that topic, and an indicator of skill in word processing is the ability to type a document using a specified word-processing program with acceptable speed and with few errors.

Figure 3.1 graphically depicts the selection process. Individuals applying for a teaching job must meet certain basic criteria before their individual qualifications are considered. All states require that applicants be certified to teach before they are hired, but when teachers are in short supply, states may issue temporary or emergency certificates to help districts fill vacancies. Most school districts now require that applicants hold a major or minor in their teaching field, and some

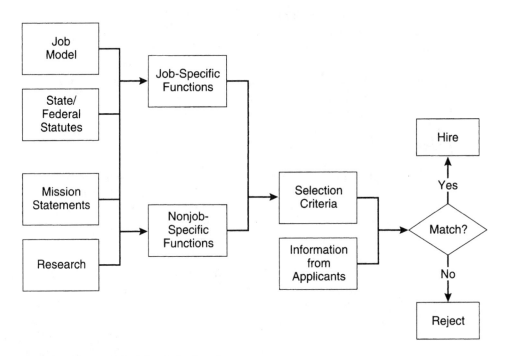

FIGURE 3.1 Model of the Selection Process

require that successful applicants must have taken and passed one or more tests covering knowledge of basic skills, knowledge of the teaching field, and familiarity with effective teaching practices.

The Americans with Disabilities Act (ADA) has brought about changes in the selection process by introducing the concept of *essential functions*. These are tasks that are fundamental to a particular job and that an employee must be able to perform in order to be considered qualified for the position.

Selection decisions have traditionally hinged on considerations of worth—that is, an individual's ability to make a contribution that is valued by the employer. If several candidates for a position were equally qualified, the candidate who was able to meet other needs of the employer, in addition to those required in the job for which he or she was applying, was hired (Scriven, 1990).

For example, an applicant for a teaching position who had experience in coaching tennis or field hockey might be chosen over an equally qualified applicant who lacked coaching experience, even though coaching was not required in the position. Under ADA, an employer who rejects an applicant with a disability who is able to perform the essential functions of a position, with or without accommodation, and hires an applicant who is not disabled, on the basis that the person hired can perform certain peripheral functions, violates the law (Jacobs, 1993). Thus, the legislation forces employers to concentrate in selection of employees on job-specific criteria.

The identification of essential functions is achieved by analyzing information from the same sources that are used to identify selection criteria (job model, state and federal statutes, mission statement, and findings of related research; see Figure 3.1). The job model specifies the results that a jobholder is expected to accomplish and describes conditions under which the work takes place. State statutes spell out mandatory preparation and licensing requirements for personnel, and research identifies school characteristics and teacher attitudes and behaviors associated with increased student learning.

Determining whether a particular task is an essential function of a job involves consideration of three factors: the tasks that the position exists to perform, the number of employees available to perform a task, and whether a person hired for the position is chosen for his or her ability to perform the task (Fersh & Thomas, 1993). Consider a high school counselor whose primary duties include counseling students and providing information to help students choose a college or make vocational plans. On three or four occasions each year, the counselor visits nearby middle schools to counsel middle school students on the transition to high school. One applicant for the position is confined to a wheelchair and is unable, without help, to travel to other schools.

Can the district reject the applicant who has a disability in favor of someone who is physically able to travel? The answer probably depends on whether visiting middle schools is considered an essential function of the job. Since little of the counselor's time is devoted to that task and the counselor is not chosen primarily on the basis of his or her ability to do it, it is unlikely that these visits would be considered an essential function. Moreover, since it is possible to make an accommodation by assigning another employee to visit the middle schools or by providing assistance for the counselor to make the trip, no rational basis exists for rejecting the applicant who has a disability.

Job-specific criteria are given more weight in the selection process under ADA than was true before that law was enacted. However, nonspecific criteria are still part of the picture, since some attributes are important to success in any undertaking. Employees who are regular in attendance, who are cooperative with other workers and with supervisors, and who are able to do their jobs without close supervision are usually successful in whatever tasks they undertake. Employers need to exercise care, however, to avoid using nonjob-specific criteria that are peripheral to successful performance.

IDENTIFYING SELECTION CRITERIA

The primary source of information about the selection criteria for a position is a job description or job model. A *job description* identifies the position and describes the duties and responsibilities associated with it. The description usually gives some information about the school and the district in which the vacancy occurs. It includes a list of qualifications required in the position, and it may describe resources available to the incumbent.

Rochester (New York) schools use a generic job description for teaching positions (Haller, 1987). The description identifies the job goal as helping students "to learn subject matter and/or skills that will contribute to their development as mature, able, and responsible men and women" (p. 184).

Among the performance responsibilities for teachers identified in the Rochester job description are the following: planning programs that meet individual needs, interests, and abilities of students; creating an environment that is conducive to learning; guiding the learning process toward achievement of curriculum goals; establishing clear objectives and communicating those objectives to students; employing appropriate instructional methods and materials; evaluating students and providing progress reports as required; diagnosing learning abilities and disabilities of students on a regular basis; working cooperatively with staff, superiors, and community; assisting in implementing the school's rules of behavior; maintaining order in a fair and just manner; maintaining and improving professional competence; and attending meetings and serving on committees as appropriate.

The Rochester document is based on the assumption that all teaching jobs in a district are alike. In fact, teaching positions vary, depending on the subject and grade level taught and the school environment. Teaching a fifth-grade class in an elementary school with a multiethnic student population is a different experience, and requires different skills, than teaching English in a college preparatory high school. The results that are expected and the resources that are available to assist teachers in the two situations differ. Position descriptions that are specific to a particular school or job can help to target the selection process and increase the probability of making successful staffing decisions.

Writing a Job Model

An alternative to the traditional job description has been developed by Dailey (1982). The job model is an improvement over position descriptions because it focuses on results and makes it possible to focus the selection process on choosing an employee who can achieve those outcomes.

The job model presents a realistic picture of the job, including both its attractive and unattractive features. If a position is located in a school in an old building with out-of-date equipment and few supplies, the job model states those facts. If parents are cooperative and supportive of teachers, that too is reported. An effort is made to avoid presenting only the positive features of a position, since once a teacher is hired he or she soon becomes aware of the less attractive features of the situation and must be able to produce results in spite of them. Employees who are informed in advance of both the negative and positive features of a new position more often experience feelings of satisfaction than those who are told only the good news about the job (Wanous, 1980).

An example of a job model for the position of high school Spanish teacher is shown in Exhibit 3.1. The job model consists of three parts. The section entitled "Results Sought" describes the outcomes the Spanish teacher is expected to accomplish. This section is the heart of the job model because it helps to focus the search on the important task of identifying a candidate who can achieve those results. "Job Environment" describes characteristics of the school and community that are likely either to facilitate or hinder performance. Interviewers use the information in this section to investigate applicants' ability and willingness to overcome barriers and to use resources effectively to achieve specified results. Applicants use the information to weigh their feelings of adequacy to face the challenge presented by the position.

The "Priority Actions" section of the job model describes tasks that must be performed on the job. These may be actions that lead directly or indirectly to accomplishment of the results described under "Results Sought," or they may be actions that help other persons in the school accomplish the results for which they are responsible. Examples of priority actions that might be required of a teacher are covering required curriculum content and assessing and reporting to parents on students' academic progress.

The first step in constructing a job model involves identifying the results sought. Schools are organizations with multiple and ambiguous goals. It is not easy in such organizations to reach consensus on results sought. The recommended procedure is to ask four or five persons who are familiar with the job to complete the following statement: "A person in this job is effective if he or she produces the result that . . . " (Dailey, 1982). Each contributor writes eight endings for

■ ■ ■ ■ ■ ▬▬

EXHIBIT 3.1

JOB MODEL: HIGH SCHOOL SPANISH TEACHER (LEVELS 1 AND 2)

RESULTS SOUGHT

1. Students listening to a speaker describing familiar activities in Spanish are able to answer questions about the main ideas of the presentation in Spanish (level 1) and about details of the presentation in Spanish (level 2).
2. Students carry on a brief conversation with a Spanish-speaking person discussing daily events at home or school using limited vocabulary (level 1) or more extensive vocabulary (level 2).
3. Students write a brief (one-page) essay using regular verbs, present tense only (level 1) or both regular and irregular verbs, present and past tenses (level 2) on a familiar topic, when provided a stimulus in Spanish.
4. In English (level 1) or in Spanish (level 2) students present oral reports on elements of Hispanic culture, including religion, dress, history, and literature.
5. Students who complete one level are prepared to succeed at the next higher level.
6. Parents are familiar with their children's progress in Spanish and afford themselves of the opportunity for conferences with the teacher as needed.

JOB ENVIRONMENT

The job is located in a high school in a rural/suburban area near a city of approximately 125,000 people. The school enrolls 1,200 students from low- and middle-income families; about one-fifth of the students are Black, Hispanic, or Asian. About 60 percent of the school's graduates attend college. Three foreign languages (French, German, and Spanish) are offered by the school. Level-1 classes typically have 25 to 30 students, and level-2 classes usually have between 20 and 25. Instructional materials that are integrated with the textbook, including audio- and videotapes and transparencies, are available for teachers' use.

PRIORITY ACTIONS

The successful Spanish teacher must speak and write Spanish fluently and must be able to motivate students from diverse backgrounds to apply themselves to the study of the language. The teacher must plan and present instruction that will enable students to attain facility in speaking and writing Spanish and must be able to diagnose students' deficiencies and provide appropriate instructional remedies. The teacher must be available to meet with students who request additional help and to confer with parents concerning their children's performance. The teacher must be able to work with teachers from other schools to develop the curriculum and select instructional materials.

the sentence and ranks these eight outcomes from most important (rank 1) to least important (rank 8).

To help in writing these statements, Dailey (1982) has offered this advice: "A 'result' should be a very *tangible* effect of work *useful to someone else* and contributing to the organization's reason for existing." Some educators focus on instructional strategies rather than results or outcomes of instruction. Statements such as "allow for individual differences" and "plan stimulating activities" describe actions, not results. Although these actions may lead to desirable outcomes, they are not tangible effects of work that are useful to others. Action statements belong under "Priority Actions."

The 6 to 10 statements that appear most often on contributors' lists are compiled under the "Results Sought" heading of the job model. Exhibit 3.2 shows examples of actions and corresponding results for several positions. Note that the results described in Column 2 of the exhibit are tangible effects that are useful to someone else. Textbooks are available for students' use, children play together in groups, assistant coaches work together, and so on. The actions described in Column 1 contribute to attaining those results, but they do not appear in the "Results Sought" section of the job model.

To prepare a description of the job environment, several individuals who are familiar with the position are asked to list forces that facilitate or hinder performance. The three most important facilitating forces are ranked +1 to +3, and the three most important hindering forces are ranked –1 to –3. These lists are then combined into a narrative statement under the heading "Job Environment." The description of the job environment should be a straightforward report of the factors that new employees will encounter in the position, including both positive and negative features.

Finally, a description of job demands is prepared by asking four or five persons who are familiar with the position to answer the questions that appear in Exhibit 3.3. When the results of this exercise are compiled, that information is written in narrative form and included in the section entitled "Priority Actions." The information generated by these three exercises is combined into a job model.

■ ■ ■ ■ ■

EXHIBIT 3.2

EXAMPLES OF ACTIONS AND RESULTS SOUGHT

ACTION	RESULTS
Assistant principal manages textbook ordering, inventory, and storage	Textbooks are available in sufficient quantities when needed
Child care provider encourages children to take part in group activities	Children interact comfortably with peers in group activities
Football coach coordinates activities of assistant coaches	Assistant coaches understand their own and others' duties and work together effectively
English teacher covers material in the approved curriculum	Students demonstrate mastery of material in the approved curriculum

■ ■ ■ ■ ■

EXHIBIT 3.3

QUESTIONS TO HELP IN WRITING JOB DEMANDS

1. How important is it that the person in this position be able to perform the following activities?
   a. Make presentations to parent or community groups
   b. Prepare detailed lesson plans
   c. Meet with parents to discuss students' progress
   d. Lead a discussion about various aspects of the school's programs
   e. Lead a team of other professionals in planning and carrying out an assigned task
   f. Develop solutions to unique problems and obtain support to implement them
   g. Deal with children who are rowdy and disorderly
   h. Plan instruction for children who are mentally or physically disabled
   i. Maintain accurate records of money, supplies, or student work
   j. Arrange public displays or performances of students' artistic work
   k. Develop and present instructional demonstrations
   l. Collect money or raise funds for special projects
   m. Monitor the school cafeteria, hallways, and parking lots
   n. Maintain a high degree of student involvement in academic tasks
   o. Conduct committee meetings to assess progress of students in special placements
   p. Arrange placements for students in community commercial businesses and government agencies
   q. Assist students in acquiring job information

2. How important is it that the person who fills this job have motivation of the type described in each statement?
   a. Wants to produce a stable level of performance and be satisfied to work within routines
   b. Desires goodwill and affection from people and cares a great deal about having close relationships
   c. Wants to acquire and use influence and to exercise leadership
   d. Wants to set objectives in order to measure progress toward a better way of doing things
   e. Wants to acquire new or more intense experiences or to try new activities and ventures

Items listed under question 2 are from *Using the Track Record Approach: The Key to Successful Personnel Selection* by C. A. Dailey. (New York: AMACOM, 1982).

Ideally, a separate job model is prepared for each vacancy, but that is not always practical. In those cases generic job models may be written for groups of positions (early childhood, special education/mentally retarded, high school physical education, and so on).

JOB-SPECIFIC SELECTION CRITERIA FOR TEACHERS

Teachers are hired to help students learn. They are expected to perform other duties as well, including maintaining records of students' attendance and academic accomplishments, serving on curriculum committees, and carrying out various managerial responsibilities. All of these are job-specific criteria, but none is more important than helping students to acquire knowledge, skill, and attitudes of respect for self and others.

The expectations held for teachers have changed in recent years, and the selection criteria for hiring should reflect those changes. Teachers are now expected to be familiar with and use technology in their teaching and to help raise test scores for all children, including those with learning difficulties. They are also expected to help children construct meaning, rather than memorize predigested content, and teachers are increasingly expected to be familiar with and use technology (Burnaford & Hobson, 2001).

The Interstate New Teacher Assessment and Support Consortium (INTASC), a collaborative effort involving the Council of Chief State School Officers and other groups, has developed a set of principles that explicitly or implicitly incorporate all of the expectations described in the previous paragraph. These principles constitute useful job-specific criteria for selection of both beginning and experienced teachers. The principles are based on research on teacher effectiveness and relate to the core task of teaching—presenting instruction that leads to student learning—while ignoring less central aspects of the teacher's role. Exhibit 3.4 shows the ten INTASC principles.

Because of the extensive amount of research on effective teaching, we know a great deal more about what to look for in prospective teachers than was true even 10 years ago. The behaviors shown in Exhibit 3.4 have been shown repeatedly to be related to teachers' ability to bring about increased student learning. Nevertheless, even with improved understanding of what makes a teacher effective, identifying individuals with potential to be effective is problematic.

If you are considering an individual for a teaching position, how do you know how much he or she knows about the subject matter or whether he or she has the ability to communicate clearly, motivate students, and maintain their interest? Some common sources of information about applicants may give clues, but there is no absolutely reliable answer to those questions. A college transcript reveals quite a bit about the extent and quality of one's knowledge, and references from previous supervisors can yield information about an applicant's instructional skill. However, if the applicant is a beginner, references are less useful. For these individuals, a statement of teaching philosophy may yield insight into the attitudes and beliefs that will shape their behavior as a teacher. All of these sources, and others, should be used to collect information and arrive at a sound selection decision.

It has not been uncommon in the past for teacher selection decisions to be made without careful consideration of valid selection criteria, in part because the criteria were not available. The attitude of those who made these decisions was "If he/she

■ ■ ■ ■ ■ ▬▬▬▬▬▬▬▬▬▬▬▬▬▬▬▬▬▬▬▬▬▬▬▬▬▬▬▬▬▬▬▬▬▬▬▬▬▬

EXHIBIT 3.4

INTASC PRINCIPLES FOR BEGINNING TEACHERS

Principle 1: Teacher understands the central concepts, tools of inquiry, and structures of the disciplines and creates learning experiences that make subject matter meaningful for students.

Principle 2: Teacher understands how children learn and develop and provides learning opportunities to support their intellectual, social, and personal development.

Principle 3: Teacher understands how students differ in their approaches to learning and creates instructional opportunities that are adapted to diverse learners.

Principle 4: Teacher understands and uses a variety of instructional strategies to encourage students' development of critical thinking, problem solving, and performance skills.

Principle 5: Teacher uses individual and group motivation and behavior to create a learning environment that encourages positive social interaction, active engagement in learning, and self-motivation.

Principle 6: Teacher uses knowledge of effective verbal, nonverbal, and media communication techniques to foster active inquiry, collaboration, and supportive interaction in the classroom.

Principle 7: Teacher plans instruction based on knowledge of subject, students, the community, and curriculum goals.

Principle 8: Teacher understands and uses formal and informal assessment strategies to evaluate and ensure the continuous intellectual, social, and physical development of the learner.

Principle 9: Teacher is a reflective practitioner who continually evaluates the effects of his or her choices and actions on others (students, parents, and other professionals in the learning community) and who actively seeks out opportunities to grow professionally.

Principle 10: Teacher fosters relationships with school colleagues, parents, and agencies in the larger community to support students' learning and well-being.

Source: The Interstate New Teacher Assessment and Support Consortium (INTASC) standards were developed by the Council of Chief State School Officers and member states. Copies may be downloaded from the Council's website at http://www.ccsso.org.

doesn't work out, we can always find a replacement." Fortunately, we now recognize the shortsightedness of that approach. Finding a suitable replacement for a teacher who doesn't work out is a difficult undertaking, and even more important, the time lost before a satisfactory replacement is found cannot be recovered. Students who are taught by a marginal teacher suffer learning losses that are seldom made up.

So the effort must be made to find ways of determining which applicants possess the critical skills necessary to ensure student learning. Chapter 4 investigates the types of information available to help human resources personnel make selection decisions.

SELECTING PERSONNEL FOR OTHER POSITIONS

One of the most difficult tasks administrators face is finding qualified substitute teachers. This is always a challenge, and as the supply of qualified full-time teachers shrinks, substitutes are often pressed into taking full-time assignments, making it even more difficult to locate individuals who can fill in for a teacher who is absent. It is not unusual for a principal to hire a substitute teacher who is not fully qualified for the assignment because no qualified substitute is available. Some communities have the benefit of a pool of retired teachers who can be called on to substitute; graduate students and their spouses are another valuable source of substitutes in districts located near a university.

The most common complaints about substitutes is that they lack knowledge of the curriculum or are not well prepared to work with children with special needs. Teachers and administrators agree that requiring substitute teachers to participate in training before they are hired as substitutes would be desirable, but district administrators are reluctant to adopt such a policy unless other districts in the area do the same (Tannenbaum, 2000).

Administrators and teachers can take actions to encourage teacher substitutes to return to their schools. Some actions that are recommended are asking regular teachers to leave assignments along with extra work for students who finish early. Substitutes appreciate receiving a clear explanation of school rules and procedures, accurate seating charts, and a guide to emergency procedures. Some substitutes also like to have the names of students they can depend on for information. To improve communication between teachers and substitutes, some schools now provide a form on which each can report suggestions, problems, or commendations that are then forwarded to the principal and transmitted to the other party (Tannenbaum, 2000).

Some personal attributes are important in many jobs. Among them are emotional maturity, self-discipline, tough-mindedness, and ability to plan. *Emotional maturity* is important for all persons who come in contact with children, including teacher aides, bus drivers, custodians, and clerical personnel. An emotionally mature person exhibits patience with children whose behavior can occasionally be trying and is able to maintain firm boundaries without feeling intimidated or reacting impulsively. An emotionally immature individual lacks the perspective to be able to look beyond his or her own needs in order to understand and respond to the needs and concerns of the child. Emotional maturity is especially vital for those who work with children who have problems of social adjustment or who are emotionally disturbed.

Self-discipline is important in jobs in which individuals work with minimal supervision and must schedule their work around frequent interruptions. Receptionists and secretaries, for example, need to possess self-discipline in order to persist in completing tasks in spite of interruptions from the telephone or from visitors. Custodians need self-discipline since they work without close supervision and must assume responsibility for monitoring heating and cooling equipment, changing lightbulbs, and, when the need arises, shoveling snow from school sidewalks, without being directed to do so.

Tough-mindedness refers to the ability to judge a situation objectively without excessive sentimentality and to persist in pursuing a course of action intended to correct a problem in the face of personal criticism. It is a trait that is especially important in those who are in personnel work or who deal with abusive individuals. Social workers who must initiate court action against families that keep their children out of school without good cause must be tough-minded and persistent in continuing to press these families to abide by the law.

Among the few jobs in which planning is not important are those that involve waiting on customers or manufacturing products on an assembly line. In those jobs, planning is usually done by someone else. In schools, planning is critical for success. Individuals in support positions must plan in order to have supplies on hand that they need in their work, and they must plan the use of their time so they will be able to finish work on schedule.

Teacher Shortages

Teacher shortages are a recurring reality that most human resources administrators must face. A recruitment program that operates year after year, during periods of both shortages and abundance, is the best way of avoiding extreme shortages, because it is difficult to gear up to recruit teachers during periods of short supply if the effort has languished during the years of plenty.

Maintaining an ample supply of qualified applicants is a primary mission of human resources managers, but, in addition to attracting applicants, school districts must also be prepared to move quickly to obtain commitments from the most highly qualified prospects. Some teacher shortages are created as a result of inefficient hiring practices. The National Commission on Teaching and America's Future concluded, after studying the problem of teacher supply and demand, that some school districts used inefficient and outdated hiring practices and as a result lost the most promising candidates to other districts that acted quickly to make an offer and secure a commitment when an especially strong applicant was interviewed (Darling-Hammond, 2000).

Teacher aides and paraprofessionals are a source of potential teachers. Many individuals in these positions would like to become teachers, and they understand better than most people what teaching entails. By offering paraprofessional tuition assistance to help offset the cost of obtaining a teaching credential, school districts can create a continuing supply of committed teachers. Some districts encourage paraprofessionals to think of their jobs as a stepping-stone to a teaching position (Black, 2002).

Recruiters must take into account the fact that the work of teachers has changed dramatically in recent years. Whereas in the past teaching was viewed as filling the "empty vessels" of children's minds, current thinking posits that teachers help students create their own knowledge. The skills called for in these two approaches to teaching are quite different, and a school administrator who hires an "empty vessel" teacher to fill a position calling for a "knowledge constructor" will likely find that that individual is a poor fit for the position (Burnaford & Hobson, 2001).

Because of the difficulty in finding qualified applicants, states and districts have devised innovative ways of recruiting qualified applicants. Massachusetts offers $20,000 signing bonuses paid over four years to teachers who meet certain criteria (National Governors Association, 1999). The South Carolina Teaching Fellows Program was created by the General Assembly of that state in 1999. It provides fellowships for up to 200 high-achieving high school seniors who receive $6,000 per year for up to four years in return for agreeing to teach in the state for a comparable length of time (South Carolina Center for Teacher Recruitment, 2000). The Department of Defense works with school districts in a collaborative "Troops to Teachers" program that provides financial assistance to former military workers and school districts to help prepare defense workers for careers in education (Taylor, 1994).

SUMMARY

Selection of personnel involves matching applicants to the selection criteria for a position. A basic objective of the selection process is to ensure that individuals who are hired possess the knowledge, skills, and abilities to perform effectively. The Americans with Disabilities Act holds employers responsible for evaluating applicants on the job-specific criteria for a position and their ability to perform the job, with or without accommodations, without regard to physical or mental disabilities. The job-specific and nonjob-specific criteria that are essential for success on a job are the basis for selection decisions.

Selection criteria for a position are obtained from a job description or job model and other sources, including state and federal statutes. A job model lists results sought in a job along with descriptions of the job environment and priority actions. A result is a tangible effect of work that is useful to someone else and that helps accomplish the unit's mission.

Among the criteria shown by research to be related to effective teaching are organizing and managing classes effectively, motivating students to learn, communicating information effectively, and maintaining student involvement in instructional activities. Among the selection criteria for support positions are emotional maturity, self-discipline, initiative, and tough-mindedness.

SUGGESTED ACTIVITIES

1. Work in teams to write a job model about a position held by one member of the group. Designate one individual to be a "resource person" and interview that person to obtain information.

2. Write an advertisement for a publication, such as *Education Week,* for the job you developed for Question 1. Point out features of the employing district and of the job that you believe would appeal to prospective applicants.

3. Obtain a job description for a support position (counselor, school psychologist, visiting teacher, etc.). Use it to identify selection criteria and indicators for the position.

4. For the job you currently hold, list job-specific criteria that could be used to choose a replacement for you. Identify sources from which information about the criteria you choose could be obtained. Which sources are most reliable? Least reliable?

5. Read Case Study I and answer the questions.

ONLINE RESOURCES

Education Week (www.edweek.org/sreports/qc99/opinion/aplus1.htm)

This site contains a report entitled "10 Recommendations for Reporting School Results to the Public."

Milwaukee Journal-Sentinel (www.jsonline.com/news/metro/feb00/teach27022600a.asp)

This is the first of a 15-part series published by the *Milwaukee Journal-Sentinel* on the experiences of Milwaukee schools' efforts to recruit and retain quality teachers.

National Clearinghouse for Paraeducator Resources
(http://www.usc.edu/dept/education/CMMR/Clearinghouse.html)

This site features descriptions of programs designed to enable instructional aides to move into teaching careers. It also has abstracts of ERIC documents related to instructional aides.

School report cards

Most states now provide online access to school report cards. Some examples of these reports are:

Colorado: reportcard.cde.state.co.us/reportcard/CommandHandler.jsp

Georgia: techservices.doe.k12.ga.us/reportcard

Oklahoma: www.schoolreportcards.org/reports.htm

Virginia: www.pen/k12.va.us/html/reportcard.shtml

REFERENCES

Black, S. (2002, May). Not just helping hands. *American School Board Journal, 189,* 42–44.

Burnaford, G., & Hobson, D. (2001). Responding to reform: Images for teaching in the new millennium. In P. B. Joseph & G. E. Burnaford (Eds.), *Images of schoolteachers in America* (pp. 229–243). Mahwah, NJ: Erlbaum.

Clement, J. R. B. (1999). Online school performance reports: Grading the schools, giving citizens data for reform. (ERIC Document Reproduction No. ED 448707).

Dailey, C. A. (1982). *Using the track record approach: The key to successful personnel selection.* New York: AMACOM.

Darling-Hammond, L. (2000). *Solving the dilemmas of teacher supply, demand, and standards.* New York: National Commission on Teaching & America's Future. (ERIC Document Reproduction Service No. ED463337).

Fersh, D., & Thomas, P. (1993). *Complying with the Americans with Disabilities Act: A guidebook for management and people with disabilities.* Westport, CT: Quorum.

Haller, E. (1987). Teacher selection in the city school district of Rochester. In A. Wise, L. Darling-Hammond, D. Berliner, E. Haller, P. Schlechty, B. Berry, A. Praskac, and G. Noblit (Eds.), *Effective teacher selection: From recruitment to retention—Case studies* (pp. 153–187). Santa Monica, CA: Rand.

Jacobs, R. (1993). *Legal compliance guide to personnel management.* Englewood Cliffs, NJ: Prentice-Hall.

Lawler, E. (1992). *The ultimate advantage: Creating the high-involvement organization.* San Francisco: Jossey-Bass.

Mood, A. M. (1970). Do teachers make a difference? In *Do teachers make a difference?* (pp. 1–24). Washington, DC: U.S. Government Printing Office.

National Governors Association. (1999). *Teacher supply and demand: Is there a shortage?* [On-line.] Available: www.na.org/pubs/issueBriefs/2000/000125Teachers.asp

Scriven, M. (1990). Teacher selection. In J. Millman & L. Darling-Hammond (Eds.), *The new handbook of teacher evaluation* (pp. 76–103). Newbury Park, CA: Sage.

South Carolina Center for Teacher Recruitment. (2000). [On-line.] Available: *www.scctr.org*

Tannenbaum, M. (2000, May). No substitute for quality. *Educational Leadership, 57,* 70–72.

Taylor, T. (1994). *Troops to teachers: Guidelines for teacher educators.* (ERIC Document Reproduction Service No. ED 366591).

Wanous, J. P. (1980). *Organizational entry: Recruitment, selection, and socialization of newcomers.* Reading, MA: Addison-Wesley.

CHAPTER FOUR

OBTAINING INFORMATION AND EVALUATING APPLICANTS

Recent educational reforms have brought attention to the issue of teacher quality. There is general agreement that the key to student achievement is quality teaching, but the experts do not all agree on how to achieve the goal of improving the quality of classroom teaching. The following comment persuasively states the case for the importance of good teaching (Lessinger & Salowe, 2001):

> There is now widespread acceptance of the fact that the teacher is the single most important school-based element in student learning, as well as in helping students gain a positive attitude toward schooling. That fact agrees with every parent's common sense as well as the best research (p. 23).

Lessinger and Salowe suggest that placing highly qualified teachers in schools as they are presently organized is unlikely to produce much improvement in student learning. They argue that schools must be "specifically designed and managed to achieve reliable classroom teaching quality" (p. 23), and add:

> There is growing evidence that some of a school's characteristics greatly influence instructional results. In healthy schools, faculty and students share a common vision of the purposes of instruction and commitment to success . . . They use what works, have lots of contact between teachers and students in class and outside, and develop high morale (p. 28).

Other authors have reached similar conclusions.

The importance of the climate of a school in mediating children's learning is discussed in Chapter 11. This chapter deals with identifying, recruiting, and retaining qualified and effective teachers.

PLAN OF THE CHAPTER

No Child Left Behind mandates that teachers of academic subjects in the public schools must be "highly qualified." Many school districts already meet that standard and are investigating ways of further upgrading the quality of the teachers in their schools. This chapter examines the processes of gathering information about applicants for teaching jobs and evaluating the qualifications of those applicants, and focuses on sources of information about applicants for teaching positions, including applications, transcripts, references, and tests. Several types of interviews are discussed, and research findings on employment interviews are presented. The chapter also contains information on criminal background checks and examines the effects of transfer policies on student achievement. Websites of organizations that help recruit teachers or that provide background information on criminals are listed.

SOURCES OF INFORMATION ABOUT APPLICANTS

The district human resources department is responsible for gathering information about prospective employees, even in districts with school-based management. Initial screening of applicants is done by district-level staff members, and information gathered about qualified applicants is made available to decision makers in the schools.

There are five principal sources of information about applicants, and each is a potential contributor of data about applicants' qualifications. This information is used to determine whether the applicant meets the selection criteria for the position and is able to perform the essential functions of the job, with or without accommodation. The five information sources are the application form, transcripts, references, tests, and interviews.

Application Form

The application form is the basic tool for collecting information about an applicant. To be of most value in the hiring process, it should include the information needed to make a hiring decision or indicate a source from which the necessary information can be obtained. The form should be designed to facilitate the hiring process by letting applicants know what additional documentation should be provided. For example, the application form should explain how many references are required and whether those references should be asked to submit a recommendation letter for the candidate. If transcripts are required, the application form should explain that. It should include enough information that a selection committee will be able to determine whether the applicant is one who should be given further consideration as a prospective employee of the district. Most importantly, the form should be designed in such a way that the applicant has adequate space to record all of the information asked for.

Questions that are not related to qualifications for performing a job should not appear on the application form since such information may be used for discriminatory purposes. Districts may ask about conviction of a crime if it pertains to a bona fide occupational qualification or business necessity, but inquiries about an applicant's arrest record should be avoided (*Education Law,* 1989). Questions dealing with race or ethnic background, religion, sex, or age should not be asked, although that information may be collected anonymously on preemployment inquiry forms. The legal ramifications of requesting this type of information are discussed in more detail in Chapter 12.

Other questions that are likely to be suspect are inquiries related to marital status or name of spouse, maiden name of female applicants, questions about the number and age of children or plans to have children, child care arrangements, organizational memberships, whether an applicant's spouse objects to the applicant's traveling, and whether an applicant is the principal wage earner in the family (*Education Law,* 1989). Employers are safe in asking if an applicant has commitments that would interfere with regular attendance on the job and, if language fluency is a requirement on the job, whether the applicant is able to read, write, or speak other languages.

Employers may ask if an applicant is over 21 years of age and whether he or she is a citizen of the United States. Noncitizens may be asked if they hold a valid work permit issued by the U.S. Citizenship and Immigration Services. Rather than ask applicants questions about their medical condition, employers are advised to describe the nature of the essential functions required on a job and ask applicants whether they will be able to perform those tasks and what accommodations, if any, they will need in order to perform them (Jacobs, 1993).

Certification

All states have legislation requiring that teachers be licensed and certified to teach. A teaching license acknowledges the fact that an individual has completed an approved course of study and meets all other requirements imposed by the state and is considered competent to teach. Certification signifies that the individual is qualified to teach in a particular field or subject specialty.

Most states now provide for alternative routes to teacher certification. These programs are designed to allow individuals from outside the field of education to become classroom teachers without being required to return to school for an extended period of time. Alternative certification programs generally involve some additional college coursework but in most cases are designed for different populations than traditional programs. Many of the people who enter these programs are older and have been in the workforce for some time. They include people who were not able, for financial or family reasons, to complete a traditional teacher preparation program earlier or who decided to switch careers.

Some alternative certification programs are specifically aimed at military personnel who wish to pursue another career after they leave military service. One such program is Troops to Teachers, which is jointly sponsored by the U.S. Defense Department and the Department of Education. The program's website contains information about the program and the criteria for participation, as well as job list-ings (see Online Resources).

A number of states offer alternative certification programs as a way of solv-ing shortages of teachers in certain subject areas or localities or as a way to increase diversity in the teaching force. Some limitations apply to personnel who obtain certification through these programs. For example, in South Carolina, an individ-ual with alternative certification in a subject area that has been identified as critical may teach in any school in the state. However, if that person's subject specialty is not deemed critical, then he or she is limited to teaching in localities with teacher shortages (www.sctreachers.org/cert/pace/degree.cfm).

In California, the Hughes-Hart Educational Reform Act grants to school dis-tricts the right to develop alternative programs for preparing teachers for middle or high school. A district that wishes to establish an alternative certification pro-gram under Hughes-Hart must verify that fully credentialed teachers are not avail-able and must work with an institution of higher education that has a state-approved program for preparing teachers. These districts are also required to provide fully certified mentor teachers for the teachers in training.

There is little evidence that teachers who enter the classroom via an alter-native route are more or less effective than those who follow a more traditional path. In fact, as critics of teacher certification are fond of pointing out, there is little evidence that certification requirements of any kind are related to teacher effectiveness (Finn & Madigan, 2001). There is some research, however, that shows that teachers with alternative certification have a higher attrition rate than teachers from more traditional backgrounds. Because alternative certification programs vary greatly in quality, it seems likely that any statement about these programs would be true of some but not of others. Research is needed to determine what characteristics are found in alternative certification programs that produce teach-ers who are effective in the classroom and who are likely to remain in the field.

Transcripts

Some districts have attempted to simplify the application process by dropping the requirement that transcripts be submitted with the application. It is important that a transcript be obtained at some point in the selection process, however, in order to verify that the individual has indeed completed an approved course of study and received a college degree. Imposters have succeeded in posing as teachers, minis-ters, and physicians without holding a degree and, in a few cases, without ever having attended college. An official transcript bearing an embossed seal from the issuing institution is acceptable as valid evidence of an applicant's having attended that institution.

The transcript provides useful information about an applicant's academic achievements and course of study. Although a high grade-point average is no guarantee that an applicant will be successful in the classroom, other things being equal, individuals who do well academically in college generally achieve better results with children than those who are average or below.

References

Administrators often discount letters of references since many of them are one-sided, praising the applicant's strong qualities and avoiding mention of any faults. One reason principals supply positive references for teachers whose performance may have been marginal is a fear of legal action. A teacher who is denied a job opportunity because of a negative reference from a former principal may seek a legal remedy. About half the states have immunity laws that protect administrators who give a negative reference for a former employee from being sued for defamation. Principals in states without such legislation may be unwilling to make any comment at all about a former teacher, either in writing or on the telephone. The desire to avoid legal entanglements has also resulted in some school districts adopting policies that limit the information they release about former employees to dates of employment and positions held (Drake, 1989). However, in spite of legitimate questions about the validity of information from references, most districts require applicants to submit the names of three or four individuals who are acquainted with their work. In some districts, the application form for a professional position specifically requests the names of supervisors in all previous positions.

Tests

Requiring prospective teachers to take and pass a test of general knowledge or knowledge of their teaching field is not new, but the practice has become more widespread in recent years. Massachusetts Tests for Educator Licensure (MTEL) cover all subject areas, including reading, English, history, general science, chemistry, physics, mathematics, moderate disabilities, bilingual education, and a number of foreign languages. Individuals preparing to teach in Massachusetts must pass the test in their teaching field. Similar tests are required in many other states. Those who oppose requiring teachers to pass a test of content knowledge argue that the tests are biased against minorities and that there is no evidence that they improve teacher quality. Teachers' associations generally acquiesce in testing prospective teachers but oppose testing employed teachers. The National Education Association (2000) adopted a resolution stating that "competency tests must not be used as a condition of employment, license retention, evaluation, placement, ranking, or promotion of licensed teachers."

One professional group has identified a set of principles that it believes should be followed when test scores are used for selection decisions (Association of Teacher Educators, 1988). Among these principles were the following:

1. Tests should be validated for the purpose for which they are to be used. A test used for selection should therefore be validated for that purpose.

2. Tests should have a rational relationship to the job to be performed. That means that tests should be chosen to measure knowledge of subject or teaching techniques.
3. Cut-off scores on tests should be determined by an accepted empirical procedure rather than by arbitrary means.
4. Individuals should not be rank-ordered on the basis of test scores unless strong evidence exists that the test possesses criterion validity (that is, accurately predicts future performance).
5. Test scores should not be used to discriminate against a group or individual.

Background Checks

Before an applicant is hired, an effort should be made to determine whether he or she has a criminal record. Failure to check can be a potentially serious error. Some states now require all applicants for teaching positions to be fingerprinted and to submit to a criminal background check (Abercrombie, 1998). Criminal databanks with information about persons convicted of child abuse, kidnapping, and other violent crimes are now available in most states, and the U.S. Department of Justice, through its National Sex Offender Registry Assistance Program, leads an effort to make information on all sex offenders available to local law-enforcement officials. Also, private firms can be hired to conduct preemployment background checks on applicants, including their criminal history, employment and credit history, drug screenings, and education verification. A list of companies that perform these services can be located on the Internet by entering "employee background" or "employee screening" in a search engine.

Even the most careful screening does not always identify potential child abusers. In the past it was not uncommon for a school district to allow an employee to resign rather than face arrest and trial for a misdemeanor involving children. In addition, criminal agencies sometimes make mistakes and an individual criminal record is lost or inadvertently destroyed (*Hiring the Right People*, 1994).

A person should not be considered guilty on the basis of an accusation alone, but if such a charge has been made against an applicant, it should be investigated and the accused given a chance to answer the charge (Hyman & Snook, 1999). Even when there is no indication that an individual has been accused or convicted of criminal activity, it is good personnel policy to question omissions or inconsistencies on the application form and to check with previous employers. Missing dates on work records and reluctance to furnish the names of previous supervisors should be investigated further. Such warning signs usually turn out to be oversights, but it is better to investigate and find nothing than wind up with a problem employee (Hughes & Ubben, 1989).

Some districts now require applicants to sign an affidavit swearing that they have not engaged in behavior that would preclude them from being hired to work in a school. An example of one such affidavit is shown in Exhibit 4.2.

■ ■ ■ ■ ■

EXHIBIT 4.1

APPLICANT AFFIDAVIT

I have not at any time pleaded guilty to or been convicted of any of the acts listed below, and I have never been terminated from a position or threatened with termination for committing any of these acts:

- rape or sexual assault
- drug or alcohol abuse
- sexual harassment
- molesting or sexually exploiting a child
- indecent exposure

Have you ever been accused of any of these actions? _____. If yes, explain below the circumstances and disposition of the charges.

_____

_____

Date _____   Signature _____

Date _____   Witness _____

_____

_____

IDENTIFYING MOTIVATORS

The internal needs or motivators that an individual brings to a job help to determine whether that person is likely to be successful on the job and experience satisfaction from the work. Someone who is highly motivated by money, for example, would not derive much satisfaction from a career in a low-paying field, just as someone with a high need for variety would quickly become bored working in a highly repetitive job. Thus the selection process should take into account the factors that motivate an applicant. Applicants whose motivations most closely match those typical of teachers are more likely than others to be effective in the classroom and will be more inclined to remain in the field.

Human resources workers can design questions that help pinpoint the motivating factors that an applicant will bring to the classroom. Among the motivating factors that are most important for teachers are the need to perform work that is interesting and socially significant, the need for comfortable and attractive surroundings and adequate resources, and the need to have contact with other people.

Teachers tend to have below average needs for money and for power and influence, and as a group they are average in the need for structure and predictability, need for variety, need for creativity, and the desire for comfortable and attractive physical surroundings. But like all human beings, teachers are individuals and what is true on average may not be true of a given person. For example, many but not all art teachers have a higher than average need for creativity and although many administrators are above average on the need for influence some are not so inclined. Some teachers prefer as little structure as possible, whereas others frequently seek reassurance that they are doing their work the right way.

The need for recognition and approval is a nearly universal trait. Teachers appreciate recognition, although most can manage without it if necessary. Supervisors should be aware that recognition serves a dual purpose. In addition to fulfilling the need for recognition, it also helps meet the need for structure. When an employee is praised for his or her work, the implied message is that the task for which he or she received praise was performed correctly, useful feedback for an employee who may not have been clear about what was expected.

Sample Questions. Examples of questions that can be used to identify factors that motivate an applicant for a teaching position are shown below.

1. Is it important to you that your job involve variety and that each day be a little different from the day before or would you be happy with a routine that doesn't change much? (Variety)
2. Is it important to you to be clear about what is expected of you on the job so there is no confusion about how you should perform your job, or can you work without clear-cut rules? (Structure)
3. Is it important to you to be able to express yourself creatively on the job so that what you produce is uniquely yours, or does it not matter that much to you? (Creativity)
4. Is it important to you to do work that helps people and is socially significant, or is that something you don't think much about? (Social significance)
5. Is it important to you to be paid well for what you do, or, if you were offered a job that you wanted, would you accept it even though the salary was less than you had hoped for? (Money)
6. Is it important to you to be able to interact with other people on the job, or would you be just as happy working by yourself most of the time? (People contact)
7. Is it important to you that the physical surroundings where you work are comfortable and attractive, or can you be just as happy in a setting where comfort is minimal? (Physical surroundings)
8. Is it important to you that you receive recognition from your boss for doing a good job, or is doing a good job enough of a reward in itself? (Recognition)

9. Is it important to you that you can influence decisions affecting your work and that you be able to tell others what to do, or are you content to leave those things to other people? (Influence)

There are no right or wrong answers to these questions, but in general applicants who are highly motivated by the need for money, recognition, variety, and influence are likely to find that most teaching jobs are not a good fit. Those who are most likely to fit well in a teaching position are applicants who express a high need for social significance, people contact, and, in most schools, comfortable and attractive physical surroundings. People with a high need for structure will find a fit in some schools but not in others. Schools in which the principal runs a "tight ship" attract teachers with high structure needs, but those teachers are often frustrated working in schools where the principal is more easy-going and rules are not always followed.

Rating the Applicant

Research has shown that note taking improves the interviewer's ability to recall information about the applicant later (Webster, 1982). Detailed note taking can be a distraction, but writing key words and phrases rather than complete statements minimizes the disruptive effect and allows the interviewer to accurately reconstruct the interview later. It is common practice to use a checklist or rating scale to evaluate applicants immediately following the interview. An example of a rating scale that can be used for this purpose is shown in Exhibit 4.2. The example draws on the job-specific criteria for teaching from Exhibit 3.4.

■ ■ ■ ■ ■

EXHIBIT 4.2
APPLICANT RATING FORM

Rate the applicant from 1 (low) to 5 (high) on each item.

(Circle One)

■ Knowledge of subject matter	1	2	3	4	5
■ Oral communication ability	1	2	3	4	5
■ Enthusiasm for teaching and learning	1	2	3	4	5
■ Maturity of judgment	1	2	3	4	5
■ Ability to motivate students	1	2	3	4	5
■ Choice of instructional methods	1	2	3	4	5
■ Relationships with parents and co-workers	1	2	3	4	5
■ Belief in students' ability to learn	1	2	3	4	5

INTERVIEWING FOR SELECTION

Interviews are employed universally to select employees. Employment interviews normally occur after the applicant's application form has been reviewed and other documents (specifically transcripts and references) have been examined. The interview is seen as a way to test and confirm impressions based on the documentary record. Applicants for a teaching position normally participate in at least two interviews, a screening interview with a team consisting of central office staff members and one or more selection interviews with principals or teachers in schools that have vacancies. Central office interviewers include one or more subject area specialists and a member of the staff of the Human Resources Department.

Interviews allow decision makers to evaluate an applicant's interpersonal skills and permit judgments about a prospect's ability to express him- or herself clearly and remain poised under stress. They also allow decision makers to judge an applicant's shyness or boldness, voice quality, and personal appearance. Answers to well-designed interview questions can reveal a good deal about an applicant's commitment to children and his or her knowledge of a subject, personal interests, and views on educational issues.

One of the main reasons interviewing is popular as a selection tool is its flexibility. Interviews allow for probes and follow-up questions that are not possible on an application form, and it is often these types of questions that are most informative. In addition, interviews evoke body language that can be revealing. A prospect's facial expressions, posture, animation, and response time can be helpful in gathering information for employment decisions.

The popularity of interviewing as a method of employee selection does not mean that interviews are necessarily more valid than other sources of information about prospective employees. In fact, the opposite may be true. When two people sit down across the table from one another, social interaction occurs that influences both individuals to form impressions that are colored by their own values, beliefs, and biases. Some of the values and beliefs that an interviewer brings to the interview are helpful in identifying high-quality teaching prospects, but others are unlikely to lead to sound selection decisions. To avoid drawing incorrect inferences from an interview, interviewers need to be aware of possible biases inherent in the process of interviewing. Researchers have identified five reactions of interviewers that can bias the judgments they reach.

Contrast effect. This occurs when an interviewer compares an applicant with an individual who was interviewed earlier. Such comparisons should be avoided and the current applicant judged solely on the basis of whether he or she matches the requirements for the position described in the job model or job description (Webster, 1982).

Halo effect. An interviewer who reacts positively to an applicant tends to discount negative information and attach disproportionately great weight to positive data (Webster, 1982).

Negative information. Interviewers tend to attach disproportionate weight to negative information obtained during an interview, with the result that promising applicants may be eliminated from consideration on the basis of fairly inconsequential information (Rowe, 1989). Interviewers can avoid this problem by carefully weighing negative information to determine whether it is important enough to disqualify the applicant. If not, it should be given appropriate consideration.

Confirmation bias. Research has shown that information obtained early in the interview has a greater influence on the interviewer's evaluation of the applicant than information that is revealed later. Put another way, interviewers tend to make their up their minds quickly and spend the remainder of the interview seeking to confirm their earlier judgment (Razik & Swanson, 2001; Rowe, 1989). This bias works to the disadvantage of prospects who, because of shyness or social anxiety, are less likely to make a positive first impression.

Social merit. Human beings are attracted to individuals with certain physical or social qualities. For example, we tend to have a positive impression of people who are tall, good-looking, and well-groomed and react less favorably to those who have physical disabilities or disfiguring conditions or who dress more simply. Because physical appearance has only a slight relationship to the ability to be an effective teacher, it should not be allowed to influence hiring decisions.

Interviews are subject to the same legal scrutiny as written tests (Arvey, 1979), but are less likely to be the subject of a legal challenge. Nevertheless, interviewers should be aware that when courts do examine interviewing practices, questioning techniques are often a subject of scrutiny. Questions should be job relevant, and the same questions should be asked of all applicants (Campion & Arvey, 1989).

Questions that are motivated by a bias on the part of the interviewer should not be asked of an applicant. Areas that are protected by antidiscrimination legislation are especially to be avoided unless questions deal with skills or knowledge that are essential for successful performance on the job. Some simple examples of questions that are not recommended are those dealing with an applicant's age, marital status, number and ages of children, and religious affiliation. Asking about age might suggest a bias against older people; questions about marital status and children could reveal a bias against women; and inquiring about religious affiliation might reveal a bias against certain religions. The University of Wisconsin—Milwaukee Office of Diversity/Compliance (1999) maintains a website that lists questions that for legal or ethical reasons should be avoided during employment interviews.

Poor reliability is a problem with certain types of employment interviews. When two interviewers come to different conclusions about an applicant—one recommends hiring the applicant, and the other recommends against—that is an indication of lack of reliability in the interview. Structured or semistructured interviews are more likely to produce agreement because all interviewers ask the same questions and attach the same weights to various pieces of information (Whetzel & McDaniel, 1999).

The best results are obtained when individuals who conduct interviews are trained in their use and are familiar with the legal requirements governing employee selection. Topics that were described as inappropriate for use on application forms should also be avoided during interviews (Campion & Arvey, 1989).

Increasing Validity of Interviews

The validity of the interview as a selection device depends in large part on the interviewer's skills. Skills of interviewing can be learned, and training should be provided for those who screen applicants for teaching positions. One of the most important skills for interviewers to possess is the ability to put applicants at ease. This is done by greeting the applicant warmly and helping to make him or her feel comfortable by talking briefly about a topic of mutual interest. Good interviewers avoid using words that are likely to create a defensive attitude on the part of an applicant. They also use body language to communicate their interest in what the applicant is saying and are sensitive to messages communicated by the applicant's body language (Moffatt, 1979).

Interviewers who are adept at their work develop the skill of using implied or embedded questions. Implied questions involve paraphrasing or repeating what the applicant has said and then pausing. This is interpreted by the interviewee as a cue to elaborate. An example of an embedded question is this statement by an interviewer: "I am curious about the reasons for your statement that teaching second-graders is tougher than teaching high school students."

Interviewers must be somewhat skeptical in order to be effective, since applicants who are eager to make a good impression are likely to be tempted to embellish the truth or omit negative information altogether. Conventional wisdom suggests that a person who is lying will give himself or herself away because of nervousness, but in fact, many people are able to lie without appearing at all nervous to a casual observer. Interviewers must rely on other means of detecting omissions and exaggerations. One such method that trained interviewers use when they suspect lack of truthfulness is to continue asking questions. The more questions an applicant must answer, the more difficult it becomes to continue to conceal the truth (Vrij, 1999).

Other methods interviewers use to tell whether an applicant is truthful are internal consistency, the amount of unfavorable information provided, and clear evidence of exaggeration. *Internal consistency* refers to the absence of conflicting or contradictory answers. Since most people have encountered some unpleasant experiences on the job, a complete *absence of negative information* may mean that an applicant is withholding information. *Exaggeration* is the opposite of withholding information—it involves blowing up positive accomplishments to make them appear more significant than is warranted (Fear & Chiron, 1990).

Interview validity can be increased by use of the *behavior description interview technique* (Janz, 1989). In this approach, the interviewer asks questions about actual events an applicant has experienced in previous jobs or elsewhere. An individual's behavior in a previous situation is a more reliable predictor of how the person will act in similar situations in the future than responses to questions about hypothetical events. Focusing on an applicant's past behavior or track record is based on the principle that "a person can do again what he or she has done in the past" (Dailey & Madsen, 1980, p. 147).

The behavior description interview mitigates the problem, which is inherent in what-would-you-do-if types of questions, of social desirability responses (Latham, Saari, Pursell, & Campion, 1980). A *socially desirable response* is one that an applicant believes will be more acceptable to the interviewer than a more honest response. Such responses may be given when an individual stands to gain something of value by creating a favorable impression on another person.

Asking an applicant to tell about a time when he or she took a particular kind of action or responded in a particular way to a problem situation reduces the possibility of the applicant's relying on socially desirable responses. For example, an interviewer might ask an applicant for a teaching position, "Tell me about a time when you helped a young child learn a new skill." Even persons who have no previous teaching experience may have taught a younger sibling to ride a bicycle or fly a kite. Descriptions of such incidents reveal a good deal about the kind of teacher a person will make.

If the applicant has taught, the possibilities for asking questions of this type are endless. The interviewer might ask, "Tell me how you taught your fifth-graders about the frontier in American history" or "How do you explain the concept of valence to your chemistry students?"

TYPES OF INTERVIEWS

In a structured or standardized interview, all applicants for a job are asked the same set of prepared questions. The interviews are sometimes conducted by a team of interviewers who keep detailed notes on applicants' responses. There are several advantages to structured interviews. Notes from the interviews can be valuable in case legal action is initiated against the district for discrimination in hiring (Herman, 1994), and the structured format helps ensure that important topics are covered.

Screening Interview

For most professional positions, at least two interviews are held before a selection decision is made. The first is a screening interview, which is used to judge an applicant's personal and professional qualifications. If the applicant has the required qualifications, then he or she may be invited to take part in a selection interview.

The application is used as the basis for the screening interview. Only candidates who are clearly not qualified should be eliminated at this time. Candidates about whom there is a question should be given an opportunity to proceed to the selection interview, since some of them may be found to have strengths that compensate for certain weaknesses (Drake, 1989). Structured questions are usually used for screening interviews.

Selection Interview

The selection interview is used to help decide whether a qualified applicant is suited to fill a specific job vacancy. Selection interviews are longer, more intensive, and less structured than screening interviews. The questions asked by interviewers in the selection interview cover much the same material as the screening interview, but they are more specific and probing. In the selection interview, principals and teachers are interested in knowing whether an applicant possesses the professional skill and experience to perform the essential functions of a job and the personal qualifications needed for a good fit.

The selection interview is the time to examine in detail an applicant's views about various facets of the job for which he or she is being considered. To do this, interviewers use probes to encourage candidates to describe, expand, and elaborate on previous answers. Some examples of interview probes are (Moffatt, 1979):

- "I'd like to hear more about your thinking on that subject."
- "I'm not sure what you have in mind."
- "Why do you feel that way?"
- "Could you elaborate?"
- "Would you describe that in more detail?"
- "Tell me more."

Examples of interview questions that can be used to elicit information about the job-specific criteria for teaching identified in Exhibit 3.4 are shown in Exhibit 4.3.

Perceiver Interview

A *perceiver interview* is a type of structured interview in which identical questions are asked of all applicants. When used to select teachers, the purpose is to identify those who will be effective in helping to increase student achievement. Questions in the perceiver interview deal with three types of content: (1) values and philosophy of life (example: "Give reasons why you believe teaching is an important job");

■ ■ ■ ■ ■

EXHIBIT 4.3

INTERVIEW QUESTIONS FOR SELECTING EFFECTIVE TEACHERS

Criterion: Is able to organize and manage a class effectively

Question: What classroom rules do you usually establish for students, and how do you introduce and explain the rules?

Criterion: Is able to motivate students to learn

Question: When you introduce a topic that is not a favorite with students, what do you do to build and hold their interest?

Criterion: Is able to communicate information effectively

Question: When you give an assignment that students are not familiar with, how do you make sure they understand what is expected?

Criterion: Is able to maintain student involvement in instructional activities

Question: How do you determine whether students understand new material, and what do you do if you find that they do not understand?

Criterion: Believes in the educability of all children

Question: What have you done in the past when you have had students who were not learning?

Criterion: Has extensive knowledge of subject

Question: What have you learned recently about the subject you teach that you did not know before, and how did you learn it?

(2) one's style of interacting with other people (example: "Do you prefer to work on a project as a member of a team or independently on your own?"); and (3) analysis of problematic situations that might be encountered in teaching (example: "How would you work with a student who loves to read and does well in his schoolwork but seems to have no friends?").

Teacher applicants who are interviewed using the perceiver protocol are rated on 12 themes. Among the themes are empathy (acceptance of others' feelings), rapport drive (ability to maintain an approving relationship with each student), and activation (ability to stimulate students to think, to feel, and to learn). Interviewees are also rated on individualized perception (perceiving students as individuals), input drive (searching for ideas and materials to help students learn), and innovation (trying new ideas and techniques in the classroom). Developers of the perceiver interview believe that applicants who are rated high on the 12 themes are more effective in the classroom. However, a recent study testing that proposition found only a modest relationship between the ratings and teachers' subsequent behavior on the job (Young & Delli, 2002).

Critical Incident Interview

An approach to a structured interview developed for business organizations can be adapted for use in teacher selection interviews (Latham, Saari, Pursell, & Campion, 1980). It is especially valuable with applicants who have not previously taught. This technique assumes that human behavior is goal oriented and that individuals choose behaviors with the intention of achieving certain results or outcomes.

The technique involves identifying critical incidents that are likely to be encountered by an employee on the job. For a teacher, critical incidents might include a student who is disrespectful or disruptive, a situation in which a teacher is seeking to encourage critical thinking on the part of students through use of higher-order questions, or a child's difficulty in grasping new material. Each critical incident is described in a written narrative. The interviewer asks the applicant to read the narrative and indicate what action he or she would take if confronted with the situation described. The interviewer scores the applicant's response against benchmark answers prepared by a group of knowledgeable individuals who are familiar with the job. If the critical incidents highlight situations that are likely to be experienced in a specific position, applicants' responses can yield useful cues to probable behavior on the job.

After the incidents have been selected, a team consisting of four to six teachers and administrators prepares "benchmark" responses to be used as an aid to scoring applicants' answers. The three benchmark responses represent excellent answers (scored 5), average answers (scored 3), and poor answers (scored 1). A response with a benchmark score of 5 represents the most complete response to the problem. It is an answer that would be given by an experienced teacher and takes into account all or most facets of the problem. A response rated 5 shows sensitivity, action aimed at resolving the problem, and a clear sense of professional responsibility. A response with a benchmark score of 1 represents a very limited response to the problem described in the narrative. It is an answer that might be given by a teacher with limited experience and knowledge of teaching or by a teacher who, despite having teaching experience, displays questionable judgment or lack of sensitivity. Such a response uses very little of the information provided in the narrative. The suggested plan of action is incomplete or addresses superficial aspects of the problem.

An example of a critical incident involving a child who is new to a school and is being harassed by other children because of his appearance and ethnic origin is shown in Exhibit 4.4, along with three benchmark responses. Applicants are asked what action they would take in the situation described in the critical incident. Because their answers to this question will vary, the benchmark responses are meant as guides to help the interviewer score the actual responses.

■ ■ ■ ■ ■

EXHIBIT 4.4

EXAMPLE OF A CRITICAL INCIDENT

Zayed is a sixth-grader who transferred to Eliot Middle School in the middle of the year from out-of-state after both his parents were killed in an automobile accident. He is living with an uncle. As Zayed's teacher, you have been visited by the school social worker who explained that the boy was depressed about the loss of his parents and is receiving therapy. Zayed is quiet and withdrawn and at present has no friends in the class. However, he is a good student and does well in his schoolwork.

The problem is that some of the boys in the class have taken to teasing Zayed about his name and his appearance. They call him "the Sheik," and some comment on his features, calling him "Big Nose."

You have spoken privately to two of the boys who seemed to be ring-leaders. Those two have stopped name-calling, but others continue to do it. At first Zayed laughed at the nicknames, but more recently he has become visibly angry. On Tuesday Paul called Zayed a "terrorist" and Zayed hit Paul, bloodying his nose. You sent Paul to the school nurse, who cleaned him up and called Paul's parents to explain what had happened. Zayed was suspended for one day by the principal.

Zayed's uncle has asked to see you, and you need to talk with your students about their behavior. Describe how you will proceed.

Benchmark Response 1 (1 point): I would tell Zayed's uncle that this was an unfortunate incident and that Zayed needs to control his temper. I would also tell him that if any students call Zayed a name in the future I will send them to the principal.

Benchmark Response 2 (3 points): I would tell Zayed's uncle that the teasing was unfortunate and that I will see that it doesn't happen again. I will also explain that, while Zayed's anger is understandable, hitting other students is not acceptable. I would explain to the students what stereotyping means and tell them that very few people of Middle Eastern backgrounds are terrorists and that most are honest, law-abiding citizens.

Benchmark Response 3 (5 points): I would promise Zayed's uncle that I will see that Zayed is not teased or insulted in the future. I would also explain that Zayed must understand that hitting other students is not acceptable. I would lead a discussion with the class about stereotyping and tolerance, explaining that America is a diverse country and that we have historically welcomed people of all races and nationalities. I would explain that name-calling is an unfriendly act and ask that they extend friendship to Zayed.

TRANSFER POLICIES AND STUDENT LEARNING

According to figures from the National Center for Education Statistics (1992), about 20 percent of teachers hired by public schools are first-time teachers. Slightly more than one-fourth reenter teaching after an absence, and the remainder are transfering from other teaching positions.

Employees seek to transfer from one school to another for a number of reasons. Some want to transfer for convenience, whereas others seek to move to schools with better programs, facilities, or equipment. Still others hope to work with particular teachers or administrators or want to be assigned to a school with school-based management.

In many districts an effort is made to act on transfer requests before decisions are made to hire new teachers. This allows teachers who are already employed by the district to have the first choice of vacancies. Such a policy is helpful in sustaining teacher morale, but it can create problems when selection decisions are delayed while employed teachers are given the option to interview for vacancies.

Preference in Transfers

Some districts have policies that specify that teachers seeking transfers must be placed before new hires are made (Darling-Hammond, Wise, Berry, & Praskac, 1987). In other districts, the bargaining agreement gives transferring teachers the right to select the school in which they prefer to teach, subject only to the condition that teachers choose in order of seniority, with the most senior teacher having first choice (Haller, 1987).

Policies that give employed teachers the right of first refusal for available vacancies can delay decisions on selection and thereby prevent the district from issuing contracts to promising applicants. For that reason, some districts attempt to solve the problem of delay by issuing open contracts to qualified candidates. An open contract secures a commitment from the teacher but leaves the district the option of making a placement decision at a later time. A potential problem with this tactic is that the more highly sought after teachers may choose to sign with a district that offers an immediate placement decision.

Delays in offering teaching contracts can occur for a variety of reasons in addition to transfers. Whatever the reason, delays increase the likelihood that a district will lose out to other districts in the competition for teaching talent. A common reason for delays in making selection decisions is uncertainty regarding need, which is a factor when enrollment projections are unavailable or are suspected of being inaccurate, when finances are tight, or when late resignations are expected.

Caution in hiring teachers who may turn out not to be needed is important when the potential cost to the district can reach $50,000 per teacher, including salary and benefits. However, if experience has shown that the number of teachers needed consistently exceeds earlier projections, a district may offer a limited number of open contracts to promising applicants. This prevents the loss of teachers with strong qualifications to competing districts.

Equity in Transfer Practices

Placement and transfer decisions almost always raise questions of equity in the distribution of teacher talent. A district that relies solely on seniority in deciding transfer requests risks having all of its experienced teachers located in the most desirable schools, except for the individuals who principals reject. The end result of such a policy is maldistribution of teacher talent, with the most experienced teachers located in the more desirable schools and those with the least experience assigned to the less desirable schools. These are oftentimes schools with large proportions of children from poor and minority families. Staffing these schools exclusively with inexperienced teachers risks loss of learning.

Of course, experience is not necessarily synonymous with ability, and many inexperienced teachers are very capable, but the problem with open transfer policies is that the most able teachers do not remain long in schools that have little to offer in the way of rewards and prestige. In a profession in which there are limited opportunities for vertical mobility, teachers gravitate toward schools with better teaching conditions, a reputation for quality programs, or better facilities. This can create a problem for administrators who may be left with no alternative other than staffing less popular schools with beginning teachers.

SUMMARY

Information about prospective employees is collected by the district office from five principal sources—application form, transcripts, references, tests, and interviews. The information is used to determine whether an applicant can perform job-specific functions.

Application forms and interviews are the most widely used methods for collecting information about applicants, but tests of knowledge of subject and methods of teaching are also used in most states.

Interviews are more reliable when interviewers are taught methods of avoiding bias. A common but subtle form of bias is giving preference to certain individuals on the basis of social merit factors.

Critical incident interviews ask applicants to describe how they would handle realistic, work-related problems. The applicant receives a detailed description of the problem, and his or her answer is scored by comparing it to benchmark responses. This technique originated in industry and is especially valuable for assessing applicants' judgment.

Teacher transfers in schools are common, and they can affect the quality of instruction. A sound policy on teacher transfers maintains a balance of experienced and inexperienced teachers in all schools in the district.

SUGGESTED ACTIVITIES

1. On the Internet locate application forms for a teaching position from three or four school districts and compare them. Can you identify a legitimate purpose for all the questions that are asked? Are any questions missing that should be included?

2. Work together with one or two other persons to write a critical incident for use in interviewing applicants for a teaching position. Identify the grade level and/or subject taught. When you finish writing the incident, write 1-point and 5-point benchmark responses.

3. Suppose you are the principal of a school and one of your teachers, whose spouse is being transferred to a position in another city, asks you to write a letter of reference. You have misgivings because the teacher is not effective. Discuss your ethical responsibilities in this situation and tell what you would do.

4. Read the following responses of two teacher applicants to the interviewer's question. What do the responses tell you about the applicants? If you were the interviewer, what follow-up questions would you ask each applicant?

   Q. Your students will take tests on reading and mathematics near the end of the school year. How will you prepare them to do well on those tests?

   Applicant 1: I don't believe in teaching to the test, so I will concentrate on covering the material in the curriculum. I hope the tests and the curriculum are aligned; if they are not, I will still focus on the curriculum. I hope it is possible to get some additional help for students who are behind in reading or math, because I will have to keep a pretty brisk pace in order to cover the curriculum. Students need to know the curriculum in order to do well on the tests, and if I slow down to bring along those who are behind we won't be able to get to everything they need to know.

   Applicant 2: I think it's important that students do well on the tests. If they don't do well, the school looks bad and so do I. I don't want other teachers to think I am the reason the school doesn't get accredited. I always look at students' cumulative records to see which ones need special help, and then I work with them in class and, if necessary, schedule some after-school sessions to help them catch up. I'll also ask their parents to work with them at home. I'm not too worried about students who are on grade level; they will do okay. I want my class to shine when the test results come back, so I intend to get them fired up so they will do well.

5. Read Case Study II and answer the questions.

ONLINE RESOURCES

AACTE Education Policy Clearinghouse (www.edpolicy.org)

AACTE (American Association of Colleges of Teacher Education) maintains this site for individuals who are interested in state and national policies that pertain to teacher quality.

Alliance for Excellent Education (www.all4ed.org)

The Alliance seeks to improve the quality of teachers and principals. Among its proposals are tax incentives, loan forgiveness for students who prepare to teach, and scholarships to educators who agree to work in high-poverty schools.

Haberman Educational Foundation (www.altcert.org/prescreeners.asp)

This site features online prescreening interviews for prospective principals and teachers. The stated purpose of the teacher interview is to identify teachers who will be able to succeed "with even the most challenging of students."

National Association of State Directors of Teacher Education and Certification (www.nasdtec.org)

The Association is dedicated to licensing well-prepared, safe and wholesome educators for schools. The website contains links showing teacher certification requirements in all 50 states. It also contains information about reciprocity for teachers across state lines and a description of actions taken by states for teachers who receive National Board certification.

National Center for Education Information (www.ncei.com/State-alt-contact.htm)

The Center is a private, nonpartisan research organization that claims to be "the authoritative source of information about alternative preparation and certification of teachers and school administrators." This site lists names and contact information about alternative certification programs available in all 50 states and the District of Columbia.

Public Education Network (www.publiceducation.org)

The Network has developed a guide for community action groups that seek to improve teacher quality in their schools

Teach for America (www.teachforamerica.org)

This organization, established by Wendy Kopp, places recent college graduates in teaching jobs for two years in under-resourced schools in urban areas and some rural locations. Participants receive five weeks of training before starting their teaching assignment.

Troops to Teachers (www.dantes.doded.mil/dantes_web/troopstoteachers/index.htm?Flag=True)

This program, jointly sponsored by the U.S. Defense Department and the Department of Education, offers opportunities for retiring military personnel to prepare for a second career in teaching. The website contains information about the program and the criteria for participation, as well as current job listings.

REFERENCES

Abercrombie, K. (1998, April 29). Right to teach in California denied without prints. *Education Week*, p. 5.

Arvey, R. (1979). Unfair discrimination in the employment interview. *Psychological Bulletin, 86*, 736–765.

Association of Teacher Educators. (1988). *Teacher assessment*. Reston, VA: Author.

Campion, J., & Arvey, R. (1989). Unfair discrimination in the employment interview. In R. Eder and G. Ferns (Eds.), *The employment interview: Theory, research, and practice* (pp. 61–73). Newbury Park, CA: Sage.

Dailey, C., & Madsen, A. (1980). *How to evaluate people in business*. New York: McGraw-Hill.

Darling-Hammond, L., Wise, A., Berry, B., & Praskac, A. (1987). Teacher selection in the Montgomery County Public Schools. In A. Wise, L. Darling-Hammond, D. Berliner, E. Haller, P. Schlechty, B. Berry, A. Praska, and G.

Noblit (Eds.), *Effective teacher selection: From recruitment to retention—Case studies* (pp. 52–92). Santa Monica, CA: Rand.

Drake, J. (1989). *The effective interviewer: A guide for managers.* New York: AMACOM.

Education law: Vol. 2. (1989). New York: Matthew Bender.

Fear, R., & Chiron, R. (1990). *The evaluation interview* (4th ed.). New York: McGraw-Hill.

Finn, C. E., Jr., & Madigan, K. (2001, May). Removing the barriers for teacher candidates. *Educational Leadership, 58,* 29–31, 36.

Grissmer, D., Flanagan, A., Kawata, J., & Williamson, S. (2000). *Improving student achievement.* Santa Monica, CA: Rand.

Haberman, M. (1987). *Recruiting and selecting teachers for urban schools.* Reston, VA: Association of Teacher Educators.

Hakel, M. (1982). Employment interviewing. In K. Rowland & G. Ferris (Eds.), *Personnel management* (pp. 129–153). Boston: Allyn and Bacon.

Haller, E. (1987). Teacher selection in the city school district of Rochester. In A. Wise, L. Darling-Hammond, D. Berliner, E. Haller, P. Schlechty, B. Berry, A. Praska, and G. Noblit (Eds.), *Effective teacher selection: From recruitment to retention—Case studies* (pp. 153–187). Santa Monica, CA: Rand.

Herman, S. (1994). *Hiring right: A practical guide.* Thousand Oaks, CA: Sage.

Hiring the right people. (1994). Malibu, CA: National School Safety Center. (ERIC Document Reproduction Service No. ED 411397).

Hughes, L., & Ubben, G. (1989). *The elementary principal's handbook: A guide to effective action* (3rd ed.). Boston: Allyn and Bacon.

Hyman, I., & Snook, P. (1999). *Dangerous schools: What we can do about the physical and emotional abuse of our children.* San Francisco: Jossey-Bass.

Jacobs, R. (1993). *Legal compliance guide to personnel management.* Englewood Cliffs, NJ: Prentice-Hall.

Janz, T. (1989). The patterned behavior description interview: The best prophet of the future is the past. In R. Eder & G. Ferris (Eds.), *The employment interview: Theory, research, and practice* (pp. 158–168). Newbury Park, CA: Sage.

Latham, G., Saari, L., Pursell, E., & Campion, M. (1980). The situational interview. *Journal of Applied Psychology, 65,* 422–427.

Lessinger, L. M., & Salowe, A. E. (2001). *Healing public schools: The winning prescription to cure their chronic illness.* Lanham, MD: Scarecrow.

Moffatt, T. (1979). *Selection interviewing for managers.* New York: Harper & Row.

National Center for Education Statistics. (1992). *The condition of education, 1992.* Washington, DC: U.S. Department of Education.

National Education Association. (2000). *NEA 2000–2001 resolutions.* Available online: www.nea.org/cgi-bin/AT-resolutionssearch.cgi

Razik, T. A., & Swanson, A. D. (2001). *Fundamental concepts of educational leadership* (2nd ed.). Upper Saddle River, NJ: Prentice-Hall.

Rowe, P. (1989). Unfavorable information and interview decisions. In R. Eder and G. Ferris (Eds.). *The employment interview. Theory, research, and practice* (pp. 77–89). Newbury Park, CA: Sage.

University of Wisconsin—Milwaukee Office of Diversity/Compliance. (1999). *Questions to avoid during employment interviews.* Available online: www.uwm.edu/Dept/OD_C/interviews.html

Vrij, A. (1999). Interviewing to detect deception. In A. Memon & R. Bull (Eds.), *Handbook of the psychology of interviewing* (pp. 317–326). New York: Wiley.

Webster, E. (1982). *The employment interview: A social judgment process.* Schomberg, Ontario, Canada: S. I. P.

Whetzel, D., & McDaniel, M. (1999). The employment interview. In A. Memon and R. Bull (Eds.), *Handbook of the psychology of interviewing* (pp. 213–226). New York: Wiley.

Young, I. P., & Delli, D. A. (2002, December). The validity of the Teacher Perceiver Interview for predicting performance of classroom teachers. *Educational Administration Quarterly, 38,* 586–612.

SELECTING ADMINISTRATIVE AND SUPPORT PERSONNEL

Finding qualified candidates to fill vacancies in schools is an ongoing challenge in most districts. This chapter examines the procedures used to fill vacancies in administrative and support positions in schools and describes the duties performed by the individuals who hold those jobs. Finding the right people for these positions is critical in order for schools to run smoothly and offer effective instructional programs.

District office personnel, current principals, and those who contemplate becoming principals will be interested in the topic of selection of principals and assistant principals, for both personal and professional reasons, and in the material on selecting aides, counselors, substitute teachers, and clerical personnel out of professional interest.

PLAN OF THE CHAPTER

Chapter 5 describes the processes involved in screening and selecting individuals to fill positions as school administrators and support staff, including school social workers, psychologists, guidance counselors, instructional aides, library/media specialists, school secretaries, and substitute teachers.

SELECTION PROCEDURES

Selection procedures for administrative and support personnel parallel the procedures in teacher selection. The steps are:

1. Prepare a job model or job description.
2. Announce the vacancy.
3. Conduct a preliminary screening of applicants and eliminate those who are not qualified.
4. Conduct first-round interviews with selected candidates.
5. Select finalists and conduct second-round interviews with them.

Preparing a Job Model

The preparation of a model follows an analysis of the position to identify major tasks performed on the job or results expected. Information for the analysis may be collected either from interviews with those who currently hold the position or from questionnaires completed by them (Gatewood & Feild, 1987). The use of a job model is important in defining the parameters of the search and selection process and in avoiding the problem of misperception of the position (Jentz, 1982).

Exhibit 5.1 provides a job model for a high school principal including results sought, a description of the job environment, and priority actions required on the job.

Announcing the Vacancy

Most districts announce all administrative, supervisory, or counseling openings to current employees in order to give those who may be interested the opportunity to apply. Some negotiated agreements contain a clause requiring that teachers be notified of administrative and counseling vacancies. An issue of concern to individuals who are interested in moving up is whether vacancies are filled from within the district or from outside. Some school districts have ironclad policies of filling all vacancies from within, whereas others hire the most qualified candidate, regardless of location. Consistently hiring from within the district has the advantage of helping maintain high teacher morale, but it runs the risk of developing inbred thinking. Hiring outsiders often brings fresh thinking into the system.

School districts are recruiting more actively to fill administrative vacancies because the pool of prospective administrators is shrinking. As older principals retire, fewer teachers are applying to fill the vacancies. In one recent survey, 60 percent of superintendents reported that their districts faced a shortage of qualified principal candidates. It is not uncommon for a district to receive fewer than a dozen applications for a principal vacancy; as a result districts that have traditionally filled administrative vacancies from within are being forced to look outside the immediate locality for replacements (Cusick, 2003).

Some districts advertise nationally in publications such as *Education Week* and *The New York Times* to attract applicants for administrative positions, and in states that allow it school districts may recruit principals from the managerial ranks of business. The requirement that principals have teaching experience eliminates that option in other states. Some experts have argued that more people could be attracted to careers in administration if starting salaries were increased and working conditions improved (Archer, 2003).

Currently, principals earn between $10,000 and $25,000 more than classroom teachers, but they also work more days each year, and their workdays tend to be longer than those of teachers. Secondary principals also spend a considerable amount of time working evenings, attending school sports events, board meetings, and committee sessions. Many teachers believe the additional compensation is not adequate for the extra work required (Cusick, 2003).

■ ■ ■ ■ ■ ▬▬▬▬▬▬▬▬▬▬▬▬▬▬▬▬▬▬▬▬▬▬▬▬▬▬▬

EXHIBIT 5.1

JOB MODEL FOR HIGH SCHOOL PRINCIPAL

RESULTS SOUGHT

1. Teachers and parents are enthusiastic about the school's mission and programs and work cooperatively to achieve them.
2. Teachers receive the support and resources they need to plan and implement an effective instructional program, including constructive feedback and regular evaluations.
3. Teachers, parents, and students are kept informed about school programs and events.
4. Community members express confidence in the effectiveness of the school's programs and are given ample opportunity to have a voice in decisions about those programs.
5. Students are polite and well-behaved and show respect to adults and one another.
6. Students regularly consult with counselors regarding personal growth issues and educational and career planning.
7. Plans for dealing with emergencies have been distributed to all members of the school community and are rehearsed at regular intervals.

JOB ENVIRONMENT

The job is principal of a high school of 1,400 students and 150 teachers and staff serving a suburb of a large metropolitan area in the Southwest. The school building is 40 years old but has been well-maintained, although it is small for the current enrollment. Temporary classrooms have been placed on-site to absorb the excess enrollment. The student body is racially mixed, with Caucasian, Hispanic, and African American students together comprising about 93 percent of the population. Almost 90 percent of the graduates attend college or pursue other educational opportunities. Economically, the area in which the school is located is thriving, with publishing, finance, and electronics being the major industries. Many residents of the area have relocated from the Eastern United States, including a large contingent of retirees living on fixed incomes, many of whom vigorously oppose property tax increases. As a result, school budgets are tight and many school buildings in the district are crowded.

PRIORITY ACTIONS

The successful candidate must provide leadership for development of an instructional programs that will enable the school to maintain its reputation as one of the best schools in the state. The principal will be expected to provide leadership to help the school reach and surpass the standards of student performance established by the state and federal governments and to prepare graduates to compete successfully for admission to the nation's most prestigious colleges and universities. The principal must be prepared to work with parents and the community to keep all stakeholders well-informed and to generate support for all phases of the school programs.

Screening the Applicants

With the growing emphasis on accountability in schools, the process of screening and selecting administrators is changing. The criteria used for selection of administrators now emphasize the ability to develop strong school cultures and to facilitate the work of teachers in order to produce gains in student achievement. Evidence of the ability to work effectively with parents and community leaders also receives more attention than in the past.

School superintendents in Georgia and Tennessee, asked what they believed were the most important qualifications for principals to possess, rated knowledge of learning theory and curriculum development among the most important. The leadership skills they rated highest included team building and the ability to communicate effectively (Lease, 2002). Other skills that the superintendents felt principals should possess included proficiency in human relations and public relations, planning, and technology. They also valued principals with knowledge of diversity, multicultural and gender issues, and school law. Budgeting, finance, and facilities management were rated lower in importance by the superintendents (Lease, 2002).

In another study, superintendents were asked what skills were most likely to lead to a principal's failure to succeed on the job. The five deficiencies cited most often by the respondents were principals' inability to work cooperatively with faculty and staff, failure to develop positive community relations, making poor decisions, and ineffectiveness in solving problems. Lack of leadership in curriculum and instruction was also cited frequently as leading to failure by a principal (Matthews, 2002).

Under No Child Left Behind, administrators are responsible for providing leadership to achieve yearly progress for all students, leading ultimately to proficiency in critical subject matter. The law does not define the process by which this goal is to be achieved, instead leaving that decision to policy makers and managers of the educational enterprise. Much of the responsibility for achieving this ambitious objective will rest directly on the shoulders of principals, and they can expect to be held accountable for progress toward the goal. Accordingly, no task the principal performs will exceed instructional improvement in importance.

The list of desirable competencies for prospective principals developed by the Interstate School Leaders Licensure Consortium (ISLLC) gives a comprehensive picture of a competent and successful principal. The ISLLC competencies are shown in Exhibit 5.2.

Interviewing and Checking References

A number of suggestions for conducting selection interviews with teachers were presented in Chapter 4. Most of the advice presented there applies equally to interviewing for administrative and support positions. The number of first-round interviews varies with the position and the number of applicants. For a principalship, it is not uncommon for 10 or more candidates to be invited to first-round interviews. For the position of teacher aide or secretary, there may be no more than

■ ■ ■ ■ ■

EXHIBIT 5.2

**STANDARDS FOR PREPARATION OF EDUCATIONAL LEADERS
DEVELOPED BY THE INTERSTATE SCHOOL LEADERS
LICENSURE CONSORTIUM**

Standard 1. A school administrator is an educational leader who promotes the success of all students by facilitating the development, articulation, implementation, and stewardship of a vision of learning that is shared and supported by the school community.

Standard 2. A school administrator is an educational leader who promotes the success of all students by advocating, nurturing, and sustaining a school culture and instructional program conducive to student learning and staff professional growth.

Standard 3. A school administrator is an educational leader who promotes the success of all students by ensuring management of the organization, operations, and resources for a safe, efficient, and effective learning environment.

Standard 4. A school administrator is an educational leader who promotes the success of all students by collaborating with families and community members, responding to diverse community interests and needs, and mobilizing community resources.

Standard 5. A school administrator is an educational leader who promotes the success of all students by acting with integrity, fairness, and in an ethical manner.

Standard 6. A school administrator is an educational leader who promotes the success of all students by understanding, responding to, and influencing the larger political, social, economic, legal, and cultural context.

Source: The Interstate School Leaders Licensure Consortium (ISLLC) standards were developed by the Council of Chief State School Officers and member states. Copies may be downloaded from the Council's website at www.ccsso.org. Copyright © 1996 by the Council of Chief State School Officers.

2 or 3 candidates. First-round interviews are intended to narrow the field to the most promising prospects, and if there are only a small number of applicants for a position, one round of interviews may be all that is needed. Discussion of selection criteria for each of the support positions will be presented later in this chapter. If needed, second-round interviews are conducted with the candidates whose qualifications appear to most nearly match the requirements of the position.

At this point, references are contacted and asked about the applicants' work record and performance in previous positions. They may also be asked to verify the accuracy of information furnished by the applicant. The final step is to check appropriate criminal justice databanks in order to verify that applicants still under active consideration have not been convicted of a crime that would disqualify them from holding the position.

Announcing Decisions

Completion of second-round interviews is normally followed in short time by an announcement of the selection decision. The decision may be delayed if two equally strong prospects are vying for the position or if none of the finalists appears qualified. In the latter case, the decision may be made to reopen the search and interview additional applicants.

When a decision is made to hire an individual, that person normally receives word promptly, but the mail moves more slowly for those who were not chosen. Courtesy dictates that all active applicants (that is, those who participated in second-round interviews and have not withdrawn) are informed when the decision is made, but this practice is by no means universally observed.

Applicants from within the district who made the list of finalists should receive a personal communication, either in the form of a letter or a telephone call, informing them of the reasons they were not chosen and suggesting ways they might improve their chances of selection in the future. Those who are unlikely to receive serious consideration for future openings should be notified tactfully of that fact and encouraged to pursue other opportunities. Candidates from outside the district should be informed when a decision has been made and encouraged to apply again in the future if their qualifications warrant that.

USE OF TESTS FOR SELECTION OF ADMINISTRATORS

Written Tests

About one-fourth of the states in the United States now require candidates for the position of principal to complete a written examination (Egginton, Jeffries, & Kidd-Knights, 1988). One such examination is the School Leaders Licensure Assessment (SLLA) developed by the Educational Testing Service in cooperation with state departments of education in several states. Some states have developed their own tests, either independently or with the assistance of a testing firm, and a few large-city school districts have adopted testing procedures to help screen prospective administrators. Some of the tests now in use combine written exercises with in-basket exercises. On in-basket exercises, an examinee responds to telephone messages, memoranda, letters, and emails similar to those that principals might receive. In addition to imposing testing requirements, some state legislatures have introduced additional educational requirements for prospective school administrators, and others have mandated internship programs.

Assessment Centers

Many school districts increasingly rely on assessment centers to help in the selection of school principals, and some states now require aspirants for school administration to successfully complete an assessment center procedure. An assessment center is a series of exercises that simulate problems that might confront a school principal. Candidates record the decisions and actions they would take and are evaluated by a team of assessors who observe them in the process of carrying out a variety of simulated tasks (Gatewood & Feild, 1987). Some examples of the kinds of attributes that are measured by assessment centers are shown in Exhibit 5.3.

Criterion validity refers to the power of a test to predict performance on a particular job. Participants in assessment centers receive ratings in 12 areas in addition

---

EXHIBIT 5.3

TYPICAL ADMINISTRATIVE SKILLS ASSESSED IN PERFORMANCE ASSESSMENT CENTERS

Oral communication
Explaining an issue, problem, or proposed action clearly and concisely using spoken language

Written communication
Clearly explaining an issue, problem or proposed action in writing using language that is appropriate for the intended audience

Leadership
Setting a course of action and influencing subordinates to support and pursue that direction

Planning and organizing
Developing a timetable and lists of tasks to be accomplished in order to achieve an objective, and assigning responsibility for completing the work

Decision making
Considering plausible options for dealing with a problematic situation and selecting the most appropriate course of action from among the alternatives

Initiative
Acting within one's authority to make a decision or carry out a plan without being prompted or directed to do so

Sensitivity
Anticipating and acknowledging the attitudes and feelings of those affected by one's actions and seeking to behave in such as way as to avoid injury to others

Collaboration
Working with members of a team toward a common goal by sharing responsibility and showing consideration for others' views and opinions

to an overall placement recommendation. A number of studies have shown that assessment center ratings are positively correlated with performance in a variety of jobs. A study of the relationship of performance of school administrators to assessment center ratings reported similar results (Schmitt, Noe, Meritt, & Fitzgerald, 1983). The dimensions most highly and consistently correlated with job performance of administrators were (1) leadership, (2) oral communication, (3) organizational ability, (4) decisiveness, (5) judgment, and (6) problem analysis. Ratings of school climate were not correlated with principals' performance on the assessment center tasks.

Although assessment procedures are considered tests in the technical sense, they avoid many of the objections that are raised to selection tests because they possess both construct and criterion validity. *Construct validity* refers to the accuracy with which an instrument measures psychological structures, functions, or traits (Landy, 1985). Assessment measures have construct validity because of the close match between the simulated tasks candidates are asked to perform and the actual work of school principals.

SELECTION OF PRINCIPALS

Most principals began their careers as teachers. Many of the skills that help one succeed in the classroom are useful in carrying out the responsibilities associated with the principalship. However, successful teachers do not always make successful principals—a fact that should be kept in mind in choosing administrators.

Principals are responsible for eight major functions related to the operation of the school. These duties may be delegated to other members of the administrative team or even occasionally to teachers, but the principal bears ultimate responsibility for the duties being carried out in a timely and effective manner. Principals and assistant principals should be selected on the basis of demonstrated evidence of successful previous performance or the potential for successful performance in these eight areas (Baltzell & Dentler, 1983):

1. Organization of the school setting
2. Resource and logistical management
3. Staff supervision
4. Staff evaluation
5. Professional development
6. Student discipline and safety
7. Instructional improvement and accountability
8. Spokesperson or symbolic agent of both school and district

The eight functions are described in the paragraphs that follow, and suggestions are made for assessing applicants on each. In all cases, the strongest predictor of success is evidence of previous successful experience in a similar setting. Assessing applicants who have had no previous administrative experience and must be judged on the basis of their potential is one of the most difficult selection decisions administrators make. Many school districts now assign teachers who aspire to become administrators to part-time or temporary duties in which they have the opportunity to demonstrate their managerial abilities without having the responsibilities of a full-time position.

Organization of the School Setting

This function involves establishing lines of authority and communication and clarifying responsibilities within a school. It is an indispensable part of effective management. Leadership experience outside of education, including volunteer work, can be useful for assessing an individual's prospects for success in this area. Those who evaluate applicants' qualifications should pay particular attention to experiences that involve coordinating or directing the activities of other adults. Some examples are serving as a volunteer coordinator for Boy Scout or Girl Scout programs, directing a United Way or other community agency fund drive, and organizing volunteer workers in community musicals, theater groups, rescue squads, and the like.

Experiences in education that are valid indicators of organizational ability include overseeing the reorganization of a department, in particular the merging of two or more specialties into a single organizational unit. The main considerations are the extent of an individual's contribution to the effort and its success.

Resource and Logistical Management

Principals are expected to manage fiscal accounts, supervise the distribution and use of equipment and supplies, and oversee the maintenance of the school building. These are managerial responsibilities that have implications for instructional effectiveness of the school. Teachers have similar responsibilities but on a much smaller scale. Few applicants will have had experience in this area unless they have held a managerial position inside or outside of education.

Staff Supervision

Supervision includes efforts to facilitate teachers' work. Other than department heads and those who have worked as administrative aides, most teachers have had little or no experience in supervising their colleagues. However, some have supervised teacher aides. In assessing supervision of aides, decision makers should consider the length, frequency, and quality of that supervision. These factors can be judged from teachers' self-reports if confirmed by other teachers or school administrators.

Summer school administrative assignments are another means by which teachers who aspire to become administrators demonstrate their supervisory ability. Ordinarily only a limited amount of supervision is carried out during summer school, but an administrator who supervises informally over a cup of coffee is demonstrating the potential for success in that area.

Staff Evaluation

In some districts, department heads are involved in teacher evaluation, and in a few cases, teachers even take part, but most teachers have had no experience with that responsibility. Some questions that can be asked of applicants for an administrative position that will help assess their readiness to evaluate teaching are:

1. What evidence would you look for in observing a fifth-grade teacher to show that students understand the material that is being presented?
2. How would you determine whether a teacher has diagnosed students' needs before presenting a lesson?
3. How would you judge whether a homework assignment given by a teacher whom you are observing is suitable for the students?
4. How could you tell during an observation how well a teacher is monitoring students' learning?
5. What would you look for as evidence that a teacher uses technology effectively in the classroom?

Professional Development

Professional development is examined in detail in Chapter 8. With school-based management, principals are assuming more responsibility for planning and presenting staff development programs. However, this is an area in which even some persons with administrative experience are novices. In fact, some teachers have had more experience as trainers and peer coaches than the principals of their schools.

An applicant with little experience in planning or conducting professional development programs might be asked to describe some programs that he or she felt were particularly effective and to identify reasons for their effectiveness. Other evidence that can be deduced from an interview includes the applicant's self-identified developmental needs and aspects of program design about which the candidate is especially enthusiastic. An important factor in this area is the individual's knowledge of human and material resources that can be used in planning staff development programs.

Student Discipline and Safety

The principal is ultimately responsible for student discipline and safety, but success in this area is dependent on his or her ability to develop among the teachers a shared sense of responsibility for the task. The most obvious indicator of future effectiveness in this area is the teacher's own record in the classroom. A teacher who successfully manages behavior of students in one classroom without being unduly repressive probably will be able to manage discipline on a schoolwide basis. However, there are important differences in the two settings. The teacher maintains a relationship with all students he or she teaches, whereas an administrator must administer discipline to students whom he or she knows only slightly.

The role of police officer is one that teachers dislike but one that administrators are often required to fill. Applicants with a strong aversion to that role will derive little satisfaction from serving as an assistant principal. Ideally, applicants for administrative positions should have experience in working with all types of children, including those from a variety of cultural backgrounds, children with physical, mental, or emotional disabilities, and children who are gifted and talented.

Instructional Improvement and Accountability

Principals often are expected to take the lead in implementing instructional improvement in their schools. This involves achieving increased student learning within an existing or redesigned curriculum framework. Knowledge of instructional materials and various teaching methods and familiarity with the research on effective teaching (described in Chapter 1) are indicators of potential success in this area. Another criterion for assessing the ability to effect instructional improvement is knowledge of subject. A teacher who lacks comprehensive knowledge of a teaching field is unlikely to bring about instructional improvement.

Spokesperson or Symbolic Agent

The spokesperson presents the organization's programs and point of view to the media and the public. Teachers rarely have the opportunity to serve as spokesperson for a school or district, but some perform that role as part of the responsibilities involved in chairing district or association committees. An individual who serves as a delegate to professional conferences or who serves as union negotiator acquires valuable experience as a spokesperson. Poise and the ability to articulate a position are important for success in this area.

An individual's ability to function effectively as a spokesperson can be inferred from oral communication skills as well as from evidence of sensitivity to the views of others. Leaders are frequently required to summarize the views of groups with divergent opinions as a way of bringing about consensus on an issue. The ability to understand and verbalize a variety of positions on an issue, including those that differ from one's own, is a valuable asset to a school administrator. Evidence of this skill can be obtained from questions in which the candidate is asked to describe two divergent positions on an issue of current interest and to explain the strengths and weaknesses of each.

SELECTION OF ASSISTANT PRINCIPALS

The selection of assistant principals has been characterized as "haphazard" and not guided by coherent policies and criteria (Hess, 1985). Assistant principals themselves acknowledge that their university coursework often fails to prepare them adequately for the job. In a recent survey, assistant principals cited several critical skills for which their preparation was inadequate including motivating teachers, resolving conflict, developing a curriculum for the "real world," working effectively with teams, improving instruction, and dealing with the politics of the job (Weller & Weller, 2002).

In the past, assistant principals' lack of expertise was not a matter of concern because the principal was ultimately responsible for the school and it was thought that the assistant principal's shortcomings could be compensated for by the principal's greater knowledge and experience. However, most school districts now expect assistant principals to be contributing members of the administrative team immediately. Successful instructional programs require the "energy, talent, and commitment of a great many actors within each school building" (Spady, 1985, p. 118), including assistant principals.

Accordingly, districts now give much more care and thought to the process of selecting assistant principals and offer workshops and internships to help novice assistant principals learn the job more quickly and with less stress (Baltzell & Dentler, 1983). In Kentucky, assistant principals serve as interns during their first year on the job, and their performance is evaluated by a committee composed of a mentor principal, the district superintendent, and a university professor of educational leadership (Kirkpatrick, 2000).

Given the scope and importance of the evolving role of the assistant principal, the selection criteria for the position should be the same as those used in selecting principals. The differences in the selection criteria used for the two positions usually have to do with depth and length of experience, with the principal expected to have more varied experience, and with counterbalancing qualifications. That is, an effort is usually made to select an assistant principal whose subject field and administrative experiences complement rather than duplicate those of the principal.

MANAGERIAL MOTIVATION

Although there is no single set of criteria that can ensure accurate selection of principals, applicants who have motivations that are similar to those of managers are somewhat more likely than persons without such motivations to succeed in managerial roles. Two well-researched psychological characteristics that identify managerial motivation are the need for power and the need for achievement (Stahl, 1983).

Need for power is not, as the name suggests, a desire to behave in arbitrary or dictatorial ways toward other people. It refers to the satisfaction that an individual receives from persuading others of the validity of his or her ideas. It might more accurately be called a "need for interpersonal influence" rather than need for power.

Need for achievement refers to the inclination to set challenging goals and strive to reach them. Individuals with this characteristic receive gratification from accomplishing demanding tasks or striving toward challenging goals. People with high need for achievement prefer goals that challenge their abilities but that they can, with hard work, expect to achieve.

In most research involving these two constructs, a projective instrument, the thematic apperception test, is used to assess an individual's placement on the achievement and power scales. Stahl (1983) developed a reliable paper-and-pencil test to measure these traits. He demonstrated that persons who hold positions as managers or who possess leadership qualities are more likely to score high on managerial motivation than nonmanagers and engineering students. Stahl operationally defined *managerial motivation* as consisting of a combination of high scores on both need for achievement and need for power. There is no difference in the incidence of managerial motivation based on gender or race. Women and minorities are equally as likely as men and whites to score high.

One trait that was found not to be related to managerial motivation was *need for affiliation.* This refers to an individual's desire to be liked and accepted by other people. One reason for the absence of an association between the two variables may be that managers occasionally need to take actions that are unpopular with those who work for them. Persons with high need for affiliation are often uncomfortable when faced with that prospect.

Even though individuals who are managerially motivated are more likely than others to seek positions as school administrators, many other factors influence those decisions. The conditions of work are an especially important consideration when an individual is considering applying for a principalship. The job of principal has become more demanding in recent years, and the rewards have failed to keep pace with the increase in the level of responsibility. Principals are responsible for the safety of teachers and students, and they are accountable for prudent management of expensive facilities and sizable budgets. A typical workday for a principal begins early and often doesn't end until late evening, after a basketball game, PTA meeting, or parent conference. Teachers are reluctant to apply for administrative jobs because many of them have decided that the modest increase in salary is not worth the longer work hours and added responsibilities.

WHY SO FEW WOMEN IN ADMINISTRATION?

A number of reasons have been advanced to explain the discrepancies in the number of females holding administrative positions as compared to the number of female teachers in the schools. Among the explanations are limited opportunities for socialization of women into administrative roles, limited visibility, and inaccessibility to informal networks (Yeakey, Johnston, & Adkison, 1986). It has also been suggested that women prefer jobs that allow them to devote time to home and family and that teaching is better suited than administration to the dual roles of careerist and homemaker (Shakeshaft, 1987).

Individuals choose to seek a career in school administration for a variety of reasons. Men and women cite different factors when they are asked to identify the attractions of an administrative career. Women cite financial factors more often than men, and women are more likely than men to give altruistic reasons for being attracted to administration. Women, much more often than men, cite the appeal of the work as a reason for their interest in administration. The opportunity to develop and use personal abilities is mentioned by both sexes about equally often (Adkison, 1985).

The Adkison study is rather dated and involved a relatively small number of administrators in one school district, and so the results should be interpreted with care, but the findings provide a clue that might help explain why more women do not apply for administrative positions. Almost 23 percent of the female respondents but only about 7 percent of male respondents cited altruistic reasons for wanting to be administrators. An example of an altruistic reason is to help children learn. Individuals with that motivation may feel they can accomplish their goal in the classroom as well as in the principal's office. For a woman who is already uncertain about her chances for promotion, such a rationalization would be easily accepted.

Need for Sponsorship

Women in positions of leadership more often than men cite the importance of encouragement from sponsors in attaining their positions. For these women, sponsorship of a relatively powerful superior appears to play a similar function in career advancement that informal networks provide for men. However, some experts suggest that sponsorship is no less critical for men than for women to advance in educational administration (Ortiz & Marshall, 1988). They argue that sponsorship limits competition and that "women have not enjoyed the benefits of the sponsorship process" (p. 126). They suggest that teaching and administration have evolved into separate, gender-specific occupations with different agendas and viewpoints.

Women who receive the support of a sponsor tend to be older than their male counterparts, since the accomplishments that bring about the recognition needed for sponsorship take time. They are also more oriented to instruction, having spent a good many years teaching and serving in quasi-administrative roles related to instruction. From the point of view of selecting promising administrative leaders for effective instruction, individuals who have demonstrated excellence in teaching and other instructional assignments over time represent a pool of talent that schools have yet to use to full advantage.

Those who make selection decisions in schools have an opportunity to bring about instructional improvement by identifying and encouraging teachers with leadership potential to apply for positions as department head, assistant principal, principal, and supervisor. It is clear that some of these people will not apply unless they are encouraged to do so and receive support from those with influence over the final selection.

Progress toward Equity

The number of women and minorities serving as school administrators in the United States continues to be small relative to their numbers as teachers, but some progress has been made in achieving a better balance. The proportion of K–12 principalships (public and private) held by women increased from 35 percent of the total in 1993–1994 to nearly 44 percent in 1999–2000 (National Center for Education Statistics, 2002). During the same period of time, the number of African American principals in schools grew from 10 to 11 percent of the total.

SELECTING OTHER SUPPORT PERSONNEL

Schools hire a wide variety of support personnel to help teachers work with students and provide various types of services to children and their families. Exhibit 5.4 lists some of the titles held by people in support positions in schools. Employees in these positions receive annual salaries in some cases but more often are paid on an hourly, daily, or weekly rate. The amount of education required for these jobs varies from high school to postgraduate, and pay and benefits vary accordingly.

Among the school personnel who have an important impact on instructional programs are psychologists and social workers, guidance counselors, library/media specialists, instructional aides, substitute teachers, and secretaries. Selection criteria for these positions are described in the sections that follow.

School Social Workers

School social workers, also known as visiting teachers, were introduced in schools in the early 1900s. They were added to school staffs to improve communication between families and the schools and to provide assistance to teachers and administrators in working with children who had academic, social, or emotional problems or whose home conditions posed a potential threat to their security and well-being.

■ ■ ■ ■ ■ ▬▬▬▬▬▬▬▬▬▬▬▬▬▬▬▬▬▬▬▬▬▬▬▬▬▬▬▬▬▬▬▬▬

EXHIBIT 5.4

EXAMPLES OF SUPPORT PERSONNEL EMPLOYED IN SCHOOLS

Adult education and literacy specialist	Equipment repair assistant
Athletic trainer	Maintenance
Behavior technician	Media specialist
Bus driver	Paraprofessional
Bus route coordinator	Secretary
Child nutrition worker	Social worker
Custodian	Teacher aide
Educational psychologist	Teacher assistant

Social workers perform liaison functions with community agencies, including social welfare organizations, law enforcement agencies, and medical service providers. If a child is in trouble with the police, a social worker will contact the police to find out what the child's offense was and will work with the family to obtain legal representation and help prevent a future recurrence. A social worker may also be called on to appear as a witness in court proceedings against families that refuse to send children to school or are suspected of neglect or abuse.

Typically, social workers work with individual students who have been referred by teachers for such problems as poor attendance, behavior problems, suspected abuse or malnutrition, social maladjustment, or health problems. They may be asked to investigate the home life of a child who falls asleep in school or who comes to school without lunch money. Often, social workers quietly collect food or clothing for children whose families are not able to buy them, or they may put the family in touch with a church or individual who can offer assistance.

Specialized training prepares social workers to use a variety of psychological techniques and casework methods to alleviate problems of children and families. They need to have strong communication skills and must be able to work effectively with a variety of people in situations that may be dispiriting or even dangerous (Allen-Meares, Washington, & Welsh, 1996).

Social workers are expected to be proactive child advocates and must be able to work effectively with families that may be suspicious or even hostile. They must maintain good working relationships with personnel in community services agencies, churches, and the courts. Among the criteria to look for when hiring a school social worker are the desire to help children, the ability to confront recalcitrant parents and officials, and the courage to take action to remove children from deplorable home conditions when necessary.

School Psychologists

Psychologists first appeared in schools near the beginning of the twentieth century. One of the first duties they were assigned—and one on which they continue to spend a good deal of time—is performing diagnostic services for special education placement. Psychologists report that, on average, they devote about 70 percent of their time to assessment activities; 20 percent is spent consulting with parents, teachers, administrators, and other professionals; and 10 percent is allocated to direct intervention with students (Fagan & Wise, 1994).

They also assist in administering, scoring, tabulating, and interpreting the results of standardized tests; help teachers to develop diagnostic tests; and offer advice on preparing instructional materials for students with particular learning needs. Psychologists are frequently asked to conduct professional development sessions for teachers on instructional strategies for children with learning disabilities, attention deficit disorder, and/or mental retardation.

A candidate for a position as school psychologist needs to have extensive professional preparation, including a master's degree or Ph.D. Among the important personal qualities necessary for success as a psychologist in schools are warmth, empathy, and ability to relate easily to a wide variety of people. Psychologists must be familiar with a wide range of psychological and diagnostic instruments and be able to administer and interpret the results of these tests. They need to be well organized and behave at all times in an ethical manner. Communication skill and adaptability are other necessary qualities.

At one time, teaching experience was considered as a requirement for school psychologists. In recent years, however, many states have eliminated that requirement and place greater emphasis on preparation and skill as a psychologist.

Guidance Counselors

The number of counselors in public elementary and secondary schools increased from about 14,600 in 1958 (*Digest of Education Statistics,* 1989) to 97,369 in 2002 (National Center for Education Statistics, 2002). However, even though counselors are more common in schools now than in the past, there is not total agreement about their role. Teachers, students, parents, and principals all have opinions about an appropriate role for counselors, but they sometimes disagree.

A study of role expectations held for middle school counselors by the four groups found that parents and students held similar expectations and that teachers and principals held similar expectations. Parents and students viewed the counselor as primarily responsible for helping students with problems. Teachers and principals, on the other hand, thought of the guidance function as only part of what the counselor does; they attached equal importance to administrative tasks such as record keeping and scheduling (Remley & Albright, 1988).

Another study compared counselors' perceptions of their own role to principal's perceptions. The respondents in this case were counselors and principals in elementary, middle, and junior high schools in one midwestern state (Bonebrake & Borgers, 1984). The researchers found a high degree of agreement among the two groups in their ranking of 15 tasks performed by counselors.

Guidance Counselor Functions.   School guidance counselors perform eight vital functions in schools. These functions demonstrate the variety of activities that counselors are involved in and the number of groups with which they work:

1. Counselors collect and record information for student records.
2. Counselors communicate with teachers and specialists about students with learning or emotional problems.
3. Counselors confer with families who request assistance with children's academic, health, and social problems.
4. Counselors meet with individuals and groups of students to discuss class schedules, educational and career planning, and academic and interpersonal problems.

5. Counselors collect follow-up data from graduates on their educational and career experiences since graduation.
6. Counselors coordinate special student services provided by specialists such as psychologists and social workers.
7. Counselors write letters of reference for students seeking admission to institutions of higher education or applying for jobs.
8. Counselors coordinate state or district testing programs and assist in administering tests and interpreting results to students and families.

Individual counseling provides students with an opportunity to have professional assistance in a caring, nonevaluative environment to solve problems and make decisions. Group guidance is developmental and preventive in nature. In group counseling, the counselor facilitates interaction among members of a group of students who are attempting to solve common developmental problems. Counselors may also train teachers to provide group guidance services.

Secondary school counselors assist students in making career plans and selecting courses appropriate for those plans, and provide guidance on how to meet high school graduation requirements. Career guidance and counseling is an organized group program that helps students prepare to select a career and enter the world of work.

Counselors often help to coordinate services provided by school and community agencies for a child. They serve as liaison from the school to community agencies and handle requests for information from community individuals and groups. Counselors also perform a public relations service by informing parents and members of the community about guidance and counseling programs and services.

Factors that are considered in selecting counselors are the recency and quality of training and, in particular, exposure to a well-planned and comprehensive internship. Positive personal qualities are especially important for counselors because of the closeness of the relationship between the counselor and the students with whom he or she works.

Traits that have been identified as essential to success in counseling include accurate empathic understanding, communication of respect, warmth, sincerity, and specific expression (Herr, 1982). Depending on the nature of the assignment, other criteria will be added to those essentials. Additional qualifications include knowledge of occupational opportunity structures, knowledge of requirements for entry into various occupations, and the ability to relate effectively to parents and teachers.

Skills in which counselors are most likely to need additional training, as determined by a survey of experts, are counseling students from single-parent families, consultation skills with teachers, small-group counseling, and planning a comprehensive career development program. More than three-fourths of respondents identified those as critical training needs of school counselors (Comas, Cecil, & Cecil, 1987).

Given the emerging demographic profile of schools, the first task (counseling children from single-parent families) is one that counselors increasingly will be called on to perform. Other skills identified by the experts in which counselors are in need of training are ethical standards, drug abuse and alcohol counseling, parent education (Comas et al., 1987), and violence in the schools. All of these are areas about which interviewers may want to question counselor applicants during the selection process.

Library/Media Specialists

As the use of instructional technology has become more common in schools, the role of the media specialist has increased in importance. The title *media specialist* is intended to convey a sense of the emerging role of librarian. In addition to such traditional tasks as maintaining collections of a variety of sources of information, librarians now are expected to be familiar with current and constantly changing ways of storing and retrieving information.

This requires that they understand the operation of computers and be able not only to access information but also to train others to use the software by which accessibility is gained. To some extent at the present time and to a much greater degree in the future, library/media specialists will be expected to provide support for teachers who wish to develop instructional software and to help solve the problems that arise in the process of using individually developed or commercially produced programs.

Two attributes should be given primacy in the selection of media specialists. The first is an attitude that encourages students and teachers to use the media center and its materials extensively and often. Usage creates extra work for the staff, since books, magazines, records, compact disks, filmstrips, fiche, recorders, and projectors that are taken from shelves and drawers must be returned to them. However, care should be taken to hire media specialists who will welcome usage of the media center as an indicator that the center is contributing to the vitality of the instructional program.

The second attribute to be looked for in a prospective media specialist is recent training. A person need not have just graduated in order to have up-to-date knowledge about instructional technology, but it is certain that anyone who completed their training more than three or four years previously and who has not had recent refresher training since graduating is out of date. This is one field in which training must be almost constant in order for a person to remain in touch.

Instructional Aides

Instructional aides represent the largest group of support personnel in schools, numbering more than 1.3 million individuals (U.S. Department of Labor, 2002). Between 1990 and 1997 the number of aides in schools increased 40 percent while the number of teachers rose only 15 percent (Ganser, 2002). Aides perform a variety of duties, ranging from helping young children don raincoats and boots on rainy days to passing out snacks and booting up computers. By relieving classroom teachers of menial tasks, aides allow them to devote more time to lesson planning and teaching. Aides are found in most special education classrooms and in non-special education settings where they work with children with disabilities to carry out provisions of individualized educational plans.

Some instructional aides tutor children or provide follow-up instruction using the teacher's lesson plan, thus providing students with individualized attention and reinforcement. Instructional aides also supervise students in hallways and the cafeteria. They record grades, set up equipment, and help prepare materials for instruction. Other duties performed by aides include grading tests and papers, checking homework, keeping health and attendance records, typing, and copying. They also stock supplies, operate audiovisual equipment, and keep the classroom in order (U.S. Department of Labor, 2002).

Qualifications for the position of instructional aide vary from state to state. Only about one-third of the states have established minimum educational qualifications for instructional aides (U.S. Department of Labor, 2002). Most of these states require aides to have a high school education or the equivalent, although many aides have some college work or even a college degree. Some aides aspire to become classroom teachers, whereas others are content to serve as assistants to classroom teachers. Some school districts offer career ladder programs that provide tuition assistance to help instructional aides make the transition to full-time teacher. The United Federation of Teachers offers a career ladder program that includes some tuition assistance and released time for study (United Federation of Teachers, 2003).

No Child Left Behind requires that instructional aides in Title I schools must have a high school diploma or the equivalent. In addition, aides who provide instructional support for students are required under NCLB to have an associate degree from an institution of higher education or to have successfully completed a test on their knowledge of reading, writing, and mathematics. These rules apply to all Title I instructional aides, regardless of when they were hired (*K–12 Principals Guide . . .* , 2003).

The demand for instructional aides is expected to grow in coming years as enrollments in special education and English as a Second Language programs expand. The continuing emphasis on accountability is also expected to spur the growth in demand for instructional aides who can help with instruction and provide remedial assistance to students. This change is already underway in many districts (Gerber, Finn, Achilles, & Boyd-Zaharias, 2001).

By raising the educational requirements for classroom aides, NCLB may have the effect of creating temporary shortages of qualified applicants, which in turn may force school districts to increase the salaries paid to these semiprofessional workers. The Bureau of Labor Statistics reported in 2000 that salaries paid to instructional aides ranged from $12,000 to $28,000, with the middle half earning between $14,000 and $22,000 (U.S. Department of Labor, 2002).

Substitute Teachers

Human resources administrators report that it is becoming more difficult to find good substitutes for teachers who are absent from their jobs. Because of the short supply of teachers in certain subject fields, some former substitutes have been pressed into full-time service, whereas others are limiting their substitute work because of difficult teaching conditions, heavy paperwork demands, and uncooperative students. Schools that provide support are the most likely to be able to find substitute teachers when they need them.

Respondents in a recent study reported that substituting is most apt to be a positive experience in schools in which teachers are helpful, materials are easily located, and the teacher leaves lesson plans and suggestions for activities for students who finish their work early. All teachers, including substitutes, appreciate having well-behaved students; substitutes also like to have the names of two or three dependable students who are familiar with homework assignments and the classroom schedule. Survey respondents also reported that being informed about classroom rules, routines, and emergency procedures and having seating charts made their work easier (Tannenbaum, 2000).

Some schools use a report form to be completed by both the substitute and regular teacher. On the form, the substitute teacher can report how much material was covered, whether any problems arose, and note questions raised by students. The regular classroom teacher uses the form to thank the substitute or to make special requests (e.g., that furniture and supplies be put back in place next time). Both teachers see the other's report, and the principal also reviews them. In this way, two-way communication is maintained and the principal is alerted to any problems that may have arisen (Tannenbaum, 2000).

Few districts provide training for substitute teachers, although school administrators believe that some training for substitutes would be useful. One district that does train its substitute teachers is Wake County Public Schools in North Carolina, which offers a four-hour orientation session for substitutes.

Districts that have developed successful strategies for locating and retaining substitute teachers are usually happy to share their ideas with professional colleagues. Some of the strategies that have worked can be found on the website for the Substitute Teaching Institute at Utah State University, Logan. See the Online Resource section at the end of this chapter for the address of the website. Ideas for attracting substitute teachers that have worked include offering higher pay, longevity pay, provision of partial benefits, and discounts on merchandise in local stores.

School Secretaries

A school secretary's is often the first voice heard by parents and others who call the school, the first person to whom new students talk, and the first individual contacted by visitors to the school (Drake & Roe, 1986). Secretaries are often known by more students than any other single individual, with the exception of the classroom teacher and possibly the principal. Given the nature of this position and the extent of the secretary's contacts with the public, teachers, and students, careful selection for this position is critical.

It has been estimated that there are four million school secretaries in the United States and that 99 percent of them are females. Their duties can be classified into five categories (Rimer, 1984):

1. Public relations (greeting visitors, explaining school rules and policies to parents of new students, dealing with community organizations and special groups)
2. Student services (attending to nonlearning needs of students; performing as nurse, friend, disciplinarian; possessor of supplies and information)
3. Clerical (filing, typing, answering the telephone, record keeping, maintaining staff and student records, requesting or sending student information, writing letters, making announcements, operating office equipment, and maintaining office supplies)
4. Financial (collecting money, writing checks, making deposits, bookkeeping, filling out requisitions)
5. Office management (maintaining an attractive and businesslike environment and supervising clerical employees and student workers)

It should be clear from the foregoing that the secretary is first and foremost a public relations expert. In schools with more than one clerical employee, one serves primarily as gatekeeper, providing or denying access to the principal, receiving and transmitting telephone messages, and dealing with walk-in or call-in requests from students and teachers. The second employee then is assigned to handle clerical duties and office management chores and, when needed, to assist the head secretary with information requests.

A necessary qualification for the position of secretary is the ability to tolerate frequent interruptions without undue frustration. Regardless of the importance of the task being worked on, the secretary is expected to put it aside to handle a request from a student or teacher. Rarely is the secretary able to finish a task without being interrupted at least once. To work in such an atmosphere requires patience, flexibility, and a sense of humor. Some of the tasks that secretaries perform, most notably financial record keeping and check writing, require an atmosphere that permits concentration. In order to keep errors to a minimum, it is necessary to provide an opportunity for the secretary who performs those chores to retreat to a quiet, out-of-the-way room where there will be no interruptions. When selecting a secretary, it is important to recognize that not all individuals operate effectively in an atmosphere as busy as school offices often are. Care must be taken to select the person who can tolerate the noise and confusion without undue feelings of stress.

Because of their location in the center of the school's information flow, secretaries obtain considerable confidential information about teachers and students.

Caplow (1976) noted that employees who have access to the manager of an organization and who possess information about other organization members acquire power that exceeds that allocated to them by the organization chart. He warned that such power can be a source of organizational problems and thus urged managers to keep the power of their assistants in check.

SUMMARY

Successful schools depend on the quality of the personnel who run them. Besides teachers, schools require administrators, counselors, secretaries, instructional aides, substitute teachers, and other support staff. The selection process for these positions is similar to that used to select teachers, beginning with preparation of a job model and announcement of the vacancy. Administrative vacancies receive priority attention in school districts because of the critical nature of the position. Principals perform eight functions, including organizing the school setting, supervising and evaluating teachers, supervising student discipline and safety, and encouraging instructional improvement. These functions should form the basis for assessing applicants for administrative positions.

Selection of assistant principals has been a neglected area, but with increasing attention to the importance of the principalship for school effectiveness, more care is being taken to select well-qualified assistants. People who possess managerial motivation (high need for achievement and power) generally gravitate toward positions of leadership. Minorities and women have made progress in increasing their representation in administrative ranks in school districts in recent years, but they are still underrepresented in comparison to their presence in the teaching force. The number of counselors in schools has grown rapidly. Counselors provide a variety of services, including personal and group counseling and career guidance.

SUGGESTED ACTIVITIES

1. Interview a school guidance counselor or social worker and prepare a list of duties performed or results expected. Then, using what you learned from the interview, identify the qualifications for a person applying for one of those positions.

2. Reread the job model for a high school principal (Exhibit 5.1). If you were hired to fill this position, how would you decide which of the tasks listed under expected results you would tackle first? Explain your reasons.

3. Brainstorm with a colleague or friend to identify actions that a school might take to secure and maintain a reliable supply of competent substitute teachers.

4. Personal qualities are important for school counselors. Explain why you believe this is true and identify the personal qualities you would look for if you were hiring a counselor for your school.

ONLINE RESOURCES

Bureau of Labor Statistics, U.S. Department of Labor (www.bls.gov/oco/home.htm)

> The *Occupational Outlook Handbook* is the authoritative source for information about occupations. Each of the thousands of entries includes a description of the type of work performed by members of the occupation, anticipated future demand for workers, qualifications, and salary ranges. It is a vital reference tool for counselors and human resource workers.

Job Interviews? (www.job-interview.net/sample/Principal.htm)

> Questions and other requests for information that applicants for a school principalship might expect are shown on this site. Among them: Tell us about your qualifications, and What is your vision for parent participation in the school? The site also offers tips on how to prepare for a job interview.

National Center for Education Statistics (nces.ed.gov//pubs2003/digest02/index.asp)

> This site shows statistics on all levels of education in the United States, including enrollments, number of personnel, and their demographic characteristics.

National Center for Research on Evaluation, Standards, and Student Testing (www.cse.ucla.edu)

> The Center promotes the development and use of evaluation and testing for informed decision making.

Substitute Teaching Institute, Utah State University, Logan (http://subed.usu.edu)

> The Institute helps school districts develop policies and best practices for recruiting, screening, training, and evaluating substitute teachers. The website contains information of value to administrators who are responsible for obtaining substitute teachers and for the teachers themselves.

REFERENCES

Adkison, J. (1985). The structure of opportunity and administrative opportunities. *Urban Education, 20,* 327–347.

Allen-Meares, P., Washington, R., & Welsh, B. (1996). *Social work services in schools* (2nd ed.). Boston: Allyn & Bacon.

Anderson, L., & Gardner, C. (1995). Substitute teachers. In L. Anderson (Ed.), *International encyclopedia of teaching and teacher education* (2nd ed., pp. 367–369). Tarrytown, NY: Pergamon.

Anderson, M. (1988). *Hiring capable principals: How school districts recruit, groom, and select the best candidates.* Eugene, OR: Oregon School Study Council.

Archer, J. (2003, June 4). Debate heating up on how to lure top-notch principals. *Education Week,* pp. 1, 12.

Baltzell, D., & Dentler, R. (1983). *Selecting American school principals: A sourcebook for educators.* Washington, DC: National Institute of Education.

Bonebrake, C., & Borgers, S. (1984). Counselor role as perceived by counselors and principals. *Elementary School Guidance and Counseling, 18,* 194–199.

Caplow, T. (1976). *How to run any organization.* New York: Holt Rinehart.

Comas, R., Cecil, J., & Cecil, C. (1987). Using expert opinion to determine professional development needs of school counselors. *The School Counselor, 35,* 81–87.

Cusick, P. A. (2003, May 14). The principalship? No thanks. *Education Week,* pp. 44, 34.

Digest of education statistics. (1989). Washington, DC: U.S. Office of Education.

Drake, T., & Roe, W. (1986). *The principalship* (3rd ed.). New York: Macmillan.

Egginton, W., Jeffries, T., & Kidd-Knights, D. (1988, April). State-mandated tests for principals—A growing trend? *NASSP Bulletin, 72,* 62–65.

Fagan, T., & Wise, P. (1994). *School psychology: Past, present and future.* New York: Longman.

Ganser, T. (2002, December). The new teacher mentors. *American School Board Journal, 189,* 25–27.

Gatewood, R., & Feild, H. (1987). *Human resource selection.* Chicago: Dryden.

Gerber, S. B., Finn, J. D., Achilles, C. M., & Boyd-Zaharias, J. (2001, Summer). Teacher aides and students' academic achievement. *Educational Evaluation and Policy Analysis, 23,* 123–143.

Herr, E. (1982). Discussion. In H. Walberg (Ed.), *Improving educational standards and productivity* (pp. 99–109). Berkeley, CA: McCutchan.

Hess, F. (1985). The socialization of the assistant principal from the perspective of the local school district. *Education and Urban Society, 18,* 93–106.

Jentz, B. (1982). *Entry: The hiring, start-up, and supervision of administrators.* New York: McGraw-Hill.

K–12 principals guide to No Child Left Behind. (2003). Alexandria, VA: National Association of Elementary School Principals. Reston, VA: National Association of Secondary School Principals.

Kirkpatrick, R. (2000, September). Recruiting and developing candidates for principal. *NASSP Bulletin, 84,* 38–43.

Landy, F. (1985). *Psychology of work behavior.* Homewood, IL: Dorsey.

Lease, A. J. (2002, June). New administrators need more than good grades. *School Administrator, 59,* 40–41.

Matthews, D. (2002, September). Why principals fail and what we can learn from it. *Principal, 82,* 38–40.

National Center for Education Statistics. (2002). *Digest of education statistics, 2002.* Washington, DC: U.S. Department of Education.

Ortiz, F., & Marshall, C. (1988). Women in educational administration. In N. Boyan (Ed.), *Handbook of research on educational administration* (pp. 123–141). New York: Longman.

Remley, T., Jr., & Albright, P. (1988). Expectations for middle school counselors: Views of students, teachers, principals, and parents. *The School Counselor, 35,* 290–296.

Rimer, A. (1984, Fall). Elementary school secretary: Informal decision maker. *Educational Horizons, 63,* 16–18.

Schmitt, N., Noe, R., Meritt, R., & Fitzgerald, M. (1983). *Validity of assessment center ratings for the prediction of performance ratings and school climate of school administrators.* (ERIC Document Reproduction Service No. ED 236777).

Shakeshaft, C. (1987). *Women in educational administration.* Newbury Park, CA: Sage.

Spady, W. (1985). The vice-principal as an agent of instructional reform. *Education and Urban Society, 18,* 107–120.

Stahl, M. (1983). Achievement, power and managerial motivation: Selecting managerial talent with the job choice exercise. *Personnel Psychology, 36,* 775–789.

Tannenbaum, M. (2000, May). No substitute for quality. *Educational Leadership, 57,* 70–72.

United Federation of Teachers. (2003). The career training program. Available online: www.uft.org/index/cfm?fid=222

U.S. Department of Labor Bureau of Labor Statistics. (2002). *Occupational outlook handbook, 2002–2003 edition.* Washington, DC: Author.

Weller, L. D., & Weller, S. J. (2002). *The assistant principal: Essentials for effective school leadership.* Thousand Oaks, CA: Corwin.

Yeakey, C., Johnston, G., & Adkison, J. (1986). In pursuit of equity: A review of research on minorities and women in educational administration. *Educational Administration Quarterly, 22,* 110–149.

CHAPTER SIX

MOTIVATION OF PERSONNEL

All of the actions of a human being originate from inner motivation. However, in spite of extensive study, there are still many unanswered questions about human motivation. Human resources managers must take human motivation into account in many phases of their work. This chapter examines our knowledge of job-related motivation and offers guidelines on applying that knowledge to the management of human resources in schools.

PLAN OF THE CHAPTER

Topics covered in this chapter are: Nature of work motivation, theories of motivation, job satisfaction in teaching, and job satisfaction and teacher turnover.

NATURE OF WORK MOTIVATION

The factors that influence people in choosing an occupation and in carrying out the tasks associated with a particular job have been studied by organizational psychologists for many years. Most of the research on motivation in the workplace has taken place in industrial settings. Nevertheless, much of what has been learned can be applied to those who work in schools.

Work motivation refers to conditions responsible for variations in the intensity, quality, direction, and duration of work-related behavior. Variations in the quality of work produced by employees may arise from either motivational or knowledge differences. If an employee is not achieving satisfactory results, it is necessary to ascertain whether the problem originates with lack of motivation, lack of knowledge, or both.

People are motivated to work for a variety of reasons, including reasons that may not be related to the job. For example, a person who continues to live and work in a small town where jobs are scarce and pay is low might find more opportunities by relocating, but the decision to stay is based on a desire to be near relatives and to enjoy the relaxed lifestyle of small-town living. These are motivating factors that affect decisions about work that are not related to the work itself.

If asked, most people could name several ways in which their work satisfies inner psychological needs, including the basic need to support themselves and their families. The degree of fit between a person's work motivation and the job is usually an indicator of how well satisfied the individual will be with the job. Selection of employees involves an assessment of this fit for a given applicant. A person who enjoys being around people probably will not be satisfied in a job that involves little people contact, and one who values exercising authority is likely to be unhappy in a position that is devoid of power. Of course, human beings are very adaptable, and it is never safe to assume that an individual will not be happy in a given job, but by considering an applicant's work motivation, a human resources specialist can increase the probability that the person who is hired will be well suited for the position.

Theories of Motivation

Psychologists have advanced several theories to explain how people become motivated to perform a job and what factors within the individual or in the work setting influence the level of motivation experienced. Three theories are of particular interest to school administrators because of their potential for improving our understanding of work motivation among teachers. The three theories are:

1. *Expectancy theory:* Advocates believe that people are motivated by the opportunity to earn incentives.
2. *Equity theory:* Advocates believe that people expect a balance between effort expended and rewards received and lose motivation when that balance is missing.
3. *Goal-setting theory:* Advocates believe that people are motivated to achieve identified goals.

Each theory has implications for administrative action. An administrator who believes that employees are motivated by expectancy will attempt to identify and distribute incentives to increase teacher motivation. One who believes in equity theory will try to provide more generous rewards to employees who work hard and withhold some rewards from those who put forth less effort. Administrators who subscribe to goal-setting theory will attempt to identify long- and short-range goals that are personally meaningful to employees and help the employees to achieve those goals.

These theories are described in more detail in the following sections.

Expectancy Theory. Psychologists who have studied human motivation have developed elaborate theories about the relationship between tangible rewards and employee performance. These theories help explain the conditions under which tangible rewards and recognition lead to an increase in employee productivity. One such theory is expectancy theory, which is based on the premise that workers perform tasks to gain incentives and that motivation is a function of the value of the incentive to the individual. Vroom incorporated three concepts into his model of expectancy motivation—valence, instrumentality, and expectancy—so the theory is sometimes referred to as VIE theory (cited in Pinder, 1984).

1. *Valence* refers to the positive or negative feelings attached to work outcomes. For example, money received for performing a job has positive valence for most workers, whereas working in a dirty environment has negative valence. For teachers, student success has positive valence. Some work outcomes that have negative valence for teachers are unnecessary paperwork and being required to monitor hallways, restrooms, and bus-loading areas.

2. *Instrumentality* refers to the perceived connection between a work outcome and some object or event that has positive valence for an employee. An employee must believe that something he or she does on the job will lead to a desirable result in order for motivation to occur. According to the theory, a teacher who has been asked by the principal to serve on a textbook committee will be more motivated to serve if he or she believes that by doing so, something pleasant will be forthcoming. The teacher must believe that the task (serving on the committee) is instrumentally related to an incentive he or she values. That might be the principal's approval, or it might be the opportunity to improve the instructional program.

3. *Expectancy* refers to the employee's perception of the probability of successfully achieving a work outcome. In the preceding example, the teacher who has been asked to serve on the textbook committee may decide not to do it if she believes that she lacks the requisite knowledge and skills, since she would not expect to be able to perform the task satisfactorily.

Expectancy theory suggests that instrumentality is a function of an individual's estimate of the probability that he or she can achieve certain results. When one's success is tied to the performance of others, as it is in programs that reward groups of teachers, then instrumentality is the sum of the individuals' estimates of success. In such a program, each teacher considers not only his or her ability to accomplish desired results but must also attempt to determine whether other teachers will be successful. In that situation, instrumentality will be influenced by cohesiveness among teachers and the level of confidence they have in one another (Kelley, 1998).

Work outcomes include tasks performed on the job, but they may also include *opportunities.* For example, the chance to attend a workshop to improve one's skills is a work outcome, but most of us would not refer to it as a task. This distinction is important because with it we can use expectancy theory to help explain why teachers are sometimes not motivated to participate in staff development activities.

Expectancy theory is illustrated in Figure 6.1. The figure shows how a work situation leads to a condition of motivation or lack of motivation for an employee. The employee considers a work outcome, which might be an in-service program offering instruction on a new way to teach music. The teacher asks first, "Can I achieve the work outcome?" This might involve several other considerations, including "Do I have the time to take this in-service class?" "Is Tuesday afternoon a convenient time for me?" "Can I learn the material?" If the answer to any of these questions is *no*, the teacher will not be motivated for this particular work outcome. If the answer to all of the questions is *yes*, the teacher moves to the next decision block.

At this point, the teacher considers whether there is an incentive to perform the outcome. The music teacher in the example might decide that the workshop could result in her acquiring new instructional techniques that would increase student interest in music or help her get a better job. If one of these outcomes has positive valence for the teacher, then she will be motivated to attend the workshop.

Consider another situation: A district offers a salary increment to teachers who agree to teach in schools with concentrations of low-achieving students. A

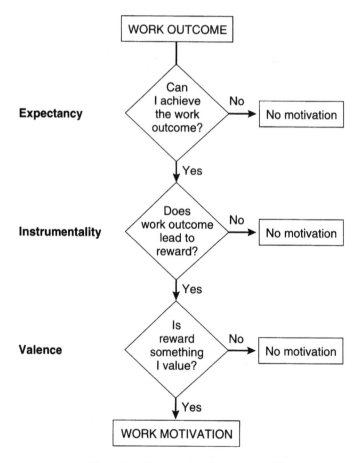

FIGURE 6.1   Flowchart Illustrating Expectancy Theory

teacher considers first whether he or she can perform the task. If the job involves working with children with learning problems, the teacher may decide that he or she lacks the necessary skills. However, if the teacher feels able and qualified to do the job and the salary increment is attractive, he or she will be motivated to accept the offer.

Applying Expectancy Theory.   Using expectancy theory to motivate teachers is more likely to succeed if administrators follow these guidelines:

   1. Select incentives that are valued by teachers. Direct financial incentives to teachers seem to have promise for attracting teachers to specific assignments, such as schools with large numbers of non-English-speaking students or schools located in neighborhoods with a high rate of crime. They can also be used to achieve specific goals, such as raising achievement test scores. However, financial incentives do not work as well in raising the overall level of quality of teaching performance (Johnson, 1986). These issues will be discussed in more detail in Chapter 10.

   2. Be sure that teachers understand the instrumental connection between work outcomes and incentives. If the connection between the work outcome and the incentive is not clear, no motivation will occur. Some merit pay programs fail because teachers do not understand what they must do to earn the merit increase.

   3. Select work outcomes that are attainable. Teachers must believe that a work outcome is attainable in order for expectancy to affect their work behavior. Choosing work outcomes that are beyond the reach of most teachers defeats the purpose of using rewards and incentives.

   4. Incentives are not effective when used to reward behavior that is expected or required of all employees. For example, teachers should not be offered incentives for arriving at school on time. Individuals may be given the choice of whether to seek a particular incentive.

Equity Theory.   When rewards are distributed on the basis of performance, employees who do not receive a reward or who receive a smaller-than-average reward may feel they have been treated unfairly. It is therefore important to be aware of the issue of equity in distributing work-related rewards. Researchers who have studied equity find that employees compare themselves to people with whom they work who perform the same or similar jobs. An employee who feels that he or she worked harder but received a smaller reward than another employee will feel unfairly treated.

Reducing Tension.   Equity theory suggests that if two employees—Allan and Barry—work equally hard but Allan receives a promotion and Barry does not, both will experience feelings of psychological tension. They may try by various means to allay this tension. One way they try to do that is by use of cognitive distortion.

Barry may tell himself, "Maybe Allan works harder than I thought," or "Allan talks about how hard he works, and the boss believes him."

A second way to relieve psychological tension is to change one's inputs. Barry may decide not to work so hard, or he may elect to change his priorities on the job in order to devote more effort to activities that are rewarded. He may also act to change the comparison. One way to do that is to tell himself, "Allan may be a better salesman, but I'm a better manager." Or he may say, "A promotion is not worth it if I have to neglect my family to get it." Finally, Barry may leave the job altogether.

Allan may experience some of the same tension that Barry feels, and if so he will probably react in some of the same ways. For example, he might distort reality by telling himself, "I always thought Barry was kind of lazy." Or he may decide to change his inputs by working less hard in order to avoid further alienation from Barry.

Equity theory helps one to understand teachers' opposition to merit pay and other forms of performance-based compensation. Since most of these programs rely on principals' ratings to determine which teachers will receive salary increases, teachers fear that principals may reward their favorites and ignore all others. Teachers seem to be less concerned about inequities in the single salary schedule than they are about possible inequities in performance-based compensation plans.

Equity theory assumes that employees have accurate information about the amount of effort their colleagues expend, but in education that assumption is often faulty. Since teachers seldom observe one another's work directly, they lack complete information about the work habits of others. Nevertheless, they form judgments about which of their colleagues work hard and which do not, basing those conclusions on inconclusive evidence, such as how late a teacher stays at school and whether he or she takes work home.

Even though an employee may be misinformed about how hard colleagues work, it is the beliefs he or she holds that provoke the responses predicted by equity theory. Thus, the perception of inequity has the same effect on employee behavior as actual inequity.

Applying Equity Theory.   Using equity theory to motivate teachers is most likely to be successful when administrators follow these guidelines:

1. Differentiating rewards on the basis of performance will increase productivity but may also increase intragroup conflict. If harmonious relations and minimal conflict are important, distribute rewards equally among members.

2. Whenever possible, give all employees the chance to work toward rewards, but if rewards are offered to some groups and not others, make certain that the individuals understand and accept the reasons for the differentiation. Providing clerical assistance to employees who serve on a curriculum revision committee is

acceptable, but providing such assistance to coaches who already receive a salary increment is likely to be perceived as inequitable.

3. Achieve a balance between the effort required and the value of the reward. Rewards that are of little value should be more easily attained than those that are of greater value. In education, the cost of incentive programs is always a concern. Costs may be capped by limiting the number of incentive awards given, but a more equitable approach is to increase the amount of effort required to gain a reward, so that fewer people try for them.

4. In education, perceived inequities most often arise in connection with evaluating performance. If no objective and valid way of measuring performance exists, managers are vulnerable to charges of unfairly rewarding favorites. To avoid the charge, appoint a committee of teachers to set standards for deciding which individuals shall receive rewards.

Goal-Setting Theory.   One reason that games are highly motivating is because they have clear and challenging goals. Whether playing bridge, video games, or touch football, participants understand the objective of the activity and enjoy the challenge of trying to attain it. A number of psychologists contend that clear-cut and challenging goals are as effective for motivating people in work settings as in recreational situations. Locke and Latham (1984) suggest that people gain a sense of accomplishment and efficacy from attaining goals, provided the goals are sufficiently challenging and success is not either impossible or meaningless.

Goal-setting theory has been shown to work in psychological laboratories as well as actual work environments when the goals are accepted by the people involved. Studies have shown that individuals who were assigned more challenging goals outperformed those who received moderately difficult or easy goals. Also, individuals who were given specific goals did better than those who were given vague admonitions such as "Do your best."

Goal setting is a form of self-leadership. Organizations use a variety of external control mechanisms for influencing employee behavior, including evaluation, rules and policies, and supervisory oversight. In recent years, however, organizations have begun to place more emphasis on internal controls. By working to achieve commitment by employees to the organizational mission and goals, it is the hope of these organizations that the need for external mechanisms of control will diminish.

Self-leadership refers to an inclination by an employee to engage in behaviors that contribute to the accomplishment of an organization's mission and that are performed in the absence of any external constraint (Manz, 1986). Employees engage in self-leadership because they are committed to the goals and purpose of the organization that employs them. In schools with school-based management, self-leadership assumes greater importance because these schools do not have access to the full range of external controls on employees that are available to districts with centralized administrative structures.

Locke and Latham (1984) stated that goals are motivating for employees even though they were not involved in setting them. Teachers may differ from other employees in that respect, however, since teachers believe that setting instructional goals is an important function of their jobs. Goals that are set by the administration are more likely to be accepted by teachers if the principal justifies the choice of goals and offers to provide support to members in attaining those outcomes.

Applying Goal-Setting Theory.   When goal setting is used as a motivational device for employees in schools, the following principles should be kept in mind:

1. Goal setting works better when employees are confident of their ability to achieve goals (Carroll & Tosi, 1973). Supervisors may need to provide interpersonal support for employees who lack confidence in their ability to achieve a goal. Individuals who are new to the job may be especially uneasy about identifying performance goals.

2. Performance goals should reflect the outcomes envisioned in the school's strategic plan and mission statement. Other documents that can be helpful in formulating goals are job models and incentive pay plans or career ladders.

3. Detailed feedback helps in several ways. It reduces uncertainty concerning which behaviors are most appropriate in the pursuit of goals, and it provides information about the relative importance of various goals (Ashford & Cummings, 1983). Feedback is more likely to be perceived accurately if it follows the performance without delay, is positive, and is given relatively frequently (Ilgen, Fisher, & Taylor, 1979). The motivational value of feedback is influenced by the extent to which it conveys to the recipient a sense of competence.

4. Employees are more committed to performance goals that are chosen consensually by members of work teams.

Goal Setting and Teacher Evaluation.   Goal setting is commonly used in schools as part of the evaluation process. Teachers choose annual goals and are evaluated on their success in achieving them. In such programs, it is advisable for principals and teachers to discuss how goal attainment will be measured and to set a date for achieving the goals (Locke & Latham, 1984). The time limit is ordinarily one year, but interim reviews of teacher performance at periodic intervals during the year are recommended. Teacher evaluation schemes that involve teacher-selected outcomes are reviewed in more detail in Chapter 9.

Goal setting as part of the evaluation process is most effective when these guidelines are followed:

1. Teachers are encouraged to select goals that conform to the school and district mission and to accountability requirements such as those found in NCLB.

2. When an organization asks employees to identify performance goals, it should commit itself to help the employees achieve the goals they choose. To avoid the frustration and discouragement that arise from seeking unrealistic results, employees should be advised to select attainable goals, and supervisors should work to obtain the resources employees need in order to achieve them (Katzell & Thompson, 1990).

3. Employees should be assisted to write goal statements that are clear and concise, describe measurable outcomes, and require a significant and continuing effort. Since most goal statements represent a year's work, a problem that is sometimes encountered is that the goals are too modest. A goal that can be accomplished within a month or two is not sufficiently challenging. Employees often think of goals as being an addition to their normal workload. In fact, the goal statement should incorporate the activities that are part of normal responsibilities.

4. Employees are understandably concerned about the possibility of being penalized if they select goals that are too difficult and they fail to achieve them. That fear can be reduced by giving individuals an opportunity to revise their goals if it turns out they are unable to accomplish as much as they had expected.

JOB SATISFACTION IN TEACHING

A persistent question in the minds of administrators and organizational psychologists has to do with the relationship between job satisfaction and performance. It is frequently assumed that by creating conditions that increase employees' levels of satisfaction, we will obtain increased productivity, but the evidence for a connection between the two is not strong.

The median correlation from studies that examined the relationship between satisfaction and performance was about 0.14 (Vroom, 1964). In practical terms, that means that when an employee's level of satisfaction increases, the job performance will improve slightly, or that when job performance improves, job satisfaction levels will rise a little. The direction of the cause-effect relationship is not clear. Some experts believe that satisfaction results from performance rather than the other way around (Lawler & Rhode, 1976).

Two explanations for the low correlation between satisfaction and productivity have been advanced. One is that in many jobs productivity is determined by the speed at which an assembly line moves or a machine operates. Employees' feelings do not influence the machines' speed (Fincham & Rhodes, 1988). A second explanation is that employees may feel satisfaction for reasons that are unrelated or negatively related to productivity. For example, a vendor in a sports stadium might prefer to watch sporting events rather than sell popcorn and peanuts. Watching teams play reduces sales but increases the employee's feelings of satisfaction with the job.

Career Anchors and Teacher Satisfaction

Schein (1990) introduced the concept of career anchor as a way of explaining the factors that motivate people in their work. A career anchor is the meaning or purpose an individual seeks through a job. A person who finds a job that allows him or her to achieve an important meaning or purpose is likely to feel a sense of satisfaction from the job. Among the career anchors identified by Schein were technical aspects of the work; opportunities to analyze and solve problems; opportunities to help people work together; job security and long-term commitment to the organization; opportunity to build or create an enterprise; setting one's own schedule and pace of work; and balancing career and lifestyle, such as spending time with family or friends.

When a person is asked to name the features of a job that are most appealing, the features he or she names helps to identify that individual's career anchors. That information is useful for making selection decisions, planning professional development activities, and making decisions about job promotions and transfers. Some of the most common career anchors are identified in the list in Exhibit 6.1 (Free-

---

EXHIBIT 6.1

COMMON CAREER ANCHORS

Challenging goals	Clearly defined goals that require mental or physical stretching
Structure	Clearly stated rules and expectations; clear chain of command
Tangible rewards	Money in the form of wages and bonuses
Security	Protection against being laid off or terminated; provision of medical insurance, retirement benefits, and so forth
Helping people	Providing a valued service to individuals in need, sometimes referred to as "making a difference"
Affiliation	Opportunity to work and interact with compatible, like-minded people
Working conditions	Having a comfortable, attractive work setting and adequate resources for the job
Personal/professional growth	Opportunity to develop and use new knowledge and skills
Recognition	Receiving praise or awards for the quality of one's work
Variety	Performing routines and tasks that are new or unexpected
Interesting work	Deriving pleasure from the nature of the work itself, including the pace, the demands of the job, and acquiring specialized skills.
Influence or control	Supervising, directing, or exerting influence over other people
Autonomy	Working without close supervision; being free to make decisions about one's job independently

mantle, 2001; Ritchie & Martin,1999). Most people have several career anchors, which they tend to rank in a hierarchy of importance.

Rewards and Security.   Tangible rewards and recognition are commonly used motivators in all types of work settings. Money and praise are powerful motivators, and although most people say that money is not the most important motivator for them, salary increases or expansion of fringe benefits are nevertheless welcomed by almost everyone. Money is valued not only for what it will buy but also as a symbol of success and approval. Few people enter teaching expecting to make a lot of money, but for many the security that teachers enjoy helps to compensate for the relatively low salaries. Most teachers are assured of continuing employment as long as they are reasonably effective in the classroom and do not break the law or violate community expectations. Fringe benefits such as medical insurance and a retirement plan add to the security of a teaching career.

Working with People.   People who like working with others often choose to teach because it is a job that involves constant interaction. Teachers spend most of every day with young people, and they also have opportunities to talk with colleagues. Contact with people is such an integral part of teaching that anyone thinking about a teaching career who doesn't enjoy interacting with others would be well advised to choose a different occupation.

Nature of the Work.   Some individuals are attracted to teaching by the nature of the job. Teaching is knowledge work, and helping students to understand new material is a fulfilling experience for many in the field. Teaching also involves a fairly high level of autonomy, although this autonomy is more limited now than in the past because of mandated curriculum prescriptions and accountability requirements. Nevertheless, teachers continue to enjoy a degree of autonomy that is absent from many other occupations. Another career anchor for some teachers is the opportunity for personal and professional growth. Teachers are expected periodically to take coursework or engage in other educational experiences in order to renew their professional credentials, a requirement that meets the need of many teachers for growth and learning.

Working Conditions.   Working conditions are a positive feature of most teaching positions. Teachers work in clean, comfortable surroundings, and many take pride in decorating their classrooms attractively. Teaching also involves variety, and people who are motivated by variety like teaching because no two days are the same. However, that is not to say teachers don't get bored. Those who crave very high levels of variety discover after a few years that the newness has worn off and boredom has set in. Some of these teachers seek a change of scenery, either by moving to a different school or grade level, or both, or they may obtain additional degrees to qualify for a supervisory or counseling position, or even leave the profession altogether to seek employment in other fields.

Exerting Influence.   Teaching requires one to influence students, and a person who genuinely dislikes influencing other people is not likely to be very happy in the classroom. Some teachers discover they are very good at persuading others, and these people often migrate to positions of greater influence within or outside of the profession. They may move into the position of department head, serve on a district curriculum committee, or accept an appointment as union representative in their school. Others choose an administrative career path and obtain a Master's degree in order to become an assistant principal or principal and eventually move to a central office administrative position.

Structure.   All workers want to know what is expected of them and how they will be evaluated. They like information about what to do and what actions they should avoid. They like consistency and predictability in the people with whom they work, particularly those in higher-level positions. One way by which a supervisor creates structure for employees is by identifying clear goals for performance. Goals also give workers a standard by which they are able to judge their own performance. Employees vary in the extent to which they are able to tolerate ambiguous goals. Some are able to "go with the flow" better than others, and those who supervise employees soon discover that some of their workers have a much greater need for clear-cut rules and deadlines than others.

Sources of Dissatisfaction in Teaching

There are several sources of dissatisfaction in teaching of which principals and other personnel administrators should be aware. Some dissatisfaction is inherent in the work, but some is amenable to change.

Teachers who anticipated having autonomy to make decisions about what and how to teach may be frustrated to find they are expected to follow a rigidly prescribed curriculum in order to prepare students to pass standardized tests on the subject matter they study. Under the No Child Left Behind legislation, schools must test students in grades 3–8 annually in reading/language arts and mathematics and at least once in grades 10–12. By 2007–2008, students must also be tested in science. Schools whose students fail to show adequate yearly progress for two consecutive years will be designated in need of improvement and will be required to develop a plan to improve their performance. For some teachers, NCLB and similar mandates increase the structure of teaching by establishing clear performance goals.

Dissatisfaction is likely to be especially intense in schools that lack resources to support their teachers. Shortages of teaching resources are common in schools and are a frequent cause of teacher complaints. Many schools lack funds with which to purchase the maps and charts, computer software, and supplemental textbooks that help to make lessons more meaningful for students and the teacher's job somewhat more manageable. One-half of the teachers interviewed in one study reported that the teaching materials in their schools were "poor" or "barely adequate" (McLaughlin, Pfeifer, Swanson-Owens, & Yee, 1986). Furthermore, schools with the greatest need for adequate resources—that is, those with high levels of student poverty—actually receive less than the schools with children from more affluent families, and the differences are substantial (Keller, 2003).

Teacher dissatisfaction is likely to intensify as teachers come under more pressure from NCLB and various state programs to improve student performance, especially if these demands are not accompanied by additional resources and the developmental opportunities that teachers need. One of the unintended outcomes of legislation such as NCLB is increased feelings of dissatisfaction on the part of teachers. These mandates can lead to the creation of incentives for teachers to cheat, arousing feelings of shame and guilt and ultimately leading to alienation (Leithwood, 2001).

Ironically, NCLB may also help to alleviate some of the problems that are associated with low teacher satisfaction. Teachers who are assigned to teach subjects for which they lack adequate preparation cite that as a cause of frustration and dissatisfaction (McLaughlin, et al., 1986), and by requiring that all teachers be "highly qualified" for the subject or grade level to which they are assigned, NCLB can help eliminate this source of teacher dissatisfaction.

Few conditions in schools arouse more teacher complaints than interruptions and distractions while they are trying to teach. Intercom announcements that interrupt instruction and required paperwork are two of the realities of teaching that cause frustration for teachers (Plihal, 1981). Special education teachers in particular devote much of their own time to filling out forms documenting the needs of their students and the services provided for them. It has been estimated that special education teachers spend a half day each week on required paperwork. Most of these teachers understand the need for extensive record-keeping and view the extra work as a necessary, if unpleasant, part of the job. Nevertheless, excessive paperwork is probably a contributing factor to the high rate of attrition among special education teachers. Professional organizations representing special education teachers have appealed to the federal government to reduce the amount of paperwork teachers are responsible for, but those requests are opposed by parents who view the record-keeping as necessary to ensure that their children receive the services to which they are entitled (Goldstein, 2003).

As stated before, teachers who are assigned to teach subjects that they are not qualified to teach or for which they lack interest are likely to cite that as a cause of frustration and dissatisfaction. Administrative decisions to assign teachers to teach courses for which they have inadequate preparation create incompetence (McLaughlin et al., 1986). Although it may not be possible to avoid misassignment of teachers in every case, it is possible to reduce the number of instances.

Teacher selection procedures should be reviewed if schools frequently find themselves short of teachers in certain fields. Problems are most likely to arise in fields with an undersupply of teachers, such as science and mathematics, and in fields that are affected by enrollment fluctuations. Changing selection procedures to give preference to teachers who are certified in more than one teaching field and helping teachers to acquire additional endorsements in fields with teacher shortages can help alleviate the problem.

Many teachers feel dissatisfied because of the pervasive sense of failure they experience in trying to work with children who have suffered deprivation either because of family failures or poverty. Teachers report that they are forced to take on parenting roles in order to respond to the needs of children from single-parent or dual-career families. Working with students who are learning disabled in mainstreamed settings and large classes are other sources of frustration for many teachers (McLaughlin et al., 1986). Unfortunately, administrators have relatively limited resources with which to attack the problems of poverty and neglect. The needs of children such as these far exceed the resources available to assist them. It may be of some help for administrators to stress to teachers the need to adopt realistic expectations. Suggestions for administrative actions that will help address teacher dissatisfaction arising from the sources discussed are shown in Exhibit 6.2.

EXHIBIT 6.2

ADMINISTRATIVE RESPONSES TO TEACHER DISSATISFACTION

SOURCE OF DISSATISFACTION	ADMINISTRATIVE ACTION
Boredom	Rotate teaching assignments Provide workshops and seminars on new content and methods Provide educational leave
Interruptions	Schedule announcements once a day Use volunteers to reduce teacher responsibility for fund raising Train teachers in classroom management
Misassignment	Provide support for training teachers assigned out of field Examine qualifications of all teachers and reassign accordingly Consider changes in curriculum Provide supervisory support for teachers out of field
Lack of Resources	Obtain support from other sources Reallocate instructional budget to most needed items Encourage sharing of supplies
Working with At-Risk Children	Frequent praise "Time out" for teachers to help them reduce stress Expert supervisory assistance

JOB SATISFACTION AND TEACHER TURNOVER

Attrition is an important problem in teaching, as it is in many occupations. It has been estimated that about 13 percent of teachers leave the profession or change jobs each year (National Center for Education Statistics, 1998). Attrition is highest among young teachers. It is estimated that about one-half of new teachers in urban schools leave during the first five years (Streisand & Toch, 1998). Recent entrants into teaching are somewhat less likely than their counterparts in the past to view teaching as a lifetime career, and they are more likely to plan to move on to other fields after a few years. Dissatisfaction with the conditions of their work can lead these teachers to exit the profession even earlier than they had originally expected. It is therefore important for administrators to take note of the factors that contribute to teacher dissatisfaction and to work to eliminate or at least ameliorate those conditions in order to retain teachers who might otherwise leave the classroom (Hardy, 2002).

Teachers as a group are more satisfied with their work than people in most other occupations (Rodman, 1986), but their satisfaction is affected by the conditions of their work. A study in Great Britain found that the more discipline problems beginning teachers encountered, the more likely they were to leave teaching (Veenman, 1984). Some teachers leave the profession because they are discouraged by what they perceive as a lack of success in the classroom, and others decide that they are not temperamentally or intellectually suited for the job. Not all teachers leave because of dissatisfaction, however. Some teachers leave involuntarily because of enrollment declines or changes in their family situation.

Inadequate salary was the most frequently cited reason for leaving teaching by those who had taken jobs in other fields in one of the few studies of the topic. Some 60 percent of respondents named that factor. Most of the individuals who left the profession had improved their financial situation as compared to a group of persons who were still teaching (Metropolitan Life Insurance Company, 1985).

Working conditions, including lack of input, nonteaching duties, and paperwork, were second in frequency of mention in the Metropolitan Life (1985) survey; they were named by 36 percent of the former teachers. Student-related reasons ranked third in frequency of mention, named by 30 percent of the respondents (Metropolitan Life Insurance Company, 1985).

There is evidence that academically able teachers are more likely to leave the profession as compared to those with less academic ability (Schlechty & Vance, 1981). The reason is not clear, but it is possible that teachers with higher levels of ability have more career options than less able individuals.

School districts that have made teacher retention the focus of a vigorous effort have seen strong positive results. LaFourche Parish Public Schools in Louisiana dropped its teacher attrition rate from 56 percent to 7 percent after introducing a program that provided support for teachers. New teachers in that parish receive a warm welcome from the superintendent and his staff, followed by four days of training on effective classroom management procedures and instructional practices. New teachers are made to feel that they are a part of the district "family." The cost in time and dollars of a program such as that adopted in LaFourche Parish is small in comparison to the size of the payoff (Wong & Asquith, 2002).

Organizational Correlates of Attrition

There has been very little research on organizational features of schools that are related to higher levels of teacher turnover, but one of the few studies that has been done found that certain working conditions in schools are positively correlated with teacher retention. In districts in which educational leaves for teachers were available and in which teachers helped select other teachers, teacher retention was higher, as compared to districts without those features. Interestingly, tuition payments for graduate study were associated with higher rather than lower teacher attrition (Seyfarth & Bost, 1986).

If a workplace allows employees to have fun and if people have a feeling of belonging, they are usually reluctant to leave. Some commercial firms do a better job than school districts in devising ways to hold employees, and school administrators might consider borrowing some of their ideas. Two actions taken by commercial firms that have helped reduce worker attrition are creating websites on which employees can post their gripes and classifying email so that employees can skip routine messages to save time. Messages that everyone is expected to read are labeled "first class." "Second class" messages are ideas and suggestions that others have found work well, and "no class" is for humor, puzzles, and classified ads. To encourage employees to "have a life" outside of the job, a Cincinnati firm displays photographs of its employees engaged in their favorite weekend activities. The photos help to heighten a feeling of family and have also turned out to be a potent recruiting device (Harris & Brannick, 1999).

A large drug retailer makes a video available to managers to show prospective employees. The video stresses the importance of a positive attitude and shows employees who have gone out of their way to help customers. The video shows all aspects of the operation of a drugstore, ranging from unloading trucks and stocking merchandise to helping customers find merchandise (Harris & Brannick, 1999).

Demographic Correlates of Attrition

Several demographic factors correlate with employee retention. Among those that have been shown to be related to attrition are length of service, age, level of skill, and education level. Workers who are younger, who have been with an employer a shorter length of time, and who have fewer skills and less education are more likely than employees without those traits to leave their jobs (Price, 1977). School districts that employ relatively large numbers of young teachers can expect to have higher than average turnover rates. However, teachers with higher levels of education are more, rather than less, likely to leave their jobs. That may be the result of increased awareness of job opportunities among teachers who hold advanced degrees.

Teacher turnover may be an indicator of teachers' lack of satisfaction with their jobs or have to do with factors in their personal lives or the economy. Many of the teachers who leave classrooms do so because of family reasons, either to bear or care for children or to move with a spouse to another locality. There is not much that principals and personnel administrators can do to reduce attrition that is related to family factors. However, in order to be able to understand fully the causes and implications of teacher attrition, it is necessary to collect detailed information on teacher mobility and the reasons for it.

In some districts, teachers who resign from their jobs are interviewed or asked to complete a questionnaire explaining their reasons for leaving. Although the validity of this information is debatable, it is an important source of data about an area of human behavior in which our knowledge is very limited. Unexplained increases in turnover may reveal previously unsuspected morale problems. An investigation is called for if turnover rates increase suddenly, particularly when the increase occurs among groups of teachers with normally low attrition.

Turnover generally refers to employees who leave a company or district altogether, but information about teacher transfers can also give clues about teacher motivation. Teachers transfer from one school to another in order to find more pleasant working conditions or greater convenience.

At the district level, a transfer has no effect on the overall composition of the teaching force, but at the school level it does. If an experienced teacher in a school is replaced by a less experienced one, the net result may be a decline in instructional effectiveness within the school. Principals should therefore be concerned with discovering the true reasons for teachers' requests for transfer and their decisions to leave the profession.

Not all attrition is to be deplored. Both from an individual point of view and from the point of view of the district, some is necessary and desirable. Individuals who discover that they have made the wrong career choice should be encouraged to seek other outlets for their talents.

The profession erects relatively few barriers to those who seek to become teachers. It is argued by some that ease of entry is desirable for reasons of equity (Sykes, 1983), but the training of individuals who are not intellectually or temperamentally suited for teaching imposes on both the individuals and the districts that employ them the cost of correcting earlier errors of choice and judgment.

SUMMARY

Motivated and knowledgeable teachers are essential elements of effective schools. Motivation refers to conditions responsible for variations in the intensity, quality, direction, and duration of work-related behavior. Expectancy theory explains variations in motivation as attributable to responses to the opportunity to earn rewards. Equity theory holds that motivation is affected by perceptions of fairness, and goal-setting theory suggests that people are motivated to achieve identified goals. It is often assumed that satisfaction is positively correlated with performance on the job, but the evidence shows that the correlation is weak. Happy employees are not necessarily outstanding performers. For teachers, satisfaction is related to reaching children, whereas dissatisfaction arises from factors that impede effective teaching.

SUGGESTED ACTIVITIES

1. Suppose you are the principal of a school located in an inner-city neighborhood. Many of the students are from single-parent families, and most do not expect to go to college. The school staff consists of two groups—older teachers who have taught at the school for years and younger teachers who have recently begun replacing teachers who retire. The young teachers work hard but are sometimes discouraged by the difficult conditions in which they work and by the negative, defeatist attitudes of older teachers. A businessperson in the neighborhood offers you $5,000 to be spent to help teachers in the school. There are two conditions: The money must be spent on teachers and must be used to help improve student achievement. You may choose to allocate the money among teachers in any way you choose. You may give all of the money to one teacher, divide it equally, or divide it among teachers who submit the best proposals telling how they would use the money to achieve the donor's goals. Write a letter thanking the businessperson for the gift and explaining how you have decided to distribute the money. Using one of the motivation theories discussed in this chapter, give reasons why you believe your plan will achieve the desired results.

2. Consider the career anchors in Exhibit 6.1 and rate each factor on its importance for teachers. Rate each item as you think the majority of teachers would rate it, using the terms "Very important," "Somewhat important," or "Not important." For example, you might rate interesting work as very important to teachers and tangible rewards as somewhat important. Would you rank your personal career anchors the same way as you think other teachers would rank them?

3. How much influence do you think a principal can have over the levels of satisfaction or dissatisfaction experienced by teachers on the job? Explain why you answered as you did.

ONLINE RESOURCES

A wealth of material on topics bearing on worker motivation can be accessed online. Much of this material is geared to business but can be adapted to schools.

Brookings Institution (www.brookings.org)

> This searchable database holds an extensive collection of materials related to public policy issues, including education. The Brown Center on Education Policy (www.brook.edu/gs/brown/brown_hp.htm) provides access to policy papers expressing a variety of points of view on educational issues.

Education Commission of the States (www.ecs.org/clearinghouse/18/24/1824.htm)

> ECS identifies states that reward or sanction school districts and individual schools on the basis of student performance. The site also tells which states give monetary rewards or bonuses to schools and districts that perform well.

ERIC Digests (www.eric.ed.gov/searchdb/index.html)

> ERIC is a widely used database that is the source of information, reports, and research related to education. Each year, between 100 and 200 new digests are published, containing syntheses of recent research on topics of general interest. The full text of most of these digests is available online. Among the topics covered in recent digests are beginning teacher induction programs, elementary teacher supply and demand, and teacher evaluation.

Workforce (www.workforce.com/index.html)

> This site provides information on topics having to do with motivation, including employee incentives, compensation plans, and satisfaction. The site is oriented to business users, but much of the material can be applied in educational settings. Free membership includes an email newsletter.

REFERENCES

Ashford, S. J., & Cummings, L. L. (1983). Feedback as an individual resource: Personal strategies of creating information. *Organizational Behavior and Human Performance, 32*, 370–398.

Bogler, R. (2001, December). The influence of leadership style on teacher job satisfaction. *Educational Administration Quarterly, 37*, 662–683.

Carroll, S., & Tosi, H. (1973). *Management by objectives: Applications and research.* New York: Macmillan.

Fincham, R., & Rhodes, P. (1988). *The individual, work and organization.* London: Weidenfeld and Nicholson.

Freemantle, D. (2001). *The stimulus factor.* London: Prentice-Hall.

Goldstein, L. (2003, May 28). Disabled by paperwork? *Education Week*, pp. 1, 23.

Hardy, L. (2002, April). Who will teach our children? *American School Board Journal, 189*, 18–23.

Harris, J., & Brannick, J. (1999). *Finding and keeping great employees.* New York: AMACOM.

Ilgen, D. R., Fisher, C. D., & Taylor, M. S. (1979). Consequences of individual feedback on behavior in organizations. *Journal of Applied Psychology, 64*, 349–371.

Johnson, S. (1986, Summer). Incentives for teachers: What motivates, what matters. *Educational Administration Quarterly, 22*, 54–79.

Katzell, R., & Thompson, D. (1990, February). Work motivation: Theory and practice. *American Psychologist, 45*, 144–153.

Keller, B. (2003, May 28). Average teacher pay skews school budgets. *Education Week*, 3.

Kelley, C. (1998, May). The Kentucky school-based performance award program: School-level effects. *Educational Policy, 12*, 305–324.

Landy, F. J. (1985). *Psychology of work behavior* (3rd ed.). Homewood, IL: Dorsey.

Lawler, E. E., & Rhode, J. G. (1976). *Information and control in organizations.* Pacific Palisades, CA: Goodyear.

Leithwood, K. (2001). School leadership and educational accountability: Toward a distributed perspective. In T. J. Kowalski and G. Perreault (Eds.), *21st century challenges for school administrators* (pp. 11–25). Lanham, MD: Scarecrow Press.

Locke, E. A., & Latham, G. P. (1984). *Goal setting: A motivational technique that works!* Englewood Cliffs, NJ: Prentice Hall.

Manz, C. (1986). Self-leadership: Toward an expanded theory of self-influence processes in organizations. *Academy of Management Review, 11*, 585–600.

McLaughlin, M. W., Pfeifer, R. S., Swanson-Owens, D., & Yee, S. (1986). Why teachers won't teach. *Phi Delta Kappan, 67*, 420–426.

Metropolitan Life Insurance Company. (1985). *Former teachers in America*. New York: Author.

National Center for Education Statistics. (1998). *The condition of education, 1998*. Washington, DC: U.S. Department of Education.

Pinder, C. C. (1984). *Work motivation: Theory, issues, and applications*. Dallas: Scott, Foresman.

Plihal, J. (1981). *Intrinsic rewards of teaching*. Paper presented at the annual meeting of the American Educational Research Association. (ERIC Document Reproduction Service No. ED 200599).

Price, J. L. (1977). *The study of turnover*. Ames: Iowa State University Press.

Ritchie, S., & Martin, P. (1999). *Motivation management*. Brookfield, VT: Gower.

Rodman, B. (1986, May 7). Teachers' job satisfaction seen greater than that of other college graduates. *Education Week*, p. 4.

Schein, E. (1990). *Career anchors*. San Diego: University Associates.

Schlechty, P. C., & Vance, V. (1981). Do academically able teachers leave education? The North Carolina case. *Phi Delta Kappan, 63*, 106–112.

Schlechty, P. C., & Vance, V. (1983). Recruitment, selection and retention: The shape of the teaching force. *The Elementary School Journal, 83*, 469–487.

Seyfarth, J. T., & Bost, W. A. (1986, Fall). Teacher turnover and quality of working life in schools: An empirical study. *Journal of Research and Development in Education, 20*, 1–6.

Streisand, B., & Toch, T. (1998, September 4). Many millions of kids, and too few teachers. *U.S. News & World Report*. Available online: www.usnews.com/usnews/issue/9809124teac.htm.

Sykes, G. (1983). Public policy and the problem of teacher quality: The need for screens and magnets. In L. S. Shulman and G. Sykes (Eds.), *Handbook of teaching and policy* (pp. 97–125). New York: Longman.

Veenman, S. (1984). Perceived problems of beginning teachers. *Review of Educational Research, 54*, 143–178.

Wong, H. K. & Asquith, C. (2002, December). Supporting new teachers. *American School Board Journal, 189*, 22–24.

CHAPTER SEVEN

INDUCTION

People who are hired to fill a job they have not previously held have many questions about the work and the organization that will employ them. For those who are entering a field for the first time, the questions focus on job duties and expectations, income, opportunities for advancement, fellow workers, and one's superiors. Some of these questions are answered in the interview or in orientation sessions, but many are not. Unfortunately, most employers provide little information to help employees feel comfortable in their new work setting. What the new employee learns is usually acquired from other employees, varies in accuracy, and reflects the attitudes of those employees toward the employing organization.

PLAN OF THE CHAPTER

Organizations that provide planned induction programs for new employees increase the chances that those employees will obtain accurate information about the job and the organization and that they will be more satisfied and productive as a result. Identifying the purposes of induction programs for teachers and principals and suggesting ways of planning programs that will help meet their needs for information are the goals of this chapter. The chapter is written for principals and district staff members who work with new teachers. The following topics are examined: (1) expectations and teaching reality, (2) purpose and types of induction programs, (3) mentors and teacher induction, (4) induction and career development, (5) administrative leadership for induction, and (6) induction for administrators.

EXPECTATIONS AND TEACHING REALITY

One of the reasons mentioned most frequently by educators for choosing a teaching career is a special interest in working with children or young people (Jantzen, 1981). Other reasons mentioned frequently are "a life-long opportunity to learn," "an opportunity for exercising individual initiative," and "the opportunity for service to mankind." In their choices of reasons for choosing a teaching career, students reveal their expectations for their lives as teachers. To the extent that these expectations are fulfilled by their experiences in the classroom, these teachers are likely to feel satisfied with their choice of career, but if their expectations are not met, they may feel disappointed and even cheated.

The New Teacher

The first years of teaching have been described as "intense and formative" (Feiman-Nemser, 2001) and a time of transition during which these young adults are learning who they are and what they wish to become (Schempp, Sparkes, & Templin, 1999). This is the period during which beginning teachers learn what behaviors are appropriate to their work and become aware of the unwritten values, norms, and operating procedures that guide interactions among the staff members in schools (Smylie, 1995). A teacher's first few years in the classroom are a critical period, when his or her identity is formed, skills are acquired, and far-reaching decisions about the future are made.

Beginning teachers have preformed impressions about the work of teaching gained from years of experience as students with a variety of teachers. From these mental images of teaching that they bring to the job, new teachers begin the work of creating a professional identity. This is one of the critical tasks of the early years of teaching. The professional identity is forged from the teacher's own experiences in school, the ideas and experiences encountered during preservice preparation, and the experience of teaching itself (Feiman-Nemser, 2001).

The creation of a professional identity is only one of many challenges that new teachers face. Feiman-Nemser (2001) has identified four other tasks that also occupy the attention of young teachers: (1) to gain local knowledge of the students, the curriculum, and the school context; (2) to learn to teach responsively; (3) to develop a beginning repertoire of teaching strategies; and (4) to create a classroom learning community. Induction programs can be designed to help beginning teachers accomplish these tasks.

Teachers acquire general knowledge about children as part of their preservice preparation, but they can only learn about the individuals whom they teach by being in daily contact with them, observing their behavior and interactions with one another and with adults, and evaluating their academic work. It is at this time that the idealistic beliefs about students held by young teachers are challenged. They find that students are not as eager to learn as they had expected them to be (Blasé, 1980).

This experience of dissonance between the expectations one brings to a new job and actual experiences at work are not limited to teaching. New entrants into most occupations report similar experiences. A term that has been applied to this experience is *reality shock*. Two types of factors have been cited as leading to reality shock (Veenman, 1984).

Personal causes have to do with the individual. They include personality characteristics that are not suited to teaching and attitudes that are uninformed and out of place. Situational factors that contribute to reality shock include inadequate professional preparation, teaching assignments for which the new teacher has no prior preparation, lack of materials and supplies, absence of clear instructional objectives, isolation, overcrowded classes, and a school climate that is not conducive to instruction (Huling-Austin, 1986; Veenman, 1984).

One of the critical elements of teaching that must be acquired in the early years of teaching is the ability to respond in useful ways to unexpected events. When a lesson doesn't go as planned or when instruction is interrupted, a teacher must be able to make adjustments to redirect the lesson or bring the group back on task. This is learned skill that requires hard work on the part of beginning teachers, but the task is easier when new teachers receive supportive feedback from colleagues.

Inexperienced teachers bring with them a limited repertoire of instructional strategies that they acquired during student teaching and from observing other teachers. They rapidly expand this repertoire through a process of trial-and-error, trying new ideas and retaining those that work while refining or discarding those that do not. Young teachers who are fortunate enough to teach in schools in which experimentation is encouraged and failure is not penalized will risk trying out new ideas, but if failure is looked down on, these teachers will play it safe and try only approaches that seem guaranteed to work. The result is that teaching is less varied and hence less likely to capture students' interest (Feiman-Nemser, 2001).

PURPOSE AND TYPES OF INDUCTION PROGRAMS

Changing conditions in education that have made teaching more difficult and stressful have underscored the need for well-designed induction programs. Among the conditions that make teachers' work more difficult today than in the past are the increasing numbers of at-risk children in the schools, the establishment of a prescribed curriculum with results measured by scores on standardized tests, and the introduction of new technologies that teachers are expected to master (Mager, 1992)

The definition of *induction* used in this book is a planned program designed to facilitate the process by which new teachers in a school acquire the social and technical knowledge and skills they need to perform effectively in their work roles and interpersonal relationships (Smylie, 1995). Three distinct types of induction programs are in use in the schools: orientation programs, performance improvement programs, and state-mandated induction programs.

These three types of programs serve several purposes. They help to improve teacher effectiveness, encourage promising new teachers to remain in teaching by offering support and assistance, promote the professional and personal well-being of new teachers, communicate district and school cultures to beginning teachers, and help to meet state and federal mandates.

Orientation Programs

The simplest of these three types of induction programs consists of orientation sessions to introduce new teachers to the school and the community. These programs provide information about the district, help new employees to become better acquainted with the community in which they will be working (Kester & Marockie, 1987), explain performance expectations and help new employees to learn what is expected of them on the job, provide some emotional support, promote employees' personal and professional well-being (Huling-Austin, 1986), and clarify the organizational hierarchy (Pataniczek & Isaacson, 1981). These programs tend to be of short duration, and the emphasis is on information dissemination.

About 80 percent of first-year teachers in one study reported they participated in orientation sessions of one kind or another (Pataniczek & Isaacson, 1981). Orientation sessions are not always well received by teachers. Although the teachers in the study reported that they valued the information they received, many felt that equally good results could have been achieved by providing the information in a faculty handbook. One administrator described traditional orientation programs as boring to old-timers and confusing to beginners (Hunt, 1968).

Performance Improvement Programs

The second type of induction program incorporates some of the features of the first type and also seeks to help new members learn the culture of the school (Schlechty, 1985). Some of these programs have multiple objectives, whereas others have limited scope and narrowly focused goals. Two of the most important of the objectives identified for this type of induction program in schools are helping beginning teachers to improve their instructional effectiveness and reducing attrition of new teachers (Huling-Austin, 1987).

Among the topics that are likely to be especially useful for beginning teachers seeking to improve their instructional effectiveness are workshops at which discipline and classroom management procedures are explained; conversations with subject-area specialists who provide an orientation to the district curriculum and help locate resources and share lesson plans and tests; explanations of performance assessment procedures; and assistance in preparing a professional development plan (Hirsh, 1990). This type of program often continues over a semester or a full year. In addition to receiving information about the school and the district, participants usually receive individualized assistance with their teaching from an administrator, supervisor, or, increasingly, another teacher.

The simplest type of assistance consists of responses to requests for help. More complex kinds of assistance include classroom observations combined with feedback. These observations may be provided by other teachers but are separate from the normal evaluation procedures. Mentoring programs are included in this category. They are characterized by intensive involvement of an experienced teacher with a beginner and may deal with many facets of the new teacher's experiences (Anderson & Shannon, 1988).

Well-designed performance improvement programs can lead to reductions in teacher attrition by helping beginning teachers to feel more successful in the classroom. A pilot program in California lowered attrition among new teachers from 37 percent to 9 percent over a five-year period, and school districts in Ohio and New York achieved similar results with their induction programs (Curran, Abrahams, & Manuel, 2000).

However, attrition is influenced by a number of factors, and induction programs may have little or no effect on some of them. Teachers who are more academically able are more likely than other teachers to leave the classroom within five years of entering the field, for reasons that are not well understood (Murnane, 1996). Male secondary teachers are more inclined than females and elementary teachers to leave the profession, possibly in order to increase their income, and teachers who work in schools in which a majority of students come from different ethnic backgrounds than their own have higher attrition rates than teachers in schools with a majority of students with similar backgrounds. Teachers who perceive themselves as receiving little support from the principal are also more inclined to leave the profession (Betancourt-Smith, Inman, & Marlow, 1994).

It is a fact of life that teachers have little contact with their peers, and many of them regard this isolation as an impediment. A study by the National Science Teachers Association found that 90 percent of the science teachers surveyed viewed isolation from peers as a limitation on their professional growth (Weld, 1998). Induction programs do not eliminate isolation as a fact of life in teaching, but they can help to ameliorate its effects on new teachers.

Induction programs should be designed to help beginning teachers master the critical tasks identified by Feiman-Nemser (2001). This is a growth process that takes place over time. Growth begins with a felt need and proceeds as the individual's insight becomes more incisive. It is important that the teacher have the opportunity to interact with experienced colleagues in a judgment-free, exploratory atmosphere.

Although not all teachers experience the same problems in the first year of teaching, their experiences are similar enough that an induction program can be developed around the issues with which beginning teachers generally are likely to need help. Veenman (1984) summarized findings from 83 studies that investigated concerns of beginning teachers. The list below shows the ten most frequently mentioned problems, arranged in order of frequency from most to least frequent.

1. Classroom discipline
2. Motivating students
3. Dealing with individual differences
4. Assessing students' work (tie)
5. Relations with parents (tie)
6. Organization of classwork (tie)
7. Insufficient materials and supplies (tie)
8. Dealing with problems of individual students
9. Heavy teaching load resulting in insufficient preparation time
10. Relations with colleagues (Veenman, 1984, pp. 154–155)

Competent mentor teachers can assist beginning teachers with most of the problems on Veenman's list, but some of the problems require administrative action. For example, a mentor teacher might help a beginning teacher deal more effectively with classroom discipline and student motivation, but the mentor teacher would likely be unable to help solve problems related to lack of materials and supplies or heavy teaching load, since those factors usually result from policy decisions.

There is some evidence that the kinds of assistance beginning teachers actually seek are different from the needs they identify on questionnaires. One study found that requests for assistance with classroom discipline constituted only 5.2 percent of beginning teachers' requests for assistance from mentor teachers, although it headed the list of problems cited by beginning teachers in the studies reviewed by Veenman (1984) (Odell, Loughlin, & Ferraro, 1986–87). That was the lowest frequency of seven assistance categories.

Beginning teachers most frequently requested assistance with instruction (35 percent), followed by system requests (20.6 percent) and resource requests (14.5 percent). System requests had to do with "information related to procedures and guidelines of the school district" (p. 53), and resource requests were related to "collecting, disseminating, or locating resources for use by the new teacher" (p. 53) (Odell et al., 1986–87).

These results suggest that teachers respond to questionnaires from a different frame of reference than has been assumed. Their responses may indicate which problems teachers believe are most critical to their success as a teacher, not necessarily those for which they are most likely to seek help. The findings also show that when a new teacher does not ask for assistance with a particular problem, it does not necessarily indicate that he or she feels comfortable with that situation. There is a good deal of evidence that teachers refrain from asking for help if they believe such requests will be interpreted as evidence of lack of teaching competence. New teachers may not ask for help with classroom discipline yet nevertheless welcome and profit from any assistance that is made available.

State-Mandated Induction Programs

The third type of induction program operates under state mandate and requires beginning teachers to demonstrate mastery of specified teaching competencies. This type of program is primarily evaluative in nature, but in some of these programs, evaluation is combined with limited assistance. An example of one such program is the North Carolina Beginning Teacher Induction Program (www.ncpublicschools.org/mentoring_novice_teachers/mntop.htm), which requires new teachers to assemble a performance-based portfolio demonstrating mastery of the ten standards developed by the Interstate New Teacher Assessment and Support Consortium (see Exhibit 3.4).

In some states, beginning teachers are required to demonstrate that they possess certain teaching competencies in order to receive a permanent teaching certificate. In most of these programs, an assessment or assistance team is designated to work with one or more beginning teachers. Usually, the team includes among its members one principal and one experienced classroom teacher. Some programs provide training for the team members, although the training is often brief and may be limited to use of a particular classroom observation instrument. Team members observe the beginning teacher and may give feedback on the teacher's performance along with recommendations on corrective actions.

Supplementing Preservice Training

Induction and staff development programs must sometimes provide training that was not incorporated into the new teacher's preservice preparation. As more schools adopt school-based management, it will be necessary for teachers to receive training in the leadership skills required by the added responsibility that structure requires. Many preservice programs presently offer little or no preparation in assuming leadership roles (Stallings, 1984).

Principals' leadership styles vary from laissez faire to directive, and teachers must learn to accommodate themselves to a variety of styles as administrators come and go or as teachers themselves transfer from school to school. Very few preservice programs address differences in principals' leadership styles, nor do they prepare new teachers to adapt to these different approaches. Induction is an appropriate time to help beginning teachers identify and respond in an appropriate way to the leadership behaviors of principals and supervisors with whom they work. In some schools, a small group of influential teachers exert leadership, and beginning teachers must be able to recognize such coteries and be able to work effectively through them (Stallings, 1984).

Other groups that new teachers must learn to take into account in their work include parents and professional organizations. Parents are more interested and involved in school affairs in some districts than in others, but in no school is it wise to ignore parents. Professional organizations are much more powerful in certain districts than in others, but they too are a force of which new teachers should be aware (Stallings, 1984).

MENTORS AND TEACHER INDUCTION

Induction programs in schools serve several different purposes, as noted earlier. The design of the program depends on the purpose for which the program was established. One of the most popular components of induction programs is the mentor teacher. This position goes by a variety of names, including *buddy teacher, support teacher, cooperating teacher,* and *teacher advisor.* Several studies have shown that mentor teachers have been instrumental in helping beginning professionals acquire increased teaching competence (Zahorik, 1987).

Mentor teachers perform a variety of functions to help new teachers feel at home and learn their jobs. They introduce the new teachers to others on the staff, provide copies or handbooks and curriculum guides, explain grading and discipline policies, and often help set up the classroom (Tickle, 1994). Mentors also provide political information and advice to their mentees, help them make contacts, and provide information to help with career decisions (Anderson & Shannon, 1988).

One of the reasons for the success of mentors is that teachers are accustomed to seeking help from colleagues. Most teachers prefer to talk to another teacher when they have a question rather than seek assistance from a supervisor or administrator (Pataniczek & Isaacson, 1981). In part, the preference for conferring with other teachers is related to convenience. It is usually easier to locate another teacher than to find a supervisor or administrator, and new teachers are often afraid that asking for help from the principal may raise questions in the administrator's mind about their competence. To avoid that possibility, some teachers avoid asking for help, or they go to a teacher whom they think they can trust (Schempp, Sparkes, & Templin, 1999).

Districts that have introduced high-quality mentoring programs have found that attrition rates for new teachers dropped more than two-thirds from their previous levels (Darling-Hammond, 1999). A study of mentoring reported that teacher mentors cited two factors that they regarded as their most useful contributions to beginning teachers: providing support and encouragement and informing new teachers about school and district policies, procedures, and paperwork (Ganser, 1993).

When mentors and new teachers were asked what qualities were most important for individuals who work with beginning teachers, the list of most-mentioned attributes included experience, sensitivity, approachability, and a calm manner (Tickle, 1994). The complete list appears in Exhibit 7.1.

Mentoring Minority Teachers

Teachers who are in a minority in a school may face special adjustment problems and need support from mentors who are well-informed about minority issues and able to discuss them freely. Some minority teachers report that they are viewed by parents and other teachers as representatives of their group whose actions and values are taken to be typical of those of the group as a whole rather than being unique to that individual. These teachers are surprised to learn that others expect them to know how other members of their group feel about a variety of educational and social issues (Brock & Grady, 2001).

Minority teachers also report that they are occasionally called on to give assistance when a majority teacher encounters a problem with a minority child. They note that they do not mind helping other teachers, but they feel put on the spot when these requests involve assisting with discipline problems that have arisen as a result of a teacher's failing to state clear expectations for his or her students (Brock & Grady, 2001). Induction programs can be designed to include opportunities for both majority and minority teachers to explore issues that arise in the course of working together.

■ ■ ■ ■ ■ ▬▬▬▬▬

EXHIBIT 7.1

**QUALITIES OF EFFECTIVE MENTORS IDENTIFIED BY MENTORS
AND BEGINNING TEACHERS**

PROFESSIONAL QUALITIES
Familiarity with school and district policies
Expertise in subject area or grade level
Knowledge of school's culture
Knowledge of "how things get done"

PERSONAL QUALITIES
Enthusiastic
Positive outlook
Patient and caring
Tactful
Accessible

TUTORIAL QUALITIES
Excellent teacher
Able to provide emotional support
Respectful of teacher's autonomy
Committed to providing time for advisee

Training Mentor Teachers

Training for mentor teachers is an important part of a successful induction program. The complexity of the skills required to function effectively in a support role
should not be underestimated. It is sometimes assumed that teachers who perform
well with children will be equally effective as mentors to adults (Wagner, 1985).
Unfortunately, that is not always true.

Even when training is provided, "school systems cannot expect that experienced teachers will be able to provide effective assistance to beginners in a systematic way" (Thies-Sprinthall, 1986, p. 13). It seems safe to say that training that is
brief and superficial is not likely to have much impact on the ability of mentor
teachers to affect the behavior of beginning teachers. The training they receive
should be designed to convey the knowledge and skill they will need in working
with beginning teachers. Two of the important skills are knowledge of a variety of
teaching models and the ability to explain and demonstrate the conditions under
which each is appropriate (Thies-Sprinthall, 1986).

Quality mentoring programs are expensive to develop and operate, but they
have a high probability of helping to retain young teachers. The features that dis-
tinguish a high-quality program from one of less quality include released time for

▪ ▪ ▪ ▪ ▪

EXHIBIT 7.2

FEATURES OF HIGH-QUALITY MENTORING PROGRAMS

School site administrators understand and support the mentoring program.
Mentors are provided for all beginning teachers.
Mentors are chosen using district criteria and receive training.
Mentors receive released time to work with new teachers.
Mentors are assigned reasonable caseloads.
Mentors are paid for work with beginning teachers.
Mentors are evaluated on effectiveness.

Source: "State-Initiated Induction Programs: Supporting, Assisting, Training, Assessing, and Keeping Teachers" by E. Fideler, Winter 2000, *State Education Standard, 1* (1), 12–15.

mentors, a reasonable caseload, and compensation for the mentor. These and other features of well-designed programs are shown in Exhibit 7.2.

INDUCTION AND CAREER DEVELOPMENT

Commercial and industrial organizations in particular emphasize the career development aspect of induction. In some firms, mentors are assigned to new employees and serve as sponsors to help the new worker establish informal networks inside and outside the company. Mentors also serve as teachers, and they are particularly helpful in assisting beginners to understand the organization's culture, including both written and unwritten rules and norms. They provide feedback on both performance and interpersonal relations and allow learners to test their assumptions about the organization. Mentors occasionally play devil's advocate by challenging an employee's perceptions or behavior. Finally, mentors play the role of coach by sharing their own career histories and struggles as a way of providing emotional support to beginning employees who experience difficulties in getting their ideas accepted (Farren, Gray, & Kaye, 1984).

Career Development in Schools

Some public school induction programs incorporate career development features. For example, the state of California has enacted legislation under which local school boards may elect to initiate a mentor program with state financial support. The legislation requires that mentors be credentialed and experienced classroom teachers who have demonstrated exemplary teaching ability as indicated by effective communication skills, subject-matter knowledge, and mastery of a range of teaching strategies, and are recommended by a teacher-dominated selection committee (Wagner, 1985). Mentors are appointed for terms of up to three years, during which time they teach a reduced classload and receive a stipend in addition to their regular salary. For most teachers in programs such as these, the opportunity to gain critical experience and acquire new skills outweighs the importance of added fiscal benefits.

ADMINISTRATIVE LEADERSHIP FOR INDUCTION

Principals play a key role in the success of induction programs in their schools. They act as facilitators by leading discussion groups or arranging for space, materials, and speakers. Principals also help facilitate induction by assigning mentors to new teachers and scheduling classes so that mentors and their charges have common planning periods. Principals who are committed to continuous learning serve as models for teachers in their schools and encourage new teachers to take advantage of the opportunities provided by induction (Payne & Wolfson, 2000).

One of the problematic aspects of programs that use mentors is helping experienced teachers to overcome a reluctance to comment on their colleagues' work. One author (Zahorik, 1987) made the following observation:

> Teachers must come not to fear exposing their classroom practices. They must see that knowledge of their classroom behavior by others as well as by themselves is essential to improvement. . . . Changing teachers' views of teaching is obviously a difficult and lengthy process, but it seems to be an unavoidable first step to developing collegiality, improving instruction, and making teaching satisfying work (p. 395).

Principals can help by encouraging all teachers to be more open in their teaching and by reassuring those who are observed by colleagues that they will not be evaluated on the basis of collegial observations.

Induction programs are subject to failure when unreasonably high expectations are held for them. They cannot be expected to overcome problems related to resource scarcity or policy limitations. Induction does not remove the need for ongoing professional development activities aimed at raising or maintaining the quality of the instructional program, and it does not take the place of performance evaluation.

Principals should be aware of the danger that induction may make poor teachers feel good about doing a poor job (Huling-Austin, 1986). Other potential problems arise when teachers without supervisory training or experience attempt to assist beginning teachers in improving their instructional practices or when narrowly defined instructional models are prescribed for all teachers, leading to standardized practice (Thies-Sprinthall, 1986).

Induction is not a substitute for instructional leadership. Clearly defined performance expectations are essential for effective instruction, and induction programs cannot take the place of that ingredient. Principals are sometimes surprised to hear teachers report that performance expectations are not clear, since they are clear to them. What is needed is continuous reinforcement of behavioral expectations as employees learn new roles (Kurtz, 1983).

Recommendations for Principals

Even in districts without formal induction programs, principals can anticipate and remove some of the obstacles to effective teaching that are frequently encountered by teachers who are in their first year of teaching. The following practices will help beginning teachers attain success during their first year in a school (Kurtz, 1983):

1. Plan special in-service sessions for beginning teachers throughout the school year with timely topics addressing the concerns of that group. Information is timely if it is presented when teachers need it. If presented before the need arises, the information is likely to be disregarded; if it is presented afterwards, it is worthless.

Beginning teachers want help in evaluating student work and assigning grades, but a presentation on that topic will be more successful if presented about halfway through the first grading period than if it is scheduled for the opening of school or the week grades are due.

2. Pair beginning teachers with experienced teachers, matching individuals for subject taught, physical proximity, and teaching philosophy. In some districts, the bargaining agreement places limits on the types of activities that teachers may be asked to participate in and the amount of time they may commit to such activities. Within the contract's limitations, attempt to involve teachers who are warm and supportive and who have demonstrated they are effective at producing student learning. Spell out what is expected of the support teacher, but avoid asking that individual to perform as a mentor unless training is provided.

3. If the school has a mentor program, plan to meet periodically with mentor teachers to review their experiences working with beginning teachers and, when necessary, to identify general problems that need attention.

4. Avoid allowing beginning teachers to end up with only the courses and students more senior teachers do not want. If the bargaining agreement permits it, limit new teachers' preparations to the fewest number possible and assign students who are known to be disruptive to more experienced teachers. Be aware, however, that this action may be controversial, since some experienced teachers will resent being imposed upon and will accuse beginners of not carrying their load.

5. Exercise care and judgment in making extra-duty assignments in order to avoid jeopardizing the teaching effectiveness of beginning teachers. The first year in the classroom is a demanding experience, and most beginning teachers require large amounts of preparation time. Burdening new teachers with extra-duty assignments will make it much more difficult for them to be effective in bringing about student learning.

6. If an induction program is offered, schedule sessions for beginning teachers separately from the sessions for experienced teachers but give beginners the opportunity to attend both. Administrators who are responsible for the programs should choose content that is relevant to teachers' needs. Refer to the research by Veenman (1984) and Odell, Loughlin, and Ferraro (1986–87), presented earlier in this chapter, for ideas on relevant content.

INDUCTION FOR ADMINISTRATORS

Most administrators learn the skills they need on the job in informal ways, either by trial and error or by observing an experienced administrator. Some are fortunate enough to begin their careers working with an experienced educator who is able to articulate issues that need to be considered as decisions are made, and who is willing to assist the beginner by talking through each new type of problem as it arises.

Principals who work with an assistant principal who has had no previous administrative experience should plan to spend time with the new assistant outlining duties and discussing the teachers' expectations of administrators. A useful guide on how to conduct such an induction activity is provided by Jentz (1982).

Interviews

Among the steps Jentz (1982) has recommended are helping the new assistant principal to learn more about the school's culture and procedures by scheduling him or her to conduct interviews with individuals with whom the assistant principal will be working in the coming months. For example, if the assistant is expected to help prepare the school's budget, interviews would be scheduled with the school bookkeeper and with the district business officer. The assistant principal would also want to talk to several department heads about budgeting, purchasing procedures, and handling of payments and fees.

These interviews serve several purposes. First, they allow the assistant to make initial contacts with individuals with whom he or she will be working in the future. Second, they serve to acquaint the assistant principal with existing rules and procedures as they are interpreted by the individuals involved and alert him or her to problems that may exist in the implementation of the rules. Since policies are sometimes ignored in practice, it is a good idea as well for the new administrator to read the district's policies on fiscal accounting in order to learn "what the book says."

Third, the interviews convey to those upon whom the administrator must rely for assistance when developing the budget that the assistant principal is interested in their opinions. This will facilitate future working relationships. Similar interviews can be conducted in connection with other duties for which the administrator will have responsibility.

Preparing Work Plans

Beginning assistant principals can also be helped by preparation of detailed work plans for the year. Jentz (1982) recommended preparing a chart that shows each of the major policy areas for which the assistant principal is responsible (e.g., budget, teacher absence, student enrollment, student discipline, and so on) arrayed along one dimension and a calendar on the second. Deadlines for completion of specific tasks related to each of the policy areas are noted.

In a separate document, Jentz (1982) recommended listing a detailed sequence of steps that must be accomplished in carrying out the duties assigned to the assistant. For example, one step in preparing a budget is to notify department heads of the date for submission of a tentative budget request along with guidelines for preparing it.

The principal very likely will not have the time to prepare this chart for the assistant, but the assistant should be asked to keep a record of the steps involved in carrying out major duties and to prepare a copy for the principal. This record can later be typed and kept for future referral.

SUMMARY

Induction involves planned activities developed for the purpose of acquainting new employees with an organization and equipping them with knowledge, skills, and attitudes to enable them to function effectively and comfortably in the work setting. Three types of induction programs are common in public schools: orientation, performance effectiveness, and state mandated. The first year of teaching is a transitional year for many teachers, and for some the experiences in the classroom create reality shock.

Mentor teachers can help reduce the impact of reality shock by giving new teachers a sounding board and a source of advice and suggestions. Mentors who are selected with care and trained to perform the functions of the role can be of value in helping new teachers to deal with the problems they encounter. The most frequently mentioned problem areas identified by new teachers include student discipline, motivating students, and providing individual assistance.

Administrators should be aware of potential problems in implementing teacher induction programs and should be aware that induction does not reduce the need for instructional leadership and does not replace performance evaluation responsibilities of principals. In schools with no formal induction program, principals can make life easier for first-year teachers by appointing a support teacher to assist the new teachers and by relieving new teachers of extra-duty assignments and unnecessarily heavy teaching duties.

Induction for administrators should provide the individual with the opportunity to learn about the responsibilities of the position by talking to people with whom he or she will work. Specific guidelines on major tasks are helpful to those who are new to an administrative job.

SUGGESTED ACTIVITIES

1. Prepare a five-minute talk to welcome new teachers to your school and to give them a brief history of the school and the community.

2. Working with a classmate, one of you interview a person who has recently completed the first year of teaching, and the other interview a person who recently served as a mentor for a beginning teacher. Ask each individual what he or she perceives as the advantages and disadvantages of mentoring for themselves and for the person with whom they worked. Compare the answers and report your findings to the class.

3. From *the Dictionary of Occupational Titles* select an occupation about which you have little knowledge. Suppose you have been selected for a job in that occupation. Write five questions you would like to have answered in an induction program. How many of your questions might also be asked by a beginning teacher? (The *Dictionary of Occupational Titles* is published by the U.S. Department of Labor and is available online.)

4. Prepare a plan for a semester-long induction program for new teachers. Specify instructional objectives for each session and identify a possible presenter.

ONLINE RESOURCES

Eisenhower Program (www.ed.gov/inits/teachers/eisenhower/index.html)

The Eisenhower Program provided support for programs designed to improve instruction in math and science. This site summarizes some of the findings from projects sponsored by the program. The program was incorporated into No Child Left Behind in 2002, and the guidelines were changed.

Massachusetts Department of Education
(www.doe.mass.edu/eq/mentor/r_teach.html)

Massachusetts maintains standards for induction programs for teachers and administrators.

National Library of Education (www.ed.gov/NLE)

This site has links to a number of information resources related to education, including the Educational Resources Information Center (ERIC) and the Gateway to Educational Materials (GEM). GEM (www.thegateway.org) offers a collection of lesson plans that can be searched by subject and grade level.

University of Northern Iowa (www.uni.edu/profdev)

Professional development courses are offered online for teachers, administrators, and educational specialists by the University of Northern Iowa. This site lists the offerings with a brief description of each one and information on registration.

REFERENCES

Anderson, E. M., & Shannon, A. L. (1988, January/February). Toward a conceptualization of mentoring. *Journal of Teacher Education, 39,* 38–42.

Betancourt-Smith, M., Inman, D., & Marlow, L. (1994). Professional attrition: An examination of minority and nonminority teachers at risk. (ERIC Document Reproduction Service No. ED 388639).

Blasé, J. J., Jr. (1980). *On the meaning of being a teacher: A study of the teachers' perspective.* Unpublished doctoral dissertation, Syracuse University, Syracuse, NY.

Brock, B. L., & Grady, M. L. (2001). *From first-year to first-rate* (2nd ed.). Thousand Oaks, CA: Corwin.

Cornett, L., & Gaines, G. (1992). *Focusing on student outcomes: Roles for incentive programs.* Atlanta: Southern Regional Education Board. (ERIC Reproduction Service No. ED 358058).

Curran, B., Abrahams, C., & Manuel, J. (2000). Teacher supply and demand: Is there a shortage? *National Governors Association Reports Online.* Available online: www.ngo.org/Pubs/Issue Briefs/default.asp

Darling-Hammond, L. (1999, Fall). Solving the dilemmas of teacher supply, demand, and standards. *Quality Teaching, 9* (1), 3–4.

Farren, C., Gray, J. D., & Kaye, B. (1984, November/December). Mentoring: A boon to career development. *Personnel, 61,* 20–24.

Feiman-Nemser, S. (2001, December). From preparation to practice: Designing a continuum to strengthen and sustain teaching. *Teachers College Record, 103,* 1013–1055.

Fideler, E. (2000, Winter). State-initiated induction programs: Supporting, assisting, training, assessing, and keeping teachers. *State Education Standard, 1* (1), 12–15.

Ganser, T. (1993). *How mentors describe and categorize their ideas about mentor roles, benefits of mentoring, and obstacles to mentoring.* Paper presented at the annual meeting of the Association of Teacher Educators, Los Angeles. (ERIC Document Reproduction Service No. ED 354237).

Hirsh, S. (1990, Fall). Designing induction programs with the beginning teacher in mind. *Journal of Staff Development, 11,* 24–26.

Huling-Austin, L. (1986, January/February). What can and cannot reasonably be expected from teacher induction programs. *Journal of Teacher Education, 37,* 2–5.

Huling-Austin, L. (1987). Teacher induction. In D. M. Brooks (Ed.), *Teacher induction: A new beginning* (pp. 3–23). Reston, VA: Association of Teacher Educators.

Hunt, D. W. (1968, October). Teacher induction: An opportunity and a responsibility. *NASSP Bulletin, 52,* 130–135.

Jantzen, J. M. (1981, March/April). Why college students choose to teach: A longitudinal study. *Journal of Teacher Education, 33,* 45–48.

Jentz, B. (1982). *Entry: The hiring, start-up, and supervision of administrators.* New York: McGraw-Hill.

Kester, R., & Marockie, M. (1987). Local induction programs. In D. M. Brooks (Ed.), *Teacher induction: A new beginning* (pp. 25–31). Reston, VA: Association of Teacher Educators.

Kurtz, W. H. (1983, January). How the principal can help beginning teachers. *NASSP Bulletin, 67,* 42–45.

Mager, G. (1992). The place of induction in becoming a teacher. In G. DeBolt (Ed.), *Teacher induction and mentoring: School-based collaborative programs* (pp. 3–33). Albany: State University of New York Press.

Murnane, R. (1996). Staffing the nation's schools with skilled teachers. In E. Hanushek & D. Jorgenson (Eds.), *Improving America's schools: The role of incentives* (pp. 241–258). Washington, DC. National Academy Press.

Odell, S. J., Loughlin, C. E., & Ferraro, D. P. (1986–87, Winter). Functional approach to identification of new teacher needs in an induction context. *Action in Teacher Education, 8,* 51–57.

Pataniczek, D., & Isaacson, N. S. (1981, May/June). The relationship of socialization and the concerns of beginning secondary teachers. *Journal of Teacher Education, 32,* 14–17.

Payne, D., & Wolfson, T. (2000, October). Teacher professional development—The principals' critical role. *NASSP Bulletin, 84,* 13–21.

Rowley, J. (1999, May). The good mentor. *Educational Leadership, 56,* 20–22.

Schempp, P., Sparkes, A., & Templin, T. (1999). Identity and induction: Establishing the self in the first years of teaching. In R. Lipka & T. Brinthaupt (Eds.), *The role of self in teacher development* (pp. 142–161). Albany: State University of New York Press.

Schlechty, P. C. (1985, January/February). A framework for evaluating induction into teaching. *Journal of Teacher Education, 36,* 37–41.

Smylie, M. (1995). Teacher learning in the workplace: Implications for school reform. In T. Guskey and M. Huberman (Eds.), *Professional development in education* (pp. 92–113). New York: Teachers College Press.

Stallings, J. A. (1984). Implications from the research on teaching for teacher preparation. In R. L. Egbert and M. M. Kluender (Eds.), *Using research to improve teacher education* (pp. 128–145). Washington, DC: ERIC Clearinghouse on Teacher Education.

Thies-Sprinthall, L. (1986, November/December) A collaborative approach for mentor training: A working model. *Journal of Teacher Education, 37,* 13–20.

Tickle, L. (1994). *The induction of new teachers.* London: Cassell.

Veenman, S. (1984). Perceived problems of beginning teachers. *Review of Educational Research, 54,* 143–178.

Wagner, L. A. (1985, November). Ambiguities and possibilities in California's mentor teacher program. *Educational Leadership, 43,* 23–29.

Weld, J. (1998, March). Attracting and retaining high-quality professionals in science education. *Phi Delta Kappan, 79,* 536–539.

Zahorik, J. A. (1987). Teachers' collegial interaction: An exploratory study. *Elementary School Journal, 87,* 385–396.

■ ■ ■ ■ ■

CHAPTER EIGHT

PROFESSIONAL DEVELOPMENT FOR EDUCATIONAL PERSONNEL

All personnel functions have a direct or an indirect impact on school effectiveness, but none has a greater potential effect than professional development and training. Professional development provides opportunities for teachers and other professional and support personnel to acquire new skills and attitudes that can lead to the changes in behavior that result in increased student achievement.

However, despite its promise, professional development often fails to achieve the results that planners hope for and expect. This chapter examines some of the reasons that professional development is less successful than it might be and reviews how these programs are changing in response to shifting expectations and the emergence of new organizational forms in schools.

PLAN OF THE CHAPTER

This chapter addresses these topics: (1) functions of professional development, (2) characteristics of effective professional development, (3) planning for professional development, and (4) professional development for administrators and support personnel.

FUNCTIONS OF PROFESSIONAL DEVELOPMENT

Professional development has been defined as any activity or process intended to improve skills, attitudes, understandings, or performance in present or future roles (Fullan, 1990). The definition emphasizes one aspect of professional development—to effect change—but ignores another purpose, which is to secure compliance with district policies and procedures (Evertson, 1986). Schlechty and Crowell (1983) called the latter the maintenance function of professional development. They explained that this function refers to activities intended to "keep things from getting worse" (p. 55) by reminding people "of what it is assumed they already knew but have forgotten" (p. 56).

Incorporating this idea into the preceding definition results in a more accurate description of professional development. In this book, *professional development* is defined as any activity or process intended to maintain or improve skills, attitudes, understandings, or performance of professional and support personnel in present or future roles. Professional development activities are intended to increase the capacity of the entire faculty of a school to strengthen student performance (Youngs & King, 2002). Thus, professional development is best viewed from a systemic perspective, taking into account the cumulative strengths and weaknesses of the total staff for the purpose of developing plans for improving the knowledge and skills of instructional staff members as a group.

Types of Change

Change may occur in more than one way. Change in the way work is performed is referred to as *technological change* (Schlechty & Crowell, 1983). Examples of technological change include revisions in the curriculum content and the introduction of new ways of delivering instruction, such as using television or computers. Changes in the design of programs as well as changes in the ways students are managed and motivated also fall under the rubric of technological change.

Changes in the way people relate to one another are referred to as *structural changes* (Schlechty & Crowell, 1983). Structural change may involve a reassignment of duties or a change in the way power and authority are allocated in schools. Addition of new positions, such as teacher aide, or changes in responsibilities and rewards, such as those that occur when a career ladder is introduced, are examples of structural changes (Schlechty & Crowell, 1983). Site-based management is another example of a structural change. Some structural changes are aimed at empowering teachers, but some authorities are skeptical of the value of these changes for improving student learning (Geisert, 1988).

Thus, professional development may be used to support technological or structural change or to serve a maintenance function. A change of one type may lead to change of the other kind. Introduction of certain technological changes in schools leads to alterations in power and authority relationships. When a school purchases computers for students' use, it is introducing a technological change, but the new technology may also trigger structural changes, as teachers begin to develop cooperative working arrangements in order to facilitate access to the machines.

Accommodating Teachers' Needs

People have different needs as they attempt to implement the two types of change, and it is necessary to design development programs that accommodate these needs. When they implement new teaching methods or content, teachers want specific and practical suggestions on how the new technology will work, to see demonstrations of it, and to be allowed to try it out in a threat-free environment and receive feedback. They prefer to adapt new techniques to their situations rather than implement them whole. Finally, teachers want to be convinced that the strategy they are being asked to adopt is superior to that they have been using.

In the case of structural change, employees need to have a clear conception of how the change will affect them. Changes that are perceived as altering relations among people have the potential to reduce security and are likely to be resisted unless teachers are convinced of the need for the change. The preferred presenter of a technological change is someone with expertise in the new technology, whereas the preferred presenter of structural change is someone who is trusted by those who will be affected. Expertise is less important in this case than a reputation for honesty and fairness. Thus, for a session involving structural change, a presenter might be an administrator in whom teachers have confidence and who can help allay feelings of threat aroused by the proposed alterations in roles, responsibilities, and relationships.

CHARACTERISTICS OF EFFECTIVE PROFESSIONAL DEVELOPMENT

Many of the professional development opportunities to which teachers have access do not incorporate the latest findings about what makes such programs effective. According to a recent study of professional development programs, the majority of teachers who participated were involved in traditional types of activities. The median number of hours spent on a single activity was 15, and most teachers (64 percent) were involved in activities that lasted one week or less. Only about 20 percent of those surveyed took part in activities that included collective participation (Birman, Desimone, Porter, & Garet, 2000).

Recent research has shown that programs that involve teachers in collaborative activities and in which all teachers in a school, department, or grade level are involved, are more likely to produce observable changes in instruction than programs that involve only a few members. This seems to be especially true when teachers are learning about new technology (Desimone, Porter, Garet, Yoon, & Birman, 2002). However, some researchers have found that technical skills are best learned, not as distinct topics of study, but with consideration given simultaneously to teachers' knowledge, experience, and beliefs (Lieberman, 1999).

Activities that emulate what takes place in classrooms are the surest way to have an impact on teaching practice. In these activities teachers take on the role of learner and experience how an explanation or demonstration by a skilled facilitator enhances their understanding of new material. Facilitators model for teachers the techniques that research and experience have shown to be effective. They pose open-ended questions about content and provide opportunities for teachers to work on activities that allow them to think as a scientist, mathematician, historian, or author (Cutler & Ruopp, 1999).

Teachers acquire knowledge about teaching from a variety of sources, of which professional development is only one. Reading, coursework, conversations with colleagues, and work with students are other sources from which teachers gain new insights, expand their knowledge, and add to their repertoire of skills. One writer distinguishes "inside" and "outside" knowledge. *Outside knowledge* comes from consultants, conferences, and books, whereas *inside knowledge* is learning that is gained from conversations with and observations of colleagues and from one's own experience in the classroom. Teachers tend to view outside knowledge as abstract and theoretical. It is advisable for planners to maintain a balance between the amount of inside and outside knowledge presented and to seek to blend information from these sources into a meaningful configuration to increase teacher interest and comprehension (Lieberman, 1999).

Feedback and Support

Research is clear on the need for feedback and support for teachers who are implementing new classroom practices. The principal is an important source of this support. Both teacher learning and behavior changes are more likely to occur when the principal is supportive of the change (Sparks, 1983).

Support from other teachers is also important. Peer coaching is a technique designed to be used by teachers and administrators to help other teachers learn new teaching behaviors. Teachers receive training in a new technique, including information about the skills and strategies and the rationale for their use. They practice the new technique in their classrooms while a coach observes. Afterwards, the observer-coach critiques the teacher's performance, demonstrates the technique, and makes suggestions for improvement. The teacher and coach then discuss appropriate ways to use the new strategy. Using coaching triads rather than pairs increases the amount of feedback each participant receives and reduces the "mutual admiration society" aspect that sometimes occurs when two teachers coach one another (Duttweiler, 1989).

Coaching offers several advantages that are not found in more traditional professional development arrangements. Because teachers who are coached are likely to spend more time practicing new strategies and are more likely to receive immediate feedback on their performance, behavioral change can be expected to occur. Joyce and Showers (1988) claimed that coached teachers use newly learned techniques more appropriately than teachers who do not have the benefit of coaching. They also suggested that coached teachers retain their knowledge of new techniques longer and have a clearer understanding of the purpose and uses of the strategies.

Showers (1985) reported that coached teachers show much higher levels of behavior change than teachers who receive the same training without coaching, but other researchers have not found the same results (Sparks, 1983). The effectiveness of coaching probably depends on the coach's skill, the complexity of the behavior being learned, and the teacher's receptiveness to change.

Peer observation alone appears to be about as effective as peer coaching in producing behavior change among teachers when it is carried out in an atmosphere of trust. There are several reasons for this. Peer observers pick up ideas that they use in their own teaching, and they often become more aware of their own teaching behavior as a result of watching others teach. Observing also helps to free teachers from the psychological isolation that pervades many schools (Sparks, 1983).

Congruence and Ease of Adoption

Teachers are more likely to adopt strategies for use in their classrooms when they fully understand them and when the strategies are congruent with their teaching philosophies. Difficulty of implementing new techniques is another consideration that influences teachers' decisions. If the time and effort required to learn or use them are excessive, teachers are unlikely to adopt them (Doyle & Ponder, 1977).

Some of the most effective programs are those in which a school district and a university reach an agreement under which the university offers coursework tailored to meet an identified need of teachers in the district. One example was the Houston Teaching Academy, which offered a program to prepare teachers to work in inner-city schools (Arends, 1990).

In Maryland, the University of Maryland and Montgomery County Schools cooperated to form the Minority Teacher Education Project. The district hired minority individuals with bachelor's degrees as teacher aides and gave them released time to participate in a two-year program at the university that led to their receiving a teaching credential (Arends, 1990).

College work is especially valuable for teachers who are assigned to teach out of their field or who entered teaching through an alternative certification route. In 1991, 39 states provided for alternative certification of teachers in at least some specialty areas. As a rule, teachers with alternative certification have a strong background in a content area but are not as well grounded in pedagogy. Many of them need coursework in instructional methodology and human learning. Teachers who came through a traditional teacher preparation program some years ago or who have been reassigned to a new teaching field often need additional training in a content area (National Center for Education Statistics, 1993).

The numbers of individuals who are teaching out of their field are not large. Even in special education, a field of chronic shortages, the majority of teachers are fully certified. Nevertheless, the lack of expertise among these teachers can be a significant area of need to be addressed by professional development.

Other resources available to developers are state departments of education, which usually have on their staffs specialists in the major subject fields who can be called on for information about instructional materials and in-service ideas. In some localities, curriculum centers are also available to help schools meet developmental needs of teachers. In whatever form professional development is offered, planners need to offer instruction in both content and process (Mell & Mell, 1990).

Most teachers would like to find methods and materials that produce better results than those they are using, and they are inclined to try innovations that promise to do that (Guskey, 1986). For staff developers, the implications of those facts are clear. They should select strategies that have been shown to be effective in increasing student learning and should plan workshops to include clear explanations and demonstrations showing how the techniques work.

The research reviewed in this section provides direction for administrators who are responsible for planning and coordinating professional development programs. The characteristics associated with more effective programs are those that should be incorporated into development programs for teachers.

PLANNING FOR PROFESSIONAL DEVELOPMENT

No Child Left Behind legislation requires all states to develop a plan for ensuring that teachers of core academic subjects will be "highly qualified" by the end of the 2005–2006 school year. School districts will be expected to offer professional development activities for teachers who do not currently meet the "highly qualified" standard, and many districts will view the mandate as an opportunity to upgrade the credentials of teachers who meet the legal requirement but who would benefit from additional growth.

Although the legislation does not specifically identify teachers of special education as being included in the category of "core" teachers, the Council on Exceptional Children has taken the position that these teachers should be required to meet that standard. If that interpretation of the legislation holds, many school districts may be required to undertake extensive efforts in order to bring underqualified special education teachers to the requisite level of preparation (Egnor, 2003).

In addition to requiring states to ensure that all teachers are "highly qualified," NCLB requires continual progress in student achievement toward the goal of 100 percent mastery. Under the law, increasingly far-reaching corrective actions are called for when students in a district fail to show adequate yearly progress (AYP) toward mastery of content in mathematics, reading, and science. In planning for professional development programs, principals and professional development personnel need to be well-informed about student achievement and should know in which content areas students are progressing satisfactorily toward mastery and in which areas progress is lagging. The planning process should allow for directing resources toward the instructional areas in which weakness is most evident.

If the students in a district fail to make adequate yearly progress in a subject for three or more years, the district may be required under NCLB to provide individual tutoring for the weaker students. High-quality professional development helps teachers to raise the achievement level of the large majority of students and limits the need for tutoring services.

Data from student assessments is now being used in many districts to guide planning for professional development activities for teachers. By using the data to identify areas in which students are underperforming and planning corrective actions that teachers can apply, planners are able to focus their limited resources on actions that will have the greatest impact on school and district performance. Teachers value such programs because they offer practical suggestions for improving low student achievement (Holloway, 2003).

Responsibility

Lawyers and doctors have a commitment to renew their knowledge of new developments in their fields. But it has been the practice in education that district administrators assume most of the responsibility for determining what kinds of professional development activities teachers need. Teachers participate in planning and may present materials to their colleagues, but as a rule they are not expected to assume responsibility for their own growth (Tucker & Codding, 1998).

Results-oriented professional development is keyed to the school's mission and goals and involves teachers and principals interacting to determine what knowledge, skills, and information they need to help students reach performance standards. This approach requires teachers to search for practices that have been shown to be effective in other settings and to adapt them to their own schools (Tucker & Codding, 1998).

A decision that must be made is whether to operate professional development as a centralized or decentralized activity. Some districts offer a unified program for all teachers, whereas others leave decisions on the content, format, and timing of developmental activities to the staff of each school.

School-Based Programs.   In districts with site-based management, much of the responsibility for staff development programs is delegated to the school; mandatory districtwide in-service programs cease to exist. The primary function of district staff members shifts from initiation and organization of training sessions to facilitation and support of activities initiated at the school level (Duttweiler, 1989; Smylie & Conyers, 1991). This change is accompanied by a shift in resources, with schools assuming responsibility for administering professional development budgets (Shanker, 1990).

The idea of assigning responsibility for development to faculty members in each school is based on the belief that "the individual school is the most viable unit for effecting educational improvement" (Goodlad, 1983, p. 36). Goodlad admits that this position cannot be defended on the basis of research or common practice but calls it "a reasonable working hypothesis" (p. 39).

Several claims for the superiority of decentralized programs are made by proponents. One is that school-based programs, by directly involving teachers in decisions about program content and format, lead to higher levels of interest and commitment. Advocates also claim that site-based programs increase collaboration among and between teachers and principals (Howey & Vaughn, 1983), that site-based programs are more flexible, and that program offerings are more relevant and practical than offerings in programs that are centrally directed.

Decentralized programs also have potential disadvantages. One of the main drawbacks is the heavy demand they make on the time of the principal and teachers who are involved in planning and presenting training workshops. Most principals feel they already have too little time for instructional leadership responsibilities, and adding more duties further complicates that problem. School-based programs are also somewhat less efficient than centralized operations since some duplication is unavoidable.

Professional developer is a new role for most teachers, and although most who attempt it are successful, problems are occasionally encountered. Moving from teacher to development leader in the same school can be difficult, and some teachers prefer not to attempt it. Further, in schools with strong individualistic cultures, the lack of cohesiveness can threaten the success of school-based development programs (Joyce, 1990).

The arrangement recommended in this book is to encourage school faculties to plan their own development activities when they have identified specific objectives that apply to the school and that are most appropriately addressed at the school level. A centralized option should also be available for schools that are not prepared to undertake their own effort.

Time for Professional Development.   Teacher time for development falls into four categories (Moore & Hyde, 1981). *Salaried work time* includes all hours during which teachers are on duty. *Released time* includes periods during which substitutes are hired to release teachers from teaching duties. *Stipend time* is time outside of regular work hours during which teachers participate in professional development and are paid a salary supplement. *Personal time* is time that is teachers' own. Negotiated contracts often limit the use of teachers' personal and stipend time for professional development. It is important to check the contract before scheduling activities during those times.

Use of teachers' personal time for developmental purposes is the least costly option for the district, but it is also the least feasible. Some teachers are willing to use their own time to work toward a master's degree, but few willingly participate in professional development activities on their own time. A better approach is to schedule occasional activities during work time before and after school, keeping in mind that teachers prefer to reserve this time for planning, conferring with parents, personal errands, and housekeeping. The other two options (stipend time and released time) are feasible options and are about equally costly.

Design of the Program

In designing in-service activities for teachers, planners must take into account three factors: form, duration, and participation.

Form.   *Form* refers to structure and content. Professional development may involve groups—as in traditional workshops, teacher networks, and task forces—or it may feature individual activities, such as mentoring, individual research projects, and internships. The size of training group appears to have little effect on the outcomes of training, but the composition of the group does seem to make a difference. More learning occurs when elementary and secondary teachers receive training together than when they are separated (Wade, 1984/1985).

Objectives of Professional Development.   The outcomes of professional development for teachers can be changes in knowledge, behavior, or attitudes for individuals or groups. A single activity may have objectives of several types, but the more different outcomes the planners envision, the more complex the venture becomes and the harder it is to ensure that the desired results will be obtained. Exhibit 8.1 summarizes examples of objectives of the three types for both individuals and groups.

■ ■ ■ ■ ■ ▬▬▬▬▬▬▬▬▬▬▬▬▬▬▬▬▬▬▬▬▬▬▬▬▬▬▬▬▬▬▬▬▬▬

EXHIBIT 8.1

**INDIVIDUAL AND GROUP OBJECTIVES
OF PROFESSIONAL DEVELOPMENT**

INDIVIDUAL OBJECTIVES

Behavior	Improved skill in assessing students' needs
	Improved ability to present instruction
Attitude	Increased confidence as a teacher
	Increased satisfaction in teaching
	Stronger commitment to teaching
Cognition	Increased knowledge of subject
	Changed beliefs about teaching
	Increased knowledge of educational trends
	Better understanding of school values and mission

GROUP OBJECTIVES

Behavior	Increased willingness to share and participate
	Greater interest in collaborating with other teachers to develop curriculum and teaching strategies
Attitude	Increased mutual trust
	Growth of team spirit
	Feeling of belonging
Cognition	Able to evaluate the effectiveness of group work
	Increased skill in analyzing group functioning
	Growing consensus on educational values

Source: School Effectiveness and School-Based Management: A Mechanism for Development by Y. Cheng, 1996, London: Falmer. Reprinted by permission.

Objectives may be stated either as individual or group outcomes. An example of an individual objective is: "All participants will demonstrate familiarity with five techniques for teaching thinking skills to students in the grade level or subject they teach and will commit themselves to try all five techniques in their classes within one month." A group objective could be stated in the following way: "Participants will collectively identify methods of increasing time on task that have worked in their own classes and will agree to try at least two new methods in their classes and discuss the results with colleagues within one month."

Plan Content.   Once the objectives of the program are selected, the decision about content is simplified. Both objectives and content should take into account the realities of the school as an organization and a social system and should recognize the teacher as a person and professional. Professional development programs are often presented with little or no thought given to school norms and teacher role relationships that affect the implementation of new technologies (North Dakota State Department of Public Instruction, 1986).

Some examples of topics related to improving instruction are the social climate of the school, revision of particular curriculum areas, teaching strategies, use of technology, student learning styles, and teaching students with special needs (Joyce & Showers, 1988). The research on effective schools suggests other possible topics, including time on task, behavior management, organization and grouping, lesson design, instructional sequencing, and teacher expectations (Mohlman, Kierstad, & Gundlach, 1982). Brookover and associates (1982) described 11 professional development modules on a variety of topics, including effective learning climate, grouping, classroom management, cooperative learning, and use of assessment data. In recent years many school districts in states with mandated curriculum standards have devoted most of their professional development resources to presenting workshops on how teachers can help students to meet those standards.

The adoption of mandated curriculum standards has created a need to better prepare teachers to plan instruction covering the content on required achievement tests. Well-planned professional development activities can help teachers to teach mandated content without unduly narrowing the curriculum. Professional publications contain many articles on this topic. Among the ideas covered in these articles are suggestions on integrating content from different fields, such as social studies and science (Drake, 2001), how to cover the standards without sacrificing creativity (Scherer, 2001), and deciding what knowledge is most worthwhile for students to learn (Raywid, 2002).

When planning professional development programs that involve technological change, it is important to bear in mind that teachers are not likely to be persuaded about the value of a new technique until they have seen for themselves that it works. If a technique works without being unduly costly of teachers' time and effort, they will be more likely to embrace it than if it is unproven. Staff developers should therefore concentrate on selecting strategies that have been shown to work and should offer assistance and support for teachers who are trying the new procedures.

Teachers are more likely to try new ideas when the presentation focuses on concrete practices rather than theoretical issues. Attention to specific rather than global teaching skills is also helpful. Presenters who have credibility with teachers and those who address teachers' personal concerns related to adopting the change are more likely to be successful in achieving teacher support for change (Guskey, 1986).

Planners should take maximum advantage of the resources available to them. An important source of assistance for professional development is local colleges and universities. At one time colleges and universities were the primary providers of professional development for school personnel, but today, with most school districts having developed their own programs, few teachers rely exclusively on colleges and universities for developmental opportunities (Little, 1990). Nevertheless, coursework should not be overlooked as one component of an effective professional development program.

To assess individual priorities, employees may be asked to identify their own growth needs, or supervisors, principals, and department heads list areas in which teachers ask for assistance. Exhibit 8.2 shows a survey instrument for collecting information from teachers to supplement data from other sources, including test results, evaluation reports, audits, and accreditation studies (Kramer & Betz, 1987).

The content of in-service programs usually consists of subject matter knowledge, the processes by which children learn, or generic teaching techniques. A key to raising student achievement is ensuring that teachers have a sophisticated understanding of the subject they teach and are well informed about the processes by which students learn the subject (Birman et al., 2000).

Teachers who have a thorough understanding of their subject are able to answer crucial questions that enable them to diagnose students' comprehension and plan instruction accordingly. Some of the questions teachers need to be prepared to answer are: Which concepts are most important for students to understand? What beliefs, conceptions, or misconceptions do students hold about the subject? and What instructional activities or techniques will increase children's curiosity about the subject matter (Solomon & Morocco, 1999)?

The National Board for Professional Teaching Standards has identified the knowledge, skills, and dispositions needed by teachers and has asked teachers to demonstrate that they meet those standards. National Board Certification is voluntary for teachers who wish to establish credible professional credentials. Teachers must prepare a portfolio and participate in assessment activities in order to achieve board certification (Jenkins, 2000).

Methods of Presentation.   Development workshops are likely to be most successful when they incorporate four components: (1) presentation of theory, (2) demonstration of a teaching strategy, (3) initial practice, and (4) prompt feedback (Showers et al., 1987). The more complex the behavior being taught, the greater is the need for a training design that incorporates all four elements. The addition to the first two

■ ■ ■ ■ ■

EXHIBIT 8.2

ASSESSMENT OF DEVELOPMENTAL NEEDS OF TEACHERS

Directions: The information you provide will be used in planning for staff development activities in the district. Please answer all questions thoughtfully and truthfully.

1. How many years (total) teaching experience do you have?
2. What grade level(s) do you teach?
3. What subject(s) do you teach?
4. What is the highest degree that you hold?
5. When did you last take a college course in your subject specialty?
6. With which of the following groups would you prefer to attend a staff development workshop?
   ❑ Teachers from your own school
   ❑ Teachers from other schools in this district
   ❑ Teachers from other districts
   ❑ Mixed groups, including teachers and administrators from this district
   ❑ Mixed groups, including teachers and administrators from other districts
7. What is your preference of day and time for professional development sessions?
8. From the following list, select the three workshops you would be most interested in attending.
   ❑ Time on task
   ❑ Classroom organization and management
   ❑ Classroom climate
   ❑ Learning styles
   ❑ Teacher-made tests
   ❑ Higher-order thinking
   ❑ Using technology in the classroom
   ❑ Effects of teacher expectations on student achievement
   ❑ Using student achievement data for instructional decisions
   ❑ Curriculum revision
   ❑ Lesson design
   ❑ Teaching students with special needs
   ❑ Preparing an individualized educational plan
   ❑ Teaching gifted children
   ❑ Site-based management
   ❑ Assessing student performance
   ❑ Working with parents and the community
9. Can you suggest presenters for any of the topics on the list? (If so, list the name of the topic and the presenter.)
10. Would you be willing to serve as a workshop leader presenting a topic in which you have received previous training? (If yes, give your name and school and the topic you can present.)

elements of the opportunity to practice and receive performance feedback dramatically increases the likelihood that teachers will retain and use what they learn (Showers et al., 1987). Practice and feedback appear to be especially important when the behavior being learned is unfamiliar to the learner (Sparks, 1983).

Sessions that are planned for beginning teachers should use a structured, directive approach. Teachers with more experience prefer to learn ways to add variety to their teaching and favor a collaborative approach (Burden & Wallace, 1983).

To prepare teachers to use specific instructional techniques, the following format is recommended (Stallings, 1985):

1. *Baseline/pretest:* Teachers are observed for target teaching behaviors. Profiles are prepared showing how frequently each behavior is used. From the profiles, teachers consult with supervisors and set goals.

2. *Information:* Information is provided to participating teachers linking research and practice. Teachers are checked for understanding.

3. *Guided practice:* Teachers adapt the new techniques one at a time to their own context and style. After trying the new methods, they assess them and are provided feedback from peer observers. Leaders obtain a commitment from participants to try the new method in their own classes and provide support and encouragement for the change.

4. *Posttest:* Teachers are observed again and a new profile is prepared. Teachers set new goals and assess the training program for effectiveness.

Duration.   Although some studies have reported that the length of training sessions has no statistically significant relationship to the effectiveness of professional development, it is reasonable to believe that more time is needed to learn material that is high in complexity as compared to simpler material (Sparks, 1983). A scheduling plan that has been shown to produce good results is a series of brief (three-hour) workshops spaced at intervals of two or three weeks over a period of several months (Mohlman, Kierstad, & Gundlach, 1982). Presenting small amounts of new material at each of several sessions rather than crowding all of it into one or two meetings helps teachers gradually integrate the new practices into their existing routines. Teachers also find it easier to cope with concerns aroused by change when the innovations are presented at a more leisurely pace (Sparks, 1983).

Participation.   The context in which development activities take place has an important bearing on the extent to which teachers are likely to see new methods and materials as relevant to their situation and make the decision to try them out. Among other things, context covers the location of training sessions, the quality and comfort of the physical facilities, and the availability of appropriate learning aids. Another important aspect of context is the participants themselves. A session in which a single representative from each school takes part is a very different experience from one in which all the teachers from a school are simultaneously involved.

A session in which all participants are beginning teachers is very different from one in which teachers from all levels of experience are on hand (Birman et al., 2000).

School districts with limited financial resources to devote to professional development programs must choose between in-depth programs for a few staff members and less intensive activities for a greater number. Most districts choose the second option, even though research shows that more intensive programs have greater impact on teachers' instructional practices (Desimone, et al., 2002). Collective participation (that is, all or most of the teachers from a single school participate in the same activity) enables teachers to discuss problems that arise in implementing new strategies and allows them to share workable adaptations with one another (Birman, et al., 2000).

It has been common practice in many districts to invite teachers to choose an in-service activity from a list of offerings, with the result that the sessions in which teachers from a school participate have no relationship to one another, thus greatly reducing the possibility of shared insights among teachers (Desimone, et al., 2002).

Evaluation and Follow-Up

When a group of teachers participates in a professional development workshop, they often feel enthusiastic about the ideas they have heard, and their comments on the end-of-workshop evaluations reflect their desire to try out these ideas in their own classrooms. However, few teachers who participate in such training adopt and continue to use the ideas they have learned about unless they receive support and encouragement to do so. The reason for this loss of momentum is not lack of interest on the teachers' part, but rather their lack of time and unfamiliarity with the new strategies. End-of-session evaluation forms are a necessary but not sufficient tool for evaluating the impact of professional development activities on teaching practice. The true effects of professional development are to be found in classrooms months after the workshop has ended. If teachers who received training are not using the techniques they learned earlier, then the resources and time that went into offering the professional development activity were wasted.

An effective method of evaluating professional development ideally should consist of four phases, as shown in Exhibit 8.3. The most widely used evaluation technique is to ask for teachers' reactions to the workshop itself, using a survey instrument to register their satisfaction with the presenters and the content. The evaluation items may be closed or open-ended. An example of an open-ended form appears in Guskey (2000). In that example, workshop participants are asked to complete five sentence stems ("I learned . . . ," "Most helpful . . . ," "Least helpful . . . ," "I would like to learn . . . ," and "Appreciations, Concerns, Suggestions"). The next phase in the evaluation of professional development activities is to determine how much teachers actually learned about the material presented during the workshop. This effort may take place at the end of the workshop or at a later date, or both. Teachers will not be able to implement material they have not learned. The third stage in the evaluation process is to determine to what extent teachers are using the strategies they studied. This information is best collected from classroom observations. The final and most difficult stage of evaluation is measuring the effect of the new practices on student learning. The only way to accurately measure this effect is by means of an experimental research design.

Evaluation of professional development programs is often carried out as an afterthought with little or no advance planning. Time spent in planning the evaluation will yield increased confidence in the findings. A comprehensive evaluation plan involves assessing four outcomes of professional development (Wade, 1984/1985). Exhibit 8.3 shows sources of data for a comprehensive evaluation of a professional development program.

■ ■ ■ ■ ■ ▬▬▬▬▬▬▬▬▬▬▬▬▬▬▬▬▬▬▬▬▬▬▬▬

EXHIBIT 8.3

INFORMATION TO BE COLLECTED IN A COMPREHENSIVE EVALUATION OF PROFESSIONAL DEVELOPMENT PROGRAMS

OUTCOME	ITEMS
Teacher Reactions	Convenience of time and day of session
	Convenience of the location
	Comfort of the room
	Ability of presenters to make concepts clear and to maintain interest
	Presenters' knowledge of subject
	Appropriateness of the content for teachers' own schools or classrooms
	Probability of using strategies presented in the workshop
	Estimated need for feedback and follow-up
Teacher Knowledge	Teachers' estimates of their knowledge of subject before and after attending session
	Pre- and posttest to measure knowledge gain
	Desire to learn more about the subject
Behavior Change	Teachers' estimate of frequency of use of new strategy one month after attending session
	Data from classroom observers showing frequency of use
	Teachers' estimates of difficulty of use (time involved, student understanding and receptivity)
	Teachers' estimates of likelihood they will continue to use strategy
Student Learning	Results of experimental research on student gains in classes with teachers using new techniques, compared to students in classes with teachers using old techniques
	Students' estimates of amount they learn when teachers use new versus old techniques
	Data from classroom observers on student interest and participation in classes using new versus old techniques

The initial presentation of a new program or technique is only the first step in implementing change. Providing regular feedback to teachers who are charged with implementing the model and providing sustained support and follow-up after the initial training are critical elements of an effective professional development program (Guskey, 1986). Feedback can be provided by other teachers who have had sufficient training in the technique to be able to guide their peers in its use.

PROFESSIONAL DEVELOPMENT FOR ADMINISTRATORS AND SUPPORT PERSONNEL

Professional development for administrators does not receive much attention in most school districts. Principals who wish to grow professionally can usually find the necessary financial support, and their schedules are flexible enough to permit them to be away from their buildings for training purposes. However, many districts do not require or even encourage principals to engage in professional development activities (Hallinger & Greenblatt, 1989).

The principal's job is a demanding one; in most schools, principals have very little time that is not already committed. Moreover, most principals feel a sense of responsibility to be available in case a problem should arise in their schools. Some principals feel that taking time for their own growth and development is selfish and deprives children and teachers of their attention.

Principals who take advantage of professional development opportunities for themselves report that they do so because it helps them to grow and learn or helps them avoid burnout. One principal commented, "It's very important to me to continue to learn. It's self-satisfying, it makes me feel good about myself." Another stated, "[I] need energy from outside, otherwise I'd be burned out or bored out" (Hallinger & Greenblatt, 1989, p. 71).

The School Leadership Program, authorized by No Child Left Behind, provides support to assist high-need school districts in recruiting and retaining principals and assistant principals. This program also is intended to help provide professional development for building administrators (*K–12 principals guide . . .*, 2003). The creation of the School Leadership Program is evidence of a growing awareness of the importance of providing high-quality professional development opportunities for school administrators and an acknowledgment of the fact that few such programs are currently available.

The National Staff Development Council (NSDC) recently identified desirable features of professional development activities for school leaders, and not surprisingly the characteristics identified by the Council are similar to those recommended for professional development programs for teachers. They include ample time (longer rather than shorter), embedding (direct tie-ins to the jobs practitioners perform), planned activities (well-thought-out rather than hastily assembled), and instructionally oriented content (focusing on ways by which by which practitioners can help improve student achievement) (Peterson, 2002).

Twenty-five states and some cities have leadership academies for principals and superintendents that incorporate some or all of the desirable features identified by NSDC. The Gheens Academy in Louisville, Mayerson Academy in Cincinnati, Ohio Principal Leadership Academy, and California School Leadership Academy are examples of well-known programs that offer workshops, mentoring, and/or individual assistance for aspiring or experienced principals or both (Peterson, 2002).

The Ohio Academy offers a two-year program based on the standards for administrator performance developed by the Interstate Leadership Licensure Consortium. The program for experienced principals consists of 28 days of training over a two-year period (Peterson, 2002).

Conferences and workshops sponsored by professional groups, such as the National Association of Elementary School Principals (NAESP) and the National Association of Secondary School Principals (NASSP), offer rich opportunities for professional growth for principals. A recent summer academy sponsored by NAESP focused on standards for leaders of learning communities, including setting high expectations, developing content and instruction that ensure student achievement, using multiple sources of data as diagnostic tools, and actively engaging the community (www.naesp.org.npa.summer2003.htm).

Periodic surveys of principals' and supervisors' needs can help those responsible for professional development to provide sessions that will help principals and supervisors to feel better prepared to deal with the dual responsibilities of school management and instructional leadership. Perennial issues of concern to both groups include evaluation of teaching performance, supervision of teachers, and conducting postobservation conferences. Other topics appear periodically as issues of interest. In one survey of principals, the following topics received frequent mention (Olivero, 1982):

1. *School climate:* Principals were interested in learning how to analyze school morale and in being able to understand the relationship between climate and school policies. Principals expressed a need to be able to take action to develop more positive climates in their schools.

2. *Team building:* Principals asked to learn more about use of interpersonal skills to achieve improved collegial relations among teachers in their schools.

3. *Internal communications:* Principals hoped to improve two-way communication among staff members and with students, community members, and other district personnel.

A newly emerging form of professional development for principals involves peer conversations aimed at helping principals to perform more effectively in their leadership roles. Small groups of administrators use structured protocols to look at their work and that of their students. A moderator convenes the group, explains the rules, and helps keep the conversation on the topic. The rules help prevent one or two participants from monopolizing the conversation by requiring that speakers take turns and listen attentively when others are speaking. Time is allowed for presenting work, listening without commenting, and giving and receiving feedback (Mohr, 1998).

The results of administrators' performance in assessment centers can also be used as a source of data on professional development needs of this group. A study of assessment center results for 94 practicing and aspiring principals found that the administrators were rated highest in group leadership and oral communication and lowest in problem analysis and creativity. The results indicated that improvement was needed in instructional leadership skills for practicing principals and in organizational ability for aspiring principals. Professional development opportunities in instructional leadership, group leadership, and organizational ability were readily available to the aspiring and practicing principals who participated in that study, but training opportunities in resourcefulness, decisiveness, creativity, and judgment were limited (Elsaesser, 1990).

Individualized Development Plans

Because individual needs and interests vary, the ideal approach to professional development is to allow each individual to design a program uniquely suited to his or her needs and interests. The Nebraska Council of School Administrators has developed such a plan, called the Nebraska Professional Proficiency Plan (Joekel, 1994), which permits administrators to plan their own professional development agenda.

Under the plan, an administrator works with a mentor to develop an individualized plan that includes, among other things, a list of career goals, descriptions of personal strengths and areas of needed improvement, and identification of one immediate goal. With the assistance of the mentor, the administrator brainstorms and lists activities that will help him or her to achieve the immediate goal and develops a means to monitor accomplishment of tasks leading to the goal (Joekel, 1994).

The administrator compiles a performance portfolio to document his or her progress toward attainment of the goal. After reviewing the portfolio, the mentor approves or recommends refinements or additional evidence. Upon completion of the individual development plan, the administrator and mentor submit a report to the state Council of School Administrators, which, after approving the report, issues a certificate of accomplishment (Joekel, 1994).

Career Counseling for Administrators

Most businesses provide extensive in-service training for their managers because they believe that it is a good investment for the individual as well as for the firm, but education lags in this regard (Daresh, 1987). Many corporations provide career counseling services to managers, but few school districts do so. The decision to leave the classroom in order to take an administrative position is a major change in career direction. Most people who consider such a career change would like to have the opportunity to discuss the decision with a sympathetic listener. Career counseling could help individuals consider all aspects of a decision more carefully and result in better quality decisions.

Some districts now arrange for prospective administrators to take part-time administrative assignments as a way of assessing their administrative potential. For the individual, such an arrangement is a growth experience; through it he or she learns what the job is like and acquires experience that can be used at a later time. The district receives the individual's services and acquires information about his or her performance.

Some new ideas are being tried in administrator in-service. One of these is a program that focuses on analyzing real-life problems. Participating administrators write short reports that describe an actual administrative problem and tell how the problem was handled. These reports become the focus of discussions that permit other administrators to relate how they have handled similar situations in the past and to suggest alternatives that might be tried. State departments of education have recognized the need for improvements in administrative development, and some now sponsor administrative academies that offer training for superintendents and other administrators (Daresh, 1987).

Some districts now recognize that many growth experiences are available to administrators other than those represented by traditional staff development. An example of one such approach is provided by Elam, Cramer, and Brodinsky (1986). It is a growth chart on which an administrator makes a record over the course of a year of a variety of activities in which he or she has participated that have led to professional growth. Some of the categories include reading, writing, research, conventions, conferences, meetings, speeches, association or community activities, travel, college courses, visits to other schools or businesses, and participation in cultural activities.

Suggestions for improving in-service training for administrators are similar to those for teachers. Planners are advised to personalize staff development activities by focusing program content on areas of identified need and providing opportunities for participants to build on their experiences as administrators. Demonstration, modeling of new skills, and providing opportunities for practice both in the training session and on the job are other recommendations. Performance feedback is important while a new skill is being learned. Administrative training should provide for both personal and professional growth and should be related to identified district instructional goals. Training should be cumulative, with sessions designed to build on previous offerings (Pitner, 1987).

Training for Staff Support Personnel

Some school districts operate comprehensive training programs that provide in-service opportunities and college courses for clerical and paraprofessional personnel. Such a program is offered to personnel in Los Angeles schools, where teachers' aides are able to participate in a program leading to an associate or baccalaureate degree from a local college. Employees who complete a bachelor's degree in an approved teacher preparation program are hired by the district as teachers. The Los Angeles school district also offers in-service training for clerical and crafts employees. These classes focus on skills development, including clerical skills, student discipline for bus drivers, computer operation, and food service operation (DeVries & Colbert, 1990).

SUMMARY

Professional development refers to any activity or process intended to maintain or improve skills, attitudes, understandings, or performance of professional and support personnel in present or future roles. It has a significant potential for influencing instructional effectiveness. Research on effectiveness of professional development programs has yielded findings related to length and scheduling of training sessions, and size and composition of the group. In districts with school-based management, responsibility for professional development is being delegated to schools. Planning for a professional development program in a school begins with creation of a planning committee and the completion of a needs assessment. A comprehensive program should include developmental opportunities for administrators and training for support staff.

SUGGESTED ACTIVITIES

1. Interview the training director of a company or agency other than a school. Some examples of agencies you might contact are a health department, social service agency, bank, electric or gas utility, or hospital. Find out who is served by the training program, the type and frequency of offerings, and the background and qualifications of the training staff. Compare the program in the agency you study to the professional development operation in a school district.

2. Visit the classrooms of two teachers of different subjects and observe each teacher's style. Note the kinds of questions each teacher asks, how much time is allowed for the student to respond, whether the teacher accepts divergent responses or expects convergent answers, and the teachers' response when a student answers a question (follow-up question, feedback, praise, additional explanation, etc.). Compare the teachers' styles. Which style seemed more effective? Why? Finally, develop a plan for a professional development session illustrating the teaching styles you observed.

3. Plan a three-hour in-service session for principals on a topic of your choice. Prepare an outline of the activities to be included and the handouts, tapes, films, or transparencies that will be used.

ONLINE RESOURCES

Education Alliance at Brown University (www.alliance.brown.edu/areas/td.shtml)

> The Alliance considers "the policies, interventions, and procedures needed to support teacher opportunities for continuous improvement."

Education Commission of the States (www.ecs.org/clearinghouse/26/93/2693.htm)

> This site lists leadership academies in 25 states with a brief description of the focus of each academy and the types of programs offered.

National Association of Elementary School Principals (www.naesp.org)
National Association of Secondary School Principals (www.nassp.org)

> These sites contain information about national developments of interest to school principals.

National Staff Development Council (www.nsdc.org/educatorindex.htm)

> Information about the Council and the text of selected articles from the *Journal of Staff Development* are available at this site.

New Teacher Center (www.newteachercenter.org/NTC.html)

> The Center advertises itself as "a national resource dedicated to teacher development and the support of programs and practices that promote excellence and diversity in America's teaching force."

Professional Development and Dissemination Network (www.jointventure.org/initiatives/21st/pddn.html)

> The Network seeks to promote "the exploration, implementation and dissemination of best practices in teacher professional development."

REFERENCES

Arends, R. (1990). Connecting the university to the school. In B. Joyce (Ed.), *Changing school culture through staff development* (pp. 117–143). Alexandria, VA: Association for Supervision and Curriculum Development.

Birman, B., Desimone, L., Porter, A., & Garet, M. (2000, May). Designing professional development that works. *Educational Leadership, 57,* 28–32.

Brandt, R. (1996, March). On a new direction for teacher evaluation: A conversation with Tom McGreal. *Educational Leadership, 53,* 30–33.

Brookover, W., Beamer, L., Efthim, H., Hathaway, D., Lezotte, L., Miller, S., Passalcqua, J., & Tornatzky, L. (1982). *Creating effective schools: An in-service program for enhancing school learning climate and achievement.* Holmes Beach, FL: Learning Publications.

Burden, P. R., & Wallace, D. (1983, October). *Tailoring staff development to meet teacher needs.* Paper presented at the Association of Teacher Educators meeting, Wichita, KS. (ERIC Document Reproduction Service No. ED 237506).

Cheng, Y. (1996). *School effectiveness and school-based management: A mechanism for development.* London: Falmer.

Cutler, A., & Ruopp, F. (1999). From expert to novice: The transformation from teacher to learner. In M. Solomon (Ed.), *The diagnostic teacher* (pp. 133–161). New York: Teachers College Press.

Daresh, J. C. (1987). Administrator in-service: A route to continuous learning and growing. In W. Greenfield (Ed.), *Instructional leadership: Concepts, issues, and controversies* (pp. 328–340). Boston: Allyn and Bacon.

Desimone, L. M., Porter, A. C., Garet, M. S., Yoon, K. S., & Birman, B. F. (2002, Summer). Effects of professional development on teachers' instruction: Results from a three-year longitudinal study. *Educational Evaluation and Policy Analysis, 24*, 81–112.

DeVries, R., & Colbert, J. (1990). The Los Angeles experience: Individually oriented professional development. In B. Joyce (Ed.), *Changing school culture through staff development* (pp. 203–217). Alexandria, VA: Association for Supervision and Curriculum Development.

Doyle, W., & Ponder, G. (1977). The practicality ethic and teacher decision-making. *Interchange, 8*, 1–12.

Drake, S. M. (2001, September). Castles, kings . . . and standards. *Educational Leadership, 59*, 38–42.

Duttweiler, P. (1989, Spring). Components of an effective professional development program. *Journal of Staff Development, 10*, 2–6.

Egnor, D. (2003, March). No principal left behind: Implications for special education policy and practice. *Principal Leadership, 3*, 10, 12–13.

Elam, S., Cramer, J., & Brodinsky, B. (1986). *Staff development: Problems and solutions.* Arlington, VA: American Association of School Administrators.

Elsaesser, L. (1990, April). *Using assessment center results to determine subsequent staff development activities for principals.* Paper presented at the annual meeting of the American Educational Research Association, Boston. (ERIC Document Reproduction No. ED 318763).

Evertson, C. (1986). Do teachers make a difference? Issues for the eighties. *Education and Urban Society, 18*, 195–210.

Fullan, M. (1990). Staff development, innovation, and institutional development. In B. Joyce (Ed.), *Changing school culture through staff development* (pp. 3–25). Alexandria, VA: Association for Supervision and Curriculum Development.

Geisert, G. (1988, November). Participatory management: Panacea or hoax? *Educational Leadership, 46*, 56–59.

Georgia State Department of Education. (1990). *School-focused staff development guide.* Atlanta: Author.

Goodlad, J. (1983). The school as workplace. In G. Griffin (Ed.), *Staff development* (pp. 36–61). Chicago: University of Chicago Press.

Guskey, T. R. (1986, May). Staff development and the process of teacher change. *Educational Researcher, 15*, 5–12.

Guskey, T. R. (2000). *Evaluating professional development.* Thousand Oaks, CA: Corwin Press, Inc.

Hallinger, P., & Greenblatt, R. (1989, Fall). Principals' pursuit of professional growth: The influence of beliefs, experiences, and district context. *Journal of Staff Development, 10*, 68–74.

Holloway, J. H. (2003, November). Linking professional development to student learning. *Educational Leadership, 61*, 85–87.

Howey, K., & Vaughn, J. (1983). Current patterns of staff development. In G. Griffin (Ed.), *Staff development* (pp. 92–117). Chicago: University of Chicago Press.

Jenkins, K. (2000, May). Earning board certification: Making time to grow. *Educational Leadership, 57*, 46–48.

Joekel, R. (1994, January). Nebraska Professional Proficiency Plan. *Design for Leadership: Bulletin of the National Policy Board for Educational Administration, 5*, 5–7.

Joyce, B. (1990). The self-educating teacher: Empowering teachers through research. In B. Joyce (Ed.), *Changing school culture through staff development* (pp. 26–40). Alexandria, VA: Association for Supervision and Curriculum Development.

Joyce, B., & Showers, B. (1988). *Student achievement through staff development.* New York: Longman.

K–12 principals guide to No Child Left Behind. Alexandria, VA: National Association of Elementary School Principals. Reston, VA: National Association of Secondary School Principals.

Kramer, P., & Betz, L. (1987). *Effective inservice education in Texas public schools.* (ERIC Document Reproduction Service No. ED 290205).

Lieberman, A. (1999). *Teachers—Transforming their world and their work.* New York: Teachers College Press.

Little, J. (1990). Conditions of professional development in secondary schools. In M. McLaughlin, J. Talbert, and N. Bascia (Eds.), *The contexts of teaching in secondary schools: Teachers' realities* (pp. 187–223). New York: Teachers College Press.

Mell, B., & Mell, C. (1990). An experience in Anchorage: Trials, errors, and successes. In B. Joyce (Ed.), *Changing school culture through staff development* (pp. 229–242). Alexandria, VA: Association for Supervision and Curriculum Development.

Mohlman, G., Kierstad, J., & Gundlach, M. (1982, October). A research-based inservice model for secondary teachers. *Educational Leadership, 40*, 16–19.

Mohr, N. (1998, April). Creating effective study groups for principals. *Educational Leadership, 55*, 41–44.

Moore, D., & Hyde, A. (1981). *Making sense of staff development: An analysis of staff development programs and their costs in three urban school districts.* (ERIC Document Reproduction Service No. ED 211629).

National Center for Education Statistics. (1993). *America's teachers: Profile of a profession.* Washington, DC: U.S. Department of Education.

North Dakota State Department of Public Instruction. (1986). *Professional development model: A wholistic approach.* Bismarck, ND: Author. (ERIC Document Reproduction Service No. ED 286868).

Olivero, J. (1982, February). Principals and their inservice needs. *Educational Leadership, 39*, 340–344.

Peterson, K. (2002, April). The professional development of principals: Innovations and opportunities. *Educational Administration Quarterly, 38*, 213–232.

Pitner, N. (1987). Principles of quality staff development: Lessons for administrator training. In J. Murphy and P. Hallinger (Eds.), *Approaches to administrative training in education* (pp. 28–44). Albany: State University of New York Press.

Raywid, M. A. (2002, February). Accountability: What's worth measuring? *Phi Delta Kappan, 83*, 433–436.

Scherer, M. (2001, September). How and why standards can improve student achievement: A conversation with Robert J. Marzano. *Educational Leadership, 59*, 14–18.

Schlechty, P., & Crowell, D. (1983). *Understanding and managing staff development in an urban school system.* Washington, DC: National Institute of Education. (ERIC Document Reproduction Service No. ED 251519).

Shanker, A. (1990). Staff development and the restructured school. In B. Joyce (Ed.), *Changing school culture through staff development* (pp. 91–103). Alexandria, VA: Association for Supervision and Curriculum Development.

Showers, B. (1985, April). Teachers coaching teachers. *Educational Leadership, 42*, 43–48.

Showers, B., Joyce, B., & Bennett, B. (1987, November). Synthesis of research on staff development: A framework for future study and a state-of-the-art analysis. *Educational Leadership, 45*, 77–87.

Smylie, M., & Conyers, J. (1991, Winter). Changing conceptions of teaching influence the future of staff development. *Journal of Staff Development, 12*, 12–16.

Solomon, M., & Morocco, C. (1999). The diagnostic teacher. In M. Solomon (Ed.), *The diagnostic teacher* (pp. 231–246). New York: Teachers College Press.

Sparks, B. (1983, November). Synthesis of research on staff development for effective teaching. *Educational Leadership, 41*, 65–72.

Stallings, J. (1985). *How effective is an analytic approach to staff development on teacher and student behavior?* Nashville: Vanderbilt University, Peabody College. (ERIC Document Reproduction Service No. ED 267019).

Tucker, M., & Codding, J. (1998). *Standards for our schools.* San Francisco: Jossey-Bass.

Wade, R. (1984/1985, December/January). What makes a difference in inservice teacher education? A meta-analysis of research. *Educational Leadership, 42*, 48–54.

Youngs, P., & King, M. B. (2002). Principal leadership for professional development to build school capacity. *Educational Administration Quarterly, 38*, 643–670.

CHAPTER NINE

EVALUATING EMPLOYEE PERFORMANCE

Evaluation of performance is a fact of life in most work settings, and even though it may be carried out in a routine and perfunctory manner, few individuals approach the experience with indifference. All employees potentially stand to gain or lose from evaluation, but in schools, it is not only teachers and other personnel who have something at stake. Parents and students can also benefit from evaluation, since evaluation procedures properly carried out lead to improved instruction.

In many schools, teacher evaluation has little effect on teacher performance. It is carried out to fulfill the requirements of state statutes, board policy, or union contracts. In such cases, evaluation

> does little for teachers except contribute to their weariness and reinforce their skepticism of bureaucratic routine . . . [and] does little for administrators except add to their workload. It does not provide a mechanism for a school system to communicate its expectations concerning teaching (Darling-Hammond, 1986, pp. 531–532).

Two of the most common problems in teacher evaluation are the relative infrequency of classroom observations and the unrealistically high ratings teachers receive. A majority of teachers report they are observed by an evaluator no more than twice a year, and a substantial number (about one in six) say they have never been observed. Elementary school teachers and younger teachers, including those with less experience, are observed slightly more often than teachers in middle and high schools and those who have been teaching longer (Educational Research Service, 1985).

All employees tend to rate themselves high on performance and are disappointed when they receive lower ratings from superiors than they feel they deserve. On the whole, however, teachers are rated high. One study showed that about 41 percent of teachers surveyed viewed themselves as belonging in the top 10 percent of all performers (a striking finding in itself); however, an even larger proportion (48 percent) reported that their superiors rated them among the top 10 percent. Put another way, the evaluators rate teachers even higher than teachers rate themselves (Educational Research Service, 1985).

There is nothing inherently wrong with high ratings, and it is human nature to prefer to avoid giving others low ratings. The problem is that personnel who receive higher ratings than they deserve may be lulled into believing that they have no need for further improvement.

PLAN OF THE CHAPTER

This chapter deals with the following topics: Purposes of performance evaluation, models of teacher evaluation, characteristics of successful evaluation programs, criteria for evaluating school personnel, state-mandated evaluation programs, evaluation of administrative and support personnel, and legal considerations in personnel evaluation.

PURPOSES OF PERFORMANCE EVALUATION

The Joint Committee on Standards for Educational Evaluation (1988) has identified the following purposes for evaluation of educational personnel: "Evaluation of educators should promote sound education principles, fulfillment of institutional missions, and effective performance of job responsibilities, so that the educational needs of students, community, and society are met" (p. 21).

This chapter examines two types of evaluation for educational personnel. *Summative evaluation* refers to assessment carried out for accountability purposes. This type of evaluation is usually conducted annually or semiannually, and the results are used to make decisions about individuals, such as whether to grant tenure, to seek termination or transfer, to place an individual on a career ladder, or to make a salary adjustment (Educational Research Service, 1978). *Formative evaluation* serves a developmental function. Its purpose is to help an individual employee improve his or her effectiveness on the job by providing feedback and coaching (Educational Research Service, 1978). (Note: Consult the Glossary at the end of this chapter for definitions of terms used in the chapter.)

The formative and summative sides of performance evaluation are sometimes in conflict. Formative evaluation relies on the creation and maintenance of a bond of trust between the employee and the evaluator. Summative evaluation, because of the high stakes involved and the emphasis on judging, risks undermining the trust that is essential to helping employees learn new job-related behaviors (Wise, Darling-Hammond, McLaughlin, & Bernstein, 1984). Some authorities believe that formative and summative evaluation cannot be reconciled in the same evaluation system and suggest that the two functions should be separated (Knapp, 1982).

Although formative and summative evaluation are the most common reasons for conducting performance evaluations, other purposes are served as well.

Evaluation is sometimes used to validate selection criteria, to provide a basis for career planning, and to select individuals to receive merit pay awards or promotions to positions of greater responsibility (Educational Research Service, 1978).

MODELS OF TEACHER EVALUATION

There are several models of teacher evaluation in use in schools. The assumptions about teaching, and about evaluation of teaching in particular, vary from one model to another. Four models that are in widespread use in schools will be examined in this chapter. They are the remediation, goal-setting, portfolio, and assessment models. Exhibit 9.1 presents a summary of the major features of each model, including the purpose, objectives, assumptions, and typical methods of operation.

Remediation Model

In districts that use the remediation model, teachers who receive unsatisfactory summative evaluation readings are required to participate in formal remediation sessions to correct identified weaknesses (Pfeifer, 1986). Assistance is provided to the teacher either by the principal or assistant principal or by other teachers or supervisors from the district office. The assistance usually consists of two parts: didactic instruction and classroom practice. The teacher tries new techniques with students while an observer provides performance-related feedback.

Under the remediation model, teachers who fail to meet performance standards may be required to demonstrate improved proficiency in specified areas or face termination. Assistance is provided to help teachers expand their skills, and if no improvement is noted after a reasonable time, action is taken. In some programs a committee of observers, including peers, evaluates the teacher's performance and makes a recommendation for continued employment or termination. In other districts the evaluation process is carried out in the usual way, with the principal observing and rating the teacher's performance and recommending appropriate action.

An assumption upon which the remediation model is based is that individuals can become effective teachers by mastering a limited number of teaching behaviors identified in the research literature as related to student learning. The object of such a program is to bring all teachers to a minimal level of competence using specific instructional criteria such as those shown in Exhibit 9.2.

The remediation model works best with teachers who have correctable problems, who are motivated, and who have the ability to profit from instruction. Classroom management is an example of a problem for which teachers can usually be helped by the remediation approach. The model is most successful when specific corrective techniques can be prescribed and when support is provided to help teachers expand their skills.

EXHIBIT 9.1
COMPARISON OF FOUR EVALUATION MODELS

Remediation Model

Purpose:	Correct identified weaknesses.
Objective:	Bring all teachers to a minimum level of performance.
Assumption:	It is possible to specify effective teaching behaviors and teach them.
Method:	Assess, provide feedback, and reassess.
Works best with:	Teachers with correctable teaching problems.
Evaluator skills:	Ability to provide clear, specific directions.
Possible problems:	Heavy demands on evaluator's time; offers no challenge to more competent teachers; deemphasizes variety in teaching.

Goal-Setting Model

Purpose:	Involve teachers and administrators in choosing individualized evaluation criteria.
Objective:	Increase teacher autonomy and commitment.
Assumption:	Teachers are professionals and able to assess their own developmental needs.
Method:	Teacher prepares annual goals statement; principal reviews, approves, or amends it and evaluates teachers' attainment.
Works best with:	Experienced, motivated teachers.
Evaluator skills:	Ability to help teachers write relevant performance objectives and guide teachers into productive channels; ability to evaluate on individualized criteria.
Possible problems:	Weak or overly ambitious goals; lack of consensus on what constitutes attainment of objective.

Portfolio Model

Purpose:	Base teacher evaluation on documented evidence of effective performance.
Objective:	Encourage teachers to cooperate in formulating high standards of practice.
Assumption:	Teachers will be able to assemble a collection of evidence that will present an accurate picture of teaching skills.
Method:	Teachers maintain a file of handouts, tests, reports, student evaluations, documentation of teaching practices, and other information and submit it to the evaluator.
Works best with:	Experienced teachers in a variety of areas; especially well suited to teachers of art, music, and vocational subjects.
Evaluator skills:	Ability to synthesize a profusion of details into a meaningful assessment of an individual's performance.
Possible problems:	Teachers: Time required to prepare portfolio; temptation to impress with flashy packaging.
	Administrators: Amount of time required to review portfolios; need to equate evidence from many different sources.

Assessment Model

Purpose:	Base teacher evaluation on amount of student learning.
Objective:	Determine amount of learning attributable to teacher's effort.
Assumption:	Each teacher contributes to students' accumulating knowledge.
Method:	Use pre- and posttests to measure student growth each year.
Works best with:	Teachers of subjects that have well-defined cognitive outcomes.
Evaluator skills:	Able to interpret and understand the limitations of achievement tests; able to take into account uncontrolled factors.
Possible problems:	Inflexible application of procedure results in loss of credibility; method does not identify teacher behaviors that affect learning.

EXHIBIT 9.2

EVALUATION CRITERIA FOR REMEDIATION MODEL

KNOWLEDGE OF SUBJECT
1. Teacher demonstrates understanding of the subject being taught.
2. Teacher helps learners to understand the significance of the topics or activities studied.

PREPARATION AND PLANNING
1. Teacher prepares instructional plans on both a daily and long-term basis.
2. Teacher makes advance arrangements for materials, equipment, and supplies needed for instruction.
3. Teacher develops teaching procedures to match lesson objectives.
4. Teacher prepares plans for use by substitute teachers in case it is necessary to be absent.
5. Teacher works cooperatively with colleagues in the school and district to develop curriculum and select instructional materials.

IMPLEMENTING AND MANAGING INSTRUCTION
1. Teacher makes the goals of instruction clear to all students.
2. Teacher monitors students' performance and adjusts the pace and difficulty level of instruction as needed.
3. Teacher reviews material previously learned before introducing new concepts.
4. Teacher maintains student interest and attention by using a variety of instructional modes.
5. Teacher frequently checks students' understanding of new material and reteaches when indicated.
6. Teacher makes use of students' ideas to introduce new concepts and reinforce previously learned material.
7. Teacher allocates instructional time to activities that produce the highest rates of student learning.
8. Teacher asks content-related questions that most students are able to answer correctly.
9. Teacher summarizes important points.

STUDENT EVALUATION
1. Teacher regularly assigns, collects, and evaluates students' homework.
2. Teacher uses both teacher-made and standardized tests to check student progress.
3. Teacher provides feedback to students.
4. Teacher uses results of student evaluations to modify the pace or scope of instruction.
5. Teacher provides detailed directions for completing assignments and evaluates students' work on the basis of specified criteria.

CLASSROOM ENVIRONMENT
1. Teacher is fair and impartial in dealings with all students, including those of different races and nationalities.
2. Teacher behaves toward all students in a friendly and accepting manner.
3. Teacher displays high expectations for the amount and quality of work to be performed by students and expresses confidence in their ability.
4. Teacher maintains a businesslike learning climate without being humorless or repressive.
5. Teacher informs students about classroom rules and procedures.
6. Teacher provides a safe, orderly, and attractive environment.
7. Teacher uses nonpunitive and preventive techniques for minimizing disruption and maintaining learner involvement.

The model requires evaluators to spend a good deal of time observing teachers and providing feedback. A few spaced observations over the course of a school year are not sufficient for solving most problems. For severe problems, observations should be scheduled two or more times per week, but for mild deficiencies, biweekly or monthly visits should suffice. Because of these time demands, the remediation model is usually not practical for use with more than a small number of teachers.

A variation of the remediation model that has received relatively little attention to date is to use professional development to remediate identified deficiencies. This approach helps overcome some of the problems with the model of individual remediation described earlier by reducing somewhat the demands on principals' and supervisors' time (Knapp, 1982).

Goal-Setting Model

Goal-setting models of teacher evaluation involve teachers in selecting the criteria for evaluation. In this approach, each teacher selects developmental goals and identifies strategies for achieving them. These strategies might include observing other teachers, coursework, workshop attendance, or readings (Darling-Hammond, 1986). This approach is used most often for formative evaluation purposes. Goal statements are prepared individually but usually reflect a current schoolwide or systemwide emphasis. A typical goal-setting plan requires a participating teacher to meet with the evaluator near the beginning of the school year to establish the year's goals. The principal may approve the proposed workplan as submitted or amend it by adding additional goals or by revising those submitted by the teacher.

Once a goal statement has been agreed to by both parties, it becomes part of the teacher's personnel file and constitutes a contract between the teacher and the district. In most such plans the principal meets with the teacher once or twice during the year to check on progress. If necessary, the goals may be amended or revised at these meetings.

The goal-setting model presumes that teachers are able to identify their own developmental needs. It is not well suited for teachers who are having difficulty with classroom management or instructional organization, and in some schools that use goal-setting plans, teachers with identified deficiencies do not participate (Tesch, Nyland, & Kernutt, 1987).

The plan is most effective when teachers' efforts are coordinated. When all teachers in a school work together toward improving questioning techniques, for example, the impact on students is far greater than when each teacher works independently of colleagues.

Several problems may be encountered in implementing a goal-setting evaluation plan. One potential problem is disparities in the difficulty of the goals chosen by teachers. Some teachers select goals that require little or no effort, whereas others identify objectives so ambitious that they exceed the time and other resources available to accomplish them. Both cases require the evaluator to exercise critical judgment in reviewing proposed workplans.

A second problem may arise at the end of the year when teachers are evaluated on the attainment of their approved goals. Unless the evaluator and teacher have agreed beforehand what will constitute evidence of achievement of goals, disagreements may occur. Evaluating goal attainment is further complicated by questions of equity when a teacher who has set ambitious goals fails to attain them, while another teacher proposes and easily achieves a modest list of accomplishments. Should the evaluator rate the more ambitious teacher lower for failing to reach all of the proposed goals, or should the difficulty of the outcomes be taken into account in evaluating the teachers?

The major strength of the goal-setting approach is that it gives teachers autonomy in identifying and working toward attainment of professional objectives. Autonomy is a key to building commitment (Hawley, 1982). Goal-setting plans involve considerably more teacher input than the remedial plan (described earlier) and allow for flexibility in the determination of the criteria upon which teachers are evaluated. Their success is dependent on whether teachers approach the program seriously. This approach is most likely to be successful when used with teachers who are experienced and willing to assume responsibility for their professional development.

Portfolio Model

Portfolios are used to document changes in students' academic performance over time, and the idea has been borrowed for use as a device in evaluating teachers. Teachers prepare a portfolio by assembling a variety of information pertaining to their teaching, normally for the purpose of applying for National Board Certification or to renew a professional license. When used for evaluation, the portfolio is presented to the principal, who reviews the information and prepares an evaluation report on the teacher.

Portfolio evaluation appeals to teachers because it gives them more control of the evaluation process, but many teachers find that collecting the information they need to assemble a file is onerous. The process is somewhat less burdensome if specific guidelines are available showing what to include and what to omit. In most portfolio plans, teachers receive a checklist or outline of the materials they are expected to include in the portfolio. Items on the list include the following (Bird, 1990; Wolf, 1996):

- Resumé
- Educational philosophy and teaching goals

- Samples of completed student work
- Grade distributions
- Student evaluations

- Professional activities
- Letters of recommendation
- Formal evaluations
- Lesson plans
- Sample tests
- Sample handouts

- Parent comments
- Teaching license or certificate
- Professional development activities
- Documentation of teaching practices, including videotapes of class sessions

The resumé contains information about educational background, professional experience, and professional leadership activities. Leadership activities include serving as an officer for a professional association or taking part in regional or statewide service activities such as serving on accreditation teams. District leadership activities that are included on the resumé include chairing committees for staff development or textbook selection. Activities for the school, such as serving as a mentor to another teacher or serving as grade-level chair or department head, are also featured.

Teachers applying for National Board Certification prepare a portfolio following guidelines provided by the Board for the specialty field in which they are seeking certification. Among the fields in which Board Certification is available are generalist, art, career and technical, English as a New Language, exceptional needs, library/media, mathematics, music, physical education, science, social studies, and world languages (www.nbpts.org/candidates/portfolios.cfm).

Portfolios have two major advantages over conventional methods of evaluation. First, they involve teachers proactively in gathering, organizing, and evaluating the material that composes the portfolio. Although most educators agree that teachers should be active participants in their own evaluation, most acknowledge that it seldom happens. Portfolios give teachers an opportunity to be active in their own evaluation. A second advantage of portfolios is that they offer a more comprehensive picture of a teacher's approach to the craft of teaching as compared to conventional means of evaluation. Even the most conscientious principals seldom observe a teacher more than three or four times in the course of a year, and although those brief glimpses of the teacher yield useful data, the picture they present is far from complete. Portfolios help fill in the gaps. The main disadvantage of portfolios is the time required in preparing and evaluating them (McNelly, 2002). A principal who must read and evaluate a portfolio for every teacher in the school may find that it is necessary to put aside other important tasks.

Teacher Assessment Model

This approach to evaluating teaching performance establishes a more exacting standard of teaching effectiveness than the three approaches just described by measuring teachers' ability to help students master challenging subject matter. Teacher assessment requires that teachers be able to demonstrate that students have actually gained knowledge from instruction.

Assessment links learning objectives and instruction so that it is possible to determine how much students have learned and whether the observed gains are attributable to an individual teacher's efforts. One other element that is considered in teacher assessment is whether the objectives that students attempt to master are worthwhile (Darling-Hammond, 1998). In practice, that often means confirming that the objectives of instruction are from a set of state-approved standards.

CHARACTERISTICS OF SUCCESSFUL EVALUATION PROGRAMS

McLaughlin (1990) pointed out that improving evaluation requires increasing the district's capacity by equipping principals and other supervisory staff members with the skills and strategies needed to carry out effective evaluation processes. Few principals are able to maintain evaluation systems that result in improved teaching outcomes without encouragement and backing from district personnel. Human resources managers need to ensure that evaluation processes are integrated in a seamless web with staff development and curriculum development, so that knowledge gained from one process informs the others. District leadership is one of several factors identified as characteristic of successful evaluation programs (Wise et al., 1984).

A second feature of effective evaluation programs is training for evaluators. Training should prepare evaluators to recognize and avoid psychometric errors, such as halo errors, first-impression errors, and leniency errors (Milkovich & Newman, 1996).

Guidelines adopted by the Connecticut State Board of Education state that general responsibilities and specific tasks of a teacher's position should be available and should serve as a frame of reference for evaluation of the teacher. The guidelines also specify that teachers should be informed about and understand the means by which they will be evaluated and that the evaluation should take into account any factors that affect evaluation results. According to the Connecticut guidelines, evaluation should be more formative than summative and should be implemented in such a way that teachers are encouraged to be creative in their approach to instruction (Iwanicki & Rindone, 1995).

Cycle of Evaluation

Evaluation of teaching personnel occurs in a regular cycle, although the phases of the cycle vary somewhat from district to district. It is helpful if teachers who are new to the system understand the timing and focus of each of the phases of the cycle and the purpose for each. In most districts, a distinction is made between evaluation that takes place in the first year or two in the classroom and that carried out in subsequent years.

Evaluation for teachers in their first two or three years in the classroom is more intensive and, as a rule, more frequent than for teachers with more experience. Observations made at this stage are usually diagnostic in nature and are intended to provide feedback to help beginning teachers improve their effectiveness. A secondary purpose is to document observations of teachers who may be at risk of being dismissed at the end of the probationary period.

Teachers with three to nine years of service follow a different pattern as compared to teachers near the beginning stages of their careers. Tenured teachers continue to be evaluated on a regular basis, but the process is more relaxed. These teachers may be observed only every other year rather than every year. The purpose of evaluation for these teachers is to ensure that they continue to be effective.

For experienced teachers who have consistently been effective over time, evaluation is aimed at encouraging professional growth and development. The emphasis is on finding opportunities for these teachers to explore new interests, try out new strategies, or take on new leadership responsibilities. The teacher and evaluator usually jointly develop a long-range plan of professional growth activities, which might call for the teacher to work toward an advanced degree or seek National Board certification. The plan might include granting leave to allow the teacher to conduct research on a topic related to his or her subject field.

Evaluating Evaluation Systems

The purpose of performance evaluation is to improve a school's ability to accomplish its mission (Stronge & Helm, 1991). If the system in use fails to do that, it should be changed or replaced. When educators consider ways of improving performance evaluation, they often assume that problems with the system can be resolved by developing a better observation instrument or rating form. In fact, what is usually needed is agreement among those who have a stake in performance evaluation regarding its purpose and uses.

Two types of performance evaluation were described earlier in the chapter. Formative evaluation helps to improve an individual's performance on the job, and summative evaluation is used for decision-making purposes. The process of evaluating a performance evaluation system should begin by determining which of the two types is needed. If both are required, then a decision must be made about whether to attempt to combine both into one plan.

If the evaluation plan is intended primarily to assist in making personnel decisions, the evaluation of it should consider how well it performs that function. Are the recommendations clear-cut and free of ambiguity, and do they result in actions that are sound and defensible? If not, the plan may need an overhaul, or those who administer it may need to be better trained in its use.

A good summative evaluation system specifies minimally acceptable performance, and employees are aware that if their performance does not measure up, they may be in jeopardy of a demotion, a cut in pay, or termination. If the reason for an individual's failure to attain a minimally acceptable level of performance is lack of skill, then consideration should be given to providing training and assistance to help correct the deficiency (Guzzo & Gannett, 1988).

If, on the other hand, the evaluation plan was meant to help improve individual performance, an evaluation of the system should consider first whether it is being used for that purpose. Evaluation plans are sometimes subverted for uses other than the intended ones, and it is not uncommon for data from a formative evaluation system to be used for summative purposes. When that happens, employees lose confidence in the evaluation program and either ignore it or resist participating in it.

If it is determined that the information collected from performance evaluations is being used as intended, the next question is whether individuals are able to perform better as a result. If evaluators can point to specific instances of increased individual effectiveness that can be traced directly to evaluation feedback, it is fair to conclude that the evaluation plan is working. But if no specific evidence is available—even though participants may feel positive about the plan—there is a question about its value. In that case, consideration must be given to ways of changing the operation of the evaluation system in order to bring it into line with the stated purpose.

Characteristics of the evaluator and the quality of information provided to teachers influence the extent to which workers benefit from performance evaluation. An evaluator's credibility, relationship to the employee, and ability to model suggestions have all been found to be positively correlated with the appropriate use of evaluation information. Characteristics of the information received by teachers from evaluation sources, including the quality of suggestions and the persuasiveness of the evaluator's rationale for improvement, are also related to the value of the evaluation process for teachers (Duke & Stiggins, 1990).

Both types of evaluation plans are more likely to be successful if they are accepted and supported by those who are evaluated. Teachers look for three features that they regard as indicators that an evaluation plan is likely to be beneficial. First, teachers consider whether it encourages self-improvement. Second, they judge whether evaluators demonstrate, both in their personal attitudes and in the mechanics of evaluating an individual's performance, appreciation for the complexity of teaching. Finally, they consider whether the procedures employed are fair and likely to provide protection of their rights (Darling-Hammond, Wise, & Pease, 1983).

Administrators should not overlook the motivating potential of performance feedback. Knowledge of results is an important motivator, and feedback sets the stage for new learning by pinpointing areas in which improvement is needed. Performance evaluation is one of the few ways by which teachers receive information about the results of their efforts. They gauge their success in the classroom by how their teaching is rated.

The design of evaluation instruments should take their potential motivating effects into account. Teachers pay heed to the criteria on which they are evaluated and adjust their performance accordingly (Hoenack & Monk, 1990).

CRITERIA FOR EVALUATING SCHOOL PERSONNEL

Workers are evaluated on the basis of possessing certain personal characteristics, demonstrating behaviors associated with successful performance, or producing specified results. The characteristics, behaviors, and results used to judge performance are called *criteria*. To identify criteria for use in evaluating an individual in a position, the job model for that position (see Chapter 3) is a logical place to start. The "Priority Actions" and "Results Sought" sections of the job model are useful sources of criteria for performance evaluation. The "Results Sought" section lists outcomes the employee is expected to achieve, and the performance evaluation should be based on the degree to which the employee has successfully attained those results.

Teachers are asked to perform a number of tasks, but none is more important than instruction. Accordingly, the main emphasis in this chapter is on evaluating performance of instructional tasks. The model of student learning depicted in Chapter 1 (Figure 1.1) showed that student learning results from teacher behaviors, which in turn are influenced by teacher knowledge and motivation. If the bottom line is student outcomes, why not measure those results directly rather than relying on indirect indicators of teaching effectiveness?

In some occupations, results are readily available and are easily measured. In sales, for example, the best indicator of employee performance is the number of units sold or the dollar value of sales completed during a given period of time. To the sales manager, a salesperson's personal characteristics are less important than the revenue the employee generates. In manufacturing operations, the quantity of a product produced is a measure of employee performance, and in clerical work the number of letters typed or the number of customer questions answered are measures of employee productivity.

However, the "product" of teaching is the content of children's minds. This output is not tangible, nor is it easily attributed to the efforts of a single teacher, since the learner's responses in a given situation are influenced by all previous experiences. Learning outcomes are not easily measured, and cause-effect relationships between teacher behavior and learning are far from clear. Learning gains achieved by a child during the course of a year result in part from the efforts of the current teacher and in part from the child's previous teachers and from experiences outside of school.

Flags and Alerts

One way to make teachers aware of criteria of effective teaching (and also of practices that should be avoided) has been developed by a school district in Colorado (Maglaras & Lynch, 1988). Desirable practices are labeled "green flags," and those that are to be avoided are called "red alerts." Examples of green flags in mathematics classes include heterogeneous grouping, high student interest and teacher enthusiasm, applying mathematics to real-life situations, use of manipulatives, and availability of enrichment activities for all students.

Red alerts are practices that "if seen consistently, call for explanation; they should usually be avoided" (Maglaras & Lynch, 1988, p. 59). Some examples of red alerts from mathematics are giving no homework or excessive amounts of homework, chalkboard work for no purpose, teacher grading papers while students do homework, no diagnostic testing, students not understanding the purpose of homework assignments, and no use of calculators.

Evaluating Personal Qualities

One of the most difficult problems in teacher evaluation is deciding what to do about an individual who has a negative or bitter outlook on life. These individuals cause others to feel frustrated and stressed, and their attitudes and behavior interfere with the work of their colleagues (Weber, 2003). Even though such people may know their jobs well and perform them satisfactorily, their negative attitudes exact a toll on the school's effectiveness. No recipe exists for dealing with such people, and over time others begin to ignore or avoid them. When a teacher with chronically negative attitudes is being evaluated, that person should receive honest yet tactful feedback to let him or her know how the negative attitude affects other people.

Selecting Evaluation Instruments

Teachers are evaluated on performance standards developed by the district or state. These standards describe teacher knowledge, attitudes, and behaviors that have been shown by research to be related to student achievement. An evaluation instrument designed for formative evaluation purposes usually contains detailed items describing observable classroom behaviors. The instrument may also include rubrics or behavioral descriptors for each item on the scale. Rubrics help to increase the reliability of the instrument.

When improved performance is the purpose of the evaluation, the items on the evaluation instrument should be designed to yield information about how often teachers display certain target behaviors and their appropriateness at that moment. Ratings that are distributed across the scale are more useful to teachers than ratings that cluster near one end of the scale. A teacher who is rated "Always or frequently" on every item has little room for improvement, and one who receives "Seldom or never" ratings exclusively is likely to feel overwhelmed, with no idea on where to start working to improve his or her performance. Evaluation instruments used for summative purposes normally contain items that are broad in scope and include fewer rating options. Terms such as *Outstanding, Satisfactory,* and *Needs Improvement* are examples of ratings that might appear on a summative evaluation form.

In order for the results of formative evaluation to be useful in helping to improve instruction, it is important that teachers understand what standards are used to evaluate them. Surprisingly, almost one-half of the teachers in one study reported they did not know the criteria on which they were to be evaluated, even though the principals of the schools in which those teachers taught indicated that they believed their teachers were familiar with the criteria (Natriello & Dornbusch, 1980/1981). The authors of that study wrote:

> Informing teachers of the criteria used to evaluate them is of prime importance if procedures for teacher evaluation are to have any impact on modifying and improving teacher performance. If teachers are unaware of the criteria and standards used to judge their performance, they are in no position to direct their energies along lines desired by the school organization (p. 2).

Classroom Observations

Principals rely on classroom observations to gather data for evaluation purposes. Although some information is obtained in other ways (e.g., teacher attendance records, parent and student comments, and comments from other teachers or department heads), by far the most widely used source of data for teacher evaluation is that gathered by principals during classroom visits.

Most principals view evaluation as part of the process of improving instruction, and most of them believe that they could be more effective as instructional leaders if they were able to observe classrooms more often. However, the time available for classroom visits is limited, and principals spend more time visiting classrooms of probationary teachers than those of tenured teachers. Tenured teachers may have one observation by the principal during the course of a year, and some may not see the principal at all. This imbalance is justified by principals as necessary to help new teachers get off to a good start and to ensure that no incompetent teacher is granted tenure at the end of the probationary period.

In some districts classroom observations are very structured, whereas in others they are more open. In districts with collective bargaining agreements principals are required to comply closely with the terms of the agreement in carrying out observations. Contracts frequently specify the number of classroom observations required during the year as well as the minimum length of each observation. It is also common for the contract to require that the principal schedule a follow-up conference with the teacher shortly after the observation.

What does a principal look for during a classroom observation? Typically, observers seek to determine whether the teacher has identified instructional objectives and whether those objectives address mandated content. Observers are also interested in the extent to which students participate in the lesson by asking or answering questions, volunteering opinions, or demonstrating processes; how well-prepared the teacher is; evidence of effective classroom management; and whether and in what ways the teacher uses technology in presenting the lesson.

Observing a class requires the observer to make evaluative judgments about the lesson and the way in which it was presented. For example, on the question of student participation, the observer watches to see whether students volunteer to participate because they are interested in the topic or because they are called on by the teacher. The observer will also want to note whether participation is limited to a few students and whether the teacher makes an effort to involve students who are reluctant to volunteer.

Stevens (2001) has developed a comprehensive list of items on which observers can evaluate a teacher while visiting a classroom. The behaviors on his list include stating the purpose of the lesson, arousing student interest in the topic, using a variety of instructional methods, providing for individual differences, and summarizing the material. Other items from Stevens' list include classroom appearance and the teacher's handling of student discipline, along with the teacher's appearance, enthusiasm, and knowledge of subject.

Many principals find that it is difficult to keep track of so many details. To make the task more manageable, they adopt an instructional model as a guide to the observation. The model helps by narrowing the list of behaviors they watch for while also giving them a mental picture of how and when certain behaviors should be enacted.

Direct instruction is an example of a model that can be used as a guide for classroom observing. Direct instruction involves these steps:

1. Teacher reviews content of previous lessons
2. Teacher states lesson objectives
3. Teacher presents new content
4. Students engage in guided practice and receive feedback
5. Students engage in individual practice and receive feedback
6. Teacher reviews content covered during the lesson.

A teacher who uses the direct instruction model may vary the amount of time spent on each step or he or she may even omit a step. For example, if the teacher decides that students need more individual practice, he or she may decide to skip the end-of-lesson review and allow time for additional practice during the next class meeting. In the context of that particular class, the teacher's decision may have been a wise one.

During the guided practice phase of the lesson, the observer should be watching to see whether the teacher designs the practice in such a way that students are able to be successful. The object of the practice phase is to give students a chance to apply ideas that they may not yet have fully comprehended. The practice itself should help the students grasp the new concepts.

STATE-MANDATED EVALUATION SYSTEMS

The law in most states requires regular evaluations of teaching and is explicit in describing the types and frequency of procedures used. Some states provide guidelines for tenured and nontenured teachers or establish performance standards by which teachers are to be judged. In addition, some state statutes specify roles for peer or external evaluators and require training for evaluators (Duke, 1995).

Tennessee adopted the Framework for Evaluation and Professional Growth of teachers consisting of six domains (Planning, Teaching Strategies, Assessment and Evaluation, Learning Environment, Professional Growth, and Communication) and the corresponding indicators (www.state.tn/us/education/frameval).

Iowa administrators who evaluate teachers using the Comprehensive Summative Evaluation Form developed by the Iowa Department of Education are provided detailed criteria for each of eight performance standards. Teachers are rated either as meeting or not meeting each standard, and space is provided for the evaluator's comments. For example: Standard 2 reads: Teacher "demonstrates competence in content knowledge." The indicators for that standard include understands and uses key concepts, underlying themes, relationships, and different perspectives related to the content area; uses knowledge of student development to make learning experiences meaningful and accessible; relates ideas and information within and across content areas; understands and uses instructional strategies that are appropriate to the content area. The complete form is available online at www.state.ia/us/educate/ecese/tqt/tc/doc/cefbt.html.

The Texas Education Agency developed the Texas Teacher Appraisal System to serve several purposes. Data from teacher observations are used for decisions about contract renewal or placement on a career ladder. The information also serves as an indicator of the need for staff development programs related to particular teaching skills (Barnes, 1987).

The instrument developed by the state education agency in Kentucky for use with that state's teacher career ladder is similar to one used in Texas. The Kentucky instrument consists of six functional areas (planning, management of student conduct, instructional organization and lesson development, presentation of subject matter, verbal and nonverbal communication, and evaluation of students). Unlike the Texas instrument, which consists of items describing behaviors associated with greater student learning or higher student satisfaction, the Kentucky instrument contains both positive and negative indicators.

The California Formative Assessment and Support System is a state program that establishes standards for practice in teaching and uses evaluation for the purpose of improving practice. Teachers cooperatively work through a series of activities involving assessment of their teaching. They observe classrooms and conduct research on creating an environment for learning in their classrooms (Olebe, Jackson, & Danielson, 1999).

A study by the Southern Regional Education Board (SREB) (1991) of state-sponsored teacher evaluation systems identified several strengths and weaknesses of these programs. Among the strengths identified by the SREB were the use of research on effective teaching; requiring beginning teachers to demonstrate satisfactory classroom performance prior to initial licensure; introducing a set of common terms and concepts with which to discuss teaching performance; and linking evaluation of teaching with professional development.

The SREB (1991) report also identified some weaknesses of state-sponsored teacher evaluation programs. Among these were the absence of attention to teachers' knowledge of the subject they teach; an overreliance on classroom observation and little use of other means of documenting teaching effectiveness; the failure to assess the relationship between teachers' practices and student outcomes; and the lack of attention to developing ways of identifying the most competent teachers.

EVALUATION OF ADMINISTRATIVE AND SUPPORT PERSONNEL

Exhibit 9.3 shows seven criteria that are used to evaluate school administrators. These are generic criteria that can be applied with appropriate adaptations to all administrators, from assistant principal to superintendent. Some of the criteria in the exhibit are taken from the Texas statute that prescribes evaluation of school administrators in that state. For each position to be evaluated, a specific list of duties or results expected would be prepared, and the administrator's performance would be rated against that list.

The scope of duties for which administrators are responsible varies. Principals and superintendents are responsible for all areas, but the director of personnel is primarily responsible only for personnel administration.

Administrators are evaluated by their immediate superiors, and the superintendent is evaluated by the board. Principals in small districts are usually evaluated by the superintendent. In larger districts, they may be evaluated by an assistant or associate superintendent.

Some administrator evaluation plans provide for input from subordinates or others who work with the individual. For example, teachers may be asked to evaluate the principal's instructional leadership or community relations skills. In some systems, administrators design their own evaluation form to collect information from subordinates, and they are encouraged to construct items that will be of use to them in planning professional development activities.

There are sound reasons why subordinates' opinions should not be the sole basis for judging administrative performance, but there are equally convincing arguments in support of giving subordinates a voice. Administrators must on occasion make decisions that leave some subordinates unhappy, and they need to be buffered from the resentment that follows such actions. Nevertheless, information from subordinates can provide a perspective on administrative performance that is not available from other sources.

Since most district office personnel provide support services for the schools, it makes sense to ask teachers and principals to evaluate their performance. Teachers are a valuable source of information about curriculum supervisors and instructional specialists, since they are the recipients of the services provided by those personnel. Principals are also in a position to evaluate at least some aspects of the operations of departments of transportation and maintenance.

■ ■ ■ ■ ■

EXHIBIT 9.3

PERFORMANCE CRITERIA FOR ADMINISTRATORS

1. *Instructional management:* Improves instruction by (a) monitoring student achievement and attendance and using the data to improve programs, (b) assisting teachers to design effective instructional strategies and select appropriate instructional materials, (c) providing mechanisms for articulation of the curriculum, and (d) supporting programs designed for students with special needs

2. *School/organizational improvement:* Brings about improvement in school programs by (a) collaborating to develop and achieve consensus for an organizational mission statement, (b) organizing to permit and encourage teamwork among staff members pursuing common goals, (c) encouraging an attitude of continuous improvement in curriculum, instruction, and operations on the part of all staff members, (d) arranging for and promoting opportunities for professional development designed to meet identified needs of staff, and (e) providing current information about innovative programs and technologies to staff members

3. *School/organizational climate:* Fosters a positive climate by (a) assessing and planning for improvement of the environment, (b) reinforcing excellence, (c) promoting an atmosphere of caring and respect for others, and (d) encouraging broad participation in decisions about school programs and operations

4. *Personnel management:* Manages personnel effectively by (a) recognizing exemplary performance, (b) encouraging personal and professional growth, (c) administering personnel policies and regulations consistently and fairly and recommending changes when needed, (d) securing necessary personnel resources to meet objectives, and (e) periodically evaluating job performance of assigned personnel

5. *Management of facilities and fiscal operations:* Responsibly manages facilities and fiscal operations by (a) compiling budgets and cost estimates that enable the organization to accomplish its mission, (b) ensuring that facilities are maintained and upgraded as needed, and (c) overseeing school operations, including attendance, accounting, payroll, and transportation

6. *Student management:* Promotes positive student conduct by (a) developing and communicating guidelines for student conduct that help students feel safe and valued, (b) ensuring that rules are enforced consistently and without favor, (c) appropriately disciplining students for misconduct, and (d) effecting collaboration among teachers and parents in managing student conduct

7. *School/community relations:* Ensures community support by (a) clarifying the mission of the school(s) to members of the community, (b) taking an active part in deliberations of school councils and advisory committees, (c) seeking support for school programs from the community, and (d) participating in activities that foster rapport between schools and the community

LEGAL CONSIDERATIONS
IN PERSONNEL EVALUATION

Because of tenure, teacher evaluation decisions more often provoke legal challenges than evaluations of other personnel. To protect teachers' rights to procedural fairness, most states impose specific requirements for conducting performance evaluations. Some states require that teachers be notified in advance of the criteria upon which they will be evaluated, and, in case deficiencies are found, that teachers be informed of the nature of the problems. Other requirements establish a minimum number of classroom observations as part of the evaluation process or specify a deadline for completing the process (Webb, 1983). Districts are allowed latitude in establishing performance criteria (McCarthy & Cambron-McCabe, 1987).

Negotiated contracts also contain provisions regulating teacher evaluation. Board negotiators generally prefer to limit such provisions to general descriptions of evaluation procedures and to avoid committing principals to make a specific number of observations, meet specified deadlines for completion of the evaluation process, or notify teachers of performance deficiencies (Deneen, 1980).

However, specifying evaluative criteria either in the contract or in a policy statement has advantages for both the board and for teachers. Publicizing the standards on which teachers will be judged allows teachers to prepare to meet them and allows administrators to assess them. It also avoids reliance on unreliable, invalid, and legally indefensible criteria (Gross, 1988).

Training for evaluators should include information about applicable provisions of state law, state or district policy, and the master contract that affect evaluation. Failure to comply with these requirements can nullify a district's attempt to terminate or place a teacher on probation. Issues related to termination of teachers are examined in more detail in Chapter 15.

Performance Criteria

Legal challenges to evaluation decisions most often take the form of questions about the performance criteria used. Basing unsatisfactory ratings on criteria for which direct links to student learning do not exist are likely to invite legal challenge. Two examples of questionable criteria that are still in use in some districts are appearance or grooming and personal lifestyle. Unless the district is able to show that a teacher's appearance or behavior outside of school has a direct relationship to teaching effectiveness or poses a threat to students, it is unlikely to be successful in a court test (Deneen, 1980).

In reviewing district actions, courts have taken into account, in addition to the factors already enumerated, whether teachers are given an opportunity to correct their weaknesses and whether they are provided with assistance and sufficient time for implementing improvements. Courts may also consider the question of whether the reasons given teachers for unsatisfactory ratings are stated clearly enough to provide direction for correcting deficiencies (Webb, 1983).

The use of student achievement gains to assess teacher performance raises legal questions that are not at issue when other criteria are employed. The use of student test results in teacher evaluation is relatively uncommon, judging by the small number of dismissal cases in which such evidence has been used to document unsatisfactory teacher performance. One authority recommends that student achievement data be used only as supporting evidence for dismissal, not as the sole or primary reason for the action (Groves, 1984, cited in Carter, 1985).

SUMMARY

Evaluations of educators should promote sound education principles, fulfillment of institutional missions, and effective performance of job responsibilities, so that the educational needs of students, community, and society are met (Joint Committee on Standards for Educational Evaluation, 1988). Performance evaluation may be either formative or summative in nature. Formative evaluations are intended to help individuals perform more effectively; summative evaluations support decisions on promotion, transfer, and termination.

Four models of teacher evaluation used in schools are the remediation model, goal-setting model, portfolio model, and assessment model. Each serves specific purposes. Successful evaluation programs are characterized by strong district support, including training for teacher evaluators. Legal challenges to evaluation decisions are less likely when teachers are informed about the procedures and the evaluation policy is carefully followed by those responsible for implementing it.

GLOSSARY OF EVALUATION TERMS

Assessment Procedures used to gain information about achievement in subject areas by students or about the relative effectiveness of personnel, teaching methods, or school programs

Personnel evaluation Systematic assessment of the performance of prospective or current employees which serves several purposes, including selection, accountability, career planning, and professional growth

Rating a numerical or qualitative value assigned to an individual or object indicating the magnitude of a specified attribute possessed by the individual or object

Rubric Scoring guidelines used to apply criteria to the performance of individuals on specified tasks.

Scale a set of related items pertaining to a single construct or object, which are rated on a continuum and used to evaluate individual attitudes, behavior or performance

SUGGESTED ACTIVITIES

1. Three characteristics of evaluation plans that are valued by teachers are (a) protection against arbitrary or biased evaluations, (b) recognition of the complexity of teaching, and (c) provision for professional growth. Describe how you would develop a design for a teacher evaluation plan incorporating these features.

2. Arrange to visit and observe a classroom for a complete lesson. Note how the teacher you observe identifies objectives for the lesson, arouses student interest in the topic, varies his or her instructional methods, provides for individual differences, involves students, and summarizes lesson content.

3. One of the problems with portfolio evaluations is deciding how to use the information submitted by a teacher in a portfolio. Select three or four items from the list of items to be included in a teacher evaluation portfolio and be prepared to discuss what you might learn from each piece about a teacher's instructional effectiveness if you were the teacher's evaluator. (*Example:* Suppose a teacher includes examples of classroom tests in a portfolio. What could you learn about his or her teaching from examining these tests?)

4. A frequently heard complaint about summative evaluation plans is that they seldom lead to dismissal of incompetent teachers. Do you agree? If so, explain why you believe it is true. Do you believe the problem is lack of training for those who administer teacher evaluations, opposition from teacher unions contesting the dismissal of members, or courts that are inclined to support teachers' rights over administrators' efforts to improve school performance?

5. Read Case Study III and answer the questions.

ONLINE RESOURCES

Cincinnati Public Schools
(www.cpsboe.h12.oh.us/general/TchngProf/TES/StndsRubrics.htm)

This site shows standards for teacher performance developed by Cincinnati Public Schools, along with ratings and accompanying rubrics.

ERIC Clearinghouse on Educational Management Trends and Issues (Instructional Personnel)
(eric.uoregon.edu/trends_issues/instpers/selected_abstracts/teacher_evaluation.html)

This site features an extensive annotated bibliography of journal articles on the topic of teacher evaluation.

Montgomery County (MD) Public Schools
(www.mcps.k12.md.us/departments/personnel/TE)

This site discusses a new teacher evaluation system adopted by Montgomery County Schools. It includes an evaluation handbook prepared by the county and a discussion of the philosophy and design of the evaluation system.

North Carolina Department of Education (www.dpi.state.nc.us/pbl/pblintask.htm)
North Carolina has developed a comprehensive set of behavioral indicators that can be used with the 10 principles for evaluation of beginning teachers developed by the Interstate New Teachers Assessment and Support Consortium (INTASC). The behavioral indicators are available at this site.

REFERENCES

Barnes, S. (1987). *The development of the Texas Teacher Appraisal System.* Paper presented at the annual meeting of the American Educational Research Association, Washington, DC. (ERIC Document Reproduction Service No. ED 294323).

Bird, T. (1990). The schoolteacher's portfolio: An essay on possibilities. In J. Millman and L. Darling-Hammond (Eds.), *The new handbook of teacher evaluation* (pp. 241–256). Newbury Park, CA: Sage.

Carter, B. (1985). *High expectations: A policy paper on setting standards for student achievement.* Stanford, CA: Stanford University School of Education, Education Policy Institute.

Darling-Hammond, L. (1986). A proposal for evaluation in the teaching profession. *Elementary School Journal, 86,* 532–551.

Darling-Hammond, L. (1998, February). Standards for assessing teaching effectiveness are key. *Phi Delta Kappan, 79,* 471–472.

Darling-Hammond, L., Wise, A., & Pease, S. (1983). Teacher evaluation in the organization context: A review of the literature. *Review of Educational Research, 53,* 285–328.

Deneen, J. (1980). Legal dimensions of teacher evaluation. In D. Peterson and A. Ward (Eds.), *Due process in teacher evaluation* (pp. 15–43). Washington, DC: University Press.

Duke, D. (1995). Conflict and consensus in the reform of teacher evaluation. In D. Duke (Ed.), *Teacher evaluation policy* (pp. 173–188). Albany: State University of New York Press.

Duke, D., & Stiggins, R. (1990). Beyond minimum competence: Evaluation for professional development. In J. Millman and L. Darling-Hammond (Eds.), *The new handbook of teacher evaluation* (pp. 116–132). Newbury Park, CA: Sage.

Educational Research Service. (1978). *Evaluating teacher performance.* Arlington, VA: Author.

Educational Research Service. (1985, September). *Educator opinion poll.* Arlington, VA: Author.

Gross, J. (1988). *Teachers on trial: Values, standards, and equity in judging conduct and competence.* Ithaca, NY: Cornell University, New York State School of Industrial and Labor Relations.

Guzzo, R., & Gannett, B. (1988). The nature of facilitators and inhibitors of effective task performance. In F. Schoorman and B. Schneider (Eds.), *Facilitating work effectiveness* (pp. 21–41). Lexington, MA: Lexington.

Hawley, R. (1982). *Assessing teacher performance.* Amherst, MA: Education Research Associates.

Hoenack, S., & Monk, D. (1990). Economic aspects of teacher evaluation. In J. Millman and L. Darling-Hammond (Eds.), *The new handbook of teacher evaluation* (pp. 390–402). Newbury Park, CA: Sage.

Iwanicki, E., & Rindone, D. (1995). Integrating professional development, teacher evaluation, and student learning: The evolution of teacher evaluation policy in Connecticut. In D. Duke (Ed.), *Teacher evaluation policy* (pp. 65–98). Albany: State University of New York Press.

Joint Committee on Standards for Educational Evaluation. (1988). *The personnel evaluation standards: How to assess systems for evaluating educators.* Newbury Park, CA: Sage.

Knapp, M. (1982, March). *Toward the study of teacher evaluation as an organizational process: A review of current research and practice.* Paper presented at the annual meeting of the American Educational Research Association, New York.

Lawler, E. (1973). *Motivation in work organizations.* Monterey, CA: Brooks/Cole.

Maglaras, T., & Lynch, D. (1988, October). Monitoring the curriculum: From plan to action. *Educational Leadership, 46,* 58–60.

McCarthy, M., & Cambron-McCabe, N. (1987). *Public school law: Teachers' and students' rights.* Boston: Allyn and Bacon.

McLaughlin, M. (1990). Embracing contraries: Implementing and sustaining teacher evaluation. In J. Millman and L. Darling-Hammond

(Eds.), *The new handbook of teacher evaluation* (pp. 403–415). Newbury Park, CA: Sage.

McNelly, T. A. (2002, December). Evaluations that ensure growth: Teacher portfolios. *Principal Leadership, 3,* 55–60.

Milkovich, G., & Newman, J. (1996). *Compensation* (5th ed.). Chicago: Irwin.

Natriello, G., & Dornbusch, S. (1980/1981). Pitfalls in the evaluation of teachers by principals. *Administrator's Notebook, 29,* 1–4.

Olebe, M., Jackson, A., & Danielson, C. (1999, May). Investing in beginning teachers—The California model. *Educational Leadership, 56,* 41–44.

Pfeifer, R. (1986). *Integrating teacher evaluation and staff development: An organizational approach.* Stanford, CA: Stanford University, Institute for Research on Educational Finance and Governance. (ERIC Document Reproduction Service No. ED 270506).

Southern Regional Education Board. (1991). *Teacher evaluation programs in SREB states.* Atlanta: Author.

Stevens, Larry J. (2001). *An administrative handbook.* Lanham, MD: Scarecrow Press.

Stronge, J., & Helm, V. (1991). *Evaluating professional support personnel in education.* Newbury Park, CA: Sage.

Tesch, S., Nyland, L., & Kernutt, D. (1987, April). Teacher evaluation—Shared power working. *Educational Leadership, 44,* 26–30.

Webb, L. (1983). Teacher evaluation. In S. Thomas, N. Cambron-McCabe, and M. McCarthy (Eds.), *Educators and the law* (pp. 69–80). Elmont, NY: Institute for School Law and Finance.

Weber, M. R. (2003, February). Coping with malcontents. *School administrator, 60*(2), 6–10.

Wise, A., Darling-Hammond, L., McLaughlin, M., & Bernstein, H. (1984). *Teacher evaluation: A study of effective practices.* Santa Monica, CA: Rand.

Wolf, K. (1996, March). Developing an effective teaching portfolio. *Educational Leadership, 53,* 34–37.

■ ■ ■ ■ ■

CHAPTER TEN

COMPENSATION AND REWARDS

Education is a labor-intensive enterprise. A larger share of school funds is spent to pay personnel than for any other purpose. Estimates of the proportion of school budgets allocated for personnel costs range from 60 to 90 percent. Personnel funds are expended in accordance with a compensation plan that, if well designed, can help schools achieve their strategic goals.

Compensation plans have three broad objectives—to attract, retain, and motivate qualified and competent employees (Cascio & Awad, 1981). It is desirable that a compensation plan be acceptable to taxpayers, who seek assurance that cost-effective compensation procedures are being followed, and to employees, who are concerned that compensation practices are orderly, fair, and consistent.

PLAN OF THE CHAPTER

Fair and adequate compensation are important issues in human resources management. Districts that offer competitive salaries and benefits are able to attract and hold well-qualified teachers, and equitable compensation plans help them to maintain employee morale and motivation. This chapter deals with the following topics: (1) sound compensation plans, (2) adequacy of teacher pay, (3) balance in teachers' salaries, (4) equity and the single salary schedule, (5) forms of incentive pay, (6) keeping costs under control, (7) administrators' salaries, and (8) constructing a salary schedule.

SOUND COMPENSATION PLANS

Sound compensation plans have six features. They are externally competitive, are internally equitable, are internally balanced, offer incentive, limit cost, and provide adequately for employees' needs (Cascio & Awad, 1981). These six features help achieve three organizational imperatives described by Katz (1973): attracting and retaining members, obtaining commitment, and motivating members to perform role-related behaviors and respond with innovative behavior when appropriate.

Competitiveness improves a district's ability to attract and retain workers; adequacy and balance are important for increasing employee commitment and retention; and equity and incentive help a district to motivate members to perform role-related tasks and to respond with innovative behavior. The sixth factor, cost, impinges on a district's ability to sustain a compensation program.

Competitive Salaries

The offered salary is an important factor influencing an individual's decision to accept or decline a job offer. Beginning teachers give more weight to salary than do more experienced teachers, who are likely also to consider fringe benefits in judging a job offer (Jacobson, 1989). A district's compensation is externally competitive when the district is able to compete with other employers for qualified applicants. If its salaries are not competitive, a district will have difficulty filling teaching vacancies with well-qualified applicants unless it offers other advantages such as a desirable location or well-regarded schools.

On the whole, teachers' salaries are relatively competitive when compared with the earnings of private sector workers. In 2001–2002, teachers in the United States earned on average more than $44,000 per year, compared to average annual earnings of about $36,000 for private sector employees. Beginning teachers earned an average of $30,700. However, teachers' salaries are low when teachers are compared to private sector employees with an equivalent amount of education. Moreover, teacher salaries have risen more slowly in recent years than the salaries of comparably educated professionals in other fields (www.aft.org./research/salary/home.htm).

Bringing teachers' salaries into line with those paid to other workers with equal education would be an expensive proposition. The American Association of School Administrators (1983b) estimated that beginning salaries for teachers would have to increase an average of 35 percent in order to attain the goal of making them competitive with the salaries of other professionals with similar levels of education. The increases required to reach that goal would have ranged from a low of 14.2 percent to a high of 58.5 percent in the 28 districts surveyed.

Some economists believe that teachers' salaries are high enough to attract an adequate supply, and one economist who has studied teachers' salaries concluded that about one-third of teachers are paid too much, and one-third are paid too little. The rest are presumably paid about right (Keller & Galley, 2003).

The salary increases won by teachers during the 1980s and 1990s moved teaching into a slightly more competitive position with respect to other occupations, but salaries for teachers continued to lag behind those of most fields that require a bachelor's degree. In 1990–91, college graduates with degrees in teaching were paid on average $10,000 less those individuals who majored in computer science and $6,100 less than persons with degrees in mathematics or physical science. However, teachers fared better in comparison with graduates holding degrees in biology, communications, and public affairs. Biology majors averaged annual salaries that were about $1,400 more than teachers, but individuals with degrees in communications or public affairs both earned slightly less, on average, than teachers (National Center for Education Statistics, 1993b).

Single Salary Schedules

It has been estimated that 99 percent of all teachers in the United States teach in districts that use single salary schedules (Murnane & Cohen, 1986). A single salary schedule uses only two factors in determining the salaries of all employees in each job classification: experience and level of education. Historically, the single salary plan is fairly young. The first use of the idea occurred in 1920, when Lincoln (Nebraska), Denver, and Sioux City (Iowa) put single salary schedules into effect. The idea spread rapidly; by 1927, 165 cities had adopted the plan (Morris, 1972).

Teachers' organizations pushed for the adoption of the single salary plan as a way of achieving a more professionalized teaching force. Supporters argued that the plan would encourage professional growth, contribute to a feeling of unity and satisfaction among teachers, equalize pay for men and women, increase tenure, attract better-quality teachers to elementary schools, and encourage teachers to teach at that level rather than aspire to teach in high school.

Critics suggested that the single salary plan was contrary to the law of supply and demand and that it was a "subterfuge" invented by administrators who wished to be freed of the burdensome task of rating teachers on merit. Those who were against the idea argued that elementary teachers did not need extensive educational preparation and that educational attainment in itself was not a criterion of teaching ability. Their bottom-line argument was that the cost of the single salary proposal was excessive (Morris, 1972).

Districts that use the single salary schedule sometimes provide a fixed dollar increment at each step. The increment represents a proportionally larger adjustment for teachers near the bottom of the scale as compared to those near the top. To provide step increments that are proportionally equal, many districts use indexed schedules in which the dollar amounts vary but the rate of increase is fixed.

In most districts with single salary schedules, regular increases are provided for the first 12 or 15 years a teacher is employed, although a recent survey by the American Federation of Teachers (1999) found that the number of steps in salary scales in the 100 largest city school districts in the United States ranged from 8 to 45. After a person reaches the top of the scale, longevity increases are granted about once every five years. Practically speaking, however, teachers in the United States reach the peak of their earning power within 15 years of entering the field. This is in contrast to most other occupations, in which salaries continue to rise throughout most of one's working life.

Since attrition is highest in the first few years after an individual is hired (Mark & Anderson, 1978), it would seem to make sense to provide proportionally larger raises to teachers near the low end of the scale and smaller increases to those at the top in order to hold teachers who might otherwise leave. However, the evidence for the effectiveness of such an approach is not strong. Jacobson (1987) found that in the two regions of New York state that he studied, proportionally larger increases in the middle of the scale were more strongly related to retention of teachers than were adjustments at either top or bottom.

Some economists argue that, because the salary curve for teachers is so steep, a disproportionate share of salary funds go to experienced teachers and, thus, are not available to attract younger, less experienced but more talented teachers. Those who express this opinion believe that there is relatively little difference in the effectiveness of a teacher with many years experience in the classroom and one who is new to the job. If one accepts the economists' premise, then it makes sense to pay higher salaries to beginning teachers and offer less lucrative rewards to more experienced individuals because the loss of experienced employees would not result in lower productivity. If experienced teachers are no more effective than beginners in the classroom, there is no justifiable reason for paying higher salaries based on experience (Ballou & Podgursky, 2002). Few educators would accept the proposition that experienced teachers are no more productive than those without experience, but they would probably agree that there is a point at which additional experience adds little in the way of increased productivity. The question is, at what point does that transition occur?

A salary schedule may be made more competitive by increasing salaries across the board or by providing targeted increases. If the district is losing experienced teachers, it may decide to provide targeted increases at the upper end of the salary schedule. On the other hand, if it is having problems attracting beginning teachers, the decision may be made to raise salaries at the bottom end of the schedule.

Another approach is to add more steps to the schedule. Experience increments might be scheduled for 20 rather than 15 years. Experience increments average about 4 percent per year (Bacharach, Lipsky, & Shedd, 1984), so adding 5 additional steps onto a 15-step scale, each providing a 4 percent increase, results in a top-of-the-scale compounded figure that is 21.7 percent higher than the 15-step maximum. However, as long as teachers' salaries lag behind those in other occupations, administrators will be under pressure to maintain or decrease the number of steps in the schedule rather than to increase them.

Critics claim that the single salary schedule lacks motivational power. None of the three motivational theories described in Chapter 6 would predict that the single salary schedule would be an effective motivator. Since the single salary schedule provides equal compensation for teachers with similar levels of experience and education without regard to effort, equity theory would regard it as demotivating for highly productive teachers.

Defenders of the single salary schedule acknowledge that it has weaknesses, but argue that there is no alternative approach that does not have even more problems. It is unlikely that the single salary schedule will disappear. Its widespread use and strong appeal to teachers and many administrators militate against its being replaced. However, we can expect to see new models of teacher compensation being adopted by school districts.

Reasons for Low Salaries

To what can the disparity between teachers' salaries and the salaries of workers in other occupations with comparable educational requirements be attributed? In part, the decline in teachers' salaries during the 1970s was the market's response to an oversupply of teachers. However, even during periods of short supply, teachers make relatively lower salaries than members of most other comparable occupations.

Teachers, of course, work fewer days per year than full-time employees in most other fields. They are on the job between 182 and 190 days per year (Educational Research Service, 1985), compared to about 225 days per year for most other workers—a difference of about 17 percent. But teachers salaries' appear to be lower than expected, even when this difference is taken into account.

One factor that appears to contribute to low salaries in teaching is the composition of the teaching force. Bird (1985) used Census Bureau data to compare salaries of teachers to those of persons with similar levels of education employed outside of teaching. Mean income from wages for the nonteaching group was 39 percent higher than teachers received. The nonteaching group had somewhat less education (16.3 years compared to 17.7 years) but included more males (60.2 percent versus 20.0 percent) and more whites (88.6 percent versus 79.0 percent).

On an annualized basis, teachers did about as well as a nonteaching group of workers with characteristics similar to those found in teaching, but they did less well than nonteachers with different demographic characteristics. Bird's conclusion was that sex discrimination accounted for the lower salaries in teaching and concluded that "the challenge facing education policymakers today is to seek a new teacher pay comparability strategy to fit a market in which the results of a history of sex discrimination may be disappearing" (Bird, 1985).

ADEQUACY OF TEACHER PAY

Adequacy refers to whether employees receive sufficient pay and benefits to permit them to maintain a decent standard of living. Workers whose salaries are too low to permit them to afford a middle-class lifestyle often take second jobs in order to supplement their earnings. This practice, called *moonlighting,* is more common among teachers than members of other occupations. About one-fourth of teachers in public schools earn income from a second, nonteaching job, and one-third earn money from extra-duty assignments for the school system, including coaching athletic teams or sponsoring student clubs. Teachers earned an average of $4,400 from nonteaching jobs and $1,900 from school-related extra-duty assignments in the 1990–91 school year (National Center for Education Statistics, 1993a).

There has been relatively little research on the extent of moonlighting among teachers or of its effects on the individual's attitudes toward the primary job. In one of the few studies of this phenomenon, researchers found that about 13 percent of the 329 Texas teachers they surveyed held second jobs after school or on weekends and holidays. They worked nearly 13 hours a week and earned slightly more than $3,500 a year at the second job. About 31 percent of the respondents also worked during the summer breaks, with average earnings of about $1,900. Teachers who moonlighted year-round thus increased their income by about $5,400 on average (Henderson & Henderson, 1986).

The most common type of outside employment among teachers in the Texas study was sales, reported by 35 percent of respondents. Next in frequency of mention were school-related work (24 percent) and music (15 percent).

Cross-National Comparisons

How do U.S. teachers fare economically in comparison with their counterparts in other parts of the world? One study compared the economic situations of teachers in the United States and Japan (Barro & Lee, 1986). The findings showed that beginning teachers in Japan make 20 to 25 percent less than the average beginning teachers in U.S. schools, but that the lower starting salaries are balanced by long-term gains.

A Japanese teacher with the equivalent of a bachelor's degree who remains in teaching will eventually earn three times the beginning salary, compared to two times or less in most school districts in the United States. The reason for this substantial difference in the long-term rewards of teaching in the two systems has to do with the "topping out" of teachers' salaries. After about 15 years, U.S. teachers no longer qualify for annual increments, but Japanese teachers continue to receive increases each year until retirement.

BALANCE IN TEACHERS' SALARIES

Although salaries are the most visible part of personnel costs and the item that employees most often consider in deciding whether to accept a job offer, they are only part of the total compensation package. Fringe benefits are an important part of the compensation picture. Benefits include immediate and deferred payments employees are entitled to receive by virtue of working in a particular organization. The best known benefits are various kinds of leave, medical and hospital insurance, and retirement contributions.

Three types of benefits are common in school districts:

1. *Collateral benefits:* These are direct and indirect forms of compensation that are received without expenditure of additional effort. Examples are sick leave, medical insurance, and retirement contributions. More than 95 percent of public schools in the United States offered medical insurance to teachers in 1990, retirement benefits were available to teachers in 99 percent of the schools, and dental insurance was offered by 67 percent of the schools (National Center for Education Statistics, 1993a).

2. *Nonsalary payments:* These are supplementary payments made to individuals who perform duties above and beyond their regular assignments. Coaching and sponsoring various activity groups are the most common examples of nonsalary payments. Data from the National Center for Education Statistics (1993a) showed that public school teachers who performed extra-duty assignments earned $1,940, on average, during the 1990–91 school year.

3. *Noneconomic benefits:* This category includes any features of a job that make it more attractive, whether or not the employer thinks of them as benefits. Intrinsic rewards are included here. Examples of noneconomic benefits are small class size, duty-free lunch, a planning period, and motivated students.

The cost of fringe benefits for workers in the private sector has increased dramatically. In 1959, for example, benefit costs for employees averaged less than 25 percent of the total payroll for industrial firms in the United States, but by 1993, that figure had increased to more than 40 percent (Milkovich & Newman, 1996). Educational personnel typically receive fewer fringe benefits than employees in the business world. (Geisert & Lieberman [1994, p. 227], however, claim that fringe benefits received by teachers are 10 to 20 percent higher than for workers in other fields.)

One reason for the increase in the cost of fringe benefits has been the surge in the cost of health care. In Minnesota schools between 1986 and 1991, the cost of medical insurance for professional staff members rose 58 percent, almost four times the rate of increase in salaries in that state over the same period (How Is Minnesota . . . ,1993).

In certain situations, increasing fringe benefits may be an alternative to raising salaries. For employees who would like to reduce their income tax, an increase in fringe benefits valued at $1,000 may be more attractive than a pay increase of that amount, since taxes on fringe benefits may be deferred or taxed at a lower rate than a salary increase. Fringe benefits are also attractive because they offer services that could not be purchased as cheaply by individuals. Group medical insurance is a good example. Although premiums for group plans are not cheap, they cost considerably less than individuals would pay for comparable coverage. Surprisingly, employees are often poorly informed about the types and value of the fringe benefits they receive, and when they are offered a job, few of them investigate fringe benefits before deciding whether to accept. Exhibit 10.1 lists examples of fringe

■ ■ ■ ■ ■

EXHIBIT 10.1

EXAMPLES OF EMPLOYEE BENEFITS GROUPED BY TYPE

BENEFIT	BENEFICIARY	TYPE
Health insurance*	Employee and family	Collateral
Dental insurance*	Employee and family	Collateral
Term life insurance	Designated	Collateral
Sick leave	Employee	Collateral
Retirement contribution*	Employee	Collateral
Tax sheltered annuity*	Employee	Collateral
Leaves of absence		Collateral
Family leave	Employee and family	
Maternity leave	Employee	
Illness	Employee and family	
Military service	Employee	
Sabbatical	Employee	Noneconomic
Tenure	Employee	Noneconomic
Supplemental income	Employee	Nonsalary payment
Coach, club sponsor, summer school instructor, etc.		
Holidays and vacations	Employee	Collateral
Automatic deduction for professional dues	Employee	Collateral
Travel to professional meetings	Employee	Collateral

*Employee may be required to share cost.

benefits to which school employees may be entitled. The exhibit classifies benefits into three categories: collateral, noneconomic, and nonsalary payments.

EQUITY AND THE SINGLE SALARY SCHEDULE

The Equal Pay Act of 1963 requires employers to refrain from discriminating against female employees by paying them less than males are paid for performing the same or similar jobs. Few cases involving teachers have been decided by the courts under the Equal Pay Act, since teachers' salaries are commonly assumed to be gender neutral. However, a study of teachers' salaries found that female teachers in public high schools school earned $1,134 less, on average, than their male counterparts. The discrepancy in salaries of female and male teachers was even greater in private high schools.

    The disparity persisted even when differences in educational attainment, experience, and teaching field were taken into account. The researchers concluded that the differences were the result of male teachers receiving more credit for previous teaching experience than females (Bradley, 1989).

In the few cases involving charges of unequal pay for female teachers under the Equal Pay Act, courts have held that schools may not pay female coaches less than male coaches for assignments that involve similar levels of effort. In one case, a plan to provide a salary supplement for male heads of household was struck down (McCarthy, 1983).

Since the passage of the Equal Pay Act, some progress has been made in closing the gap between men's and women's incomes, but discrepancies remain. Women who work in occupations that are dominated by women, including teaching, nursing, and secretarial work, generally earn less than men. However, a female employee has no redress under the Equal Pay Act unless her employer pays a male more to do a similar job.

Aside from adequacy, employees value equity more highly than any other feature of compensation. Opposition of teachers to merit pay is based on a fear of potential inequity. There is no widely accepted objective measure of equity, since people's perceptions vary depending on their definitions of their own and others' contributions and rewards. Moreover, objective judgments of equity are difficult when individuals have access to incomplete information about an organization's compensation policy and practices.

FORMS OF INCENTIVE PAY

Employers use a variety of compensation plans designed to increase employee motivation and commitment or to strengthen the relationship of pay to performance. Business corporations use compensation to help them achieve certain strategic objectives. Pay-for-performance plans, group and individual incentive plans, profit sharing, and various types of bonuses are widely used by private employers.

The field of education has been more cautious than the private sector about adopting alternative pay arrangements. The forms of alternative compensation used most widely in schools are pay for performance, incentive pay, and career ladders. These plans are described in detail here.

Taxpayers are in favor of providing differentiated pay for teachers. In their report entitled *Time for Results*, the National Governors Association recommended developing compensation plans that would recognize differences in function, competence, and performance of teachers (Alexander, 1986).

Pay for Performance

Pay for performance, also known as merit pay, rewards individuals on the basis of their performance on the job and avoids relying on principals' ratings of teachers.

In Denver, the school board and teachers' union developed and implemented a plan to award bonuses of up to $1500 to teachers whose students reach or surpass specified achievement goals (Gorman, 2001). Proponents of pay for performance plans believe that tying salaries directly to student achievement will result in greater teacher effort and, ultimately, increased learning.

Several questions have been raised about the psychological assumptions on which pay for performance plans are based. It is not clear, for example, whether people work harder when they have the opportunity to earn a monetary reward, which advocates of pay for performance maintain, or if the reward simply has the effect of making goals more salient to workers, as goal-setting theory suggests. If the latter is true, then the bonus teachers receive for reaching student achievement goals will have little effect on teacher effort, and the same results could be obtained by making learning goals clearer and stressing them more forcefully.

A second question is whether offering rewards for performing a task that an individual finds inherently interesting will lead to a reduction in the individual's satisfaction (Deci, 1972). For example, if you enjoy playing chess for the mental challenge it presents, you are likely to find that your interest wanes once someone starts paying you for each game you win. The application to teaching is straight-forward. Presumably teachers who are effective enjoy what they do and do it well, but when a reward is introduced for student achievement, the teachers' interest in the work itself is likely to drop.

Still another question is whether salary is the most highly motivating reward available for teachers. Some researchers have concluded that at least some teachers prefer other rewards over salary bonuses. A small study that looked at teachers' preferred rewards found that tuition grants, time off to attend conferences, the opportunity to work with student teachers, and money for purchasing instructional materials were all preferred over salary bonuses by a majority of teachers in the sample (Kasten, 1984). Because only 26 teachers were surveyed by Kasten, the results cannot be generalized to all teachers, but further study is needed to determine which rewards are most highly valued by teachers.

Proponents believe that pay for performance motivates teachers to improve their teaching practices and that, as a result, students benefit. The available research offers little evidence to support that conclusion, but some studies have suggested that merit pay does influence other work-related behaviors, including recruitment, attendance, and retention (Jacobson, 1996).

Objections to pay for performance for teachers focus on the subjective nature of teacher evaluation and the divisive nature of the competitive motives merit pay is believed to arouse. Since there are few truly objective measures of effective teaching performance, merit pay plans usually rely on principals' judgments regarding which teachers deserve merit raises. This requires trust on the part of teachers in the principal's ability to fairly and accurately rate their performance. Some teachers lack confidence that principals can be trusted to administer merit pay plans equitably, but most administrators themselves believe they are capable of doing so.

Incentive Pay

Incentive pay is a salary supplement or bonus paid to teachers who fulfill specified conditions established by the district to help it attain certain goals or solve particular problems (American Association of School Administrators, 1983a). Examples include payments to teachers who are willing to teach in schools with high concentrations of educationally disadvantaged children or who are in fields with teacher scarcity, such as special education, mathematics, and science. Incentive pay is also given by some districts to teachers who attain certain educational or professional growth objectives. The amount of these awards varies. For teaching in a difficult school, a teacher may receive a bonus of $1,500 to $2,000 per year, and for achieving professional growth objectives, the payment is often equivalent to the cost of tuition for a graduate college course.

Houston Independent School District successfully used an incentive plan to recruit teachers with scarce subject specialties. The Houston plan paid salary supplements ranging from $600 to $1,000 per year for teachers of mathematics, science, bilingual classes, and special education.

Career Ladders

The best-known example of a career ladder is that adopted statewide in Tennessee in 1984. That plan provides five levels of teaching competence: Probationary, Apprentice, and Career Levels I, II, and III. Teachers on the top three rungs of the ladder earn from $1,000 to $7,000 per year in salary supplements (Thornton, 1986). Advancement in the Tennessee plan is based on performance and experience. Teachers move from the Probationary to the Apprentice stage in one year and remain at that level for three years. A minimum of five years of experience at Career Levels I and II is required before a teacher can advance to the next higher step. All promotions on the ladder require demonstration of satisfactory performance and a review of performance conducted by assessment teams that consist of teachers, principals, and supervisors (Thornton, 1986).

Most career ladder plans, including the one in Tennessee, assign additional responsibilities to teachers as they advance up the ladder. These duties may include supervising other teachers or planning and leading curriculum or staff development activities.

Advantages and Disadvantages

All compensation plans have both advantages and disadvantages. Single salary schedules have the advantage of being easily administered and acceptable to most teachers. These plans also have one major weakness: They fail to attract and hold enough high-quality teachers.

Pay for performance plans have three potential advantages. By rewarding employees who have above-average productivity, they help attract quality employees, provide an incentive for greater effort by current employees, and reduce the level of attrition among more productive employees (Bishop, 1986).

However, any plan that bases compensation on performance evaluation is likely to encounter problems. It is expensive to obtain data on worker productivity, and the information that is obtained is often low in reliability. Even in industry, supervisory ratings are often used to assess productivity, and research shows that those ratings are not very reliable. An added complication of the use of pay for performance for teachers is the evidence that teacher performance is not consistent over time. Teachers who achieve above-average learning gains with their students one year may be average or even below average the next.

Aside from the technical difficulties involved in implementing pay for performance, there are questions about the soundness of the psychological assumptions on which it is based. Some researchers (Deci, 1972) have found that activities that are intrinsically motivating—that is, those that are performed only for the pleasure of performing them—lose some of their intrinsic motivation if a reward is offered for performing them. Moreover, the research has shown that individuals who are given tangible rewards for engaging in activities that are intrinsically motivating engage in the activities less often after they are rewarded. Some educators interpret these findings to mean that teachers who derive pleasure from teaching may experience less satisfaction from it when pay for performance is implemented, and hence may lose interest in teaching well.

Nonsalary rewards may have greater motivational potential for teachers than salary bonuses, according to a study of teachers' preferences of performance rewards (Kasten, 1984). That study involved 26 teachers, 15 of whom reported no interest in merit pay. "Strong interest" in tuition grants was reported by 20 of the teachers, and 21 were strongly interested in the opportunity to have time off to attend conferences. The opportunity to work with student teachers was also of strong interest to 20 of the teachers, and 21 reported a strong interest in receiving money to be spent on classroom enrichment.

One of the problems with pay for performance is that many more employees believe they should receive awards than qualify for them. A study of teachers' ratings of themselves and their colleagues (Hoogeveen & Gutkin, 1986) found that teachers rated themselves higher than they rated their peers and that their self-ratings were higher even than the average ratings given all teachers by the principal.

A question investigated by Hoogeveen and Gutkin (1986) had to do with whether teachers agree on the identity of superior performers. In all three of the small elementary schools involved in the study, one teacher was nominated by more than one-half of his or her colleagues as deserving a merit bonus. This finding suggests that there is a reasonably high degree of consensus in some faculties. Whether similar results would be obtained in larger elementary schools or in high schools, however, is not known.

Career ladders are meant to provide opportunities for teachers to move through a series of positions of expanding responsibility, greater task variety, and increasingly attractive monetary rewards. They are designed for the purpose of attracting and retaining able teachers. However, career ladders, like pay for performance, are more expensive to operate than single salary schedules and, if not adequately funded, can result in greater competition and less cooperation among teachers. Moreover, if advancement on a career ladder is based on the results of performance evaluation, teachers are likely to experience the same concerns that they report for merit pay (Timar, 1992).

Incentive pay has the advantage of being effective in attracting better quality applicants for positions that are normally difficult to fill. Incentive pay has no effect on teacher performance, except indirectly, and it is more costly than the single salary schedule (although potentially less expensive than merit pay or career ladders).

KEEPING COSTS UNDER CONTROL

A sound compensation plan must provide for careful monitoring of compensation costs in order to ensure that all monies are expended legally and that they yield the maximum possible benefits for students. If salaries are excessive given local market conditions, the district will be paying more than it should for the services it receives, and if salaries are too low the most highly qualified prospects will be lost to other districts and the quality of services received for the dollars spent will be diminished. Merit pay and pay for performance can substantially increase the cost of personnel salaries in a school district, and the additional cost of such plans cannot always be projected accurately.

In recent years a number of school districts have discovered that they owe back pay to classified employees for overtime work. Some districts have had to pay millions of dollars to employees who worked more than 40 hours a week as a result of claims brought under the Fair Labor Standards Act (FLSA). Human resources managers need to be familiar with provisions of this legislation, which governs conditions of work and employee compensation. Districts that do not pay classified employees for overtime work may be subject to legal action under FLSA and, if found in violation, will have to pay a lump sum to the employees who have accumulated overtime (Cavanagh, 2003; Cook, 2003).

Under the law, classified employees who volunteer to serve in positions such as coach, assistant coach, or yearbook sponsor may qualify for overtime pay if they perform these services on an ongoing basis. Districts that do not have contracts with classified employees will need to take action to ensure that they will not be liable for a substantial one-time payout if these employees decide to go to court over the issue of back pay.

ADMINISTRATORS' SALARIES

Table 10.1 shows the average salaries for central office and school level administrators in large districts (enrollments of 25,000 or more) and small districts (enrollments between 2500 and 10,000) in 2002–2003. It also shows the ratio of salaries

TABLE 10.1   Average Salaries of Selected Administrators by District Size

STAFF POSITION	LARGE DISTRICTS	SMALL DISTRICTS	RATIO
Superintendent	$170,024	$121,853	1.40:1
Assistant Superintendent	107,469	96,288	1.12:1
Director of Finance & Business	95,986	80,648	1.19:1
Director of Instructional Services	94,133	81,086	1.16:1
Director of Staff Personnel Services	93,090	81,697	1.14:1
Director of Technology	94,413	69,751	1.35:1
Principals:			
Elementary	79,138	77,429	1.02:1
Junior High/Middle	83,274	83,242	1.00:1
Senior High	91,063	90,258	1.01:1
Assistant principals:			
Elementary	63,271	63,497	1.00:1
Junior High/Middle	67,115	68,730	.98:1
Senior High	70,543	72,393	.97:1

Note: Large districts are those with enrollments of 25,000 or more students; small districts enroll between 2500 and 10,000 students.

Source: Salaries Paid Professional Personnel in Public Schools, 1998–99. Arlington, VA: Educational Research Service, 2003. Reprinted by permission.

paid by large districts to those paid by small districts. Superintendents of large districts earn almost $50,000 per year more on average than the superintendents of small districts, and large district central office personnel in general earn more than their small district counterparts. However, the salaries of principals and assistant principals in the two sizes of districts are very similar.

Pay for performance for administrators is more common than for teachers. A 1978 study found that 15.3 percent of school districts offered such pay for administrators, compared to only 4 percent with similar plans for teachers (Kienapfel, 1984). At least one state has adopted a statewide career ladder plan for administrators and supervisors (North Carolina Department of Public Instruction, 1984). The North Carolina plan consists of four steps, beginning with Provisional status and advancing through Career Statuses I, II, and III.

An individual must spend a minimum of two years at each step before being eligible to advance to the next higher level. Advancement is based on satisfactory performance and demonstrated professional growth, including completion of continuing education credits appropriate for the position and related to the needs of the individual (Kienapfel, 1984). Advancement from one career status level to the next results in a salary increase of 10 percent in addition to the normal 5 percent step increment.

Some districts have abolished salary schedules for principals and offer only minimum and maximum salaries. Salaries are determined individually, based on several factors such as the size of the school served and the quality of the individual's performance.

CONSTRUCTING A SALARY SCHEDULE

Salary schedules are usually developed by firms that specialize in employee compensation. The task is one that requires a considerable amount of expertise and a great deal of data. The first decision to be made in developing a salary schedule is the number of grades or levels to be included. Henderson (1985) defined *pay grades* as convenient groupings of a wide variety of jobs that are similar in difficulty and level of responsibility but with little else in common. The number of grades to be incorporated into a schedule varies depending on the number of employee specialties and the extent to which the district administration wishes to be able to make small distinctions in compensation.

Each grade is subdivided into 10 to 15 steps to provide for differences in experience and level of educational attainment. The difference between the lowest step in adjacent grades in school district salary schedules typically ranges from 2.5 to 4 percent, and there is obviously considerable overlap across grades.

The procedure used to establish salaries for dissimilar jobs is *job evaluation* (Landy, 1985). A job evaluation involves these steps:

1. Select the jobs to be evaluated and choose the evaluation factors. The factors should be skills or abilities that are required to varying degrees in all of the positions and for which salary differences can be justified. An example of a factor that is frequently used is education; people who hold jobs requiring higher levels of education receive higher salaries than those whose jobs require less education, other things being equal.

2. Collect information about the positions from a variety of sources, including interviews, job descriptions, and observations.

3. Using information collected in step 2, rate the jobs being evaluated by assigning points for each criterion. Sum the points to obtain a total for each position. This activity is normally carried out independently by members of a committee who compare their ratings after they are completed and discuss differences until a consensus is reached.

4. Rank the positions by point totals agreed upon in step 3. Select a few key positions and assign salaries to those by investigating salaries for similar positions in nearby districts.

5. Assign salaries to the remainder of the positions by comparing the point totals for those positions to the point totals for the key positions.

Job evaluation should result in a salary schedule that is internally consistent and externally competitive. It is necessary to repeat the procedure about every 10 years because jobs change over time and their relative importance to the district shifts. As duties evolve and new specialties emerge, some positions must be moved up or down on the scale to preserve internal competitiveness.

SUMMARY

A well-designed compensation plan should help a district to accomplish the objectives of attracting and holding employees and helping employees engage in reliable task-related behavior and, when appropriate, to be spontaneous and innovative in carrying out a job. Six features of a sound compensation plan are competitiveness, adequacy, balance, equity, incentive, and reasonable cost. A competitive salary structure enables an organization to attract employees; adequacy and balance help to hold them; and equity and incentive assist in motivating employees to higher productivity. Reasonable cost permits the organization to continue to offer an attractive compensation package to its employees.

Most school districts in the United States use single salary schedules, in which teachers are paid on the basis of education and experience. Three other approaches to teacher compensation are being tested in some districts. Merit pay rewards teachers who are judged above average in effectiveness; career ladders establish steps in which teachers may advance in both income and prestige; and incentive pay involves salary supplements for teachers who possess scarce skills or fulfill specific contractual requirements such as accepting a difficult teaching assignment. All of these plans have advantages and disadvantages that should be considered before a decision is made to implement one or more of them.

Job evaluation is a procedure by which a school district equates jobs with different content for purposes of compensation. It is used to eliminate inequities in salaries and to ensure that all salaries are commensurate with level of responsibility.

SUGGESTED ACTIVITIES

1. In trying construct a salary schedule that is externally competitive, a school district must sometimes sacrifice internal equity. Discuss the relative importance of these two features. Under what conditions is it advisable to increase external competitiveness at the cost of internal equity? What problems may arise as a result?

2. The argument is sometimes made that dollars spent increasing beginning salaries have a bigger payoff for a school district than those spent on raises for experienced teachers. Discuss the merits of that argument and cite reasons why you believe it is or is not true. How do you explain research showing that increases in the middle of the salary schedule have more impact on retention than those at the lower or upper ends?

3. Adding additional steps to existing salary schedules has been proposed as a way to make teaching more competitive with other occupations. However, that idea has

little support among teachers. Why do you think teachers do not favor adding steps?

4. A study cited in this chapter showed that some school personnel hold two jobs during the academic year. What are the factors that contribute to teachers and other employees working at two jobs? What is the likely effect of a second job on teachers' effectiveness? What policy should districts adopt with regard to second jobs?

5. Read Case Study IV and answer the questions.

ONLINE RESOURCES

American Federation of Teachers (www.aft.org/research/salary/home.htm)

The AFT conducts salary surveys annually and publishes detailed results on its website. The surveys compare salaries paid beginning and experienced teachers by state and show the amount of increase in recent years.

Consortium for Policy Research in Education (www.wcer.wisc.edu/cpre/tcomp/)

This site describes research on teacher compensation being conducted by CPRE at the University of Wisconsin-Madison. The Center publishes an online newsletter that seeks to facilitate communication among educators who are interested in issues related to teacher compensation.

Joint Task Force on Teacher Compensation (http://denverteachercompensation.org)

A plan developed jointly by Denver Public Schools and the Denver Classroom Teachers Association bases teachers' salaries on four components: skills and knowledge, professional evaluation, market incentives, and student growth.

Salary Expert (www.salaryexpert.com)

This site lists average salaries of teachers (kindergarten, primary, and secondary) and teacher aides for cities in the United States. It also shows average national salary and fringe benefits. This is a useful source of information for comparing salaries of competing districts.

REFERENCES

Alexander, L. (1986). Time for results: An overview. *Phi Delta Kappan, 68,* 202–204.

American Association of School Administrators. (1983). *Some points to consider when you discuss merit pay.* Arlington, VA: Author.

American Federation of Teachers, Department of Research. (1999). *Survey and analysis of teacher salary trends 1999.* Available online: www.aft.org/research/survey99/tables.

Bacharach, S., Lipsky, D., & Shedd, J. (1984). *Paying for better teaching: Merit pay and its alterna-* *tives.* Ithaca, NY: Organizational Analysis and Practice.

Ballou, D., & Podgursky, M. (2002, Fall). Returns to seniority among public school teachers. *Journal of Human Resources, 37,* 892–912.

Barro, S., & Lee, J. W. (1986). *A comparison of teachers' salaries in Japan and the U.S.* (ERIC Document Reproduction Service No. ED 273630).

Bird, R. E. (1985). *An analysis of the comparability of public school teacher salaries to earning opportunities in other occupations.* Research Triangle

Park, NC: Southeastern Regional Council for Educational Improvement. (ERIC Document Reproduction Service No. ED 256070).

Bradley, A. (1989, December 13). New study finds a gender gap in teachers' salaries. *Education Week*, pp. 1, 12.

Cascio, W., & Awad, E. (1981). *Human resources management: An information systems approach.* Reston, VA: Reston Publishing.

Cavanagh, S. (2003, September 17). Overtime debate puts old problem back in spotlight. *Education Week*, pp. 1, 18.

Cook, G. (2003, July). Overtime overdue. *American School Board Journal, 190*, 12–15.

Deci, E. (1972). The effects of contingent and non-contingent rewards on intrinsic motivation. *Organizational Behavior and Human Performance, 8*, 217–220.

Educational Research Service. (1983). *Merit pay plans for teachers: Status and descriptions.* Arlington, VA: Author.

Educational Research Service. (1985). *Scheduled salaries for professional personnel in public schools, 1984–85.* Arlington, VA: Author.

Educational Research Service. (1999). *Salaries paid professional personnel in public schools, 1998–99.* Part 2. Arlington, VA: Author.

Geisert, G., & Lieberman, M. (1994). *Teacher union bargaining: Practice and policy.* Chicago: Precept.

Gorman, S. (2001). How teachers should be evaluated. In W. Evers, L. Izumi, and P. Riley, *School reform: The critical issues* (pp. 198–202). Stanford, CA: Hoover Institution Press.

Henderson, R. (1985). *Compensation management* (4th ed.). Reston, VA: Reston Publishing.

Henderson, D., & Henderson, K. (1986). *Moonlighting, salary, and morale: The Texas teachers' story.* (ERIC Document Reproduction Service No. ED 269374).

Hoogeveen, K., & Gutkin, T. (1986). Collegial ratings among school personnel: An empirical examination of the merit pay concept. *American Educational Research Journal, 23*, 375–381.

How is Minnesota spending its tax dollars? (1993). St. Paul, MN: Office of the State Auditor.

Jacobson, S. (1987). *The distribution of salary increments and its effect on teacher retention.* Paper presented at the annual meeting of the American Educational Research Association, Washington, DC.

Jacobson, S. (1989). Change in entry-level salaries and its effect on teacher recruitment. *Journal of Education Finance, 14*, 449–465.

Jacobson, S. (1996). Monetary incentives and the reform of teacher compensation: A persistent organizational dilemma. In S. Jacobson, E. Hickcox, and R. E. Stevenson (Eds.), *School administration: Persistent dilemmas in preparation and practice* (pp. 89–100). Westport, CT: Praeger.

Kasten, K. (1984, Summer). The efficacy of institutionally dispensed rewards in elementary school teaching. *Journal of Research and Development in Education, 17*, 1–13.

Katz, D. (1973). The motivational basis of organizational behavior. In M. Milstein and J. Belasco (Eds.), *Educational administration and the behavioral sciences: A systems perspective* (pp. 319–346). Boston: Allyn and Bacon.

Keller, B., & Galley, M. (2003, May 28). Economists: Scrap single salary schedule for teachers. *Education Week*, p. 12.

Kienapfel, B. (1984). *Merit pay for school administrators: A procedural guide.* Arlington, VA: Educational Research Service.

Kohn, A. (2003, September 17). The folly of merit pay. *Education Week*, pp. 44, 31.

Landy, F. (1985). *Psychology of work behavior.* Homewood, IL: Dorsey

Mark, J., & Anderson, B. (1978). Teacher survival rates: A current look. *American Educational Research Journal, 15*, 379–383.

McCarthy, M. (1983). Discrimination in employment. In J. Beckham and P Zirkel (Eds.), *Legal issues in public school employment* (pp. 22–54). Bloomington, IN: Phi Delta Kappa.

Milkovich, G., & Newman, J. (1996). *Compensation.* Chicago: Irwin.

Morris, L. (1972). *The single salary schedule: An analysis and evaluation.* New York: AMS Press. (Original work published 1930).

Murnane, R., & Cohen, D. (1986). Merit pay and the evaluation problem: Why most merit pay plans fail and a few survive. *Harvard Educational Review, 56*, 1–17.

National Center for Education Statistics. (1993a). *Schools and staffing in the United States: A statistical profile, 1990–91.* Washington, DC: U.S. Department of Education.

National Center for Education Statistics. (1993b, March). Teacher salaries—Are they competitive? *Issue Brief*, pp. 1–2.

North Carolina Department of Public Instruction. (1984). *North Carolina career development plan for administrators, supervisors and other certified personnel.* Raleigh: Author.

Thornton, R. (1986). Teacher merit pay: An analysis of the issues. In R. Thornton and J. Aronson (Eds.), *Forging new relationships among business, labor and government* (pp. 179–199). Greenwich, CT: JAI Press.

Timar, T. (1992). Incentive pay for teachers and school reform. In L. Frase (Ed.), *Teacher compensation and motivation* (pp. 27–60). Lancaster, PA: Technomic.

CHAPTER ELEVEN

CREATING PRODUCTIVE WORK ENVIRONMENTS

"In fundamental ways, the U.S. educational system is structured to guarantee the failure of teachers" (McLaughlin, Pfeifer, Swanson-Owens, & Yee, 1986). That indictment was not written by a disgruntled teacher. It was authored by four educational researchers in one of the nation's leading universities, who reached that conclusion after interviewing 85 teachers about the conditions of their work. Despite evidence that the charge is not true in many schools, it is difficult to deny that in too many cases it accurately describes reality.

Why do many people find psychological success in their work so elusive? To what extent are structural conditions in schools responsible for the sense of frustration and defeat that teachers and members of support staffs experience? What can administrators do to make schools more conducive to success? These are questions that are addressed in this chapter.

PLAN OF THE CHAPTER

Chapter 6 described three theories of employee motivation and their effect on human performance. However, working conditions in some schools are such that even motivated employees are unable to achieve maximum productivity. This chapter examines how environments in schools facilitate or inhibit employee productivity and it suggests ways of creating more productive work environments. The chapter considers four topics: (1) psychological success and work environments, (2) qualities of productive work environments, (3) teacher stress and burnout, and (4) employee assistance programs in schools.

PSYCHOLOGICAL SUCCESS AND WORK ENVIRONMENTS

All human beings strive to experience psychological success. One way by which they are able to do that is by performing competently in some personally valued task (Hall & Schneider, 1973). Teachers as well as students gain self-esteem when they believe they are performing capably a task that they value, and they experience satisfaction from the feeling that they are using their abilities appropriately and effectively (McLaughlin et al., 1986).

The environments in which people work may either increase or decrease the likelihood that they will experience psychological success. When conditions in the work environment prevent them from meeting their expectations, disappointment and frustration follow. Self-esteem suffers and the individual withdraws emotionally and perhaps physically by leaving the organization (Hall & Schneider, 1973). If the employee is not able to change jobs, continued frustration produces stress that may eventually lead to job burnout.

Unfortunately, the work environment in some schools does little to help employees experience psychological success. Surveys have shown that teachers believe that working conditions in schools limit their effectiveness and contribute to feelings of frustration (Corcoran, 1990).

Among the conditions about which teachers have expressed most concern in these surveys are low salaries and limited opportunities for advancement; heavy workloads; limited contacts with colleagues; shortages of materials and supplies for teaching; limited input into school decisions; lack of support from administrators; unfair or unhelpful evaluation practices; unavailability of stimulating professional development opportunities; run-down or outdated facilities; and lack of respect from administrators, students, and parents (Corcoran, 1990). Similar concerns are expressed by other school employees, including counselors, aides, nurses, and secretaries. Many of the conditions that limit employee productivity in schools are so common that they are taken for granted as characteristic of these occupations.

Some conditions found in schools prevent employees from doing their best work, whereas others simply make it more difficult to do a good job. Many teachers manage to be effective in spite of large classes by taking work home on evenings and weekends, and they overcome the lack of materials and supplies by buying them from their own funds. Other employees cannot solve their problems as easily, however. A counselor who is assigned to an office in which his or her conversations with students can be overheard by others is unable to conduct confidential counseling sessions with students, and a teacher who cannot be confident of receiving support from the principal must avoid teaching topics that offend sensitive parents.

Fortunately, the prospects for creating and sustaining productive work environments in schools have improved as our knowledge of the factors that contribute to employees' feelings of psychological success have increased. Based on recent research, we can identify elements of the work setting that employees rank as most important, and it should come as no surprise that some of these are factors about which teachers expressed concern. The elements identified by employees as most important were having a good relationship with one's supervisor; being treated as an important person; receiving adequate and fair compensation; working in a safe, healthy, and stress-free environment; having a job that is socially relevant; and having opportunities for growth and development (Bruce & Blackburn, 1992). Other job factors to which employees attach importance are good relationships with co-workers, having a job with variety, being involved and informed, and being able to maintain a balance between work and family responsibilities (Bruce & Blackburn, 1992).

School administrators, in general, and personnel administrators, in particular, need to find ways to create more productive working environments in schools. Although it may be true that administrators have little or no control over some conditions that cause psychological stress for employees, they are able to influence others.

QUALITIES OF PRODUCTIVE WORK ENVIRONMENTS

Productive work environments are those that enable employees to perform their jobs effectively and to experience psychological success while doing it. These environments generally have seven characteristics:

1. Continuous learning culture
2. Supportive administrative leadership
3. Opportunity to work collaboratively with others
4. Mutual respect among employees and managers
5. Opportunity to use one's knowledge and skill and to receive feedback on one's performance
6. Comfortable, attractive, and well-equipped physical space
7. Adequate and equitable compensation

When one of these conditions is missing, teachers are less likely to be able to carry out their work successfully and hence are not as likely to experience psychological success.

Continuous Learning Culture

In organizations that value learning, employees share ideas about new techniques and procedures that may help to increase productivity. The culture of these organizations encourages employees to listen to one another's ideas and to try out those that sound promising. Learning organizations provide extensive learning opportunities for employees, either through internal training and professional development programs or by supporting employee access to external opportunities (London, 1998). A large number of school districts encourage teachers to pursue National Board Certification, and most of them provide financial support to help teachers defray the expenses incurred in obtaining the certification or provide salary increments for those who receive Board certification.

Types of Leadership

Leaders achieve results by influencing members of the group to work toward attaining group goals. Four types of leadership behavior may be involved (House, 1971):

1. *Directive leadership:* The leader spells out expectations to subordinates.
2. *Supportive leadership:* The leader treats subordinates as equals and shows concern for their well-being.
3. *Participative leadership:* The leader involves subordinates in advising about or actually making decisions concerning their work.
4. *Achievement-oriented leadership:* The leader identifies challenging work-related goals and communicates to subordinates confidence in their ability to achieve them.

Supportive, participative, and achievement-oriented leadership are the critical elements of a productive work environment. Directive leadership is also necessary on occasion. Leaders must be able to determine which type of leadership is needed in a given situation. Some principals rely primarily on participative leadership to achieve results, by delegating instructional duties to department heads and teachers. Others identify a small group of innovative teachers and use achievement-oriented leadership to encourage them to try new ideas and share with other teachers those that work (Little & Bird, 1987).

A large body of research suggests that when workers are given the opportunity to make decisions about how to organize and carry out their work, their satisfaction and commitment increase. In most cases, their performance also improves, but occasionally changes are limited to reductions in sick days, turnover, and other indirect indicators of performance (Louis & Smith, 1990).

Participative leadership is particularly important in schools, but the evidence indicates that few teachers believe they have much influence over decisions about their work. Data collected nationally in 1990–91 showed that fewer than 40 percent of teachers in public schools reported they had a great deal of influence over decisions about discipline policy, in-service training, ability grouping, and curriculum development. However, the level of self-reported influence varied somewhat across district types (National Center for Education Statistics, 1993b).

The number of teachers who reported having a lot of influence changed slightly between 1987 and 1990, increasing by a small amount in two areas, decreasing slightly in another, and remaining unchanged in the fourth (National Center for Education Statistics, 1993a). This finding was surprising, since during this time school-based management was widely adopted in U.S. schools (Caweiti, 1994).

Although a participative style of leadership has several important benefits, there are also limitations. Participative decisions take more time than directive decisions, and if employees are called on to make decisions for which they lack the necessary interest, knowledge, or experience, the quality of their decisions is likely to be poor (Landy, 1985).

Increasing Trust. Supportive leadership helps build trust between administrators and employees. Leaders gain employees' trust by exhibiting consistent and predictable behavior and by demonstrating a commitment to helping individuals do a better job. Trust is important; workers who trust their boss are more willing to accept his or her influence since they believe the supervisor will not suggest a course of action that will harm them.

Principals use a variety of strategies to demonstrate support for teachers, including involving them in important decisions; doing things with them; being positive, cheerful, and encouraging; being available and accessible; and being honest, direct, and sincere. They also exercise supportive leadership by collecting and disseminating information to staff members, assisting teachers with their tasks, facilitating communication within the school and between the school and community, and establishing procedures to handle routine matters (Leithwood & Montgomery, 1986).

Principals who wish to become more effective in supportive leadership should make a point of talking with teachers often about their personal and instructional interests and concerns. Teachers would like opportunities to discuss a variety of issues, including their own career plans and training needs, their concept of education, and the content of their courses. However, most teachers have relatively few chances to talk with administrators even about issues of immediate concern, including adjustments in work assignments, their own performance, their need for materials and supplies, instructional problems, and teacher/parent relationships. On only two topics do teachers report having fairly frequent conversations with principals. Those are student achievement and behavior (Bacharach, Bauer, & Shedd, 1986).

Administrators exhibit achievement-oriented leadership by alerting employees to new practices and encouraging them to experiment. They help obtain the resources employees need in order to try out new ideas, and they provide advice on implementation of innovative practices. Principals who make opportunities for teachers and other professional employees to attend conferences are also exhibiting achievement-oriented leadership.

Teachers' morale is higher in schools in which principals provide support by offering constructive suggestions, displaying interest in improving the quality of the educational program, encouraging superior performance standards in the classroom, maintaining egalitarian relationships, offering social and managerial support, and standing behind teachers in conflicts with students and parents (Gross & Herriott, 1965).

Even though the press of managerial duties limits the time available for principals to perform as instructional leaders (Deal, 1987) and even though involving teachers in a participative style of leadership makes sense, the principal must retain the title of leader both symbolically and in fact. No other individual carries the authority to speak for the school as a whole in resolving differences of opinion regarding allocation of resources and in making decisions regarding goals. The role of instructional leader is one that the principal can and should carry.

Professional Cultures in Schools

Teaching has traditionally been thought of as a solitary occupation with little interaction with other adults. However, that is changing. One of the characteristics human resources managers look for in today's teachers is the ability to work cooperatively with others. It is less acceptable today than in the past for a teacher to retreat into his or her own classroom and ignore other teachers. Teachers must be prepared to work with their colleagues to plan the curriculum, develop and present professional development sessions, and serve on committees charged with everything from developing instructional plans for special-needs children to interviewing applicants for teaching or paraprofessional vacancies (Monson & Monson, 1993).

Teachers welcome the opportunity to connect with colleagues and often describe the school in which they work in terms of how close teachers are to one another and how willing they are to work together. Professional cultures in schools influence whether teachers work collaboratively and the extent to which assistance and support are available to new teachers. Recent research has identified three types of professional cultures in schools. *Veteran-oriented professional cultures* are typical of schools in which a group of veteran teachers have taught together for many years. In these schools, long-time teachers form a closely-knit social group, and although they may be friendly toward new teachers, there is usually little effort made by the older teachers to offer assistance and support to beginners. Some experienced teachers in these schools are confident and competent in their work, whereas others indicated that they were tired and were waiting for retirement. In schools with this type of culture, new teachers received little support or encouragement (Kardos, Johnson, Peske, Kauffman, & Liu, 2001).

A second type of professional culture described by Kardos et al. (2001) was the *novice-oriented culture,* characterized by high proportions of young teachers. Teachers in these schools tended to be idealistic and hard-working. Professional interaction was frequent but characterized by an absence of expertise. The wisdom born of experience common among teachers with years of experience was missing from novice-oriented schools. As was true in schools with veteran-oriented professional cultures, new teachers in novice-oriented schools received little assistance or support from their colleagues.

New teachers in schools with the third type of professional culture, in contrast to the first two types, did receive support and assistance from colleagues. This type of culture was labeled *integrated* by Kardos et al. (2001). Experienced teachers in schools with an integrated culture understood the importance of mentoring new teachers, but they also engaged in exchanges with their experienced colleagues.

The atmosphere in integrated schools was one characterized by conversations and deliberations among teachers at all levels of experience about many aspects of instruction and the school curriculum.

Principals can help develop an integrated culture in a school by creating opportunities for collaborative work. However, they may also need to provide guidance and train teachers in the skills that make for effective collaboration. Specifically, training in communication, team building, and conflict resolution may be needed for teachers to share with one another in beneficial ways (Rallis & Goldring, 2000). Most teachers are willing to share with colleagues what they are doing in their classrooms but prefer to speak with those whom they know well and for whom they feel an affinity. Few are willing to speak out in school-wide faculty meetings unless group norms support such sharing.

Teacher communities such as those that are found in schools with integrated professional cultures enhance teachers' sense of professionalism. Talbert and McLaughlin (1996) described the advantages of and necessary conditions for maintaining these professional communities in this passage:

> We expect that strong teacher communities foster a shared knowledge base or technical culture, shared commitment to meeting the needs of all students, and durable professional identities and commitments. Conversely, without opportunities to acquire new knowledge, to reflect on practice, and to share successes and failures with colleagues, teachers are not likely to develop a sense of professional control and responsibility (p. 133).

Accepting a collaborative mode of operation in schools requires first adopting an attitude that improvement is necessary and desirable. If teachers have not fully accepted that value, the principal should make its adoption the first priority. After that, administrators can suggest activities that will permit teachers to work collaboratively for more effective instruction. Some examples of ways teachers collaborate appear in Exhibit 11.1.

Respect for Individuals

Teachers and other school employees desire respect from others, including their colleagues on the job, administrators, parents, students, and the community at large. Lack of respect has led many teachers to believe that their work is unimportant and unappreciated (Louis & Smith, 1990).

Lack of respect for others is demonstrated in a number of ways, both obvious and subtle. An individual who is shown disrespect by others whose opinions he or she values experiences an erosion of self-confidence and a loss of feelings of efficacy. The individual may feel marginalized, which may carry with it feelings of powerlessness. Teachers who are marginalized often feel stigmatized, and they may retreat to their classrooms and, as much as possible, avoid interacting with other teachers (Bailey, 2000).

■ ■ ■ ■ ■

EXHIBIT 11.1

EXAMPLES OF COLLEGIAL COOPERATION IN TEACHING

Design and prepare instructional material
Design curriculum units
Research material and ideas for curriculum
Write curriculum
Prepare lesson plans
Review and discuss existing lesson plans
Persuade others to try a new idea or approach
Make collective agreements to test an idea
Invite other teachers to observe one's classes
Observe other teachers
Analyze practices and effects
Teach others in formal inservice
Teach others informally
Talk publicly about what one is learning or wants to learn
Design inservice sessions
Evaluate the performance of the principal

Source: The Power of Organizational Setting: School Norms and Staff Development by J. W. Little, April 1981. Paper presented at the annual meeting of the American Educational Research Association, Los Angeles. ERIC Document Reproduction Service No. ED 221918.

Employees who experienced fear related to their work reported that their concerns had created negative feelings about the organization or about themselves or had a negative impact on the quality or quantity of their work. Some reported that, as a result of the fear, they were taking more care to avoid actions that might expose them to repercussions or were engaging more often in politically oriented behavior by cultivating "connections" with powerful individuals in the organization. Others reported that they were contemplating a transfer to a job outside the organization or had engaged in petty revenge or sabotage (Ryan & Oestreich, 1991). The researchers also found that employees who reported being fearful less often put forth extra effort to complete a task, more often attempted to hide mistakes, and less often engaged in creative thinking or risk-taking behavior on the job (Ryan & Oestreich, 1991).

Supervisory behaviors are a source of anxiety for many employees. Behaviors that are especially likely to arouse fear, whether the supervisor intends it or not, are silence, glaring, abruptness, insults and put-downs, blaming, yelling and shouting, and an aggressive, controlling manner.

Suggestions for administrators that will help lessen the level of fear in an organization include recognizing its presence and harmful effects and avoiding behaviors that are known to increase it. Administrators who wish to lower the level of anxiety are also advised to reduce ambiguous behavior, to talk about sensitive issues that are likely to arouse fear and that employees may be embarrassed to bring up on their own, and to welcome criticism (Ryan & Oestreich, 1991).

Using Knowledge and Skill

Few experiences are more important for employees' feelings of well-being than holding a job that allows them fully to use their knowledge and skill. Most young workers are less satisfied in their jobs than more experienced individuals, and the reason is that entry-level jobs tend to be less demanding and offer fewer opportunities for these workers to use the knowledge and skill they have acquired from their training.

Employees who are required to stretch in order to meet challenging aspects of their jobs are generally happier in their work and more productive than those for whom the job is a familiar routine. Of course, mastery is partly a function of one's experience, and the longer an individual is in a job, the less likely it is that he or she continues to be challenged by it. For that reason, the opportunity to move into new positions or take on demanding new duties that force the employee to acquire new skills and knowledge are important for maintaining employee interest and involvement.

Some teachers find that the emphasis on a mandated curriculum and the drive to increase test scores limit their opportunities to use their creativity, knowledge, and skill and lead to a decrement in their job satisfaction. Principals who help teachers view mandated testing as a way of improving learning for all students can help minimize the negative effects of the legislated curriculum (Hargreaves & Fink, 2003).

Physical Facilities

Teachers are more productive when the school building and its surroundings are clean and attractive and repairs are made promptly to malfunctioning physical systems. A maintenance schedule that includes painting at regular intervals and improvements to run-down classrooms, workrooms, and restrooms sends a message to teachers that their work is valued.

Although amount of space is a more common problem, the quality of space is also a concern of teachers (Bacharach et al., 1986). *Quality* refers to availability of electrical outlets, running water, telephone, adequate lighting, and privacy. It also encompasses furnishings, including desks, and electronic equipment such as computers. Updated networked computers with Internet and email capability are increasingly important in classrooms as teachers are expected to take advantage of the extensive instructional resources available through the Internet. A school that fails to provide these resources for its teachers is out-of-date.

Good teaching is hindered by the shortage of textbooks, equipment, and supplies. It is not uncommon for teachers to have too few microscopes, maps, and computers for their classes, and in some schools even textbooks must be shared. Adequate facilities and resources do not by themselves guarantee teacher satisfaction or effectiveness, but they help (McLaughlin & Yee, 1988).

Adequate Compensation

It is true that few people enter teaching for financial reasons, but it would be a mistake to assume that salary and benefits are unimportant to teachers. Teachers, like most other occupational groups, desire to maintain a comfortable middle-class lifestyle and need decent salaries in order to do that. Teachers who must make a financial sacrifice in order to teach often feel resentful, a condition that is not conducive to high productivity. Many teachers must hold a second job in order to pay their bills, and the strain of long working hours may further reduce their effectiveness in the classroom and their satisfaction with the job.

TEACHER STRESS AND BURNOUT

Teachers have historically been attracted to the profession because of their desire to work with children, and that factor is still an important motivation for teachers. In the last 30 years, however, a number of changes in families and society have made it more difficult for teachers to reach students as effectively as they could in the past, with the result that some teachers feel their work is less rewarding. Today's teachers have less freedom to decide what to teach and how to teach it, and they feel more pressure from administrators and parents. Much of what they teach is prescribed, and teachers are held accountable for preparing students to pass standardized tests on the prescribed content. Teachers feel less like professionals who exercise their judgment and more like clerks who carry out directives from superiors (Provenzo & McCloskey, 1996).

Some teachers are better prepared, both by temperament and training, to deal with stress, but excessive and prolonged stress saps any teacher's energy and sharply reduces productivity. Stress also contributes to teacher attrition. According to one report, stress was cited more often by teachers who had decided to leave the field than either working conditions or low salaries (Darling-Hammond, 2001).

The stress experienced by teachers varies depending on the type of teaching position a person holds and the extent to which the individual is able to shrug off job-related stressors. Teachers with large classes and many disruptive students are likely to experience more stress than those with smaller classes and more well-behaved students. Yet, even in comparable teaching situations, two individuals may experience different levels of stress because of individual variations in the tolerance for stress. Thus, no action is likely to reduce stress for all teachers, although some actions have more promise for relieving stress than others.

Types of Stress

There are at least four sources of stress in schools (Albrecht, 1979). *Time stress* occurs when the time allotted for completing a task is insufficient or when inflexible deadlines are established for completion of work assignments. Employees experience *situational stress* when the demands of the job exceed the individual's perceptions of his or her ability to cope. Special education teachers are especially susceptible to situational stress because of the demands of their jobs. It is estimated that special education teachers spend five or more hours per week filling out paperwork that other teachers are not required to complete. Recent efforts by professional groups to change the law to reduce the amount of paperwork required of special education teachers have been resisted by parents and by district administrators concerned with the legal consequences of failing to adequately document the rationale for decisions affecting children with disabilities (Goldstein, 2003). One teacher expressed the frustration felt by many special education teachers: "I am supposed to keep perfect paperwork, collaborate with regular education teachers, train and grade peer tutors, keep in constant touch with parents, and still find time to teach my students!" (Sack, 2000).

Teachers who have been well-prepared for the job of teaching are less likely to experience high levels of situational stress because they are better prepared to handle the demands of the job. However, recent research has shown that a significant number of new teachers are not very well prepared. In a national survey, only 61 percent of new teachers reported they had been adequately prepared to teach. They felt better prepared to maintain order and discipline in the classroom than to use newer instructional methods, implement state or district curricula, address the needs of students from diverse cultural backgrounds, or integrate educational technology (National Center for Education Statistics, 2000).

Any teacher who is assigned to teach a subject in which he or she lacks adequate background preparation is by definition unprepared. Adequate preparation to teach a high school subject is usually defined as a major or at least a minor in the subject area, but about one-third of high school mathematics teachers and one-fourth of English teachers do not have even a minor in the subject (Ingersoll, 2001). The additional work required to plan lessons in a subject with which one is unfamiliar adds to teachers' stress levels, to say nothing of the loss of learning experienced by students.

Situational stress may be also induced by poor hiring practices. When teachers are hired late, either shortly before classes start or later, they are more likely to feel unprepared for the job and thus experience situational stress. This is especially likely to be a problem for people who are new to the field. A study of hiring practices in four states determined that about 62 percent of new hires occurred within 30 days of the start of classes and that one-third of new teachers were hired after the school year was underway (Viadero, 2003). Not all last-minute hires can be avoided, because late resignations, budget problems, and enrollment surges may force a district to make last-minute offers. However, last-minute hires that result from lack of proper planning should be avoided.

Encounter stress is experienced when a person is forced to deal with other individuals whose behavior is unpleasant or unpredictable (Albrecht, 1979). An example of encounter stress is a teacher who is confronted by a student who is angry about a grade received on a test or a parent who is hostile and abusive. Negative colleagues may also contribute to encounter stress experienced by teachers. Efforts to address these teachers' concerns sometimes help, but with certain individuals negativism has become so ingrained that no intervention seems to help (Weber, 2003).

Anticipatory stress occurs when an individual experiences anxiety about an upcoming event (Albrecht, 1979). Teachers may experience anticipatory stress prior to issuing report cards or before a classroom observation visit by the principal.

Symptoms of Stress

The experience of stress is manifested in feelings of fear, anxiety, depression, and anger. The individual subjected to prolonged stress experiences fatigue, reluctance to go to work, withdrawal, hypersensitivity to criticism, and hostility and aggression toward others (Cedoline, 1982).

Stress also produces physiological effects, such as changes in skin conductance, heart rate, and blood pressure. Individuals are unlikely to be aware of physiological changes except when the level of stress experienced is quite high. However, the physiological manifestations of stress exact a cumulative toll on mental and physical health.

Stress can also affect cognitive functioning. Some stress is desirable for optimal performance, but exposure to unrelenting stress results in a marked decrease in performance (Lazarus, 1968).

Over time, the frustration, anger, disappointment, and guilt that teachers experience have a cumulative effect on their feelings about themselves and about their work that results in a condition known as *burnout*. Burnout has been defined as a form of alienation characterized by the feeling that one's work is meaningless and that one is powerless to bring about change that would make the work more meaningful. The experience of meaninglessness and powerlessness is intensified by the feeling that one is alone and isolated (Dworkin, 1987). Teachers who are experiencing job burnout often exhibit cynicism and negativism. They are likely to be inflexible and rigid and to demonstrate reduced concern for students and fellow workers.

Factors in Burnout

Factors that contribute to teacher burnout are role ambiguity (having a job in which duties are not clearly spelled out); responsibility/authority imbalance (having insufficient authority to carry out the responsibilities one has been assigned); a workload that is either too heavy or too light; inability to obtain information needed to carry out one's responsibilities; and job insecurity (Milstein, Golaszewski, & Duquette, 1984). Interactions with superiors can also lead to stress for some teachers. Teachers who receive no performance feedback from principals and who feel that they are unable to influence the administrators' decisions about their work are more likely to experience stress (Litt & Turk, 1985).

Administrators can help reduce the stress teachers experience by following some commonsense precautions:

1. Reduce time pressures by alerting teachers early to upcoming deadlines and by providing directions and assistance to help teachers complete paperwork requirements.

2. Assist teachers in obtaining help for students with emotional and psychological problems; if district resources are not available, appeal to community service agencies and service clubs for help.

3. Provide training to help teachers deal with disruptive students and, when necessary, provide support for teachers who are experiencing problems with student behavior.

4. Remove the dread of performance evaluation by pointing out that everyone can improve in some area; give teachers the opportunity to evaluate the school administration.

5. Provide feedback to teachers on their classroom performance, including specific suggestions that will help them be more effective teachers.

6. Offer to participate in parent conferences when teachers request it; provide training in planning and carrying out parent conferences.

7. Make time for informal conversations with teachers and give them a chance to talk about whatever they wish to talk about, bearing in mind that the most conscientious teachers are most subject to burnout.

8. Plan faculty outings that provide a break from the routine and allow teachers to have a good time with colleagues.

9. Help discouraged teachers maintain perspective by reminding them of past successes. Invite former students who have done well back to the school to talk about their successes and how their teachers helped them succeed.

Teacher Absenteeism

One of the symptoms of excessive stress on the job is absenteeism. Although not all absences can be attributed to on-the-job stress, when chronic absenteeism is encountered, administrators should consider the possibility that teachers are under excessive stress. A number of factors are involved in absenteeism, including individual characteristics, characteristics of the job, motivation to attend, and ability to attend (Steers & Rhodes, 1978).

Individual factors that may contribute to absence from work include gender, age, marital status, and size of family. An employee may be unable to attend work because of illness, transportation problems, or family responsibilities. Job characteristics that have an impact on employee absences are work-group size, peer relations, and the scope of work. Individuals who work with a small group of people are likely to feel a greater sense of responsibility to the group and thus miss work less often. Peer relations have a similar effect; employees who like and get along with fellow workers will tend to have more regular attendance than employees who do not feel as close to other workers.

Motivation to attend is related to sick-leave policy (whether one receives wages for days missed because of illness), work-group norms, an individual's personal work ethic, and his or her commitment to the organization.

Job satisfaction does not appear to be closely tied to employee attendance. Individuals who are members of cohesive groups with high satisfaction have low absenteeism, but when a group of cohesive workers express dissatisfaction with the job, absenteeism is usually higher (Steers & Rhodes, 1978).

Does teacher absenteeism translate into loss of student learning? The research on this question shows mixed results. Some studies show that students of teachers who miss school frequently have lower achievement test scores than those whose teachers were regular in attendance, whereas other studies found no relationship between the variables. However, there are at least two good reasons why excessive teacher absences should be discouraged and efforts made to reduce them. First, absenteeism costs the district money. A district with 500 teachers and a 4 percent absenteeism rate that pays substitutes $90 a day incurs additional costs of $324,000 a year for substitutes. Second, teacher absenteeism is related to student absences. Students of teachers who miss school frequently tend to have poor attendance records, too, and since school funds are usually distributed on the basis of attendance, schools with poor attendance receive less money from the state (Steers & Rhodes, 1978).

Of course, some absenteeism is legitimate and necessary. No employee should be encouraged to go to work when he or she is ill. To do so puts other workers at risk and increases the chances that the employee's condition will worsen. There are also times when a "mental health" day is in order. Taking a day off to rest can help a teacher feel relaxed and improve his or her ability to concentrate.

Principals of schools in which teachers are absent frequently can work to change the culture that permits or encourages absenteeism. During World War II, workers were reminded that missing work hindered the American war effort. This appeal to patriotism reduced the amount of time lost to absences and improved the output of both military and civilian goods. In the same way, if teachers understand that their contributions to student learning are important, most will respond to appeals to maintain continuity of instruction by reducing unnecessary absences.

EMPLOYEE ASSISTANCE PROGRAMS IN SCHOOLS

Employees' productivity may be affected by problems that originate on the job or elsewhere. In the past, supervisors could suggest that an employee with problems seek help, but if the worker chose not to do so, there was little the supervisor could do about it. Individuals with medical problems were usually willing to seek help because in most cases the employer provided insurance to cover the cost of medical care. But when the problem was not a medical one, many employees did not know where to go to find help, or if they did, they avoided going. Many of these cases involved individuals with problems of alcohol abuse, for which treatment was expensive and not readily available.

A number of companies instituted counseling programs to assist individuals whose work was affected by alcohol or drug abuse and other mental health or personal problems. Gradually, these programs came to be known as *employee assistance programs*. They are now widespread in industry and are becoming more commonplace in school districts.

An employee assistance program consists of policies and procedures for identifying and assisting employees whose personal or emotional problems hinder their job performance. Counselors in an employee assistance program also provide a valuable service by advising principals and other administrators about how to work more effectively with employees who have various kinds of mental health or personal problems (Hacker, 1986). Most administrators are not trained to work with problem employees, and they can perform their jobs more effectively if they have access to professional advice on dealing with such workers.

Wellness Programs

Because of escalating costs of all types of health care, many industrial concerns and some schools districts are now offering wellness programs, which emphasize good health practices for all employees. The idea of a wellness program is to help employees prevent illness by using sound judgment in decisions on nutrition, weight control, exercise, and use of drugs, tobacco, and alcohol.

SUMMARY

All human beings want to experience psychological success. One of the most common ways by which they seek to do that is by performing competently in some personally valued task. Schools are structured in such a way that teachers frequently experience failure in their efforts to help children grow and develop.

Productive working environments are characterized by a continuing learning culture; supportive administrative leadership; opportunities to work collaboratively with others and receive respect from others, including administrators, colleagues, and parents; opportunities to use one's knowledge and skill and to receive feedback on one's performance; and the resources one needs to do the job.

Four types of leadership used by administrators to achieve desired results are directive, supportive, participative, and achievement-oriented leadership. All four types are appropriate in particular situations. Directive and achievement-oriented leadership behaviors provide clear guidelines for teachers to follow and make goals more salient. Supportive leadership increases trust between teachers and administrators and helps to foster norms of collegiality, which in turn facilitate the introduction of participative leadership. Participative leadership increases commitment to group decisions.

Teachers often experience stress because of the conditions under which they work. Conditions that are particularly conducive to stress are pressure to produce learning gains and disruptive and disrespectful students. Prolonged stress leads to physical and emotional symptoms characterized by a loss of interest in work and in the welfare of others. Administrators should be sensitive to the need to provide supportive leadership to alleviate teacher stress.

Employee assistance programs help individuals whose job performance is affected by personal or mental health problems. Wellness programs are designed to help all employees avoid illness by observing sound health practices.

SUGGESTED ACTIVITIES

1. An item that almost always shows up on lists of desirable characteristics of work environments in schools is *supportive administrative leadership*. Explain what is meant by that phrase and give one or two specific examples of it from your own experience. Tell what you think are the necessary ingredients of supportive leadership and why school employees attach so much importance to it. Are school personnel different from people in other occupations in this respect?

2. Think about a school you are familiar with. Would you describe the culture of the school as more like a veteran-oriented, novice-oriented, or integrated culture? What characteristics of the school suggest that type of culture? Given your preference, which type of school culture would you choose to work in?

3. A number of people have observed that some stress is desirable and that the total absence of stress makes life boring. Nevertheless, individuals vary in their tolerance for stress. Is some stress acceptable to you? Think of one or two situations in which you have experienced "pleasant" stress and an equal number in which you have experienced "unpleasant" stress. What is the difference between the two? Do you deal with "pleasant" stress differently from the way you handle "unpleasant" stress? If so, why? Do you agree that teaching is a "stressful" occupation? Why or why not?

4. Most teachers agree that the leadership style of the principal has a strong effect on a school environment. Rank-order the four styles of leadership described in this chapter according to teachers' preferences by assigning number 1 to the leadership style that more teachers prefer and number 4 to the one fewer teachers prefer. Explain the reasons for your ranking.

ONLINE RESOURCES

British Petroleum (www.bpfutures.com/glob/you_environment.asp)

This statement appears under "What to Expect," on this company's website: "Everyone who works for BP should know what's expected of them in their jobs and have open and constructive conversations about their performance. Everyone should be helped to develop their capabilities and be recognized and competitively rewarded. We also believe everyone has a right to offer input, and be involved, in helping their team's growth. We think all employees should feel supported in the management of their personal priorities."

University of California at San Francisco (www.ucsf.edu/swe/cms/index/cgi?)

The University maintains this website for the Supportive Work Environment Initiative. The site includes a description of a supportive work environment, offers details of a contest on creative ways to say "thank you," and asks for comments from employees on such questions as "What do you need at work in order to feel supported?"

University of Oregon (eric.uoregon.edu/publications/digests/digest120.html)

ERIC Digest 120 discusses factors that affect teacher job satisfaction and proposes steps to raise the morale of school employees.

REFERENCES

Albrecht, K. (1979). *Stress and the manager.* Englewood Cliffs, NJ: Prentice Hall.

Bacharach, S. B., Bauer, S. C., & Shedd, J. B. (1986). The work environment and school reform. *Teachers College Record, 88,* 241–256.

Bailey, B. (2000). The impact of mandated change on teachers. In N. Bascia and A. Hargreaves (Eds.), *The sharp edge of educational change* (pp. 112–128). New York: Routledge Falmer.

Bogler, R. (2001, December). The influence of leadership style on teacher job satisfaction. *Educational Administration Quarterly, 37,* 662–683.

Bruce, W., & Blackburn, J. (1992). *Balancing job satisfaction and performance: A guide for human resource professionals.* Westport, CT: Quorum.

Cawelti, G. (1994). *High school restructuring: A national study.* Arlington, VA: Educational Research Service.

Cedoline, A. J. (1982). *Job burnout in public education.* New York: Teachers College Press.

Corbett, H. D. (1982). Principals' contributions to maintaining change. *Phi Delta Kappan, 64,* 190–192.

Corcoran, T. (1990). Schoolwork: Perspectives on workplace reform in public schools. In M. McLaughlin, J. Talbert, & N. Bascia (Eds.), *The contexts of teaching in secondary schools: Teachers' realities* (pp. 142–166). New York: Teachers College Press.

Darling-Hammond, L. (2001, May). The challenge of staffing our schools. *Educational Leadership, 58,* 12–17.

Deal, T. E. (1987). Effective school principals: Counselors, engineers, pawnbrokers, poets . . . or instructional leaders? In W. Greenfield (Ed.), *Instructional leadership: Concepts, issues, and controversies* (pp. 230–245). Boston: Allyn and Bacon.

Dworkin, A. G. (1987). *Teacher burnout in the public schools: Structural causes and consequences for children.* Albany: State University of New York Press.

Freudenberger, H. (1977). Burn out: Occupational hazard of the child care worker. *Child Care Quarterly, 6,* 90–99.

Garubo, R. & Rothstein, S. (1998). *Supportive supervision in schools.* Westport, CT: Greenwood.

Goldstein, L. (2003, May 28). Disabled by paperwork? *Education Week,* pp. 1, 23.

Gross, N., & Herriott, R. (1965). *Staff leadership in public schools: A sociological inquiry.* New York: Wiley.

Guglielmi, R. S., & Tatrow, K. (1998, Spring). Occupational stress, burnout, and health in teachers: A methodological and theoretical analysis. *Review of Educational Research, 68,* 61–99.

Hacker, C. (1986). *EAP: Employee assistance programs in the public schools.* Washington, DC: National Education Association. (ERIC Document Reproduction Service No. ED 281267).

Hall, D. T., & Schneider, B. (1973). *Organizational climates and careers: The work lives of priests.* New York: Seminar Press.

Hargreaves, A., & Fink, D. (2003, May). Sustaining leadership. *Phi Delta Kappan, 84,* 693–700.

Ingersoll, R. M. (2001, May). The realities of out-of-field teaching. *Educational Leadership, 58,* 42–45.

Kardos, S. M., Johnson, S. M., Peske, H. G., Kauffman, D., & Liu, E. (2001, April). Counting on colleagues: New teachers encounter the professional cultures of their schools. *Educational Administration Quarterly, 37,* 250–290.

Landy, F. J. (1985). *Psychology of work behavior.* Homewood, IL: Dorsey.

Lazarus, R. S. (1968). Stress. In D. L. Sills (Ed.), *International encyclopedia of the social sciences* (Vol. 15, pp. 337–348). New York: Macmillan.

Leithwood, K. A., & Montgomery, D. J. (1986). *Improving principal effectiveness: The principal profile.* Toronto: Ontario Institute for Studies in Education.

Litt, M. D., & Turk, D. C. (1985). Sources of stress and dissatisfaction in experienced high school teachers. *Journal of Educational Research, 78,* 178–185.

Little, J. W. (1981, April). *The power of organizational setting: School norms and staff development.* Paper presented at the annual meeting of the American Educational Research Association, Los Angeles. (ERIC Document Reproduction Service No. ED 221918).

Little, J. W., & Bird, T. (1987). Instructional leadership "close to the classroom" in secondary schools. In W. Greenfield (Ed.), *Instructional leadership: Concepts, issues, and controversies* (pp. 118–138). Boston: Allyn and Bacon.

Louis, K., & Smith, B. (1990). Teacher working conditions. In P. Reyes (Ed.), *Teachers and their workplace: Commitment, performance, and productivity* (pp. 23–47). Newbury Park, CA: Sage.

Maslach, C., & Pines, A. (1977). The burn-out syndrome in the day care setting. *Child Care Quarterly, 6,* 100–113.

McLaughlin, M. W., Pfeifer, R. S., Swanson-Owens, D., & Yee, S. (1986). Why teachers won't teach. *Phi Delta Kappan, 67,* 420–426.

McLaughlin, M. W., & Yee, S. M. (1988). School as a place to have a career. In A. Lieberman (Ed.), *Building a professional culture in schools* (pp. 23–44). New York: Teachers College Press.

Milstein, M. M., Golaszewski, T. J., & Duquette, R. D. (1984). Organizationally based stress: What bothers teachers. *Journal of Educational Research, 77,* 293–297.

Monson, M. P., & Monson, R. J. (1993). Who creates curriculum? New roles for teachers. *Educational Leadership, 51*(2), 19–21.

National Center for Education Statistics. (1993a). *America's teachers: Profile of a profession.* Washington, DC: U.S. Department of Education.

National Center for Education Statistics. (1993b). *Schools and staffing in the United States: A statistical profile.* Washington, DC: U.S. Department of Education.

National Center for Education Statistics (2000). *Teacher preparation and professional development.* Washington DC: Department of Education, Office of Educational Research and Improvement.

Provenzo, E., & McCloskey, G. (1996). *Schoolteachers and schooling: Ethoses in conflict.* Norwood, NJ: Ablex.

Rallis, S., & Goldring, E. (2000). *Principals of dynamic schools.* Thousand Oaks, CA: Corwin.

Ryan, K., & Oestreich, D. (1991). *Driving fear out of the workplace.* San Francisco: Jossey-Bass.

Sack, J. (2000, October 25). CEC report tracks "crisis" conditions in special education. *Education Week,* 15.

Steers, R., & Rhodes, S. (1978). Major influences on employee attendance: A process model. *Journal of Applied Psychology, 63* (4), 391–407.

Talbert, J., & McLaughlin, M. (1996). Teacher professionalism in local school contexts. In I. Goodson and A. Hargreaves (Eds.), *Teachers' professional lives* (pp. 127–153). London: Falmer.

Weber, M. R. (2003, February). Coping with malcontents. *School Administrator, 60*(2), 6–10.

CHAPTER TWELVE

LEGAL ISSUES IN HUMAN RESOURCES MANAGEMENT

The legal authority to employ, assign, transfer, suspend, and terminate teachers is assigned by the states to local school boards, and the boards are given wide latitude in the exercise of that power (Hudgins & Vacca, 1995). The large majority of personnel decisions are made by school boards on the recommendation of an administrator. For that reason, principals and district administrators who are involved in human resources management activities should be aware of legal ramifications of personnel decisions.

Although they delegate considerable power over personnel matters to school boards, the states set professional preparation requirements for teachers, counselors, and administrative personnel. The states also prescribe other qualifications for those positions, including age, moral character, and citizenship (*Education Law,* 1989).

Most of the actions taken during the process of recruitment, selection, and placement of employees—including advertising, preparation of application forms, and conducting interviews—are potential areas of legal vulnerability. Also included under the aegis of the law are decisions to transfer, promote, discipline, or dismiss employees. The best protection against violating these laws is to be well informed about statute and case law relating to the various facets of human resources management, which is the subject of this chapter.

PLAN OF THE CHAPTER

This chapter covers the following topics: (1) state legislation and school boards, (2) antidiscrimination legislation, (3) types of discrimination, (4) defending personnel practices, and (5) affirmative action and reverse discrimination.

STATE LEGISLATION AND SCHOOL BOARDS

The states delegate to school boards the authority to hire and assign or reassign and terminate employees. The states also establish rules governing the preparation and certification of professional personnel, including teachers, counselors, school social workers, school psychologists, and administrators. State laws and regulations specify the course of study that the various personnel must complete and stipulate licensing procedures, including tests of general or professional knowledge. School boards may establish higher standards than those specified by the state, but they may not lower the standards.

Most states require school personnel to be free of communicable diseases, and school boards sometimes establish other policies dealing with employee health. Some states prohibit school boards from establishing a residency requirement, but where it is permitted, courts have usually upheld residency rules as long as the boards were able to establish a rational basis for the policy (*Wardwell* v. *Board of Education of the City School District of Cincinnati,* 1976).

School boards have authority to assign teachers to a school, grade level, or subject, and may transfer teachers at will, as long as the individual is qualified to hold the position to which he or she is assigned. In some states the law places limitations on the board's freedom to transfer a teacher from a higher-paying to a lower-paying job or from a position of more to a position of less responsibility. In Colorado, for example, state law allows transfers of teachers upon the recommendation of the chief administrative officer of the district, provided the teacher's pay is not reduced from its current level for the remainder of that school year. Arizona, like many other states, permits governing boards to reduce salaries or eliminate positions in order to save money, but a board may not lower the salary of a certified teacher who has been employed by the district for three years, unless all salaries are reduced by a commensurate amount.

State laws also provide a number of safeguards and incentives for teachers, including the protection against a reduction in salary. Michigan law invalidates any contract or agreement between a teacher and a board under which the teacher would agree to waive any rights or privileges granted by state law. It also forbids school districts from assigning a teacher to more than one probationary period, thus denying districts the option of extending the probationary period for a teacher whose performance is not satisfactory. It is common for states to require that probationary teachers be notified by a certain date if their contracts will not be renewed for the following school year. If a district fails to notify a teacher that he or she will not be renewed, the contract is automatically extended for one year.

Alaska is one of the more generous states in providing incentives and protections for teachers. The law of that state requires school boards to provide information on the availability and cost of housing in rural areas and to assist teachers in finding a place to live; school districts are even empowered to lease housing in order to rent living space to teachers. Alaska law also guarantees a 30-minute duty-free lunch period for teachers in schools with four or more teachers and requires districts to pay moving expenses for teachers who are involuntarily transferred to a school that is more than a 20-minute drive from their current location. In Arizona, a teacher who returns to teaching in public schools after a stint in charter schools is protected against loss of certification, retirement, salary status, or any other benefit provided under the law or school board policy.

Some state legislation also provides incentives for substitute teachers. In Michigan, a substitute who teaches for 60 days in one assignment is granted the same privileges as full-time teachers, including leave time and a salary equal to or higher than the minimum salary on the district salary scale.

ANTIDISCRIMINATION LEGISLATION

Antidiscrimination legislation is intended to protect identified groups from bias in selection, salary, and promotion decisions. The federal government, most states, and many localities have laws that prohibit discrimination on the basis of race, color, religion, gender, disability, or national origin. Discrimination based on age, marital status, and sexual preference is also prohibited under some state laws (Hauck, 1998).

These laws make it illegal to recruit employees in such a way that protected groups are discouraged or prevented from applying. Employers may decide to recruit new workers by asking current employees to tell friends and relatives about a vacancy, but they may not legally limit recruiting to that method, since workers seldom recommend people of a different race. The employer is expected to advertise the vacancy widely so that all qualified prospects have a chance to learn about it (Sovereign, 1999). Discrimination occurs when decisions about selection, placement, promotion, compensation, discipline, or dismissal of individuals are made on the basis of characteristics other than qualifications, ability, and performance (McCarthy, 1983). A number of state and federal statutes, regulations, and executive orders forbid discrimination in recruiting, selecting, placing, promoting, and dismissing employees. In this section, some of the more important federal statutes relating to discrimination will be reviewed.

Civil Rights Act of 1964 and Pregnancy Discrimination Act of 1978

The most significant piece of legislation dealing with discrimination in employer/employee relations is the Civil Rights Act of 1964, as amended. Title VII of that act covers all employers with 15 or more employees, including state and local governments as well as schools and colleges. Religious institutions are exempt with respect to employment of persons of a specific religion.

The law prohibits discrimination with respect to compensation and terms, conditions, or privileges of employment on the basis of race, color, national origin, gender, or religion. The legislation also prohibits limiting, segregating, or classifying employees or applicants for employment in any way that deprives an individual of employment opportunities or otherwise adversely affects his or her status as an employee.

Title VII is administered by the Equal Employment Opportunity Commission (EEOC), which administers most federal legislation dealing with employment rights. Title VII requires that a charge of discrimination be investigated by a state or local agency if the employer is covered by a state or local fair employment practice law. Most states have such laws, which prohibit discrimination by employers on the basis of color, religion, gender, or national origin. Some also ban discrimination related to age, disability, marital status, physical appearance, sexual preference, and political affiliation (Hauck, 1998).The EEOC has no adjudicatory authority, but most claims of discrimination under Title VII must be reviewed by the EEOC before legal action is taken against an employer. If, following an investigation, the Commission concludes that the law has been violated, it attempts to persuade the employer to eliminate the illegal practice. If this approach does not work, the Commission will issue a finding confirming that a basis for legal action exists (van Geel, 1987).

The Pregnancy Discrimination Act of 1978 extended the protections of Title VII of the Civil Rights Act to pregnant employees. This law requires employers to treat pregnancy the same as other temporary medical conditions. Except where state law establishes conditions that make separate policies necessary, school divisions are advised to establish a single policy on medical leave, including maternity leave (Hubbartt, 1993).

Title VII of the Civil Rights Act was amended by the Civil Rights Act of 1991. One of the amendments made it unlawful for an employer to adjust scores on employment tests or to set different cut-off scores for the purpose of benefiting applicants of a particular race, color, religion, gender, or national origin. Some affirmative action plans had adopted these practices for the purpose of giving minorities a slight advantage in selection, but Congress has outlawed that practice.

Age Discrimination in Employment Act of 1967 and Older Workers Benefit Protection Act of 1990

The Age Discrimination in Employment Act (ADEA) of 1967, as amended in 1986, enjoins discrimination against individuals above the age of 40 in hiring, assignment, training, promotion, and the terms and conditions of employment (McCarthy & Cambron-McCabe, 1992). In 1990 Congress passed the Older Workers Benefit Protection Act, which amended ADEA to prohibit employers from discriminating against older workers in provision of fringe benefits. This legislation requires employers to grant equal benefits to workers of all ages, unless the employer can show that the cost of providing the benefit for older workers is greater than for younger workers (Twomey, 2002). ADEA also provides that employees who are discriminated against on the basis of age in employment decisions may sue for monetary damages. However, the Supreme Court ruled in 2000 that ADEA does not grant that right to employees of state and local governments (Twomey, 2002).

The legislation makes it unlawful to give preference to a younger person over an older one if the older person is within the protected range. For example, a district that promotes a 45-year-old employee rather than a 60-year-old because of the latter's age when the two are equally qualified would be guilty of age discrimination, just as it would be for promoting a 25-year-old employee over an equally qualified 40-year-old. The act offers no protection against discrimination based on age for individuals who are outside the protected range. Thus, refusing to hire a 21-year-old applicant on the basis of age is not unlawful.

An employer charged with violating the Age Discrimination in Employment Act may disprove the charge by showing bona fide occupational qualification (BFOQ). For example, a director hiring an actor to play the part of a 25-year-old man in a play could lawfully select a younger person over an applicant within the protected age range solely on the basis of age. An employer who uses age as a qualification for employment must be able to show a reasonable relationship between the requirement and job performance. This is usually done by citing a connection between employee age and safe performance (van Geel, 1987).

In the Civil Rights Act of 1991, Congress expressed a preference for submitting claims under ADEA to arbitration rather than litigating those charges in the courts. Employers have followed that advice as a way of reducing litigation costs (Thorne, 1996).

Equal Pay Act of 1963

The Equal Pay Act of 1963 forbids an employer from paying higher wages to employees of one sex than it pays to those of the opposite sex for jobs that require equal skill, effort, and responsibility and that are performed under similar working conditions. Employers may not attempt to comply by reducing the wages of any employee. Exceptions are allowed for wages that are based on a seniority system or a merit pay plan. The Equal Pay Act applies to federal, state, and local governments as well as to private commercial and industrial firms. Enforcement of the act became the responsibility of the Equal Employment Opportunity Commission in 1979, but the statute is less frequently used than Title VII since a violation of one is also a violation of the other and most attorneys prefer to bring suit under Title VII (McCulloch, 1981).

A question that frequently arises in litigation having to do with equal pay is how similar duties must be in order for two jobs to be considered as meriting equal pay. Courts have not always been consistent in defining the degree of required difference (Schlei & Grossman, 1976). It is common for female custodians to be assigned tasks that are less physically demanding than those assigned to males. For example, male custodians may be responsible for removing snow from school sidewalks and driveways, whereas female employees escape that duty. Males may be required to climb a ladder to change lightbulbs, install wiring, repair air conditioning equipment, and perform other tasks that female employees are not asked to perform.

Given these differences in assigned duties, is it justifiable to pay higher wages to the male employees? In the cases that have been tried under the Equal Pay Act, the answer to that question given by the courts has most often been *no*. The courts have held that the differences in the duties required of male and female custodians were not great enough to justify wage differences favoring males.

As a general rule, wage differences in favor of one sex are more likely to be sustained by the courts if the additional duties of the higher paid sex require a significant percentage of the employees' time or if they can be shown to require significant extra effort (Schlei & Grossman, 1976). For example, a school board could justify paying a male soccer boys' coach more than it pays a female girls' soccer coach if it could show that the boys' team played more games and spent more time practicing than the girls' team.

Rehabilitation Act of 1973 and Americans with Disabilities Act of 1990

Section 504 of the Rehabilitation Act applies to federally funded programs and government agencies and prohibits those employers from refusing to hire an individual with a disability solely because of the disability. The Americans with Disabilities Act requires employers to make reasonable accommodations for employees with disabilities who are otherwise qualified for the job. The ADA defines *disability* as a physical or mental impairment that substantially limits one or more of the major life activities, which include seeing, hearing, speaking, walking, breathing, learning, and working. In determining whether an individual is regarded as having a disability, the Supreme Court has ruled that employers may consider the individual's condition in its corrected state. Thus, if wearing eyeglasses or a corrective brace or taking medication removes the limitations on major life activities, the individual is not regarded as having a disability and is thus not protected by the ADA (Twomey, 2002).

The Vocational Rehabilitation Act (VRA) of 1973 and the Americans with Disabilities Act (ADA) of 1990 prohibit discrimination in employment decisions against qualified individuals with disabilities. The VRA applies to federal contractors and agencies that receive financial assistance from the federal government, whereas the ADA applies to most employers with 15 or more employees.

Both acts provide that an individual with a disability who is able to perform the "essential functions" of a position, with or without reasonable accommodation, is qualified for consideration for a position and may not be refused employment solely on the basis of the disability. *Essential functions* are defined as primary duties that are intrinsic to a specific job, not including those of a peripheral nature (Jacobs, 1993).

Three questions that are used to help identify essential functions of a job are (Fersh & Thomas, 1993):

1. Does the position exist to perform the function?
2. Are there only a limited number of employees available to perform the function?
3. Is the function so highly specialized that the person holding the position is hired for his or her ability to perform that particular function?

To help answer those questions, consider information obtained from written job descriptions, estimates of time devoted to various functions, suggested consequences of not performing a particular function, and the terms and conditions of collective bargaining agreements (Fersh & Thomas, 1993).

Some jobs have a limited number of essential functions. For a school nurse, essential functions include the ability to apply first aid and make decisions regarding follow-up actions when a child is ill or injured—for example, whether to contact parents to take the child home or call emergency services. Other jobs have multiple essential functions. School counselors discuss problems of personal adjustment with students and work with them to find solutions. But counselors also help students locate information about prospective careers, calm anxious or upset parents, prepare and mail transcripts, and administer and interpret standardized tests. All of these functions are essential, but the position of counselor does not exist solely to perform one of these functions to the exclusion of the others.

The EEOC defines *reasonable accommodation* as a modification or adjustment in the way a job is ordinarily performed that enables a qualified individual with a disability to perform the job without imposing an undue hardship on the employer (Schneid, 1992). Examples of accommodations are providing entrance ramps to allow access to persons in wheelchairs, granting time off for medical treatments or physical therapy, and purchasing special equipment or adapting existing equipment to enable people with disabilities to perform a job.

Other forms of accommodation include hiring an assistant to perform the tasks that the employee with disabilities is unable to perform and restructuring work assignments to limit those employees' responsibilities to tasks that are within their capabilities. An employer is not required to make accommodations that are unduly costly or disruptive to the operation of the business or agency (Schneid, 1992).

A person is considered to be disabled if he or she has a physical or mental impairment that substantially limits one or more major life activities or is regarded as having such an impairment. Individuals who have undergone drug rehabilitation are considered to be disabled, but those who are currently using drugs are not. Homosexuality is not considered a disabling condition, but AIDS is (Schneid, 1992).

The law does not require an employer to hire a person with disabilities who is less qualified than a person with no disabilities, but it forbids employers from refusing to employ individuals solely on the basis of their possessing a disability. Employers may legally refuse to hire an applicant with disabilities whose employment in a particular position would result in creation of a safety hazard for the employee or others when it is not possible through reasonable accommodation to eliminate the danger (Gordon, 1992). However, the employer should be prepared to produce evidence that the claimed hazard is real and not simply a pretext.

Deciding whether to employ individuals with disabilities as teachers requires administrators to consider the safety and well-being of students as well as the rights of the disabled. Districts that are able to show that they have carefully weighed a disabled applicant's qualifications to perform the job with reasonable accommodation against the potential risk to students created by hiring the person stand a good chance of prevailing in court.

On the other hand, districts that refuse to consider a disabled applicant's qualifications are almost certain to lose a legal challenge. A district that declined to allow a blind applicant to take a qualifying examination for a teaching position on grounds that her blindness made her incompetent to teach sighted students lost its suit and was required by the court to hire the teacher and provide back pay and retroactive seniority (*Gurmankin* v. *Costanzo*, 1997).

Interviewers should ask applicants with disabilities to indicate how they will perform essential functions of the position for which they are applying and what accommodations they will need in order to carry out their duties. Requests for accommodation should be treated on an individual basis and decisions should take into account both the expected cost and the potential for creating hardships for other employees (Sovereign, 1999).

One question that is still largely unanswered is to what extent the law protects employees who contract contagious diseases. The Eleventh Circuit Court held that the legislation did not exclude persons with such conditions as long as their presence did not pose a risk to other people. The case involved a teacher who had been dismissed from her job because she had tuberculosis (*Arline* v. *School Board of Nassau County*, 1985).

Family and Medical Leave Act of 1993

The Family and Medical Leave Act (FMLA) was enacted to allow families to balance the demands of their jobs with the needs of their families. The act grants eligible employees up to 12 weeks of unpaid leave during a 12-month period to care for a newborn child, adopted child, or foster child; for personal illness; or to care for a parent, spouse, or child with a serious health problem. The legislation covers private employers with 50 or more employees and state and local government employers without regard to the number of people they employ. A *serious health condition* is defined by FMLA as a condition that requires in-patient care or continuing treatment by a health care professional. An individual may have a serious health condition under FMLA without qualifying for coverage under the Americans with Disabilities Act of 1990. To be eligible for leave under FMLA, an individual must have been employed for 12 months or more and must give advance notice if practicable.

School Safety

In recent years, violent attacks against teachers and students by other students and, in a few cases, by intruders in schools, have raised public awareness of the importance of implementing measures to make schools safer. In 1994, Congress passed the Improving America's Schools Act, which included Title VII, known as the Safe and Drug Free Schools and Communities Act. The purpose of this legislation was to prevent violence in and around schools and to strengthen programs designed to prevent illegal use of alcohol, tobacco, and drugs. The legislation provides funds for programs designed to achieve those goals.

Several states have also enacted legislation intended to reduce the threat of violence in schools. Kentucky established a Center for Safe Schools, which collects data on school violence, conducts research, and disseminates information about successful school safety programs. The center also provides technical assistance to local schools in the state and administers grants to school districts. The center maintains an extensive clearinghouse on issues and best practices in school safety. The Internet address for the clearinghouse appears in the Online Resources section of this chapter.

Colorado law requires school boards to adopt and implement a safe school plan and mandates that principals report annually in writing about the learning environment of their schools, including attendance figures; dropout rate; disciplinary violations; possession of dangerous weapons, alcohol, drugs, or tobacco; and destruction or defacement of school property. The Colorado law also directs boards of education to adopt procedures to be followed in case a teacher is assaulted, harassed, or falsely accused of child abuse. The law requires that all new school employees be screened for previous criminal activity. The legislation is contained in Section 22–32–109.1 of Colorado Revised Statutes and can be accessed online.

Constitutional Protections

All U.S. citizens have certain protections under the Constitution. Freedom of speech, association, and religion are guaranteed by the First Amendment, and the rights of due process and equal protection are secured by the Fifth and Fourteenth Amendments, respectively. Privacy rights also derive from the Constitution (Sorenson, 1987).

The Supreme Court has held that the free speech right of school employees must be balanced by consideration for the efficient operation of schools. In reviewing a case in which a teacher was dismissed for making public statements critical of the school board and the administration (*Connick v. Myers,* 1983), the Supreme Court held that discussion of issues related to public concerns was protected under the First Amendment but that comments about issues of a personal nature were not so protected. Unfortunately, the distinction is clearer in theory than in practice.

Criticism by teachers of student grouping practices and of the quality of the educational programs have been held to be matters of public concern and thus entitled to protection (*Cox v. Dardanelle Public School District,* 1986; *Jett v. Dallas Independent School District,* 1986). However, statements that were critical of school officials for changing registration procedures and for delays in purchasing teaching materials were judged to be matters of personal concern and thus not protected (*Ferrara v. Mills,* 1986; *Daniels v. Quinn,* 1986).

The Seventh Circuit Court held that a district action prohibiting teachers from holding prayer meetings at school before the school day started did not infringe on the teachers' right of free speech (*May* v. *Evansville-Yanderburgh School Corporation,* 1986). The right to privacy has been cited as protecting women who choose to bear a child out of wedlock from adverse employment decisions (*Eisenstadt* v. *Baird,* 1972). Policies that require pregnant teachers to begin mandatory maternity leave at a specific point in the pregnancy have been held to deny teachers' rights to equal protection under the Fourteenth Amendment (Director, 1973).

Protecting Privacy.   Privacy is increasingly a concern of civil libertarians and ordinary citizens because of the widespread availability of information about individuals on the Internet and the enactment of legislation that allows the federal government extensive access to personal information. Most Americans regard the right to privacy as a fundamental freedom and resent what they regard as intrusions into their private affairs, whether by the government or others, yet when a person accepts a job, he or she surrenders the right of absolute privacy. Privacy on the job is limited, and employers can legally collect and act on information about their employees that many employees might prefer not to share (Hubbartt, 1998).

Disputes having to do with privacy usually arise over holding second jobs, use of alcohol, tobacco or illegal substances, criminal behavior, and, for teachers in particular, behavior that violates community norms and expectations. An employee of a grocery store who is arrested for DUI arouses a legitimate concern for his or her employer, who is bothered by the potential damage to the company's image, but if the employee is a teacher, the board will also be concerned about the effect the teacher's behavior might have on students.

One of the most contentious issues involving privacy concerns of employees has to do with lifestyles and off-duty activities. Most employees assume that what they do after working hours is their own business, but employers also have an interest in after-hours activities of their workers. Some school districts are reluctant to hire teachers with same-sex partners out of concern for the community's reaction and the fear that the teacher's presence might influence impressionable students to adopt a homosexual orientation, even though there is no evidence to support the latter fear.

School administrators should be well-informed about the provisions of state laws dealing with employee privacy, and they would benefit also from knowledge of case law pertaining to the issue. Although there are no hard-and-fast rules for dealing with situations that involve employee privacy, knowledge of the law and previous court actions, combined with sound judgment, can help avoid legal entanglements.

Administrators who have access to personnel records have a responsibility to take precautions to prevent unauthorized persons from having access to the information contained in them. Failure to exercise care in maintaining records that contain personal information can result in liability for the district. An employee has a personal privacy interest if disclosure of information results in embarrassment, damage to his or her reputation, or loss of employment (National Center for Education Statistics, 2000).

The interest of the individual employee is one of several elements to be considered in making a decision about releasing private information. The degree to which releasing the information might intrude on the employee's personal privacy must also be considered, as must the public's interest in having access to the information. Consider an example: Releasing information about an employee's past criminal record has the potential to be embarrassing and costly for the employee, but, depending on the nature of the crime, the public's interest in the information may be equally important. In weighing these factors, most reasonable people would conclude that the public's interest in knowing about the employee's background outweighs the individual's desire for privacy. The district is less likely to be held liable for releasing private information about an employee if that information is available from other sources.

All districts that do not have it should develop a policy on responding to requests for information about employees. Districts are required to release information about staff members when a law enforcement agency asks for it unless state law forbids its release. The policy should identify the person who is responsible for determining whether to release the information being requested, and it should tell who should be informed about the release of the information (National Center for Education Statistics, 2000).

TYPES OF DISCRIMINATION

Title VII of the Civil Rights Act of 1964 prohibits overt discrimination, also known as *disparate treatment*. This is the most flagrant and, fortunately, also the least common form of discrimination. It occurs when an individual who is a member of a protected group and who qualifies for or holds a job is discriminated against for legally indefensible reasons.

A more common form of discrimination is *adverse impact*, which occurs when employment practices that are neutral in intent have a discriminatory effect on a protected group. This is the most common form of discrimination (Miner & Miner, 1978). Among actions that can lead to charges of adverse impact are using screening tests on which members of one group score lower than other groups and establishing educational or experience requirements that adversely affect members of a protected group.

Once an adverse impact claim is established, the district must show that the practice is valid for the purpose intended. This is a "business necessity" defense. The Supreme Court accepted such a defense in allowing the use of the National Teachers Examination (NTE) for teacher certification and to determine employee salaries (*United States* v. *State of South Carolina*, 1978). However, in *Griggs* v. *Duke Power Company* (1971), the Supreme Court held that the use of a test of general intelligence for selection purposes was discriminatory because the test had an adverse impact on minority applicants and had not been validated for use in employee selection. The use of an arbitrary cutoff score as part of a selection process without prior investigation of the potentially harmful effects of such a decision is likely to be successfully challenged (Beckham, 1985).

Perpetuation of past discrimination refers to the lingering effects of discriminatory practices after the practices themselves have ended. Under segregation in the South, for example, African American staff members were assigned to schools that enrolled only African American students. These were often schools with outdated facilities and limited budgets. After integration took place, the effects of previous personnel assignment practices lingered until districts took action to reassign personnel in order to achieve balance in the racial distribution of staff members.

The fourth type of discrimination is *failure to make accommodation.* Section 504 of the Rehabilitation Act of 1973 and the Americans with Disabilities Act of 1990 require employers to make reasonable accommodations in order to enable employees who have disabilities to perform a job. Reasonable accommodations include improving accessibility, restructuring jobs, modifying work schedules, designing flexible leave policies, adjusting or modifying examinations and training materials, and providing qualified aides or assistants (Fersh & Thomas, 1993).

Sexual Harassment

When it occurs on the job, sexual harassment is considered discrimination and is prohibited under Title VII of the Civil Rights Act. Charges of job-related sexual harassment may be analyzed under either the disparate treatment or adverse impact theories, depending on the situation (Lindemann & Kadue, 1992).

Sexual harassment claims are usually one of three types: unwelcome sexual advances, gender-based animosity, or a sexually charged workplace. *Quid pro quo* discrimination occurs when an employee is the object of sexual advances that involve explicit or implicit promises of employment benefits in return for sexual favors. Hostile environment discrimination results from other employees or supervisors engaging in conduct that is offensive to an employee because of his or her gender, even if the conduct is not sexual in nature. For example, a woman who joins a previously all-male work group may be subjected to hostile comments and treatment by the male members of the group because of her gender (Lindemann & Kadue, 1992). Even if the actions of employees are not sexually suggestive, they constitute sexual harassment if the intent is to embarrass or humiliate another employee or to prevent that individual from doing his or her best work.

The Supreme Court, in *Meritor Savings Bank* v. *Vinson* (1986), held that sexual harassment violates Title VII's prohibition against sex discrimination even if the loss incurred by the offended employee is psychological and not financial. *Meritor* involved a sexual harassment claim against a supervisor by a female employee. The woman admitted that she had voluntarily had sexual relations with her boss on numerous occasions. The bank argued that the voluntary nature of the liaison freed the bank from liability, but the Supreme Court held that the test for sexual harassment was whether the woman had indicated that the sexual advances were unwelcome (Lindemann & Kadue, 1992). In *Harris* v. *Forklift Systems, Inc.* (1993), the Court clarified somewhat the conditions under which sexual harassment creates a hostile or sexually charged working environment. In the Court's words:

> Whether an environment is "hostile" or "abusive" can be determined only by looking at all the circumstances, which may include the frequency of the discriminatory conduct, its severity, whether it is physically threatening or humiliating . . . , and whether it unreasonably interferes with an employee's work performance. The effect on the employee's psychological well-being is relevant in determining whether the plaintiff actually found the environment abusive. But while psychological harm, like any other relevant factor, may be taken into account, no single factor is required.

Employer Liability. Employers may be held liable for harassment of an employee by a supervisor or another employee. In *Faragher* v. *Boca Raton* (1998), the Court reversed an Eleventh Circuit decision after a female lifeguard quit her job, charging that two male supervisors, by unwelcome touching and suggestive remarks, had created a sexually hostile workplace. The question was whether the employer (the city of Boca Raton, Florida) was liable for the actions of the supervisors. The lower court held that the city was not liable, but the Supreme Court reversed the appellate court, ruling that, since the employer had failed to exercise "reasonable care" to prevent and promptly correct any sexually harassing behavior, it was liable for the supervisors' actions. Increased litigation involving charges of sexual harassment has led to greater awareness of this problem but has also created confusion about what types of behavior are appropriate in the workplace.

Although the majority of sexual harassment charges are made by women against men, a male employee may bring a charge of sexual harassment against a female supervisor, and employees of either gender may bring charges of sexual harassment against a supervisor of the same sex (*Oncale v. Sundowner Offshore Services, Inc.*, 1998).

If a hostile environment exists in a workplace and the employer knew about the harassment and took no action to prevent it, the employer may be held liable. In defending against a charge of sexual harassment of an employee by a supervisor or co-worker, the employer must show that he or she exercised reasonable care to prevent harassment and that action was taken promptly when harassment was reported. Alternatively, the employer may develop a valid defense by showing that the harassed employee failed to promptly report incidents of harassment to the employer (Twomey, 2002).

A key element in cases involving sexual harassment of an employee by a supervisor is whether the harassing behavior was unwelcome. The fact that an employee did not object to sexual advances by a supervisor or a co-worker does not establish that the employee welcomed the behavior. In fact, courts are inclined to give the employee the benefit of the doubt in cases involving charges of harassment against a supervisor because of the disparity in power between the employee and the supervisor (Twomey, 2002).

Harassment of Students.   Although sexual harassment of students by school staff members has received little attention, the problem is more widespread than many people realize. One authority has estimated that about 15 percent of all students (more than one out of seven) are sexually abused by a school employee by the end of the twelfth grade (Hardy, 2002). Clearly this is a problem about which administrators need to be aware.

Administrators should be prepared to investigate charges of sexual harassment made by students against teachers, counselors, or other school personnel. Failure to take action may result in legal penalties against the district. In one such case a student recovered damages under Title IX as a result of sexual advances made by a school employee (*Franklin v. Gwinnett,* 1992), but in *Gebser v. Lago Vista Independent School District* (1998), the Supreme Court held that a student who had been sexually harassed could recover damages only if a school official knew about the harassment and failed to take steps to correct the problem (Dowling-Sendor, 2002).

Charges of sexual harassment made by students against school personnel must always be thoroughly investigated and, when appropriate, corrective actions taken. However, it should not be assumed that the accused employee is guilty before the evidence has been reviewed. Students have occasionally lodged false charges of sexual harassment against a teacher or coach out of anger. Students may also misinterpret an innocent gesture by an adult as being sexually motivated. The investigator's first task is to establish that the student understands sexual harassment. Most children today have a pretty clear understanding of acceptable and unacceptable behavior, and most educators are wise enough to avoid actions involving students that might be misinterpreted.

Establish Policy.   All school districts should have a policy on sexual harassment, spelling out what constitutes sexual harassment and explaining the procedures by which incidents are to be reported. The policy should designate the official responsible for investigating charges of sexual harassment and provide for protection against retaliation of the employee (Hubbartt, 1993). A new area of sexual harassment litigation has recently appeared, the distribution of sexual jokes or pornographic images by email. The policy dealing with sexual harassment should remind employees that the computer network is operated by the school district and is to be used only for school-related business (Towns & Johnson, 2003).

A comprehensive policy may cover sexual harassment affecting both employees and students. The Northstar School District in Alaska has such a policy (*www.northstar.k12.ak.us/eeo/sexual_131_1011.html*). Among the provisions of this policy is one permitting an employee to report harassment to a district office administrator in case the person accused of harassment is the employee's own supervisor. The policy also protects the confidentiality of employees who file harassment charges and spells out possible disciplinary actions against those who are found guilty of harassment.

Montgomery County (MD) Public Schools' policy on sexual harassment advises students who believe they are the subject of sexual harassment or "the focus of inappropriate behavior" to report the facts either verbally or in writing to their parents or to the principal, a guidance counselor, or a teacher. Students are also asked to provide supporting details, including the dates and times of any incidents, descriptions of the actions of the offending person, and names of witnesses. The policy defines sexual harassment and lists sexually suggestive actions that are prohibited (*www.mcps.h12.md.us/departments/publishingservices/sexharas.shtm*).

DEFENDING PERSONNEL PRACTICES

If a district is charged with discrimination in hiring practices, it may be able successfully to defend its actions by showing that the relevant characteristics of the applicant pool are comparable to the characteristics of the employees hired. Thus, for example, if 15 percent of applicants are members of a protected group and the district can show that an equal or greater percentage of persons hired were members of that group, that constitutes *prima facie* evidence of the absence of disparate treatment.

A more stringent test involves a comparison of the characteristics of those hired with the characteristics of members of the labor pool. This was the test used by the courts in the *Hazelwood* case. Hazelwood School District was charged by the Justice Department with violating Title VII of the Civil Rights Act by failing to recruit and employ African American teachers. The district's attorneys argued that, since the percentage of African American teachers employed by the district equaled or exceeded the percentage of African American students, the district was in compliance. The Supreme Court ultimately ruled that the relevant comparison was not the ratio of teachers to students but rather the ratio of minority teachers employed by the district to the number of qualified minority persons in the labor pool in the St. Louis metropolitan area. Hazelwood lost the suit and was required to hire and give back pay to minority applicants who had previously been rejected (*Hazelwood School District v. United States*, 1977).

Preventing discrimination before it happens is preferable to correcting it after it has occurred. School districts can help prevent discrimination by adopting an equal employment opportunity policy and publicizing it in advertisements and employee handbooks and by ensuring that personnel practices conform to the policy. Adopting practices that advance the goal of equal opportunity ensures that the policy will have its intended effect.

Human relations personnel should be reminded periodically that all records—including personnel files, correspondence, and computer files—are subject to subpoena when a suit is filed against the district. Even email messages can be obtained by attorneys in the search for evidence that the district has performed actions that are illegal. A standard rule for human relations personnel should be: Never place anything in an employee's personnel file unless the individual has seen the document and signed a statement indicating that he or she is aware that it will be part of the personnel file. It is also recommended that employees have access to their personnel files periodically (Thome, 1996).

Establishing a Defense

Personnel practices that have disparate impact may nevertheless be allowed by the courts, provided that the district is able to show a bona fide occupational qualification (BFOQ) or business necessity. One school district was upheld by the courts after hiring a male applicant without a master's degree over a female with the degree by arguing the male could be hired at a lower salary and could also perform coaching duties. To successfully use business necessity as a defense, an employer must be able to show that the practice is necessary for the efficient operation of the district and that no acceptable alternatives with lesser adverse impact are available (Valente, 1980).

Exclusion refers to the degree of pervasiveness of a particular practice. If personnel practices occasionally result in adverse impact to members of protected groups, there is a lower level of legal vulnerability than if the practices consistently result in adverse impact upon those groups. Employers are most likely to win a legal challenge when a practice involves a low degree of exclusion and a high degree of business necessity. Employers are most vulnerable when exclusion is high and business necessity is low (Schlei & Grossman, 1976).

Other factors that are sometimes considered in discrimination cases are the degree of potential risk to human health and safety or the potential for economic loss resulting from employee performance. An airline company may be able to justify exclusionary selection practices in hiring pilots by showing that the practices are necessary to reduce the chance of injury or death to passengers resulting from performance of inadequately trained employees. A hospital might support exclusionary hiring practices by showing that they are necessary to protect the health of patients. Exclusionary practices may also be defended by showing that they reduce the amount of potential economic loss to the employer resulting from employees who lack essential skills. Employers whose work involves lower levels of risk would be held to a correspondingly lower level of exclusionary practice in hiring.

Accurate and detailed records are a necessity to a successful defense if a district is charged with discrimination in employment practices. It is recommended that the district human resources office maintain charts showing the age, race, color, sex, and national origin of all applicants and similar information about those hired. Since collecting such information on the application form itself may itself constitute *prima facie* evidence of discriminatory intent, it is advisable to use a pre-employment inquiry form to collect that data. This is a form that all applicants are asked to complete and return separately from the application form itself. The applicant has the option of filling out the preemployment inquiry anonymously in order to avoid the possibility of being identified.

AFFIRMATIVE ACTION AND REVERSE DISCRIMINATION

The intent of affirmative action is to open job opportunities that have traditionally been closed to minorities and women. The purpose is not, as some have assumed, to achieve "proportional representation through preferential hiring" (Fullinwider, 1980, p. 159). There is little disagreement on the need for and importance of providing educational and employment opportunities to members of groups that have been subject to discrimination. However, preferential hiring, which is one element of affirmative action, arouses strong feelings from both proponents and opponents (Fullinwider, 1980).

Amendments to Title VII of the Civil Rights enacted by Congress in 1991 made it unlawful for an employer to adjust scores on employment tests or set different cut-off scores for the purpose of benefiting applicants of one race, color, religion, sex, or national origin. Such actions are known as *reverse discrimination,* and the Supreme Court has placed limitations on such actions unless they serve a "compelling governmental interest" and are "narrowly tailored" to correct specific instances of past discrimination.

Reverse discrimination occurs when members of a protected group such as African Americans or females are given preference in employment decisions in order to correct the effects of previous discrimination. These actions have been approved by the courts when they have been designed specifically to correct past discrimination and do no unnecessary harm to the rights of other employees.

Actions by school districts to protect the jobs of minorities when layoffs occur were the subject of Supreme Court review in *Wygant* v. *Jackson Board of Education* (1986) and *Taxman* v. *Piscataway* (1996). In both of those cases, a white teacher was laid off while a minority teacher with less or equal seniority was retained in order to maintain or increase the proportion of minority teachers in the district. The action was justified as a means of correcting past societal discrimination. In both cases, courts rejected the Board's actions. In the Piscataway (NJ) case, the Third Circuit Court stated (Moran, 2002):

> [T]he harm imposed upon a nonminority employee by the loss of his or her job is so substantial and the cost so severe that the Board's goal of racial diversity, even if legitimate under Title VII, may not be pursued in this particular fashion.

The Court added:

> [W]e recognize that the differences among us underlie the richness and strength of our Nation. . . . Although we applaud the goal of racial diversity, we cannot agree that Title VII permits an employer to advance that goal through nonremedial discriminatory measures.

SUMMARY

Local school boards have the authority to employ, assign, transfer, suspend, and terminate teachers, and they are given wide latitude by the courts in the exercise of those powers. States require teachers to have a valid teaching certificate. Boards may assign teachers to schools as long as there is no violation of the bargaining agreement or the teachers' contract. Reassignments are subject to legal challenge if they involve a demotion, but most courts have upheld the board in these cases.

Title VII of the Civil Rights Act affords protection against discriminatory employment decisions based on race, color, gender, religion, and national origin for all employees. The Pregnancy Discrimination Act extended the same protections to pregnant employees. The Age Discrimination in Employment Act protects employees above the age of 40 from age discrimination in personnel decisions, and the Equal Pay Act requires employers to pay women the same as men when they perform similar jobs. The Rehabilitation Act and Americans with Disabilities Act make it illegal for employers to refuse to hire persons with disabilities because of their disabilities and require employers to make reasonable accommodations for such employees. The Family and Medical Leave Act of 1993 allows employees to take time off from work when they have illness in the family or a newborn or adopted child.

SUGGESTED ACTIVITIES

1. Examine the State Code of your state and identify the qualifications for teachers, counselors, and administrators. What qualifications are listed besides educational ones?

2. All states require teachers and other professional personnel to be licensed. They also provide for revocation of the license. What are the conditions in your state for which a professional license may be revoked? Does the State Code spell out due process rights of employees whose licenses are revoked? If so, what are they?

3. Obtain a copy of a sexual harassment policy for a school district and answer these questions:
   a. What actions does the policy require a supervisor to take when he or she first learns about a charge of sexual harassment by a person whom he or she supervises?
   b. What procedures are recommended to ascertain the facts about a harassment charge?
   c. What corrective actions are suggested or required when a charge of sexual harassment is confirmed?

4. Suppose that you are the principal of a middle school. One of your teachers belongs to a religious group that requires its members to observe six holy days each year. Members are required to be absent from their work on those days. The bargaining agreement provides for three religious holidays and three days for conducting "necessary personal business." Personal business days are granted only if the employee can demonstrate need. The teacher in your school asks that he be allowed to use the personal business days for religious observance. This has not been done previously in the district. What will you tell the teacher? (The Supreme Court decided a similar case in *Ansonia Board of Education* v. *Philbrook*, 1986.)

5. A teacher has asked for a one-month leave under the Family and Medical Leave Act of 1993 while she recuperates from cosmetic surgery. If you were Director of Human Resources, what additional information would you need before recom-

mending approval of the teacher's request? Suppose the teacher had asked for leave while her 5-year-old son recuperates from surgery for strabismus. What would you recommend in that situation?

ONLINE RESOURCES

These sites provide information on legal issues in human resources management.

American Association of University Women
(http://www.aauw.org/ef/harass/schoolresources/cfm)

AAUW provides a description of several publications dealing with preventing sexual harassment of students by other students.

Centers for Disease Control (www.cdc.gov/ncipc/dvp/yvpt/partner.htm)

This resource provides links to organizations and agencies that supply information on and assistance in preventing and coping with youth violence.

Cornell University Legal Information Institute
(www.law.cornell.edu/topics/employment.html)

This comprehensive site provides information about all aspects of employment law, including federal and state statutes, judicial decisions, and agency regulations.

Employment Law Information Network (www.elinfonet.com/)

News items pertaining to employment law and links to sites with information about various aspects of employment law are featured on this site.

Equal Employment Opportunity Commission (www.eeoc.gov/index.html)

This site contains information on federal laws prohibiting job discrimination enforced by EEOC. News of recent EEOC decisions and information on technical assistance and training are also given.

Findlaw (www.findlaw.com)

Searchable databases of state statutes and court decisions as well as federal laws and court rulings are provided. Advice on various aspects of human resources management is given at (http://smallbiz.biz.findlaw.com).

Kentucky Center for Safe Schools (http://kysafeschools.org/clear/index.html)

The Clearinghouse locates and evaluates information on school safety practices and disseminates the information through the Internet and by CDs, print, and email newsletters.

Library of Congress (lcweb.loc.gov/global/state/stategov.html)

The Library of Congress website contains full texts of state statutes as well as legislative updates.

Uniform Guidelines on Employee Selection
(http://www.dol.gov/esa/regs/cfr/41cfr/toc_Chapt60/60_3_toc.htm)

The Guidelines were developed jointly by the EEOC, the Civil Service Commission, and the Departments of Justice and Labor to meet the need for consistency in personnel selection procedures.

REFERENCES

Ansonia Board of Education v. *Philbrook*, 478 U.S. 1034, 1047 (1986).

Arline v. *School Board of Nassau County*, 772 F.2d 759 (1985).

Beckham, J. (1985). *Legal aspects of employee assessment and selection in public schools.* Topeka, KS: National Organization on Legal Problems of Education.

Connick v. *Myers*, 461 U.S. 138 (1983).

Cox v. *Dardanelle Public School District*, 790 F.2d 668 (1986).

Daniels v. *Quinn*, 801 F.2d 687 (1986).

Director, J. (1973). Mandatory maternity leave, rules or policies for public school teachers as constituting violation of equal protection clause of Fourteenth amendment to Federal Constitution. *American Law Reports federal cases and annotations* (17 ALR 768). Rochester, NY: Lawyers Co-operative Publishing.

Dowling-Sendor, B. (2002, August). School law. What did they know? *American School Board Journal, 189,* 40–42.

Education law (Vol. 2). (1989). New York: Matthew Bender.

Eisenstadt v. *Baird*, 405 U.S. 438 (1972).

Faragher v. *Boca Raton*, 111 F.3d 1530 (1998).

Ferrara v. *Mills*, 781 F.2d 1508 (1986).

Fersh, D., & Thomas, P. (1993). *Complying with the Americans with Disabilities Act: A guidebook for management and people with disabilities.* Westport, CT: Quorum.

Franklin v. *Gwinnett County Public Schools*, 503 U.S. 60 (1992).

Fullinwider, R. (1980). *The reverse discrimination controversy: A moral and legal analysis.* Totowa, NJ: Rowman & Littlefield.

Gebser v. *Lago Vista Independent School District*, 524 U.S. 274 (1998).

Gordon, P. (1992). The job application process after the Americans with Disabilities Act. *Employee Relations Law Journal, 18,* 185–213.

Griggs v. *Duke Power Company*, 401 U S 424 (1971).

Gurmankin v. *Costanzo*, 556 F.2d 184 (1977).

Hardy, L. (2002, June). Trust betrayed. *American School Board Journal, 189,* 14–18.

Harris v. *Forklift Systems, Inc.* 510 U.S. 17 (1993).

Hauck, V. (1998). *Arbitrating sex discrimination grievances.* Westport, CT: Quorum.

Hazelwood School District v. *United States*, 433 U.S. 299 (1977).

Hubbartt, W. (1993). *Personnel policy handbook.* New York: McGraw Hill.

Hubbartt, W. S. (1998). *The new battle over workplace privacy.* New York: AMACOM.

Hudgins, H., Jr., & Vacca, R. (1995). *Law and education: Contemporary issues and court decisions* (4th ed.). Charlottesville, VA: Michie.

Jacobs, R. (1993). *Legal compliance guide to personnel management.* Englewood Cliffs, NJ: Prentice Hall.

Jett v. *Dallas Independent School District*, 798 F.2d 748 (1986).

Lindemann, B., & Kadue, D. (1992). *Primer on sexual harassment.* Washington, DC: Bureau of National Affairs.

May v. *Evansville-Vanderburgh School Corporation*, 787 F.2d 1105 (1986).

McCarthy, M. (1983). Discrimination in employment. In J. Beckham and P. Zirkel (Eds.), *Legal issues in public school employment* (pp. 22–54). Bloomington, IN: Phi Delta Kappa.

McCarthy, M., & Cambron-McCabe, N. (1992). *Public school law: Teachers' and students' rights* (3rd ed.). Boston: Allyn and Bacon.

McCulloch, K. (1981). *Selecting employees safely under the law.* Englewood Cliffs, NJ: Prentice Hall.

Meritor Savings Bank v. *Vinson*, 106 S. Ct. 2399 (1986).

Miner, M., & Miner, J. (1978). *Employee selection within the law.* Washington, DC: Bureau of National Affairs.

Moran, J. J. (2002). *Employment law* (2nd ed.). Upper Saddle River, NJ: Prentice-Hall.

National Center for Education Statistics. (2000). *Privacy issues in education staff records: Guidelines for education agencies.* Washington DC: U.S. Department of Education.

Oncale v. *Sundowner Offshore Services, Inc.*, 83 F.3d 118 (1998).

Schlei, B., & Grossman, P. (1976). *Employment discrimination law.* Washington, DC: Bureau of National Affairs.

Schneid, T. (1992). *The Americans with Disabilities Act: A practical guide for managers.* New York: Van Nostrand Reinhold.

Sorenson, G. (1987). Employees. In S. Thomas (Ed.), *The yearbook of school law* (pp. 1–44). Topeka, KS: National Organization on Legal Problems of Education.

Sovereign, K. (1999). *Personnel law.* Upper Saddle River, NJ: Prentice Hall.

Taxman v. *Board of Education of the Township of Piscataway*, 91 F.3d 1547 (3rd Cir. 1996).

Thome, J. (1996). *A concise guide to successful employment practices* (2nd ed.). Chicago: CCH Inc.

Towns, D. M., & Johnson, M. S. (2003, Summer). Sexual harassment in the 21st century—e-harassment in the workplace. *Employee Relations Law Journal, 29,* 7–24.

Twomey, D. P. (2002). *Employment discrimination law: A manager's guide* (5th ed.). Cincinnati, OH: West.

United States v. *State of South Carolina,* 434 U.S. 1026 (1978).

Valente, W. (1980). *Law in the schools.* Columbus, OH: Merrill.

van Geel, T. (1987). *The courts and American education law.* Buffalo, NY: Prometheus.

Wardwell v. *Board of Education of the City School District of Cincinnati,* 529 F.2d 625 (1976).

Wygant v. *Jackson Board of Education,* 476 U.S. 267 (1986).

CHAPTER THIRTEEN

COLLECTIVE BARGAINING IN SCHOOLS

The work of most teachers in schools in the United States is governed by negotiated contracts between teachers' organizations and boards of education. The process by which the parties reach agreement on a contract is known as *collective bargaining*. Collective bargaining originated early in the twentieth century as industrial unions fought successfully for better working conditions and the right to participate in decisions about their work.

The National Education Association (NEA), the larger of two national organizations that represent teachers, is not affiliated with the labor movement, preferring the designation "professional organization." However, in its actions, NEA resembles industrial unions; its tactics and objectives are quite similar to those of the American Federation of Teachers (AFT), which is the other, smaller organization for teachers. The AFT is affiliated with the national labor movement.

Board negotiators are sensitive to the dollar costs of union proposals but pay less attention to their potential impact on instructional quality. The unions seek provisions to protect job security, establish satisfactory conditions of work, and guarantee generous salaries and benefits. These and other similar provisions may create barriers to improved instruction by limiting the district's power to dismiss or transfer employees, change job descriptions, or alter staffing patterns. Once incorporated into the contract, they are difficult to change, and improving instruction becomes dependent on the willingness of the union to accept modifications in the contract.

PLAN OF THE CHAPTER

This book advocates an approach to collective bargaining that encourages negotiators to consider the potential effects on instruction of contract proposals, in addition to the usual attention given to issues of cost and security. The following topics are covered in this chapter: (1) public sector bargaining, (2) scope of bargaining, (3) new forms of collective bargaining, (4) negotiating processes, and (5) impact of collective bargaining on schools.

PUBLIC SECTOR BARGAINING

Public sector employees in the United States won the right to bargain collectively with their employers long after their private sector counterparts had secured that right. The passage of the National Labor Relations Act in 1935 recognized labor–management bargaining in the private sector, but it was not until 25 years later that states began to authorize bargaining for public employees. According to the most recent count, 40 states have statutes that provide for collective bargaining or some variant of it for public employees (Najita & Stern, 2001).

Wisconsin was the first state to authorize collective bargaining between teachers' unions and school boards. That legislation took effect in 1959, and other states soon followed Wisconsin's lead (Creswell & Murphy, 1980). Thirty-four states provide for collective bargaining by teachers' unions, whereas only five prohibit bargaining between teachers and school boards. The other states have no provision of any kind (Marczely & Marczely, 2002). Collective bargaining has been called one of the three most significant developments in public education. The other two are desegregation and the introduction of categorical aid programs (Mitchell, Kerchner, Erck, & Pryor, 1981).

Public sector collective bargaining laws vary in the degree of regulatory specificity and in the types of rights accorded to the unions. Some states grant teachers' unions the right to "meet-and-confer" with school boards, whereas others provide detailed prescriptions of what may and may not be negotiated. In states with meet-and-confer laws, teachers' unions may present the case for better pay and working conditions, but the boards are free to ignore their suggestions. A number of states copy the language of the National Labor Relations Act and provide for discussion of "wages, hours and other terms and conditions of employment."

The development of collective bargaining in schools typically followed a path that began with an imbalance of power between the parties, with the school board holding much more power than the teachers' union. Over time, the balance shifted so that power is now more evenly divided between unions and management (Mitchell, et al., 1981).

Most states specifically prohibit public employees from striking, but 14 states have provisions that allow strikes by some employees. Employees who provide essential services and those whose absence from the job would create a danger to public safety are forbidden from walking off the job. Work stoppages by teachers are fairly common because teachers' work is not usually considered essential (Najita & Stern, 2001).

SCOPE OF BARGAINING

Topics of discussion between teacher organizations and boards of education are determined by the legal framework governing bargaining, the history of the relationship between the parties, and their willingness to negotiate an issue (Cresswell & Murphy, 1980). Legislation may specify mandatory topics (those about which the parties must negotiate) and exclude others from the bargaining table. Any topic that is not specifically mandated or forbidden is subject to negotiation if the parties agree. A list of items that are often included in teacher contracts appears in Exhibit 13.1.

Unions like to widen the scope of the negotiations to cover as many aspects of the work situation as possible. However, management generally prefers to limit the scope of the talks in the belief that anything not covered in the contract remains a prerogative of management (Mitchell et al., 1981). In addition to negotiating salaries and conditions of work, teacher unions favor including in the contract policies relating to the curriculum, student placement, and teacher selection and assignment. Almost half (46 percent) of agreements in effect during the 1981–82 school year contained provisions on curriculum. About 64 percent had policies on student placement, and 96 percent provided for policies relating to teacher selection and assignment (Goldschmidt, Bowers, Riley, & Stuart, 1984).

Some contract provisions have more impact on instruction than others. Examples of proposals that could have an effect on instruction are shown in Figure 13.1. The figure shows the positions taken by the union and the board of education on each issue. In the middle, a marker indicates the position that would be most likely to promote instructional quality. The nearer the mark appears to the position taken by one of the parties, the greater the likelihood that that party's position is instructionally responsible. The issues are discussed in the paragraphs that follow.

Teacher Evaluation

Through collective bargaining, teachers' unions push to include in the contract restrictions on evaluation practices that they believe are unfair or that might be used by administrators to punish teachers. The restrictions include limiting when and where teacher observations can be held and what data may be included in written evaluations. Unions also seek to write into the contract prohibitions against evaluating teachers on the use of one approved model of instruction, arguing that teachers may achieve equally good results using a variety of approaches (Black, 1993).

The agreement between the Salida (Colorado) School Board and the Salida Teachers Association contains a detailed provision dealing with teacher evaluation. The contract identifies several purposes for teacher evaluation, including self-improvement, documentation for possible termination of tenured teachers, improved instruction, and assistance in implementing a revised curriculum. The contract also establishes rules for classroom observations. All observations are to be conducted by the school principal, who may not use video- or audio-recording devices without the teacher's permission. The agreement requires three observations each year of probationary teachers and two observations of tenured teachers. Each observation must be followed within five days by a joint principal-teacher evaluation conference. If the principal observes deficiencies in the teacher's classroom performance, those must be identified in writing along with objectives for improvement and a plan for assistance, and must allow a reasonable amount of time for improvement. Teachers are given the right to append written comments to the principal's evaluation, both of which are to be placed in the teacher's file.

EXHIBIT 13.1

TYPICAL PROVISIONS OF NEGOTIATED AGREEMENTS

    I. Recognition of the union and union rights

    II. Management rights

    III. Rules governing negotiations

    IV. Shared decision making

    V. Staffing
       Class size
       Placement of children with disabilities
       Common planning time
       Teaching load
       Duty-free lunch

    VI. Teacher assignments
       Transfers
       Layoffs and recall procedures

    VII. Professional development

    VIII. Performance evaluation
       Teacher discipline and reprimands

    IX. Working conditions
       Class size
       Work day
       Academic freedom
       Books and supplies
       Teacher personnel files
       Parent conferences
       Telephones
       Parking
       Mail
       Classroom environmental control
       Student discipline

    X. Compensation and benefits
       Credit for previous work experience
       Salary schedule
       Advancement on the salary schedule
       Pay for extra duties
       Mileage
       Severance pay
       Retirement benefits
       Insurance

    XII. Leaves of absence and sick leave

    XIII. Dispute resolution
       Grievance procedure
       Mediation
       Arbitration

FIGURE 13.1 **Location of Most Instructionally Effective Position between Opposing Demands of Teacher Union and Board on Selected Issues**

ISSUE	TEACHER POSITION
Teacher evaluation	Limited number of classroom observations with advance notice
Transfer and reassignment	More senior teachers have choice of teaching assignments; no involuntary transfers
Selection and hiring	Teacher committee interviews applicants and recommends person to be hired
Class size	Specified upper limit; class divided or aide provided if limit exceeded
Lesson preparation	Limit on number; additional planning time provided if exceeded
Extra-duty assignments	Duties required only if stated in agreement; pay for all extra duty
Planning time	Minimum number of minutes per week; no exceptions
Curriculum and text-book committees	Teachers volunteer and are paid extra
Reduction in force	Enrollment loss and program change only basis for reduction Reductions absorbed by attrition whenever possible; otherwise seniority governs
Working conditions	Require daily preparation period for elementary and secondary teachers; limit classroom interruptions; provide teaching supplies and individual desk, filing cabinet, and storage space for all teachers
Employee leave	Allowed for illness of employee or family member; no proof of illness required; personal leave granted for any reason
Safety and security	District will reimburse all teachers for medical expenses and loss or destruction of property from a physical attack occurring on or near school property; district will take action leading to arrest and conviction of individuals involved in physical attack on a teacher

FIGURE 13.1   Continued

INSTRUCTIONALLY EFFECTIVE POSITION	BOARD POSITION
— — — — X —	No limit, no advance notice
— — — — X —	Administrators decide, considering teachers' expressed preferences
— — X — — —	Principal interviews applicants and decides who to hire
— — — X — —	Principal decides optimum size based on teacher skills, budget, and student needs
— — X — — —	Principal considers number of preparations but no absolute limit on number
— — — X — —	Duties performed as needed upon assignment by principal; pay only if contract requires
— X — — — —	Provided within limits of available resources
— X — — — —	Teachers volunteer or are appointed; no extra pay
— — — — X —	Enrollment loss, program change, budget cutbacks, and other factors allowed
— — — — X —	Reductions absorbed by attrition if possible; otherwise seniority and other factors govern
X — — — — —	Provide preparation period for secondary teachers when practicable; provide teaching supplies, furniture, and equipment appropriate for the type of instruction
— X — — — —	Sick leave for illness of employee only; proof of illness required; personal leave for specified reasons only
— — — — X —	District will provide free insurance to cover medical expenses and loss or destruction of personal property resulting from a physical attack on school property; district will provide assistance of the association attorney in pursuing legal action against an attacker

Transfer and Reassignment/Selection

Teacher transfer and reassignment policies have long been an area of contention between boards and unions (McDonnell & Pascal, 1979). Teacher unions prefer limiting involuntary transfers to situations involving declining enrollment or changes in programs and favor making seniority the sole criterion for deciding who is transferred (Cresswell & Murphy, 1980). Board negotiators favor allowing administrators to make these decisions under more general guidelines.

The importance for teacher morale of contractual safeguards against arbitrary decisions on transfer and reassignment should not be underestimated, but neither should the potential negative consequences for the quality of instruction be overlooked. A principal who is prevented from selecting the most qualified teacher is hampered in trying to improve the quality of learning in the school.

Some negotiated contracts contain clauses prohibiting discrimination against employees by either the union or the board. When discrimination is suspected, the employee has a choice of filing a grievance, which may ultimately be decided by arbitration, or bringing suit under a state or federal statute such as Title VII. The U.S. Supreme Court has on at least one occasion voiced concern about handling discrimination claims through arbitration. Since the procedures used in arbitration are somewhat less formal than those followed in court proceedings, the justices questioned whether arbitration would result in a thorough and fair outcome. As a general rule, transcripts of arbitration proceedings are less complete, and procedures that are routinely followed in a courtroom—such as discovery, cross-examination, and testimony under oath—are often ignored in arbitration hearings. The Supreme Court was concerned that the more lax rules and procedures common to arbitration proceedings might result in questionable decisions (Hauck, 1998).

Class Size/Preparations

Class size is another contentious issue between boards and teachers' representatives. Teachers prefer smaller classes over larger ones, and they attempt to persuade boards of education of the benefits to student learning from reducing class size. Board members tend to be skeptical of these claims, and researchers who have studied the question are also divided about the possible benefits of small classes. There is agreement about the cost of reducing class sizes—it is expensive—but there is less agreement about the effects.

The best-designed study on class size was conducted in Tennessee in the mid-1980s. In this four-year study, students in the early grades were randomly assigned to one of three conditions (1 teacher to 20 students, 1 teacher to 20 students with an instructional aide, and 1 teacher to 15 students). Seventy-nine schools enrolling 6300 students participated in the study. Students who were in small classes scored substantially better on standardized tests in reading, word-study skills, and mathematics than those in larger classes, including those in classrooms with an instructional aide. Moreover, the researchers found a strong relationship between the length of time children remained in small classes and their test scores. Each additional year that children were in small classes added to their learning advantage (Biddle & Berliner, 2002).

Limits on the number of different preparations a teacher may be assigned make sense from the point of view of instructional effectiveness. Again, however, such a policy is difficult to administer if expressed in absolute terms with no room allowed for administrative judgment.

Extra Duty

Unions prefer that the contract specify the extra duties teachers are required to perform and include rules to ensure fairness in the assignment of those duties. They also favor provisions for additional pay for noninstructional tasks.

Duties that have traditionally been a part of teachers' responsibilities, such as sponsoring clubs and meeting with parents, have become optional under most negotiated agreements. In districts that do not pay extra for them, these jobs are often not done. Even teachers who are willing to donate their time are discouraged from doing so by union officers anxious to preserve the principle of extra pay for extra work (Mitchell, et al., 1981).

Some extra duties are necessary for the efficient operation of the school, but an excessive number can interfere with good instruction. It is not always possible to anticipate what duties may be necessary, so some flexibility is needed. Everything considered, the best solution seems to be to include in the contract a statement acknowledging the administration's responsibility for fair and judicious use of extra duty and providing extra pay for the more time-consuming tasks. The statement should also acknowledge teachers' responsibility to perform the duties.

Planning Time

Teachers seek to include in the contract a statement that guarantees a minimum number of minutes of common planning time each week. Adequate planning time is essential for effective instruction, and allowing common planning periods leads to increased collaboration among teachers, thus further contributing to improved student learning. However, it is not always possible to develop a schedule that allows for common planning time, and some flexibility must be permitted.

Curriculum and Textbook Committees

The majority of contracts contain no provision dealing with curriculum revision and textbook selection committees (Cresswell & Murphy, 1980). These committees perform important functions, and teachers who serve on them should receive payment for their time.

Reduction in Force

Both sides have an interest in limiting the impact of reduction in force on employee morale. Usually both teacher and board negotiators are willing to discuss the order of release, but they sometimes disagree on the criteria to be used. Unions prefer that seniority be the only factor considered, whereas management argues for allowing considerations of performance and program needs in making reduction-in-force decisions (Cresswell & Murphy, 1980).

Reduction in force can impact instruction by depleting the faculty of a school of persons qualified to teacher certain subjects and by triggering bumping, which may lead to less qualified teachers taking over for those who are more qualified. Chapter 15 discusses this topic in more detail.

Working Conditions

Negotiations over working conditions are sometimes tedious because of the variety of issues covered. Working conditions include use of telephones, delivery of mail, parking rules, parent conferences, and student discipline. The last two items on that list are the most likely to stir controversy. Teachers prefer to have scheduled times for parent conferences and do not like to be called on to confer with parents without advance notice. The administration, on the other hand, strives to address parents' concerns promptly, even when it means a teacher must remain after school on short notice to meet a parent. The issue is usually resolved via compromise, with teachers agreeing to meet parents on days reserved for that purpose and at other "mutually convenient times" as the need arises.

On matters pertaining to student discipline, teachers seek to establish rules that give them flexibility and support in dealing with student disruptions. Teachers want to be able to send a child out of the classroom when they believe it is necessary in order for instruction to proceed smoothly. Administrators argue that, because the school has no means of supervising students who are not in class, teachers should not be allowed to dispatch students at will.

Safety and Security

Teachers are justifiably concerned about their safety and that of the students with whom they work. Although the number of violent attacks in schools is small, the possibility of one is always present, and teachers are reasonable in asking boards to take action to reduce the risk. However, legal action against those who perpetrate attacks is the province of civil authorities and not the school board.

NEW FORMS OF COLLECTIVE BARGAINING

In recent years, a search has been undertaken to find new approaches to collective bargaining that will permit the parties to reach agreements more quickly and encourage boards and unions to cooperate in the interest of improving education. Several new models have been tried, with varying degrees of success. Among the new approaches are expedited bargaining, progressive bargaining, the win/win approach, principled negotiations, and strategic bargaining.

In *expedited bargaining,* the parties agree to limit the amount of time available to reach an agreement and the number of issues that will be discussed. The time limit is usually two to three weeks and the number of items to be discussed is usually no more than 10. Expedited bargaining avoids the protracted discussions that have in the past held up school operations and planning while negotiations were underway (National Education Association, 1991).

Progressive bargaining is the opposite of expedited bargaining. Progressive bargaining is intended to permit full discussion of any issue that either party wishes to raise. Because of the number of issues examined and the amount of time spent on each one, progressive bargaining sometimes continues for months. Issues are referred to subcommittees for study, and if a stalemate is reached, fact finding and mediation are used to resolve the impasse (National Education Association, 1991).

Win/win bargaining was developed by a sociology professor, Irving Goldaber, who specialized in conflict resolution and hostage intervention. This form of bargaining is highly structured, and includes detailed rules that govern negotiating sessions. At the outset, participants must agree that the needs of the institution take precedence over individual goals (Booth, 1993). Some authorities describe win/win bargaining as an "attempt to bring civility to teacher bargaining" but criticize it because unions attempt to use the process to increase teacher power at the expense of the board's prerogatives. According to these critics, a school board that accepts limitations on its authority in order to maintain a collaborative relationship with the teachers' union is likely to find itself hamstrung in trying to improve educational quality or introduce efficiency measures (Geisert & Lieberman, 1994).

Principled negotiations was developed by the Harvard University Negotiation Project and is intended for use in any setting, including negotiations between employers and employees. The objective of this approach is to allow both parties to benefit without compromising their interests (Fisher & Ury, 1981, 1988). The principled negotiations approach provides a set of guidelines for negotiators that help remove the most common stumbling blocks to agreement. Among these guidelines are the following (National Education Association, 1991):

1. *Separate the people from the problem.* Negotiators are encouraged to accept emotions expressed by the other side and to allow people to let off steam without reacting angrily. Negotiators are urged to listen actively and speak clearly.

2. *Focus on interests, not positions.* An individual's or group's position on an issue is a way of advancing an underlying interest. By trying to identify the interest, bargaining partners can identify other, more acceptable, positions that may be equally effective at advancing their interests.

3. *Invent options for mutual gain.* The idea here is to create new choices that satisfy both shared and separate interests. This guideline helps avoid situations in

which both parties lock in to positions early and refuse to yield. It also helps the parties refrain from the assumption that a win for one side necessarily signifies a loss for the other.

4. *Evaluate options, not power.* The parties to the negotiations should establish a set of criteria by which proposals will be judged. The criteria might include fairness, cost, and practicality. In the absence of criteria, the final outcome is often determined by which party is more unyielding in its positions.

Strategic bargaining is the negotiating counterpart to strategic planning. In this approach, the parties are urged to develop a vision of the future for their organization and to identify potential hurdles that might be encountered in trying to actualize that vision. The power of strategic bargaining is its focus on the future and the underlying assumption that labor and management must contribute to building the future, that neither can do it alone (National Education Association, 1991).

NEGOTIATING PROCESSES

Both sides in collective bargaining know that they have the power to inflict damage on the other. The board can withhold the concessions teachers seek, and teachers can strike. (Even in localities in which strikes are unlawful, unions are sometimes willing to risk them in order to extract concessions.) Most of the time, collective bargaining works because the two sides develop a level of trust that allows them to work cooperatively to reach a mutually acceptable agreement. This trust does not emerge immediately, however. As with most human exchanges, development of trust between negotiators takes time.

Successful negotiations occur in three stages, as depicted in Figure 13.2. In the first stage, demands are heard and the parties agree on the issues to be negotiated and the order in which items are to be taken up (Lipsky & Conley, 1986). Board representatives sometimes try to postpone negotiating economic issues in hopes that the union will make concessions on other items in order to proceed more quickly to wages and benefits (Geisert & Lieberman, 1994). During the second stage, parties come to acknowledge one another's legitimacy and begin developing trust. In the third stage, serious bargaining takes place, with both parties making concessions on less vital issues in order to prevail on more important questions (Lipsky & Conley, 1986).

Both sides learn what the other side hopes to gain from the negotiations early in the process, but it takes longer for them to begin to get a picture of what the other is willing to accept. Bargaining proceeds through a series of give-and-take exchanges with each party yielding on some demands in return for concessions from the other side (Mitchell et al., 1981). Teacher negotiators, for example, may demand a 10 percent salary increase, expecting to settle for 7 or 8 percent and pre-

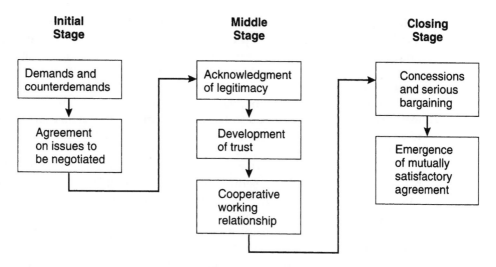

FIGURE 13.2   **Stages in a Successful Collective Bargaining Relationship**

pared to strike if the board does not come through with at least 6.5 percent. The board, on the other hand, may approach the table prepared to offer 6 percent but preferring to settle for 5.5. Obviously one side must yield if a settlement is to be reached. However, neither side wants to make a concession too early in the process for fear of appearing weak.

As the distance between the parties narrows, bargaining becomes more difficult because the negotiators are nearing their final positions. Impasses are not uncommon at this point and are more likely to occur when one or both sides is poorly informed about the other's true position.

When the board signals that it is making its final salary offer, for example, union negotiators must decide whether the board is bluffing or will, under pressure, agree to a higher amount. Teachers' representatives may propose a figure they believe is slightly above the board's predetermined limit in hopes that board negotiators will yield in order to reach a settlement, but this strategy has some risks. If the teachers miscalculate, they may provoke a strike that neither side wants (Mitchell et al., 1981).

If the differences are resolved and an impasse avoided, an agreement is finally reached. The work is now finished unless the teachers or board members reject the settlement. If negotiators have stayed in close touch with their constituencies throughout the process, however, that should not happen.

Processes for New Forms of Bargaining

Negotiating models vary in the degree of importance attached to each of the stages in Figure 13.2. Several of the newer models of collective bargaining attempt to reduce the total amount of time devoted to bargaining. In win/win bargaining, identification of issues takes place prior to the initiation of bargaining. In the process of deciding which issues to negotiate, the bargaining teams begin to develop a cooperative working relationship, so that when negotiations start, the participants are ready to move immediately to the closing stage.

In progressive bargaining, the initial stage is prolonged as members of both teams discuss a variety of issues. These preliminary discussions allow the parties to become acquainted and to develop trust, so that by the time bargaining gets underway, an agreement can be reached quickly.

Expedited bargaining attempts to speed up negotiations by limiting the number of issues discussed and setting deadlines for reaching agreement. However, since this model does not provide for preliminary discussions, the parties are not always able to reach a satisfactory consensus on the issues they wish to resolve.

In its emphasis on principles and deemphasis on power, the principled negotiations model expands the middle stage of negotiations and devotes less time to the initial and closing stages. This approach is particularly effective at building trust and encouraging the emergence of cooperative working relationships.

Strategic bargaining shifts the focus of attention away from current issues toward consideration of the organization's future. It places considerably more emphasis than other models on the middle stage of bargaining. In arriving at an agreement about the future, the parties often are able to develop a trusting, cooperative relationship that permits them to move to the final stage of negotiations with confidence that they will be successful.

Resolving Impasses

The climate of negotiations is affected by several factors, including the personalities of the participants, the pressure each side feels from its constituencies, and the nature of the situation (Cresswell & Murphy, 1980). When trust breaks down and union and management representatives find themselves at an impasse, outside intervention may be needed.

Mediation, fact-finding, and arbitration are tools for resolving differences between two parties. The mediator's role is clarifying the issues that prevent the parties from reaching an agreement and helping the parties arrive at a mutually acceptable solution. A fact finder gathers information about the issues on which the contending parties disagree and proposes a solution to resolve their differences. In some states the law defines criteria for settling impasses. These may include availability of funds, the interest and welfare of the public, and comparisons of salaries and working conditions in the same or similar positions in the region (Marczely & Marczely, 2002).

Neither mediation nor fact-finding impose solutions to a dispute. However, some forms of arbitration do involve such imposition. In *compulsory* or *binding arbitration,* the arbitrator hears presentations by both sides and then makes a decision that is binding. An alternative approach is *final offer arbitration,* in which the arbitrator reviews final offers from both parties and chooses one to be implemented (O'Reilly, 1978).

In preparing for final offer arbitration, each side must consider how the other side is likely to respond. Teacher representatives making a final offer on salaries are aware that if they are unreasonably demanding the arbitrator will be likely to adopt the board's position. Similarly, board representatives must try to anticipate the position the teachers are likely to take in order to present an offer that has a reasonable chance of being accepted. Thus both parties are prevented by self-interest from making offers that are unreasonable or nonresponsive.

IMPACT OF COLLECTIVE BARGAINING ON SCHOOLS

Collective bargaining has had a major impact on the operation of schools in the United States, but observers disagree on the question of whether, on balance, the effect has been positive, negative, or neutral. Three questions that are often asked about the impact of collective bargaining are: (1) What has been its effect on teachers' salaries? (2) How much and in what ways does collective bargaining affect the quality of instruction in schools? and (3) What effect has it had on principals' power? The following paragraphs try to answer those questions.

Teachers' Salaries

Stone (2000) recently reviewed research on the effect of collective bargaining on teachers' salaries and found that teachers employed by districts with collective bargaining received salaries that ranged from 5 to 12 percent greater than those of teachers in districts without collective bargaining. The research also showed that teachers from districts with collective bargaining enjoyed an even greater advantage over nonunionized teachers in size and number of fringe benefits paid to them by their employers. Teachers in collective bargaining districts also received advantages in nonmonetary benefits such as more planning time and fewer students.

Student Learning

If quality of instruction is measured by student academic achievement, then the research evidence suggests that the effect of collective bargaining on student learning is, for the most part, positive. Stone (2000) cited studies that showed slightly higher scores on standardized mathematics tests for students from districts with collective bargaining teacher contracts and a difference of between 6 and 8 percent in scores on SAT and ACT tests favoring students from districts with collective bargaining. However, the studies cited by Stone also found that average students in districts with collective bargaining for teachers benefited most whereas students who were either above or below average actually learned less on average than similar students in districts without collective bargaining. The research also suggested that the dropout rate was higher in districts with negotiated contracts.

Potentially, the most damage to student learning occurs when negotiators reach an impasse and a work stoppage results. Strikes are traumatic events for school personnel. Everyone loses, and it may take years to repair the damage. Student learning is affected both by the length of a strike and by whether or not striking teachers are replaced by substitutes.

There has been relatively little research on the subject, but the available studies show, as one would expect, that shorter strikes are less harmful than longer ones. Mathematics achievement seems to be more sensitive to loss of instruction than reading. Mathematics is negatively affected both by the length of strike and by the presence of substitute teachers, whereas reading achievement appears to be affected more by the length of a strike than by the presence of substitute teachers (Crisci & Lulow, 1985). That may be because substitute teachers are less likely to be proficient in teaching mathematics.

For principals and human resources managers, the obvious lessons from this research are, first, to take actions that will prevent or limit the length of teacher strikes and, second, if strikes occur to seek to maintain normal instructional routines to the extent possible.

Work of Principals

Negotiated agreements limit the power of principals to make decisions related to administration and organization of the school by forcing the administrators to become interpreters of the contract (Ubben & Fulmer, 1985). District administrators pressure principals to adhere closely to the contract because of fear that leniency by one principal will lead to demands from teachers in other schools for similar treatment (Mitchell et al., 1981).

Principals sometimes express concern about the difficulty of dismissing incompetent teachers, whom they feel are protected by the unions. The teachers' organizations deny the charge and insist that they will support dismissal of teachers whose incompetence is adequately documented.

The truth is probably somewhere between these positions. Most administrators know of cases in which ineffective teachers have managed to keep their jobs with union support. However, it is also true that administrators have occasionally been careless in documenting poor performance or have simply lacked the courage to take action against an incompetent employee out of fear of the union's reaction.

Principals who are accustomed to a free-wheeling style of management may have difficulty adjusting to life under a negotiated agreement. Being successful in such a situation requires an individual with considerable flexibility—one who is careful to abide by the provisions of the master contract, yet able to inspire teachers to give more than the minimum effort in order to increase learning.

Most administrators will admit that collective bargaining has some positive features. Among these are the increased security that teachers feel and the increased clarity of teachers' work responsibilities. Principals who work in districts with contracts that detail duties teachers are expected to perform report that they have no problems in getting those duties carried out (Jessup, 1981).

All in all, administering a school that operates under a negotiated agreement probably require skills that are no different from those required in schools in which there is no agreement in effect. In both cases, the administrator must attend to details and provide leadership to move the faculty toward a goal of improved instruction.

SUMMARY

Collective bargaining has been called one of the most significant developments in education in the past half century. The content of negotiated contracts is regulated by state statutes but generally covers compensation and working conditions. Some agreements may impinge on the quality of instruction in schools, and board negotiators should take those effects into account, along with attention to cost and administrative prerogatives, in reaching a settlement.

Negotiations proceed through three stages: (1) an initial stage in which the sides state their positions and agree on the issues to be negotiated, (2) a middle stage in which trust emerges and a cooperative working relationship is established, and (3) a closing stage in which both parties begin to bargain seriously, granting the concessions that are needed to reach a mutually acceptable agreement.

New approaches to collective bargaining are being tried in a number of school districts. Among these approaches are expedited bargaining, progressive bargaining, the win/win approach, principled negotiations, and strategic bargaining. Several new forms of bargaining are designed to speed the negotiation process by setting deadlines for reaching an agreement and limiting the number of issues to be discussed.

When the two sides are not able to reach agreement, outside assistance may be required. Mediation, fact finding, and arbitration are all used to help resolve impasses.

SUGGESTED ACTIVITIES

1. Following is a statement on class size proposed by the teachers' union. Take and defend a position for or against the proposal as written. (You are not allowed to rewrite it.)

   "We believe instruction is most effective when class sizes are kept small enough to permit teachers to diagnose students' needs and plan instruction to meet them. To permit the level of teacher attention needed for learning to occur, we ask the board to agree to place a limit of 20 students in classes in reading and English in grades

1–12 and to limit all other classes in grades 1–12 (except special education) to no more than 24 students. Each special education student assigned to a regular class will count as two students for purposes of calculating size limits."

2. Principals are sometimes excluded from joining the board's negotiating team because board members believe they might be inclined to side with teachers. Principals argue that they could help the board's representatives understand how proposed contract provisions might affect instruction, and thus avoid language likely to harm learning. Take and defend a position on this proposition:

"Principals should be represented on the board's negotiating team."

3. Consider the statement on teacher evaluation that follows. If you were a member of the union bargaining team, what changes would you propose in the statement? If you were a member of the board team, what changes would you want made?

"The union and the board recognize the importance of teacher evaluation for sound instruction. Teachers will be evaluated in the following way: The principal will observe each teacher at least twice during the school year, will evaluate the teacher after each observation, and will inform the teacher of the results. No later than April 15, the principal will prepare a written narrative describing the teacher's strengths and weaknesses and include the statement in the teacher's personnel file. If the teacher is completing the probationary period, the principal shall recommend that the teacher be tenured or terminated."

4. No Child Left Behind requires that all subgroups of students in a school make adequate yearly progress (AYP) on mandated tests each year. Schools in which students fail to make progress for two years may be identified as in need of improvement, with corrective actions to follow. What effect do you anticipate this legislation will have on contract provisions relating to teacher evaluation?

5. Locate contract provisions from two master contracts relating to one of the topics listed below. Read the provisions from each contract and compare and contrast them. Tell which provision is more favorable to teachers and which is more favorable to the board. (You may wish to use one of the online master contracts listed under Online Resources.)

   a. Evaluation of teachers

   b. Teacher safety and security

   c. Teacher transfer and promotion

   d. Extracurricular duties of teachers

6. Locate additional information about one of the new forms of collective bargaining described in the chapter (expedited, progressive, win/win, and principled).

ONLINE RESOURCES

American Federation of Teachers
   (www.aft.org/research/models/contracts/conindex.htm)

Sample bargaining agreements between employers and teachers, nurses and other health professionals, employees of institutions of higher education, and public employees are available at this location.

Cherry Creek (CO) School District (www.ccsd.k12.co.us/employ/vol2policies/teacherpolicies.lasso)

The full text of collective bargaining agreement between the Cherry Creek School District and the teachers' association can be found at this site.

Cornell Law School Legal Information Institute (www.law.cornell.edu/topics/collective_bargaining.html)

This site has links to federal statutes, federal agency regulations, and U.S. Supreme Court and Appeals Courts decisions pertaining to collective bargaining.

Education Commission of the States (www.ecs.org/clearinghouse/37/48/3748.htm)

Information about state policies on collective bargaining for teachers is available here. The site covers the scope of bargaining, procedures for resolving impasses, and policies on teacher strikes for all 50 states.

Iowa State Department of Education (www.edinfo.state.ia.us/tcdiscussion/faq_post.asp?g=3&sb=5)

This site addresses frequently asked questions about teacher quality. It includes information about mentoring, induction, professional development, and collective bargaining.

ThoughtBridge (www.thoughtbridge.net/tpneg-collective.htm)

This site features an article on interest-based negotiation.

REFERENCES

Biddle, B. J., & Berliner, D. C. (2002, February). Small class size and its effects. *Educational Leadership, 59*, 12–23.

Black, S. (1993, October). How teachers are reshaping evaluation procedures. *Educational Leadership, 51*, 38–42.

Booth, R. (1993). *Collective bargaining and the school board member.* Springfield, IL: Illinois Association of School Boards.

Cresswell, A., & Murphy, M. (1980). *Teachers, unions, and collective bargaining in public education.* Berkeley, CA: McCutchan.

Crisci, P. E., & Lulow, R. J. (1985). The effect of school employee strikes on student achievement in nine Ohio school districts. *Journal of Collective Negotiations, 14*, 197–212.

Fisher, R., & Ury, W. (1981). *Getting to yes: Negotiating agreement without giving in.* New York:Penguin.

Fisher, R., & Ury, W. (1988). *Getting together: Building relationships as we negotiate.* New York: Penguin.

Geisert, G., & Lieberman, M. (1994). *Teacher union bargaining: Practice and policy.* Chicago: Precept Press.

Goldschmidt, S., Bowers, B., Riley, M., & Stuart, L. (1984). *The extent and nature of educational policy bargaining.* Eugene, OR: University of Oregon, Center for Educational Policy and Management.

Hauck, V. (1998). *Arbitrating sex discrimination grievances.* Westport, CT: Quorum.

Jessup, D. (1981). *Teacher unionism and its impact: A study of change over time.* Washington, DC: National Institute of Education.

Lipsky, D. V., & Conley, S. C. (1986, April). *Incentive pay and collective bargaining in public education.* Paper presented at the annual meeting of the

American Educational Research Association, San Francisco. (ERIC Document Reproduction Service No. ED277111).

Marczely, B., & Marczely, D. W. (2002). *Human resource and contract management in the public sector.* Lanham, MD: Scarecrow Press.

McDonnell, L., & Pascal, A. (1979). *Organized teachers in American schools.* Santa Monica, CA: Rand.

Mitchell, D., Kerchner, C., Erck, W., & Pryor, G. (1981). The impact of collective bargaining on school management and policy. *American Journal of Education, 89,* 147–188.

Najita, J. M., & Stern, J. L. (2001). *Collective bargaining in the public sector: The experience of eight states.* Armonk, NY: M. E. Sharpe.

National Education Association. (1991). *Collaborative bargaining: A critical appraisal.* Washington, DC: Author.

O'Reilly, R. C. (1978). *Understanding collective bargaining in education.* Metuchen, NJ: Scarecrow Press.

Stone, J. (2000). Collective bargaining and public schools. In T. Loveless (Ed.), *Conflicting missions?* (pp. 47–68). Washington, DC: Brookings Institution.

Ubben, G. C., & Fulmer, B. (1985). The relationship of collective bargaining to the decision-making power of the public school principal. *Journal of Collective Negotiations, 14,* 141–150.

CHAPTER FOURTEEN

MANAGING CONFLICT IN SCHOOLS

Conflict occurs in all organizations, and although managers work to resolve or eliminate it, it is important to recognize that some conflict is inevitable and may even have beneficial effects (Pneuman & Bruehl, 1982). Conflict occurs when people disagree regarding values, information, and goals, or when individuals compete for scarce resources (Rahim, 1986). Organizational managers usually become involved when conflict occurs among members of the organization, and managers themselves are sometimes parties to conflict.

Conflict may occur between individuals, within or between groups, or between an individual and a group. The focus of this chapter is with conflict involving school personnel and, in particular, that which involves two teachers or groups of teachers or a teacher and an administrator such as a principal. Conflict involving parties outside of the school is beyond the scope of this book. For example, issues of conflict between teachers and parents will not be addressed, even though many of the principles for handling various types of conflict are identical.

PLAN OF THE CHAPTER

This chapter discusses the nature of conflict in organizations and methods for resolving common types of organizational conflict. Grievance arbitration, a method of conflict resolution that is used in many organizations including schools, is examined in detail.

Exhibit 14.1 shows examples of the four types of on-the-job conflict.

NATURE OF CONFLICT IN ORGANIZATIONS

In any human activity, disagreements and conflict are inevitable. In the workplace, much conflict centers on one of four issues: disagreements about the application of laws, rules, and policies; disputes regarding the allocation of resources and

EXHIBIT 14.1

EXAMPLES OF FOUR TYPES OF CONFLICT IN SCHOOLS

DISPUTES OVER ALLOCATION OF RESOURCES AND PRIVILEGES

Example 1. A teacher in the mathematics department and the department head both request permission to attend a regional conference sponsored by the math teachers' association. There is not enough money in the budget for both to attend. The principal approves the department head's request and denies the teacher's application. The teacher protests this action and accuses the principal of favoritism.

Example 2. Department heads were asked to limit requests for instructional materials for the next school year to essential items because of the tight budget. The foreign language department's request is the largest of any department, although its enrollment is small. The department head justifies the materials as essential for good instruction and says that language materials are more expensive than materials for other subjects. The head of the science department states that, although the biology laboratory needs new equipment, he did not include the equipment in his request and suggests that, because the school's accreditation is based in part on students' performance in biology and chemistry, his department should receive more support than foreign language.

DISPUTES OVER APPLICATION OF LAWS, RULES, AND POLICIES

Example 3. Board policy states that high school teachers may not leave school until 15 minutes after students have been excused "except in case of emergency." A teacher who left school early argued that she needed to have a prescription filled and that that should qualify as an "emergency."

Example 4. Members of the marching band held a car wash and collected $170 for new uniforms. Board policy requires that clubs obtain advance approval for fund-raising activities, and, because the band members did not have approval for the car wash, the principal told the band instructor that he would cancel a second fund-raiser for the band scheduled for the Spring. The instructor objected and pointed out that the band had sponsored car washes for at least seven years and that, under the previous principal, he never had to obtain permission because it was understood that car washes were part of the band's fund-raising activities.

CONFUSION ABOUT DUTIES AND RESPONSIBILITIES

Example 5. A teacher's aide complains that the teacher asked her to help two students with a reading assignment. The aide says she is not qualified to teach and that her job description does not mention instruction. The teacher says the aide was asked to help two students with difficult words, which she argues is tutoring, a duty aides are expected to perform.

Example 6. District budget cuts have forced the elimination of drivers for vans to carry students to away football and basketball games. Coaches of other sports have been told they must drive the vans to transport their teams to games. The district has agreed to pay for liability insurance to cover the coaches. The coaches argue they should be paid extra for driving their teams to games, especially because basketball and football coaches are exempt from the added duty.

DISPUTES OVER PERFORMANCE EVALUATION

Example 7. A biology teacher has been absent from school 21 days during the year, most of the absences resulting from an infection contracted during a summer trip to Latin America. The teacher's evaluation is downgraded from "Excellent" to "Average" as a result of his absences. The teacher protests that he should not be penalized for illness.

Example 8. An English teacher is rated "Average" by the principal. The teacher points out that the principal's only visit to her classroom was very brief and that she therefore cannot possibly evaluate her fairly. The principal responds that she had input from other sources, including a district supervisor who observed the class one time, as well as parents and students.

privileges, confusion about duties and responsibilities of employees, and disagreement about performance evaluation.

The principal or human resources administrator must act as conflict manager when disputes arise. There are certain actions the administrator may take that are more likely than others to lead to resolution of the conflict. If the dispute centers on something the administrator did, then he or she must be prepared to defend that action by citing the policy or rationale for it. If the decision was made in haste and not well thought out, it may be necessary for the administrator to change it. After hearing all sides, however, if the administrator continues to feel that the decision was correct, it should be left intact. Most employees will accept adverse decisions without bitterness if they have received a respectful hearing from a decision maker who has no "hidden agenda" (Yates, 1985).

The role of the principal or human resources administrator in attempting to resolve conflict depends on the nature of the strife. Some conflict involves disagreements about events, as when two witnesses give different accounts of an altercation between two students. Other disagreements are technical in nature, involving arguments over the best way to perform an action. For example, a teacher and supervisor may disagree over the preferred method of teaching reading. Interpersonal conflict occurs when a disagreement between two individuals erupts into threats and recriminations. Disputes about work rules or the correct interpretation of a collective bargaining agreement fall under the rubric of legal conflict (Stitt, 1998).

Methods of Resolving Conflict

Disagreements are common in work settings. Employment discrimination lawsuits are the second most common form of civil litigation, after petitions by prisoners. About 21,000 such suits are filed each year. With the cost of legal proceedings rising, employers are seeking alternative methods of settling disputes (Downey, 2003). Three methods of resolving on-the-job conflict that are in common use are negotiation, mediation, and arbitration. In addition, some business corporations have developed their own mechanisms that combine elements of two or more of these approaches.

Negotiation

Negotiation is the most widely used means of conflict resolution in organizations and is the least costly both in terms of time and money. Exhibit 14.2 lists the steps involved in negotiation. The first step in the process is to decide who should participate. If the dispute involves an employee and his or her immediate supervisor, at least those two must be involved, and, as the negotiations proceed, it may be necessary to involve other people to help clarify policies and procedures or to verify events. People at a higher level of the organization may become involved later in the negotiations to approve a tentative agreement reached by the contending parties. If an agreement reached by an employee and supervisor affects other

■ ■ ■ ■ ■

EXHIBIT 14.2

STEPS INVOLVED IN SETTLING CONFLICT VIA NEGOTIATION

1. Decide which individuals or groups should be involved in the negotiation
2. Define the problem in terms that all parties agree to
3. Rank the issues and begin by discussing the most important ones
4. Identify alternative solutions without committing to any one course of action
5. Evaluate the alternatives, taking all points of view into consideration
6. Choose the alternative that is most acceptable and least costly
7. Implement the chosen alternative

employees, it may also be necessary to hear their views before the agreement is finalized. At the very least, those affected must be kept informed regarding any changes in work rules or job requirements that result from the settlement (Isenhart & Spangle, 2000).

The second step in negotiations requires that the parties agree on a definition of the problem. Framing a problem in terms that all the disputants can accept is an important prerequisite to reaching a solution. Because many disputes are rooted in the different assumptions and interpretations held by the parties, exposing those assumptions and interpretations can help bring the parties closer to agreement on the nature of the problem (Isenhart & Spangle, 2000).

An example of how disputes arise from differences in definitions held by the parties is found in Example 5 in Exhibit 14.1, where the instructional aide objects to helping two students with reading, which she considers to be an instructional task, whereas the teacher regards it as tutoring. Resolving this disagreement requires clarifying the meanings of the terms *instruction* and *tutoring,* as applied in this setting.

Example 4 shows how individuals define a problem by the assumptions they make. The band teacher in that example assumed that the rules on fund-raising that had applied in the past under the previous principal were still in effect. Because the new principal is enforcing the board policy on fund-raising, a conflict has arisen.

Example 8 from Exhibit 14.1 also illustrates the important part that assumptions play in a dispute. The teacher in the example assumed that classroom observations are the most (or perhaps the only) valid method of evaluating teaching. The principal believed that information from other sources is equally useful. If the master contract or board policy requires multiple classroom observations for evaluation or forbids the use of information from other sources, then the teacher's assumption is correct and the problem is the principal's violation of the provision. If the contract and board policy are silent on the issue, then the question is whether evaluating a teacher on the basis of one observation is fair to the teacher.

Step 3 in the negotiation process is to rank the issues and begin discussing the most important one (Isenhart & Spangle, 2000). Example 2 in Exhibit 14.1 describes a situation in which several issues are involved. The department heads in this example were instructed to keep their budget requests modest, but that was insufficient guidance to avoid disagreements over priorities. The question that the participants must now tackle is how to decide which values will prevail in the distribution of scarce resources. The foreign language chair believes that cost of materials should be considered in formulating instructional requests, whereas the science department chair stresses the need to base requests for materials on their potential contribution to accreditation. Size of enrollments is suggested as still another criterion by which funds might be allocated. Identifying alternative solutions to the problem is Step 4 in the negotiation process, and evaluating potential solutions is Step 5 (Isenhart & Spangle, 2000). These steps are often combined. All reasonable solutions should be examined, with both advantages and disadvantages explored. Participants should be asked to withhold committing to a solution until all the possible solutions have been evaluated. This may not be easy to accomplish, but if the participants can reserve judgment, it will make it easier for the parties to eventually arrive at a solution that is acceptable to all.

Mediation

In mediation a person who is not a party to the dispute and who has no stake in how it is resolved presides over discussions among the parties to reach a resolution. Professional mediators are trained to help parties to a dispute examine the issues involved in an objective manner and identify common interests that can be used as the basis for developing a satisfactory settlement. A mediator must be impartial and able to help those involved in the conflict to understand their adversaries' points of view. Mediation normally occurs only after negotiation has failed, so the problems that mediators are asked to resolve are usually fairly complex, and the positions of the contending parties tend to be strongly held. A mediator has no power to impose a solution and depends on his or her ability to bring the parties together through a discussion of the salient issues in the dispute.

An important contribution that mediators make is to get the parties to agree to discuss their differences in an atmosphere free of hostility. By requiring that the discourse be civil, the mediator can defuse the atmosphere and allow calm, rational discussions to take place. It is through a respectful discussion of differences that the parties begin to understand the diverse points of view represented and to envision solutions that contain elements acceptable to all parties (Masters & Albright, 2002).

When emotions run high, mediators may first meet separately with the disputants in order to gain a clearer understanding of their fears and concerns. During these early meetings, the mediator can often identify issues that, in themselves, are minor but stand in the way of a settlement and on which the parties are unwilling to yield, either for fear of being seen as weak or because they feel the other party has not understood and accepted the legitimacy of their position. Separate meetings with each group help the mediator to begin to identify solutions that each side might accept and to develop a proposed solution that contains elements that appeal to each of the parties.

Arbitration

An arbitrator acts as a mediator in some respects, but arbitrators have power that mediators lack: They can impose a settlement that the disputing parties are obligated to accept. A party to a dispute will be likely to avoid arbitration if he or she believes that the arbitrator's decision will go against his or her interests. For this reason, arbitration is usually reserved for disputes in which the lines are firmly drawn and neither party has shown a willingness to make concessions. Arbitration is a more formal process than mediation, usually involving hearings at which witnesses may be heard and the parties represented by counsel. The arbitrator may also refer to documents that provide background information on the dispute.

The advantages of arbitration are that it leads to a resolution of a dispute rather quickly and at a lower cost than legal action. A disadvantage is that neither party may be happy with the solution that the arbitrator announces. A method that helps avoid this problem is final-offer arbitration, in which each side presents its final offer and the arbitrator must choose one of the offers. Each side is inclined to present an offer that it believes the arbitrator will find responsive to the other side's demands in order to increase the odds of its being accepted.

MANAGING CONFLICT THROUGH THE GRIEVANCE PROCESS

Negotiated contracts between school boards and teachers' unions normally include a grievance procedure, an orderly process for resolving disputes over interpretation and administration of the contract (*Contract Administration,* 1983). Grievance procedures have a long history in industry. The first record of their use dates back to the early years of the twentieth century, but they did not come into widespread use in this country until World War II. A recommendation of the President's Labor-Management Conference that all labor contracts include a procedure for settlement of grievances gave impetus to their adoption. The U.S. Supreme Court gave additional support to their use when it held in a series of decisions that courts should not rule on the merits of disputes between labor and management but should limit themselves to enforcing arbitration awards and reviewing questions of arbitrability (Lovell, 1985)

At the present time, grievance procedures are pervasive in industries with negotiated labor agreements, and they are increasingly used to resolve employee/ employer disputes in schools. In districts without negotiated agreements, written grievance policies govern the resolution of disputes. The grievance process is favored by most employers and many unions because it is a quicker and less costly way of settling disputes than strikes and lengthy litigation (Lovell, 1985).

Arbitration has a number of advantages over litigation. Arbitration is faster than pursuing a resolution through the courts and is usually less complicated. The disputants are not required to hire attorneys, and because of the flexibility of the proceedings, facts are obtained more quickly and easily. Decisions arrived at by arbitration are announced soon after the hearing, whereas a court decision may be delayed for several months. Moreover, arbitration decisions are seldom appealed, since courts are inclined to uphold arbitrators' decisions (McDermott, 1996).

One of the most important advantages of grievance arbitration from an employer's point of view is its potential for avoiding strikes. When employees can seek redress from unfair actions of management, they are less likely to walk off the job. If a strike does occur, an employer who has agreed to settle disputes through binding arbitration is usually able to obtain injunctive relief through the courts (*Boys Markets Inc.* v. *Retail Clerks*, 1970).

The operational assumptions of SBM (School Board Modification) are different from the assumptions used in grievance processes. In schools with SBM, disputes are resolved through informal discussion, cooperation, and compromise. The search for solutions usually takes into account the interests of teachers, students, and parents. Grievance procedures, on the other hand, use an adversarial approach and ultimately rely on an objective outside party to hear the evidence and decide the issue. The procedures focus on faithfully interpreting an agreement rather than seeking the best solution to a problem. Resolving conflict in a school with SBM involves evaluation of options, with attention given to the school's mission and the well-being of the parties involved. Finding a solution often requires compromise.

In Dade County (Florida) Schools, a grievance committee composed of administrators and union representatives hears grievances appealed from schools with SBM plans. If a dispute is not resolved by the grievance committee, it is appealed to a two-person panel composed of the district superintendent and a union vice president. Only if the panel fails to resolve the issue does it go to binding arbitration (Fossey, 1992).

Administering Grievance Procedures

A grievance clause in a master contract usually consists of a definition of *grievance,* tells who may initiate a grievance, and establishes deadlines for filing and processing employee complaints. The clause also details the procedural steps that are followed in processing the grievance, including the final step, which in many districts is binding arbitration.

Unions favor grievance plans that include binding arbitration as the final step because they feel that it guarantees employees a fair hearing for their complaints. However, most school boards prefer advisory arbitration, which leaves the final decision on a dispute in the hands of the board (Lovell, 1985). The grievance clause also specifies which parties may file grievances. In some districts, teacher associations and unions are allowed to file, whereas in others only individuals are permitted to grieve the employer's actions.

Steps in Resolving Grievances.   Most grievance policies provide three or four steps through which a grievant may appeal a complaint. Step 1 commonly includes both an informal and a formal stage. The employee initiates action informally by bringing to the attention of the supervisor the decision or situation that originally aroused the employee's concern. If not satisfied with the response received, the employee may then proceed to Stage 2 of Step 1 by formally filing a written grievance with the same supervisor. In the case of teachers, Step 1 involves the principal of the school in which the grievant works.

In most districts, a form is provided on which the employee is asked to (1) describe the incident, decision, or practice that gave rise to the complaint; (2) cite the contract or policy provision that has been violated; and (3) explain what corrective action is being requested. Since there is usually a time limit for filing a grievance, the grievant must specify the date of occurrence of the precipitating event or the date on which the employee first learned about it.

Appeals Procedures.   If the employee is unhappy with the decision at the first step, he or she proceeds to Step 2 by appealing to the next higher level, usually either the director of human resources or an assistant superintendent. Step 3 involves a hearing before the superintendent. Step 4 in the grievance procedure is a hearing before the board of education or an arbitrator or arbitration panel. In districts with binding arbitration, the decision of the arbitrator is final, but in districts that use advisory arbitration, the recommendation of the arbitrator is reviewed by the school board, which has the final word about the employee's complaint.

Grievance hearings become more formal as the complaint advances from one administrative level to the next. The only written documentation required at the first step is the supervisor's written decision, but at the final step, a transcript of the hearing is prepared (Salmon, 1983). The transcript, along with the superintendent's written decision on the employee's complaint, is reviewed by the arbitrator or arbitration panel if the grievance is appealed to arbitration.

Grievance Arbitration in Schools

When an employee fails to achieve a satisfactory solution to a grievance after following all of the steps provided in the policy, the final step is arbitration. The rules on arbitration vary, depending on the state in which the individual works and on the provisions of the bargaining agreement. Some states require boards to include binding arbitration in contracts with employees, whereas others leave the decision to the negotiators. A few prohibit binding arbitration.

Certain powers of school boards are nondelegable and are considered nonarbitrable unless state law specifically permits review. Among these are the power to hire, promote, and discharge employees; establish the curriculum; and set standards of service (Lovell, 1985).

Courts generally prefer to allow arbitration procedures to operate without interference, but if nondelegable powers of school boards have clearly been abridged in the process of arbitration, courts are likely to intervene. In some states, the courts are less ready to grant arbitration the acceptance in the public sector that it has traditionally been accorded in the private sector (Lovell, 1985).

Selection of Arbitrators.   A grievance may be heard by a single arbitrator or by a panel consisting of several arbitrators. The procedures followed in selection of arbitrators are those established by state legislation or by a professional organization such as the American Arbitration Association or an agency such as the Federal Mediation and Conciliation Service. The usual practice is for the designated organization or agency to submit a list of five to seven names of qualified arbitrators, from which representatives of the grievant and the board alternately delete names until only the required number remains (Ostrander, 1987).

The arbitrator's function is to determine whether the administrative decision or practice to which the employee objects is a violation of the bargaining agreement. Most disputes involve rights that union members claim to have received at the bargaining table and that management denies were granted. The arbitrator thus has the task of determining which interpretation is the one intended by the parties at the time the contract was signed (Ostrander, 1987).

Guidelines for Interpreting the Contract.   In arriving at an interpretation of the contract, arbitrators are guided by several rules of contract interpretation. Among them are the following (Elkouri & Elkouri, 1973):

1. If the intent of the parties is clear, it should govern.
2. Words are given their ordinary and accepted meaning unless other meanings are specifically indicated.
3. The meaning given to a passage in the contract should be consistent insofar as possible with the intentions expressed in other parts of the contract.
4. When the agreement specifically includes something, it is assumed that which is left unstated is excluded.
5. When there is a conflict between specific and general language, specific language should govern.
6. When there is no evidence to the contrary and the meaning of a term is unclear, the intentions of the parties should be viewed to be the same as those held during the negotiations that led to the agreement.
7. No consideration should be given to compromise offers or to concessions offered by one party and rejected by the other during the process that led to arbitration.

Exhibit 14.3 contains a summary description of a grievance filed by a middle school reading teacher in a California school district that was referred to arbitration. Arbitrator Norman I. Lustig's decision on the grievance and the reasoning that led him to his conclusions are described below, but before you read about

■ ■ ■ ■ ■

EXHIBIT 14.3

SANGER UNIFIED SCHOOL DISTRICT AND SANGER UNIFIED TEACHERS ASSOCIATION

BACKGROUND

The grievant is a tenured teacher who is qualified to teach middle and high school Language Arts and Reading and had taught since 1978 at a middle school in the district. Her principal regarded her as an "excellent" teacher. In 1997 the grievant was voluntarily reassigned to a position as Teacher on Special Assignment (TSA) at the middle school, a position she held for the 1997–98 and 1998–99 school years. This was a nonclassroom teaching assignment that involved oversight of reading development activities in the middle school. The offer of employment indicated that the TSA position was financed from regular education funds, but in fact some of the money for the grievant's salary came from categorical rather than regular funds.

In Spring 1999 the principal of the middle school decided to eliminate the TSA position for lack of funds, and the grievant was offered the position of teacher of language arts at the middle school, the same assignment she had held prior taking the TSA position two years earlier, although with a different teaching team.

The grievant was not happy about being reassigned and investigated the possibility of requesting a transfer to the high school. However, there was no opening at the high school for a reading development specialist, so she accepted the middle school assignment. In February 2000 she informed the middle school principal that she did not wish to return to the middle school as a classroom teacher for the 2000–2001 school year. She also completed a transfer request, asking to be reassigned to Sanger High School for the 2000–2001 school year as English teacher or to be in charge of the reading laboratory. In April 2000 she was interviewed by a two-person team for one of five vacancies in the English department at the high school.

The grievant claimed that she regarded the interview as *pro forma* and that she did not understand why she was asked to participate. She expected to be given preferential consideration for the position because she believed she had been involuntarily transferred to a regular middle school teaching position when the TSA assignment ended. She believed that, because she had more seniority than the other applicants and had an excellent teaching record, she would be granted preferential consideration for the high school position.

However, the interviewers felt that the grievant was not seriously interested in teaching at the high school level and had applied for the position as a way to escape the middle school. They reported that, of the six people they interviewed for a position at the high school, all except the grievant came prepared to explain how they would handle the demands of the job and brought with them sample lesson plans. The grievant did neither, and she admitted that she had not tried to "sell" herself to the interviewers.

Although the grievant's credentials were superior to those of the other applicants and although she had more seniority than any of them, she was not offered one of the five openings, whereas all five of the other applicants, including three who were new to the district, did receive offers. Later, during the summer, the district announced several reading-related vacancies in the district for Fall 2000. The district claimed that notice of the vacancies was sent to every certificated employee in the district, but the grievant did not receive it. One of these positions was a reading position at Sanger High School, and, although the grievant had asked for a transfer to a reading position at the high school, neither the principal of the school nor the district reading director was aware of her interest. The person who was chosen to fill that position, who lacked the grievant's qualifications, resigned the position after one day, and the position was filled by an applicant from outside the district who did not go through an interview.

The grievant argued that, because her reassignment from the TSA to a classroom teaching position was an involuntary reassignment, she should have received priority placement rights when she requested a transfer to a high school position in 2000. She claimed that the district had violated the collective bargaining agreement by employing three junior unit members in the English Department at Sanger High and refusing her request to transfer to the school.

The district argued that involuntary reassignment provisions apply only to reassignments between regular assignments, not to temporary support positions such as the TSA position. The district indicated that the involuntary reassignment provision of the contract was interpreted to mean that individuals who had been involuntarily transferred would have the right to an interview but no right to preferential consideration after that. The district further claimed that involuntary reassignment provisions of the contract apply to changes in grade level but not to temporary assignments. The district stated that the provision did not apply in the grievant's case because the decision to discontinue the TSA position was made by the principal, not district administrators.

QUESTIONS

1. Did the district violate the collective bargaining agreement between the district and the teachers' association by failing to transfer the grievant to the position of classroom English teacher at Sanger High School for the 2000–2001 school year, either under the involuntary transfer/reassignment provisions or under the voluntary transfer provisions?
2. If so, what should the remedy be?

CONTRACT PROVISIONS

Article III (3.1) It is understood and agreed that the District retains all of its powers and authority to direct, manage and control to the full extent of the law. Included in those duties and powers are the exclusive right to:

> Determine the number and kinds of personnel required;
>
> Maintain the efficiency of district operations;
>
> Hire, classify, assign, evaluate, promote, and terminate employees.

Article XII (12.1) For purposes of this provision "transfer" shall be defined as a change in work site from one school site to another; "reassignment" is defined as a change in the specific duties of any bargaining unit member.

(12.2) An involuntary transfer or reassignment of a bargaining unit member may be initiated by the District at any time such transfer or reassignment is in the best interests of the District.

(12.11) Teachers who must be involuntarily transferred from their current positions shall be given priority placement in future job openings in the district.

a. Teachers shall receive notification of all openings as they become available.
b. Teachers shall have first right to be interviewed for openings.
c. All involuntarily transferred or reassigned teachers shall be placed prior to outside hires (except for affirmative action needs).
d. All involuntarily transferred or reassigned teachers shall remain on the priority placement list until they have been placed to their satisfaction.

(12.23) When two or more current employees apply for a particular position, the teacher with the longest unbroken span of employment in the teacher bargaining unit shall normally be allowed to fill the vacancy. Any denial of a teaching position to the most senior applicants as defined herein shall be for good and sufficient reason based on the educational needs of the District.

them you may want to test your skill as an arbitrator by reviewing the case to see if you would have reached the same conclusions as the trained arbitrator.

Arbitrator's Reasoning and Decision

The arbitrator held that the grievant's transfer to the TSA position was not a temporary assignment. The arbitrator noted that the district did not, either orally or in writing, indicate to the grievant that the TSA position would be of limited duration. The fact that on elimination of the TSA position the grievant was returned to a parallel classroom teaching position and not to her original position, which was then occupied by another teacher, indicated, according to the arbitrator, that the district did not regard the TSA position as temporary.

It was the arbitrator's view that the reassignment of the grievant to a classroom teaching position after the elimination of the TSA assignment was an involuntary reassignment under terms of the agreement. The arbitrator noted that the duties performed by the grievant in the classroom teaching position were very different from those she performed while in the TSA position, which involved program coordination and reading-related activities. Hence, using the definition in the agreement, the grievant's return to a classroom qualified as reassignment.

The arbitrator held that, because the grievant requested a transfer for 1999–2000 and had indicated that she did not wish to continue teaching at the middle school, she retained priority placement rights under the agreement until she was given a placement that she felt was satisfactory. However, the arbitrator reasoned that the district was not required to give absolute preference to a transferred teacher over an outside hire or a teacher with less seniority.

The arbitrator held that the district did not violate the agreement by not appointing the grievant to a vacancy in the Sanger High School English Department for the 2000–2001 school year but that it did violate the agreement by failing to appoint the grievant to the reading development vacancy. The arbitrator reasoned that interviewing applicants for a position in the English Department would have served no purpose if the decision were simply *pro forma*. He also pointed out that the district had the right to value selection criteria of its own choosing. The fact that the grievant did not perform well enough in the interview to be recommended by the committee was a sufficient reason for offering positions to the other applicants.

The arbitrator ruled that the district did violate the agreement in not considering the grievant for appointment to a reading development position at the high school for the 2000–2001 school year. The agreement required the district to notify all individuals who had been involuntarily reassigned or who had voluntarily requested reassignment about any vacancies that they might have been qualified to fill. In this case the grievant did not receive notice of the opening for a reading development specialist at the high school. The arbitrator held that, to remedy this violation, the district would be required to place the grievant in a reading development teacher position at the high school.

ARBITRATION INVOLVING WORK RULES

Many grievances have to do with application of work rules. It has been noted that principals are expected to discuss disagreements concerning work rules with the involved parties and that doing so increases the chances that the principal will be successful in mediating future disputes (Lutz & Caldwell, 1979). Disagreements over work rules usually involve these three questions (Turner & Weed, 1983):

1. What action or activity is covered by the rule?
2. Under what conditions is the activity appropriate?
3. To whom does the rule apply?

Consider a policy that states, "Teachers will confer with parents upon request and at a mutually convenient time regarding students' academic performance." What actions are covered by the rule? If a teacher discusses a child's work with a parent by telephone, does that constitute conferring? What about an exchange of notes? If the request for a conference originates with the principal rather than a parent, does that constitute a "request" within the meaning of the policy?

Under what conditions is the activity appropriate? Suppose a teacher tells an inquiring parent that there is no need for a conference since the child in question is doing well. Has the teacher violated the rule? Suppose the teacher has a second job and cannot arrange a mutually satisfactory time for a conference. Is she exempt from the rule?

To whom does the rule apply? Are both part-time and full-time teachers obligated by the rule? Is a teacher who has a child for one period a day under a mainstreaming arrangement equally as bound by the rule as the child's base teacher? Is an itinerant teacher who spends only three or four hours per week in a school required to meet with parents who request it?

Deciding Which Rule Applies

In some disputes, a question arises regarding which of two or more rules governs. In one such case, the contract between teachers and the board of the Anoka-Hennepin District in Minnesota contained a provision stating that "teachers shall not be disciplined, reduced in rank or compensation without just cause." Teachers who missed school because of snow requested they be granted personal leave for the half-day they missed. The request was denied and the teachers lost one-half day's pay. They filed a grievance that ultimately went to arbitration. The teachers cited the "just cause" clause, but the district argued that its action was justified by a clause governing emergency leave. That provision held that absence from school because of the effects of weather on transportation would not be approved for emergency leave purposes. The arbitrator supported the district in this case (Coulson, 1986).

Interpreting Just Cause

Arbitrators are frequently confronted with the necessity of interpreting "just cause" clauses, such as the one in the Anoka-Hennepin contract. The intent in using this phrase is to allow administrative discretion while protecting employee rights granted by the contract. Several criteria are used by arbitrators to determine whether administrative action meets the "just cause" standard. Among the questions an arbitrator is likely to ask are the following:

1. Was the employee informed of management's rules and expectations?
2. Were management's rules and expectations reasonable?
3. Was adverse action necessary to maintain orderly, efficient procedures in the organization?
4. Was the employee given a chance to improve his or her conduct?
5. Was the imposed penalty reasonable? (Ostrander, 1981, p. 41)

Teachers' Use of Force

Teachers are expected to take action to prevent students from fighting or to stop fights when they occur, yet the rules about the use of force in such situations are often unclear. In a junior high school in Michigan, a teacher who encountered two students fighting sent another child to the principal's office for help. The principal came and stopped the fight, but on the following day the principal placed a letter of reprimand in the teacher's file because he felt she should have been more aggressive and stopped the fight herself (Coulson, 1986).

A teacher in a school in Iowa got into trouble with the school principal for the opposite reason: He was too aggressive in separating two youngsters who were fighting. The teacher grabbed one of the students by the shoulder and pulled him away from the other boy, causing the student to fall and strike his head. He wrapped his arm around the other boy and pulled him into the office. The teacher was reprimanded for excessive use of force (Coulson, 1986).

Both teachers filed grievances seeking to have the reprimands removed from their personnel files. How would you rule if you were the arbitrator? It might help you to know that the first teacher had taught for a total of 30 years, 13 in the same system, and had never been previously reprimanded. The teacher in the Iowa school, however, had been warned by the principal about excessive use of force and had previously received a reprimand for the same offense.

The arbitrator in the first case decided, as you probably did, that the teacher should not have been reprimanded, but in the second case the arbitrator held that the reprimand was justified. In both cases, teachers were operating on the basis of expectations that were not very clear or explicit, but the second teacher, because of the principal's previous warning, was especially vulnerable to disciplinary action. Some use of force in these situations may be required, but a fine line exists between suitable or appropriate force and excessive force. In this case, the teacher crossed that line.

Grievances on Evaluation

A good many grievances filed by teachers concern evaluation procedures. In handling these disputes, administrators must be guided by the language of the contract. When contract language is specific with regard to evaluation procedures, any departure from the provisions will probably be rejected in arbitration. If the language is permissive, then an administrative decision is more likely to be upheld.

Some contracts specify who is responsible for making classroom observations but do not forbid others from observing in classes. It is common for contracts to state that the principal is responsible for making classroom observations as part of the evaluation process. In one case, a principal called in a central office supervisor to make an additional observation of a teacher, and the teacher filed a grievance, claiming that the use of the supervisor for a classroom observation violated the contract. The administration was upheld in that case on grounds that the contract did not specifically forbid the use of observers other than the principal (Ostrander, 1981).

Another complaint that teachers sometimes make is that principals use information for evaluation purposes that was not obtained by means of classroom observations. Arbitrators have held that such use of information from other sources is justified unless specifically prohibited by the contract.

Guidelines for Action

Being aware of the factors that arbitrators consider in deciding disputes over work rules can help administrators make better decisions and avoid some of the emotional cost of confrontations with employees. In disputes that involve employee absence or tardiness, arbitrators look for a pattern of employee behavior and are not inclined to support the board when an employee's infraction is limited to a single incident. Advance notification is also considered. A teacher who fails to notify the principal when she is absent from school is less likely to win an appeal of a reprimand than a teacher who has been more conscientious about notification (Ostrander, 1981).

Negative Norm Setters

Arbitrators also consider an individual employee's behavior in light of the behavior of other employees. A reprimand of a teacher who has accumulated "excessive" absences is unlikely to be sustained if other teachers in the district with equal or greater numbers of absences were not reprimanded. Employees whose behavior is poorest set the standard by which all employees are judged, so administrators must first take corrective action against these negative norm setters.

Noncompliance with work directives is a charge that most often arises in connection with noninstructional duties. Teachers are expected to monitor hallways, cafeterias, and restrooms in most schools. In some schools they also supervise the playground and bus-loading ramps. If the contract defines particular duties as voluntary, teachers may refuse to perform them without being subject to penalty. A question arises, however, when a teacher has agreed to perform a duty and later discontinues the activity before the task is complete. Consider a teacher who agrees to serve as sponsor of a cheerleading squad and resigns at midyear because of an increased workload related to a part-time job just taken on. Would a reprimand issued to a teacher in such a situation be sustained?

There is no way to predict what an arbitrator will decide in a given case, but if the contract is silent on the issue in question, then the arbitrator will use other information, including past practice, in making a decision. In this case, several factors must weigh on the decision. The arbitrator might consider whether the teacher understood that the assignment was for the full year, whether the teacher received supplemental pay for sponsoring the cheerleaders, and whether the teacher gave advance notice of her impending resignation and offered to help train a successor.

OTHER ISSUES IN ARBITRATION

Arbitrability

One of the issues that frequently confronts arbitrators is the question of arbitrability. *Arbitrability* refers to whether a grievance is subject to arbitration. Grievances that deal with powers granted to the board by statute are not arbitrable, and those that are not timely are also likely to be judged nonarbitrable. Most grievance policies limit the number of days that may elapse after occurrence of an event before a grievance is filed. If the allowable number of days for filing a grievance is exceeded, it may be declared nonarbitrable unless the teacher failed to learn of the precipitating event until after it occurred.

Arbitrabilty also hinges on definitions of what is or is not arbitrable as stated in the negotiated contract or contained in state statutes. Certain disputes may be grievable but not arbitrable (*Contract Administration,* 1983). In those situations, teachers have no appeal beyond the steps provided in the grievance procedure within the district.

Timeliness

Just as teachers must file a grievance within a specified number of days after the occurrence of the event they are grieving, administrators are required to respond to formal grievances within a few days of receiving them. Even though a grievance may arrive at a time when a principal is overwhelmed with other responsibilities, an answer must be given within the required time or the administration faces the possibility of losing in arbitration because of delay.

Questions of Law

Grievances frequently involve claims that state laws have been violated, but there is no unanimity of opinion regarding whether arbitrators should attempt to interpret the law in settling such disputes. Some people believe that arbitrators should not consider issues of law but should rather confine themselves to interpreting the collective bargaining agreement. Others argue that arbitrators are uniquely qualified to interpret the law as it applies to the parties to a collective bargaining agreement.

Past Practice

Past practice is frequently used by arbitrators as a guide in resolving disputes. If a particular practice has been consistently followed and there is nothing in the contract to indicate that the negotiators intended to change it, then any deviation from the practice by the administration is likely to be rejected. On the other hand, if the bargaining agreement specifies a procedure that is a clear departure from past practice, and the evidence suggests that both parties agreed to the change, then grievances appealing to past practices are unlikely to be upheld.

Problems most often arise when contract language appears to sanction a departure from previous practice but it is not clear that the negotiators meant to initiate the change. In one district, the contract specified that the "principal shall meet with the teacher following each classroom observation to discuss the results." When a new contract was negotiated, the language was changed slightly. In the new version, the provision read: "The principal shall meet with the teacher to discuss the results of classroom observations."

A teacher complained that the principal had not held a postobservation conference with her following a visit to the classroom and had informed her that a conference following every observation was no longer required. When the question reached arbitration, the arbitrator had to decide whether the negotiators had intended to drop the requirement. The board representative argued that such a change was intended, but the teacher representative denied it. In the absence of agreement that a change in practice was intended, the arbitrator held that principals should continue meeting with teachers after every observation.

In some cases, arbitrators have upheld departure from past practice when conditions warranted unusual actions. In one case, teachers participating in a mass "sick-out" to protest an action of the board were required by the administration to produce a physician's statement or have their pay docked for the time they were not at school. The penalized teachers grieved the decision, claiming that it violated past practice. The arbitrator upheld the administration on grounds that the teachers' actions justified the board's response (Ostrander, 1981).

Teacher Allegiance

Some issues are more important to teachers than others, and they will demonstrate flexibility on certain provisions of the contract while holding firm on others. Teachers are most likely to grieve what they believe to be violations of contract provisions affecting job security, transfers, class size, and assignment to noncontractual duties (Johnson, 1984).

However, most teachers feel allegiance to their school and to the principal and will try to work out disagreements before resorting to filing grievances. On occasion, teachers have even overridden the objections of union officials and performed duties that were not required by the contract in order to help facilitate a school's program (Johnson, 1984).

Effects of Arbitration on the District

Arbitrators' decisions can have considerable impact on district personnel policies. For that reason, most district administrators attempt to include in the contract language that narrowly defines which disputes may be taken to arbitration. Some administrators make it a practice never to go to arbitration unless they are certain of winning (Salmon, 1983). There is some wisdom in that position. Although the contract language may appear to be straightforward and clear to district administrators, there is no guarantee that the arbitrator will agree with their interpretation, and once an arbitrator's decision has been announced, it establishes a precedent that may be difficult to change (*Contract Administration*, 1983).

SUMMARY

Conflict in work settings usually involves one of four issues: interpretation and application of work rules, allocation of resources, duties and responsibilities, and assessment of performance. The effort to solve work-related conflict requires clarification and discussion of underlying issues, a search for shared values, exploration of possible solutions, and selection of one solution.

Increasingly, schools are relying on grievance procedures developed through the process of collective bargaining to resolve disputes. Arbitration is a component of the grievance procedure in many districts with bargaining agreements. A grievance process permits employees to have their complaints heard by managers or administrators in the organization and, ultimately in most cases, by an impartial arbitrator. Grievance procedures reduce the cost of settling disputes for both employees and employers by taking issues out of the courts and reducing the time required for resolution.

Arbitrators who review disputes between management and labor must decide whose interpretation of the contract is correct. Guidelines that are used by arbitrators to help them arrive at an accurate interpretation of contract language include the rule of consistency and the rule of intent. Arbitrators must frequently deal with complaints that involve interpretation and application of rules. Questions they must answer include to whom rules apply and what actions are either required or forbidden by a rule. "Just cause" complaints refer to contract clauses in which the administration is prohibited from withholding an employee benefit without good reason. These grievances are usually decided on the basis of reasonableness in behavior.

One of the principles used by arbitrators in resolving grievances is past practice. Unless it is clear that the board and the teachers' union intended to institute a new practice, the arbitrator usually holds that previous practice will remain in effect.

SUGGESTED ACTIVITIES

1. Suppose you are representing one of the parties in the dispute with the administration over whether coaches should be required to drive team buses to away games without extra pay (described in Exhibit 14.1.) Write a final offer from your side to be submitted to the arbitrator, who will choose one of the two offers. Bear in mind that the side that submits the offer that the arbitrator regards as most fair and most responsive will have its offer accepted. Designate a member of the class to serve as arbitrator and choose one of the two offers submitted for his or her consideration.

2. The principal of an elementary school informs teachers that he is concerned about student behavior in the cafeteria and proposes that they sit with their students while they eat rather than sitting together at one end of the room. There are strong objections from some teachers. There is no policy or contractual agreement that prevents the principal from directing teachers to sit with their students, but he prefers to avoid conflict if possible. How would you advise the principal to resolve this conflict?

3. Interview a principal or director of human resources to learn more about the types of conflict situations that arise with regard to interpretation and application of work rules and how they are usually resolved.

4. Read the following rule and answer the three questions on page 265 regarding work rules.

   Teachers who plan field trips must secure administrative and parental approval in advance and must take necessary precautions to ensure the children's safety while away from school. No trip will be approved that does not have a logical tie-in with the curriculum. Teachers are responsible for making up any missed class time.

ONLINE RESOURCES

A number of sites with information on dispute resolution are listed below.

American Arbitration Association (http://www.adr.org/publications.html)

This site shares a list of AAA periodicals that address the latest developments in alternate dispute resolution.

CPR-Institute for Dispute Resolution (http://www.cpradr.ord/welcome.htm)

This site provides information about a nonprofit alliance of corporations and firms using alternate dispute resolution.

Department of Education (www.ed.gov/database/ericdigest/ed339791.html)

This site provides information on educational resources and guidelines on dealing with conflict resolution within educational institutions.

Equal Employment Opportunity Commission (http://www.eeoc.gov)

Information about the use of alternate dispute resolution in the EEO complaint/appeal process is given on this website.

Federal Mediation and Conciliation Service (FMCS) (www.fmcs.gov/about fmcs.htm)

FMCS is a federal agency that provides mediators free of charge to parties at impasse in contract negotiations. It also provides parties with lists of grievance arbitrators.

Mediation Information and Resource Center (http://www.mediate.com)

Information about mediation and a list of mediator resources are given.

Office of Personnel Management (http://www.opm.gov/er)

Information is presented about the Office of Personnel Management. The site contains a resource guide for alternate dispute resolution.

Society of Professionals in Dispute Resolution (SPIDR).
(http://www.spidr.org/pubs.htm)

Publications of the Society are listed.

REFERENCES

Boys Markets Inc. v. *Retail Clerks, Local 770,* 398 U.S. 235 (1970).

Chicago Board of Education and Chicago Teacher Union Local 1, AFT, 108 LA1193 (1997).

Contract administration: Understanding limitations on management rights. (1983). Eugene, OR: University of Oregon, Center for Educational Policy and Management. (ERIC Document Reproduction Service No. ED 271842).

Coulson, R. (1986). *Arbitration in the schools: An analysis of fifty-nine grievance arbitration cases.* New York: American Arbitration Association.

Downey, K. (2003, September 21). Workers' moment. *Washington Post,* F1, F14.

Elkouri, F., & Elkouri, E. (1973). *How arbitration works.* Washington, DC: Bureau of National Affairs.

Isenhart, M. W., & Spangle, M. (2000). *Collaborative approaches to resolving conflict.* Thousand Oaks, CA: Sage.

Johnson, S. (1984). *Teacher unions in schools.* Philadelphia: Temple University Press.

Lexington Local Board of Education and Lexington Support Association, 111 LA 411 (1998).

Lovell, N. (1985). *Grievance arbitration in education.* Bloomington, IN: Phi Delta Kappa.

Lutz, F., & Caldwell, W. (1979). Collective bargaining and the principal. In D. Erickson and T. Reller (Eds.), *The principal in metropolitan schools* (pp. 256–271). Berkeley, CA: McCutchan.

Masters, M. F., & Albright, R. R. (2002). *The complete guide to conflict resolution in the workplace.* New York: AMACOM.

McDermott, E. P. (1996). *Alternative dispute resolution in the workplace.* Westport, CT: Quorum.

Ostrander, K. (1981). *A grievance arbitration guide for educators.* Boston: Allyn and Bacon.

Ostrander, K. (1987). *The legal structure of collective bargaining in education.* New York: Greenwood Press.

Papa, M., & Canary, D. (1995). Conflict in organizations: A competence-based approach. In A. Nicotera (Ed.), *Conflict and organizations* (pp. 153–179). Albany: State University of New York Press.

Pneuman, R. W., & Bruehl, M. E. (1982). *Managing conflict.* Englewood Cliffs, NJ: Prentice-Hall.

Rahim, M. (1986). *Managing conflict in organizations.* New York: Praeger.

Salmon, H. (1983, April). A *superintendent's perspective of the grievance process.* Paper presented at the annual meeting of the National School Boards Association, San Francisco. (ERIC Document Reproduction Service No. ED 251927).

Stitt, A. (1998). *Alternative dispute resolution for organizations.* Toronto: John Wiley.

Tjosvold, D. (1993). *Learning to manage conflict.* New York: Lexington.

Turner, S., & Weed, F. (1983). *Conflict in organizations.* Englewood Cliffs, NJ: Prentice-Hall.

CHAPTER FIFTEEN

TERMINATION AND REDUCTION IN WORKFORCE

The emphasis in this book has been on how to improve teacher quality and performance through the application of sound principles of human resources management. This positive approach, when carried out consistently over time, will produce significant gains in the quality of instruction in schools.

However, there are times when less pleasant actions must be taken. When enrollments decline or funds are lost, reductions in force may be necessary, and when a teacher who appeared promising proves to be unable to manage a classroom successfully, termination must be considered. These actions are the subject of this chapter.

PLAN OF THE CHAPTER

This chapter deals with the following topics: (1) carrying out a reduction in workforce, (2) reduction in force and employees' rights, (3) dealing with employee misconduct, (4) dismissal and nonrenewal, (5) anticipating court challenges, (6) documenting unsatisfactory performance, and (7) rights of dismissed teachers.

CARRYING OUT A REDUCTION IN WORKFORCE

The purpose of a reduction-in-force (RIF) policy is to permit the district to achieve necessary cutbacks in the number of employees on the payroll without disrupting services. That outcome is most likely to be achieved if a policy providing fair, efficient, and consistent procedures for carrying out cutbacks has been developed in advance of the need (DeKalb County School System, 1979).

The need for reductions in the number of employees can arise in several ways. Developments that most often result in layoffs are declining enrollments, funding shortfalls, discontinuation of programs, and reorganization or consolidation of school districts. About four-fifths of the states have legislation that legitimizes reductions in force for one or more of those reasons (Zirkel & Bargerstock, 1981).

If a state statute does not expressly identify a particular factor as a legitimate basis for laying off an employee, then the school district may be on shaky ground if it implements reductions for that reason. A Pennsylvania court reinstated a teacher who had been laid off by a district that had experienced a budget shortfall because financial exigency was not identified in the state statute as an acceptable reason for laying off employees (Zirkel & Bargerstock, 1981). However, some state courts have held that declining enrollments in one program may justify staff reductions, even though total enrollments are not declining (Caplan, 1984). The seven steps involved in carrying out a reduction in force and the individual or department responsible for each are shown in Exhibit 15.1 and discussed in the sections that follow.

■ ■ ■ ■ ■

EXHIBIT 15.1

STEPS INVOLVED IN IMPLEMENTING REDUCTION IN FORCE

STEP	RESPONSIBLE INDIVIDUAL OR DEPARTMENT
1. Determination that surplus exists	Superintendent (in consultation with principals and other administrators)
2. Identification of position classifications and certification fields affected	Human resources department (or official designated by superintendent)
3. Review of alternative actions	Superintendent, human resources department, finance department, and principals
4. Identification of a potential reduction-in-force pool	Human resources department, director of instruction, and union officials
5. Rank individuals in the pool using criteria established by law and policy	Human resources department with assistance from principals and others
6. Review of ranked list to remove protected individuals and groups	Human resources with assistance from superintendent, principals, and other administrators
7. Implementation of reduction in force	Superintendent, human resources department, and principals

Determining That a Surplus Exists

The first step in carrying out a reduction in force is determining that layoffs are needed. If enrollment drops or funding is cut, the district may need fewer employees. When the number of excess personnel is small, normal attrition may achieve the needed reductions, but if it doesn't, other possibilities, including reduction in force, must be considered. The decision to lay off personnel is made by the district superintendent after consultations with other administrators. Among the factors to be considered before a final decision is made are enrollments, state statutes, accreditation standards, financial condition, court rulings, and program priorities (DeKalb County School System, 1979).

Identifying Classifications Affected

Once the superintendent has declared a personnel surplus, the human resources department is faced with the task of determining surplus personnel by position classification and certification field. Wake County (NC) Public Schools classifies certificated employees into six groups: PreK–5, 6–8 middle school, 9–12 high school, K–12, Vocational, and Special Services, which includes administrators and counselors (Wake County Public Schools, 2002).

Within each category, employees are grouped separately by certification area. For example, in the 6–8 middle school group, mathematics and language arts teachers are placed in different categories. If enrollments drop in only one subject, then staff reductions would take place in that subject area and no other, whereas if declines have occurred in several subject areas, reductions would occur in all of the affected fields. The number of teachers to be laid off varies, depending on the size of the enrollment loss or the amount of the reduction in funding.

Reviewing Alternatives

Layoffs are a traumatic experience for individuals involved. When layoffs occur, even employees who are not directly affected may experience feelings of depression and anxiety out of empathy for colleagues who are being laid off and feelings of concern for their own future security. It is sometimes possible to avoid the stress of layoffs by taking action to postpone or avoid the need to carry out a reduction in force. Among the actions to be considered are early retirement, unpaid leaves of absence, half-time employment, assistance in finding alternative employment, and retraining.

Early Retirement.   Early retirement is one of the most widely used methods for avoiding reductions in workforce because it solves the problem of surplus personnel without the trauma of layoffs. On the other hand, early retirement is expensive and is not always a satisfactory solution. It works best when enrollments are declining at an equal rate in all grade levels and programs and when the district has a relatively large number of employees nearing retirement age. If personnel surpluses are concentrated in a few programs or grade levels or if few individuals are close to retiring, early retirement is less likely to be a viable solution.

Leaves of Absence. Unpaid leaves of absence have the advantage of allowing employees to continue in-force insurance policies that are provided by the district. An employee is thus able to secure health insurance for self and family at rates below those that are available to individuals. Normally, the individual must pay the premium for the policy, but in some instances that cost is borne by the district. Employees on unpaid leave will be reinstated if a position is available at the expiration of the leave. Unpaid leaves offer psychological support at a crucial time by letting employees know that the district still values their contributions and wishes to continue the employer/employee relationship.

Part-Time Employment. Half-time or substitute positions are sometimes offered to employees who otherwise would be laid off, in the belief that most people would rather work part time than not work at all. If one position is assigned to two half-time employees, both have some income, whereas an employee who is laid off receives no income. As a temporary measure to give employees time to find alternative employment, half-time work helps.

Job-Hunting Assistance. Providing assistance to help individuals who are laid off to find new jobs is a psychologically sound strategy, since it motivates these employees to take action and move forward. Employees who receive layoff notices are sometimes immobilized by the hope that they will quickly be recalled. Rather than try to find another job, they sometimes waste months waiting for a recall notice. Beginning a systematic and wide-ranging job search can help them cope more realistically with their situation by assessing their strengths and examining their options.

Retraining Teachers. Retraining teachers who are about to be laid off is a viable strategy if enrollments in the subjects in which they are retrained are expected to remain stable. Teachers who are near to being certified in critical subjects are sometimes allowed to begin teaching classes in those subjects on temporary teaching certificates while they continue to take courses to qualify for full certification. However, teachers who lack the necessary subject matter competence should not be permitted to teach until they acquire it.

Identifying the Potential Pool

If alternative actions are not feasible, or if after such actions are taken an oversupply of teachers remains, the district then begins the crucial step of preparing a list of employees who are subject to being laid off. The list is prepared by reviewing personnel files of all individuals in the affected positions, using criteria established by the reduction-in-force policy. For example, the pool might include all business education teachers or, in a large district, business education teachers with fewer than a specified number of years seniority.

It is wise to involve the director of instruction early in the process. Some programs require teachers who are certified in certain subspecialties in order to operate effectively, and the director of instruction can provide that information. A good example is a music program that involves offerings in chorus, band, and orchestra. A school with several tenured band teachers and no tenured chorus or orchestra teachers may end up with an oversupply of band teachers if seniority is the sole criterion for making reduction-in-force decisions. The director of instruction can identify needed adjustments in the pool in order to maintain a well-balanced instructional program.

Determining Order of Layoffs

The reduction-in-force policy normally identifies the criteria to be used in deciding which employees will be laid off. Among the criteria used by districts to rank-order the employees in the groups selected for reductions in workforce are performance (as determined by annual performance evaluations), length of service, and experience in extra-duty assignments such as coaching or yearbook sponsor. Thus, a teacher with favorable performance evaluations, long years of service, and experience in extra-duty assignments would be protected against being laid off, whereas a teacher with less than stellar performance reviews and limited service in the district would have a greater chance of being dismissed.

Reviewing Ranked List

At this point, a final review of the ranked list is carried out, with involvement of principals and various district staff members. The purpose of the review is to make deletions and additions that may be needed in order to avoid violating provisions of state law, negotiated agreements, and district policy, and to provide safeguards against disruptions of programs and unnecessary harm to program quality. When the review is complete and the superintendent has signed off, the list goes to the human resources department, which initiates the process of notifying affected employees.

Implementing the Reduction

The final step in the process is to notify the individual employees who are to be laid off from their jobs. This is usually done by letter from the superintendent or the director of human resources. The letter identifies the date that the reduction in workforce becomes effective and outlines the employee's rights under the law and the bargaining agreement.

Staffing Adjustments Required

When a reduction in workforce takes place, principals are required to make adjustments in staffing by redistributing instructional and noninstructional assignments among the remaining staff members. In the case of elementary schools, this may involve nothing more than reducing the number of classes in the affected grade levels and reassigning students, but it often involves much more. In middle and high schools, principals are faced with making adjustments in the master schedule to reflect shifting enrollment patterns brought about by the elimination of some course offerings. For example, if fewer classes are offered in the business education department because of staff reductions, existing classes in that department as well as in other departments may increase in size, as a result of the reduced number of elective options available to students.

These changes in enrollment patterns also have implications for the purchase of equipment, materials, and supplies. If available business education classes increase in size, it may be necessary to purchase additional computers to accommodate the increased enrollment.

If teachers who were laid off were sponsors of student clubs or activities, it will be necessary for the principal to arrange to recruit other teachers to take over those duties rather than let the programs languish. If the layoffs involved non-teaching personnel, such as guidance counselors, the principal must see to it that the workload is redistributed equitably among remaining staff members.

The decision to carry out a reduction in workforce is not an easy one, but it is simple compared to the difficulty and distress that faces an administrator who attempts to terminate a teacher. A subsequent section addresses the topic of teacher discipline and termination.

REDUCTION IN WORKFORCE AND EMPLOYEES' RIGHTS

Collective bargaining agreements and state statutes grant certain rights to employees who are subject to being laid off. These rights include privileges earned through seniority, the opportunity to continue health insurance in effect at the employee's expense, and future reinstatement when funding permits.

In general, more senior workers are protected against layoffs when other employees with less seniority hold the same job. However, administrators sometimes decide to lay off a teacher with more seniority while retaining one with less seniority. When that happens, the district may expect to face a court challenge.

An example involved a Pennsylvania school district. The superintendent retained a teacher with less seniority as coordinator of a program for gifted students and laid off teachers who had more seniority. The administrator's rationale was that the teacher who was retained was more qualified for the position because she had been involved with the program since its inception, had more experience with arts and humanities, and was better at interacting with students and members of the community. Those arguments might have prevailed in some states, but the Pennsylvania Supreme Court held that the law of that state required the district to lay off employees with the least seniority (*Dallap* v. *Sharon City School District*, 1990).

Under collective bargaining agreements in workforce in many school districts, employees who are threatened with layoffs may replace or "bump" an employee with less seniority. However, this right has limitations. The bumping teacher must possess a valid certificate to teach the subject taught by the teacher being bumped and must have more seniority than the bumped teacher. It is common to require teachers who bump other teachers to have had recent and successful experience teaching the subject to which they are requesting to transfer. In some districts, the bargaining agreement gives the principal of the school receiving a replacement teacher the prerogative of reviewing the transferring teacher's credentials to determine whether that individual's qualifications are sufficient to maintain program quality (Johnson, 1982). In districts with such a policy, a teacher who received certification to teach a subject many years earlier but has never taught in that field and has taken no recent coursework would not be permitted to replace a teacher with more up-to-date credentials and experience.

Minority employees who have been hired under affirmative action programs often have the least seniority in their districts and therefore are most vulnerable to reductions in workforce. Bargaining agreements sometimes provide protection from layoffs for these individuals. In one case involving such a policy, the Supreme Court held that the board failed to show a "compelling purpose" in arguing that past societal discrimination justified the plan and so rejected it. The Court stated:

> Societal discrimination alone is [not] sufficient to justify a racial classification. Rather, the Court has insisted upon some showing of prior discrimination by the governmental unit involved before allowing limited use of racial classifications in order to remedy such discrimination (*Wygant* v. *Jackson (MI) Board of Education*, 1986).

However, in a case tried under Title VII of the Civil Rights Act, the Supreme Court upheld a plan that benefited individuals who had not been identified as actual victims of discrimination (*Geier* v. *Alexander*, 1986).

DEALING WITH EMPLOYEE MISCONDUCT

School employees on the whole abide by the law and carry out their responsibilities conscientiously and with relatively few errors in judgment. However, when a staff member breaks the law or exercises poor judgment, the individual's supervisor has the duty to initiate corrective action. Minor infractions by staff members usually are handled informally at the school level, but more serious offenses are referred to central administration or to law-enforcement authorities. Whether the resolution of the problem involves district administrators or law-enforcement officials depends on the nature and seriousness of the offense and provisions of the law, board policy, and the master contract. Needless to say, administrators who have responsibility for human resources management need to be familiar with all provisions of the contract and board policies that deal with employee conduct.

It is important to bear in mind that the purpose of employee discipline is to correct any damage that may have been done by the employee's actions and to prevent future occurrences. Its purpose is not to punish an employee. Nothing is gained if the employee perceives that the disciplinary action was unfair, unduly harsh, or taken for the purpose of retribution. If the episode results in an employee who is alienated and nonproductive, then the discipline has not been successful.

Types of Offenses

Actions of staff members that require disciplinary action fall under one of three levels of severity. The least severe type of offense includes actions that are inappropriate or reflect poor judgment but which require no action by the administration other than a reminder. Occasional absence from work and tardiness fall into this category. Failure to turn in information on student attendance, failure to issue receipts for money brought by students, and missing meetings are examples of offenses that belong in the least severe category. However, these offenses can escalate into actionable charges if repeated often enough.

More serious offenses include the use of inappropriate language with students, parents, or colleagues; leaving the school during the school day without signing out or notifying the office; carrying a concealed weapon in school; conducting fund-raising activities without securing advance approval; abusing drugs or alcohol; leaving students unsupervised; and using excessive force with a student. For these offenses, teachers would receive a written reprimand to be placed in the personnel file.

The most serious offenses are those for which a staff member receives a written reprimand and may be temporarily suspended with or without pay. In extreme cases the staff member may be terminated for an offense of this type. Among the offenses that belong in this category are being arrested for commission of a felony or morals offense, taking money from school funds for personal use, and misrepresenting one's professional credentials.

Levels of Discipline

Disciplinary actions start with a conference between the staff member and his or her immediate supervisor. The conference serves three purposes: (1) to collect information about the precipitating incident and hear the staff member's explanation, (2) to explain to the staff member the reasons that the behavior is unacceptable, and (3) to inform the staff member of disciplinary actions to be taken and warn of more severe consequences in the future should the behavior be repeated.

Verbal Reprimand.   The mildest disciplinary action for a staff member who has violated a school board policy or a provision of the master contract is a verbal reprimand. When issuing a verbal reprimand, the supervisor identifies the action that violated the policy or contract and informs the staff member that this is a verbal reprimand. The supervisor then warns the staff member to avoid repeating the behavior and suggests the possibility of more severe consequences if the behavior recurs.

Written Reprimand.   Above the verbal reprimand is a written reprimand, which consists of a letter addressed to the employee that identifies the action that is in violation of the law, policy, or contract. Typically the letter presents a detailed description of the action or actions for which the employee is being reprimanded, including dates and times, and identifying any other persons who were involved. The letter also cites the specific provision or provisions of board policy or the master contract that the employee violated. Finally, the staff member is urged not to repeat the behavior and is warned of more serious consequences should that happen. A written reprimand is placed in the staff member's personnel file but may be removed after a period of time if the behavior has not been repeated. Exhibit 15.2 shows an example of a letter of reprimand to a middle school math teacher, Barbara Finch.

Involuntary Leave.   Employees who are accused of or charged with breaking the law may be placed on leave until the case is resolved. The leave may be with or without pay, depending on the seriousness of the offense. When an employee is suspended without pay, the individual's salary is held in escrow until he or she is cleared or found guilty. If found guilty of a moral offense, abuse, or misuse of public funds, the employee will be terminated and may have his or her professional license revoked.

DISMISSAL AND NONRENEWAL

Many employers operate under an employment-at-will doctrine that allows the employer to terminate an employee at any time for any cause or no cause. The employer who is protected by the doctrine incurs no legal liability for terminating an employee. The exception to employment-at-will occurs when an employee is under contract or is protected by statute (Sovereign, 1999). Nontenured teachers are usually employed under contract, and if a district determines that the teacher's performance is not satisfactory and acts to terminate the individual before the contract expires, the district generally must be prepared to defend its action. The exception occurs if a teacher is hired without a written or implied contract.

Nonrenewal occurs when a nontenured teacher's contract expires and the district chooses not to renew it. No reason need be given, and the teacher generally

■ ■ ■ ■ ■

EXHIBIT 15.2

LETTER OF REPRIMAND FOR A TEACHER

MEMORANDUM

TO: Barbara Finch, Math Teacher

FROM: Richard Stein, Principal

On November 12 and again on March 3, you left a math class unattended. On the most recent occasion, when I learned that you were not in your classroom, I investigated and found you talking on the telephone in the teachers' workroom. I remind you that leaving your classroom with students present is a violation of the master contract, which states: "For safety reasons, teachers will be in their classrooms at all times when students are present. Should it be necessary for a teacher to leave the room during class time, arrangements must be made for another adult to supervise the class in the teacher's absence."

Because you have violated this provision twice this school year, I am issuing this written reprimand to caution you against repeating this behavior. Although I understand that you were phoning your doctor's office to make an appointment, that is not a justifiable reason for leaving your classroom. Furthermore, your explanation that you were out of the room for only five minutes was contradicted by a teacher and several students, all of whom told me that you were away for at least 15 minutes. I am sure I do not need to remind you of the possible harm that might have come to your students while you were out of the room. Your behavior betrayed the trust that parents of your students have placed in you. I hope that you will not be guilty of such reckless behavior in the future.

A copy of this letter will be placed in your personnel file.

cc: Dr. Anthony Raisin
       Director of Human Resources
       Mary Alice Barron, President
       Professional Teachers Association

has no recourse. Administrators should exercise care not to imply to an employee that his or her contract will be renewed. Suggesting that a contract will be renewed is referred to as an *implied contract* and may require that the district furnish reasons for its decision not to renew the individual's contract (Sovereign, 1999).

The first step for an administrator contemplating dismissing a tenured teacher is to become thoroughly familiar with the applicable policy and/or statute and to carefully follow the procedures outlined therein. Human resources administrators need to know what kinds of behavior are specified in the law as justifiable grounds for dismissing a teacher and should be familiar with the procedures to be followed in conducting a hearing. A timely notice should be delivered to the teacher who is subject to dismissal, and due process guarantees required by the law must be followed.

State statutes identify specific causes for which teachers may be dismissed. Arizona law states that a teacher who is charged with unprofessional conduct, conduct in violation of laws or rules, or inadequate classroom performance must be given specific examples of the actions or omissions that led to the charge and a list of the rules or laws that the teacher is alleged to have violated. The purpose of this provision is to allow the teacher to prepare a defense. Arizona also grants any teacher receiving such a notice the right to a hearing (Dismissal of Certificated Teacher, 2000).

According to the American Federation of Teachers (1996), the five most common reasons for dismissing teachers reported by union officers for the years 1993–1996 (from more to less frequent) were incompetence, physical or mental incapacity, insubordination, professional misconduct, and conviction of a crime. Abuse of drugs or alcohol was also frequently cited as cause for dismissal. These reasons are discussed below.

Incompetence refers to lack of ability, knowledge, or fitness. An inexperienced person may lack skill but is likely to improve over time, whereas someone who is an incompetent performer seldom improves noticeably unless remediation is available. In evaluating competence, we normally consider what are called the "essential tasks" of a position. For a computer programmer, these tasks include the ability to use programming language to produce desired results, and for a baseball player, essential tasks include hitting and fielding the ball. Essential tasks for a bus driver are collecting fares, operating the bus safely, and adhering to a schedule.

The essential tasks of teaching are preparing lesson plans, presenting information, and producing learning in the students. However, there are other expectations of teachers that are equally as important as these tasks. Teachers are professionals, and, as such, they are expected to place the well-being of their clients (the students) above other considerations. Teachers are guided in their work by a statement of ethics that defines their responsibilities as professionals. The Code of Ethics published by the National Education Association holds teachers responsible for protecting students from conditions that are harmful to their health and safety and for allowing students access to varying points of view. Codes of ethics published by the NEA and the State of South Dakota are available online (see Online Resources at the end of this chapter).

By requiring that school districts certify that all teachers are "highly qualified," No Child Left Behind puts pressure on school administrators to address the problem of incompetent teachers. For critics who believe that teacher quality in the schools is so low that it impedes instructional improvement, NCLB is welcome news. These critics believe that school administrators have been lax in ridding the schools of teachers who are not performing satisfactorily and that government action to correct the problem is needed (Johnson, 1984). Bridges (1985) has argued the point forcefully:

Most teachers in our nation's schools are competent, conscientious, hard-working individuals. All too often their efforts are overshadowed by the poor performance of a relatively small number of incompetent classroom teachers. These incompetents must be identified and assisted, and if they fail to improve, they must be dismissed (p. 19).

Scriven (1980) took an even more critical position:

The current state of teacher personnel policies is that they are reasonably fair to teachers—a great improvement over the pre-union situation—and extremely unfair to students, parents and taxpayers. They protect all, but they excessively protect the congenital incompetent, the once-but-no-longer competent and the competent non-performer. . . . We have teacher policies that ruthlessly sacrifice productivity for equity. Productivity without equity is morally intolerable; equity without productivity is socially irresponsible (p. 2).

Fewer than 10 percent of Americans questioned by the Gallup Poll in annual surveys between 2000 and 2003 reported that difficulty in hiring "good" teachers was a major problem for the public schools. The number of respondents who mentioned the teacher quality problem ranged between 4 and 8 percent, as compared with 11 percent who cited the teacher quality problem in the 1988 survey (Gallup & Elam, 1988; Rose & Gallup, 2003).

In the 2003 Poll, respondents were also asked specifically whether their local public schools had a hard time getting and keeping good teachers. Sixty-one percent of the respondents answered "yes" to the first question, and 66 percent answered in the affirmative to the second question (Rose & Gallup, 2003).

Unions and Teacher Accountability.   Many administrators and some teachers believe that unions protect both incompetent teachers and those who have lost interest in teaching but remain in the classroom. However, others, including many administrators, believe that poor teachers can be removed from classrooms if the procedures that are available are put into use by principals (Johnson, 1984).

One of the concerns expressed by administrators and union leaders alike is that in the current concern for school accountability, teachers' rights are likely to be overlooked. Gross (1988) pointed out the danger and suggested a possible solution:

Requiring fact rather than assumption as a basis for disciplinary action may appear on the surface to make it more difficult to dismiss immoral or incompetent teachers. On the contrary, identifying and eliminating unfairness in the current disciplinary system for tenured teachers will require school districts to develop hiring, evaluation, promotion, and disciplinary policies and practices that can be validated with competent evidence (p. 2).

If selection and evaluation procedures are in place and working well, there should rarely be a need to dismiss teachers. Yet, even when care and thought are exercised in selecting and placing teachers, and when opportunities for professional growth are provided, there will still be a few who do not perform the job satisfactorily or who lapse into substandard performance after a time. Districts should monitor the performance of all teachers and be prepared to take action against those few who fail to meet their standards of performance.

School boards review recommendations for dismissal of school employees and decide whether the action is warranted. Traditionally, boards have also heard appeals of a decision to dismiss an employee. Teachers believe that school boards have a conflict of interest that lessens the chance that a person who is terminated will receive a fair hearing. As a result of these concerns, legislatures in more than half of the states have in recent years enacted laws to change the procedures by which termination decisions are made and appeals heard (Lopez & Sperry, 1994).

A variety of alternative practices for ensuring due process to teachers who have been terminated have emerged to replace the practice of lodging all authority with school boards. In most of the states that have revised their procedures, hearing officers or panels, usually individuals with legal training who are not employees of the board, serve as objective fact finders, and school boards determine whether the facts justify dismissal of an employee. In a small number of states, school boards have been removed from the process of teacher termination altogether (Lopez & Sperry, 1994).

Administrators sometimes argue that the protections enacted to safeguard teachers' academic freedom make it difficult or impossible to dismiss incompetent teachers. They claim that the elaborate and time-consuming procedures required to document poor performance and the cost of hiring attorneys to handle court actions arising from termination decisions discourage them from trying to remove poor teachers from classrooms. To achieve balance, legislatures in several states have adopted laws eliminating or restricting tenure for public school teachers. In some cases, teachers receive a renewable one- or two-year contract and may be terminated with or without cause upon expiration of the contract (Hirsch, 1998).

Immoral or Unprofessional Behavior

Dismissing a teacher on grounds of immoral or unprofessional conduct places on the board the burden of showing that the teacher's behavior had an adverse impact on students or other teachers. There is no absolute standard against which such behavior is judged. Rather, the courts take into account such factors as age and maturity of the students, degree of adverse impact, motive for the behavior, and the likelihood that it will be repeated (Alexander & Alexander, 1985).

Teachers have been discharged on grounds of immoral behavior for engaging in sexual misconduct with students. Some courts have held that when sexual involvement occurs between teacher and student, a presumption of adverse impact is justified without additional proof (McCarthy & Cambron-McCabe, 1987). Other examples of immoral behavior for which teachers have been discharged are physical abuse of students, use of profanity, misconduct involving drugs or alcohol, and misappropriation of funds.

Homosexual behavior has been allowed as grounds for dismissal in some courts, but not in others (Landauer, Spangler, & Van Horn, 1983). As a general rule, private sexual behavior, whether homosexual or heterosexual, is regarded by the courts as grounds for dismissal only to the extent that it affects the individual's effectiveness as a teacher. But it should also be noted that teachers are regarded as exemplars and that their actions "are subject to much greater scrutiny than that given to the activities of the average person" (*Chicago Board of Education* v. *Payne*, 1982).

A teacher who is convicted of a crime of moral turpitude may be dismissed. However, an arrest alone is not usually sufficient grounds for dismissal, although it may be justifiable grounds for suspension. Sexual crimes are considered irremediable and are sufficient to justify dismissal. Use of drugs can justify immediate suspension pending dismissal (*Education Law*, 1989).

Insubordination

Insubordination is a lawful cause for dismissal of teachers in many states. Actions that may be construed as insubordinate include failing to follow rules and regulations pertaining to use of corporal punishment, absenteeism, tardiness, and failing to complete required reports.

Insubordination also includes a teacher's refusal to perform properly assigned duties. Administrators may assign duties that are not specified in a bargaining agreement as long as they are reasonably related to the instructional program and are not unduly time consuming or burdensome. However, a teacher may not lawfully be dismissed for refusing to perform duties for which he or she lacks competence or that are unrelated to the school program (*Education Law*, 1989).

Some courts have held that a single incident of insubordination is sufficient to justify dismissal. A teacher in Kansas was dismissed after he had his wife call the school to report that he was ill while he was actually in Texas interviewing for another job. The teacher had earlier requested and been denied leave. The principal of the school at which the teacher taught learned of the deception when the principal of the Texas school in which he interviewed called for a recommendation. The Kansas Court of Appeals upheld the decision to terminate the teacher's contract, noting that a single incident of insubordination could be sufficient to justify termination (*Gaylord* v. *Board of Education*, 1990). A similar conclusion was reached by the Colorado Supreme Court, which held that a district was justified in dismissing a teacher who had used profanity in front of several students after having been ordered by the superintendent to refrain from doing so (*Ware* v. *Morgan County School District,* 1988).

A board is most likely to win a legal test of a decision to dismiss a teacher for insubordination if it can show that the teacher knew about but repeatedly violated a rule, regulation, or directive, thereby causing harm to the school. The board's case will be further buttressed if the teacher's behavior is considered irremediable (Landauer, et al., 1983).

ANTICIPATING COURT CHALLENGES

The decision to dismiss a teacher is almost invariably followed by a legal challenge, and the district must be prepared to defend its actions by showing that all applicable laws and policies were followed in carrying out the dismissal action. Failure to adhere to every provision is likely to result in the teacher's being reinstated to his or her position by the court.

A problem that is unfortunately encountered all too often in these cases is the discovery by opposing attorneys of critical material in an employee's personnel file that the employee has not seen. If an unsatisfactory performance evaluation or a written reprimand is located in the personnel file of a teacher who has been terminated and there is no evidence that the employee has read the document, the teacher's attorney will attempt to use the discovery to depict district administrators as sloppy or biased or both. To avoid such a problem, employees should be asked to read and initial any document that is to be included in the personnel record. It is also a good idea to allow the employee to include a rejoinder in the file (Sovereign, 1999).

DOCUMENTING
UNSATISFACTORY PERFORMANCE

Most teachers occasionally violate school rules and policies, but most of those violations are minor and many of them are ignored by principals. When serious or repeated violations occur, the principal is obligated to take action. This involves preparing written documentation of the teacher's actions and the actions taken by the principal or others to remediate the problem, sending a copy to the teacher, and placing a copy of it in the individual's personnel file. Performance evaluation reports and descriptions of classroom observations are also included in the personnel file.

Five types of records prepared by principals are involved in documenting unsatisfactory performance: specific incident memoranda, private notes, descriptions of classroom observations, evaluation reports, and summary memoranda. If a teacher takes an action (or fails to take action) that constitutes violation of policy, the principal should immediately hold a conference with the teacher to discuss the infraction and to remind the teacher of the policy that has been violated. If the teacher's behavior is serious enough, this conference may be followed by a specific incident memorandum in which the principal summarizes the actions taken by the teacher that violated policy and describes any corrective action the principal has taken, including issuance of a reprimand (Frels & Cooper, 1982).

Specific Incident Memoranda

The specific incident memorandum should contain an objective description of the teacher's act or failure to act, a comment on the detrimental effect of the action on students, a description of suggestions or directives given the teacher by the principal or supervisor, and a statement indicating whether the teacher complied with the directives or followed through on suggestions (Neill & Custis, 1978).

It is advisable to ask the teacher to acknowledge receiving the memorandum by signing a copy to be placed in the individual's personnel file. The teacher should also be given the opportunity to prepare a written response explaining circumstances surrounding the incident and presenting the teacher's version of the facts. This response is also placed in the personnel file (Frels & Cooper, 1982).

Private Notes

Brief private notes about teachers may be kept by a principal as reminders for follow-up action but should be destroyed as soon as possible. For example, a principal may make a note to remind a teacher that students must be given at least one day's notice before being assigned to after-school detention in order to allow them to arrange transportation home. If the teacher continues to violate the rule after meeting with the principal, the administrator may reprimand the teacher or may place a note in a private file that serves as a reminder to comment on the teacher's actions in the performance evaluation report (Frels & Cooper, 1982).

Observation Reports

In most school districts, principals are required to observe teachers' classroom performance and to note the results of these observations in a memorandum or on a form provided by the district. These records are retained in teachers' personnel records and, if a teacher is dismissed, are used as part of the documentation. Notes prepared by the principal should be as detailed as possible, since relying on memory to recall events from an observation that occurred several months or years earlier is extremely risky.

Evaluation Reports

Evaluations of teachers' performance become part of a permanent documentary record. Evaluations are usually based on classroom performance but may include ratings on other aspects of a teacher's work. Some teachers may perform satisfactorily in the core tasks of teaching, such as planning and presenting instruction, but have problems working with administrators, teachers, and parents. These problems should be noted in the evaluation summary since they may be central to a subsequent action to dismiss.

Most teachers receive satisfactory performance ratings, even though their performance does not always justify them. It is extremely difficult to convince a court that a teacher's performance falls below the minimally acceptable standard when over a period of years the teacher has consistently received satisfactory performance ratings from principals. This problem is not exclusive to schools; it happens in most organizations (Bridges, 1984). However, organizations that do not grant tenure to their employees have more discretion in discharging unsatisfactory performers. When the decision is made to terminate a tenured teacher, the district should be able to produce evidence over a period of at least three years showing a pattern of unsatisfactory performance. Moreover, the board should be prepared to show a connection between identified deficiencies and loss of learning (Barton, 1984).

Summary Memoranda

A summary memorandum outlines the results of several incidents or classroom observations. It is used when the principal wishes to call to the teacher's attention several related instances of rule or policy violations or to summarize several classroom observations. The summary memorandum is used when the individual actions are not serious enough to warrant writing a specific incident memorandum but which, taken together, constitute a pattern of behavior that requires attention.

The documentary record should be a complete, accurate, and specific compilation of facts about an individual's performance. Complete and accurate records benefit both the district and the individual, since courts will uphold a termination action when documentation exists to show that a teacher's performance fails to meet the standards required by the district. Courts will dismiss the action when documentation is not available to substantiate the charge.

Principals who are documenting unsatisfactory performance by a teacher should be prepared to write objective, factual descriptions about what is observed in classrooms or in other areas of the school. Global descriptions are likely to be challenged in court and should be avoided. In their place, principals should use specific descriptions of classroom events or teacher actions. Sample descriptions of both types are provided in Exhibit 15.3.

RIGHTS OF DISMISSED TEACHERS

A district may refuse to renew the contract of a nontenured teacher without stating reasons for the decision, except in states with statutes that require notification.

EXHIBIT 15.3

GLOBAL VERSUS SPECIFIC DOCUMENTATION

GLOBAL	SPECIFIC
Had poor classroom management procedures	Three students were out of their seats and four others were talking, ignoring the teacher.
Violated the school policy on collection of payment and fees	Failed to issue receipts to three students who paid $5 locker fee.
Inadequately prepared for teaching	Had not prepared a lesson plan for the class; used part of class time to show a movie that was only tangentially related to the topic being studied.
Classroom appearance poor	Bulletin board displays unchanged for six months; books and papers piled atop bookcases and teacher's desk.

Tenured teachers, however, are entitled to certain protections prior to dismissal. Successful dismissal of a tenured teacher requires that the district strictly observe these procedural requirements.

The following list enumerates the due process protections that are provided tenured teachers by various state statutes (Cambron-McCabe, 1983):

1. A statement of charges
2. Access to evidence and names of witnesses
3. A choice of an open or closed hearing
4. Opportunity to be represented by counsel
5. Opportunity to introduce evidence, call, and cross-examine witnesses
6. A transcript of the hearing upon request
7. A written decision
8. Right of appeal

A teacher may be suspended without a hearing if his or her presence in the school represents a potential threat to students or other persons, or if the individual is charged with a crime involving moral turpitude.

Constitutional Protections

The Constitution grants certain rights to all American citizens, and employees are protected from employers' actions that infringe on those rights. The Fourteenth Amendment provides that government shall not "deprive any person of life, liberty, or property without due process of law." Tenured teachers and nontenured teachers under contract have potential property and liberty interests that are jeopardized by termination, and thus they are entitled to procedural due process before being terminated. Due process involves, at a minimum, notice of charges and an opportunity for a pretermination hearing at which evidence must be presented to show that the charges are true and support the proposed action (Hill & Wright, 1993).

The First Amendment guarantees freedom of speech, but the Supreme Court has held that right must be balanced with employers' interest in maintaining an efficient operation. In *Pickering* v. *Board of Education* (1968), the Court held that speech that interfered with employee performance, created disharmony, or undercut supervisory authority was not extended the same protections as other forms of expression.

In *Connick* v. *Myers* (1983), the Court held that to be protected, an employee's statement must deal with public—and not merely private—concerns. Determining which issues are private or public involves considering whether the expression advances a purely personal or community interest and whether or not there is general public interest in the issue (Frels & Schneider-Vogel, 1986).

A legal challenge under the First Amendment is likely to occur when an employee is terminated after openly criticizing district policy. The district may argue that the decision to dismiss was based on performance deficiencies and not on the employee's statements, but if the two events are proximate in time, questions are certain to be raised about the district's true motives (Frels & Schneider-Vogel, 1986).

In 1990, 40 states required prospective teachers to pass a test in order to be certified (National Center for Education Statistics, 1993), and a few states have enacted legislation that requires testing of practicing teachers. Both types of laws have been challenged in court.

In Texas, state law requires public school teachers and administrators to pass the Texas Examination for Current Administrators and Teachers (TECAT), which tests basic reading and writing skills. An organization representing teachers and administrators challenged the law, claiming that it was an unconstitutional impairment of teachers' and administrators' contracts. The Texas Supreme Court rejected the claim and upheld the test (*State* v. *Project Principle*, 1987).

In Alabama, the required test was the National Teachers' Examination (NTE). The Supreme Court of that state held that the board had properly refused to renew contracts of 106 teachers who had failed to attain the required score on the examination (*York* v. *Board of School Commissioners*, 1984).

Teachers who are threatened with dismissal are often given the option of resigning in order to avoid embarrassing and damaging publicity. Administrators should use care in attempting to persuade a teacher to resign, because courts may view the resignation as coerced and order the teacher reinstated. Courts have held that when an employer makes working conditions so unpleasant that an employee resigns rather than continue to work under such adverse conditions, the employer's action is unfair. Employers can avoid such an outcome by counseling and, if necessary, disciplining employees for cause rather than trying to force them to resign. If an employee can demonstrate that an employer's actions were taken for the purpose of forcing the employee to resign and conditions were so bad that the employee had no choice, then the employer may be held liable (Thorne, 1996).

Remediation

A question that is often raised in dismissal cases is remediability. If the behavior for which a tenured teacher is dismissed is considered remediable, then the board has an obligation to permit the teacher the opportunity to correct the behavior before it takes action to dismiss. The board's decision on the question of remediability is subject to judicial review. If there is a question about remediability, administrators are wise to assume that the behavior in question is remediable and to permit the teacher the opportunity to correct it. There is no absolute standard for judging how much time should be allowed for remediation. Although five weeks was found to be insufficient in one case, eight weeks was considered adequate by another court (Landauer et al., 1983).

Eight types of remediation are provided for teachers whose performance is judged to be unsatisfactory. They are listed in Exhibit 15.4 along with examples of actions appropriate for each. The first six remediation actions in Exhibit 15.4 should be carried out together. Although districts sometimes take one of these actions alone (for example, goal setting or instructional input), the chances of success are much greater if all six are used.

Goal setting was discussed in Chapter 6 as a motivational technique. In working with a teacher who has significant deficiencies in instructional performance, it is advisable to help the individual establish learning and behavior goals to achieve better classroom control and increased student achievement.

Instructional input equips the teacher with the knowledge and skill needed to achieve the goals. Modeling, practice, feedback, and reinforcement help the teacher to refine the skills and acquire facility and confidence in their use. Teachers who are having difficulty implementing instruction effectively may need to be reminded about the conditions under which learning occurs. Teachers help students to learn by establishing clear learning objectives, choosing appropriate learning tasks, expressing confidence in students' ability, providing rewards to practice new skills, and creating conditions under which transfer of learning can occur (Tyler, 1985).

Therapy/counseling and environmental change are less often used. They may be applied together, in conjunction with other techniques, or alone, depending on the nature of the teacher's problem. Teachers whose problems are related to their life situation may profit from therapy or counseling, and those whose difficulties emanate from their work assignment often perform better in a different setting. Sometimes it is necessary to provide psychological support along with environmental change.

■ ■ ■ ■ ■ ■

EXHIBIT 15.4
ACTIONS AND EXAMPLES FOR TEACHER REMEDIATION

Goal setting:	Help the teacher establish instructional and behavioral goals for students.
Instructional input:	Arrange for the teacher to take a class or attend a workshop to learn new skills.
Modeling:	Provide released time for the teacher to observe a colleague who has the skills the teacher is learning.
Practice:	Arrange time for the teacher to practice new skills in a non-threatening environment.
Feedback:	Provide feedback to the teacher who is attempting to master new skills.
Reinforcement:	Provide rewards, including praise, for correct use of newly learned skills.
Therapy or counseling:	Arrange for intensive emotional support for the teacher who has severe emotional problems.
Environmental change:	Arrange for the teacher to transfer to a different assignment.

Source: Managing the Incompetent Teacher by E. M. Bridges, 1984, Eugene: University of Oregon ERIC Clearinghouse on Educational Management.

SUMMARY

Reductions in workforce and termination of employees are occasionally necessary personnel actions. Policies governing both contingencies should spell out the actions to be taken and define the rights of employees involved. The purpose of a reduction-in-workforce policy is to permit the district to achieve necessary cutbacks in the number of employees on the payroll without disrupting services. Reduction-in-workforce policies should describe a procedure for declaring that a surplus of employees exists and for identifying the employee classifications and positions affected. They should also specify alternatives that may be taken to avoid layoffs. Preparation of a layoff pool should be done in consultation with the director of instruction in order to avoid harm to instructional programs.

Teachers may be dismissed for reasons related to incompetence, immoral or unprofessional behavior, and insubordination. Tenured teachers who are dismissed must be accorded due process rights, and all teachers are protected against loss of constitutional rights.

Principals anticipating the need to dismiss a teacher should prepare a detailed documentary record of the individual's performance deficiencies. Specific incident memoranda, private notes, observation and evaluation reports, and summary memoranda are all used to establish a record of evidence. An effort must be made to provide remedial assistance to tenured teachers if the deficiency is considered remediable.

SUGGESTED ACTIVITIES

1. Suppose you were composing a code of ethics for teachers. Write three statements describing expected behaviors of teachers to be included in the code and give your reasons for choosing those three statements. Tell what corrective actions would be appropriate for a teacher who violated one of the three expected behaviors.

2. Explain the procedures that must be followed in terminating a tenured (continuing contract) teacher and compare those to the procedures used in terminating a nontenured teacher.

3. Review the actions used for teacher remediation (Exhibit 15.4). Explain under what circumstances goal setting would be the best approach for helping a marginal teacher improve his or her performance. When would instructional input and environmental change be most appropriate?

4. Explain how dismissal under a reduction-in-force policy differs from termination of a teacher for cause.

5. Read Case Study VI and answer the questions.

ONLINE RESOURCES

Montana Code 20-4-110 (data.opi.state.mt.us/bills/mca/20/4/20-4-110.htm)

This section of the Montana Code lists eight reasons for which a teacher may be given a letter of reprimand; it also details the steps involved in suspending or revoking a teacher or other employee.

National Education Association Code of Ethics (http://www.nea.org/code/html).

The Code describes the responsibility of professional educators for students' health, safety, and learning.

South Dakota Code of Professional Ethics for Teachers
(www.state.sd.us/deca/OPA/ethicsteach.htm)

The Code of Ethics developed and administered by the State Professional Teachers Practices and Standards Commission defines teachers' obligations to students, the public, and to the profession.

Wake County (NC) Public School System (www.wcpss.net/policy-files/series/policies/3430-bp.html)

Board Policy No. 3430 is the Wake County Schools' reduction-in-force policy.

REFERENCES

Alexander, K., & Alexander, M. (1985). *American public school law* (2nd ed.). St. Paul, MN: West.

Barton, M. (1984, April). *What you ought to know about termination and due process.* Paper presented at the annual meeting of the National School Boards Association, Houston. (ERIC Document Reproduction Service No. ED 247641).

Bridges, E. (1984). *Managing the incompetent teacher.* Eugene: University of Oregon, ERIC Clearinghouse on Educational Management.

Bridges, E. (1985, January). It's time to get tough with the turkeys. *Principal, 64,* 19–21.

Cambron-McCabe, N. (1983). Procedural due process. In J. Beckham and P. Zirkel (Eds.), *Legal issues in public school employment* (pp. 78–97). Bloomington, IN: *Phi Delta Kappan.*

Caplan, G. (1984). Current issues in reduction-in-force. In T. Jones and D. Semler (Eds.), *School law update . . . preventive school law* (pp. 15–22). Topeka, KS: National Organization on Legal Problems of Education. (ERIC Document Reproduction Service No. ED 244321).

Chicago Board of Education v. *Payne,* 430 N. E.2d 310, 315 (111. App. 1982).

Connick v. *Myers,* 461U.S. 138 (1983).

Dismissal of Certificated Teacher, Ariz. Rev. Stat. ss 5-15-539-E (2000). Available online: www.azleg.state.az.us

DeKalb County School System. (1979). A *policy and administrative procedure for reduction in force.* Decatur, GA: Author. (ERIC Document Reproduction Service No. ED 228690).

Education law (Vol. 2). (1989). New York: Matthew Bender.

Elam, S., Rose, L., & Gallup, A. (1993, October).The 25th annual Phi Delta Kappa/Gallup Poll of the public's attitudes toward the public schools. *Phi Delta Kappan, 75,* 137–152.

Frels, K., & Cooper, T. (1982). A *documentation system for teacher improvement or termination.* Topeka, KS: National Organization on Legal Problems of Education.

Frels, K., & Schneider-Vogel, M. (1986). *The First Amendment and school employees: A practical management guide.* Topeka, KS: National Organization on Legal Problems of Education.

Gallup, A., & Elam, S. (1988). The 20th annual Gallup Poll on the public's attitudes toward the public schools. *Phi Delta Kappan, 70,* 33–46.

Gaylord v. *Board of Education, School District 218,* 794 P.2d 307 (Kan. App. 1990).

Geier v. *Alexander,* 801 F.2d 799 (1986).

Gross, J. (1988). *Teachers on trial: Values, standards, and equity in judging conduct and competence.* Ithaca, NY: ILR Press.

Hill, M., & Wright, J. (1993). *Employee lifestyle and off-duty conduct regulation.* Washington, DC: Bureau of National Affairs.

Hirsch, E. (1998, February). Teacher policy: A summary of current trends. *State Legislative Report, 23* (5), 1–10.

Hubbartt, W. (1998). *The new battle over workplace privacy.* New York: AMACOM.

Johnson, S. (1982, March). *Seniority and schools.* Paper presented at the annual meeting of the American Educational Research Association, New York. (ERIC Document Reproduction Service No. ED 221931).

Johnson, S. (1984). *Teacher unions in schools.* Philadelphia: Temple University Press.

Landauer, W., Spangler, J., & Van Horn, B., Jr. (1983). Good cause basis for dismissal of education employees. In J. Beckham and P. Zirkel (Eds.), *Legal issues in public school employment* (pp. 154–170). Bloomington, IN: *Phi Delta Kappan.*

Lopez, C., & Sperry, D. (1994). *The use of hearing officers in public educator termination actions.* Salt Lake City: University of Utah, Utah Education Policy Center.

McCarthy, M., & Cambron-McCabe, N. (1987). *Public school law: Teachers' and students' rights* (2nd ed.). Boston: Allyn and Bacon.

National Center for Education Statistics. (1993). *Digest of education statistics.* Washington, DC: U.S. Department of Education.

Neill, S., & Custis, J. (1978). *Staff dismissal: Problems and solutions.* Arlington, VA: American Association of School Administrators.

Pickering v. *Board of Education,* 391 U.S. 563 (1968).

Rose, L., & Gallup, A. (2000, September). The 32nd annual Phi Delta Kappa/Gallup Poll of the public's attitudes toward the public schools. *Phi Delta Kappan, 82,* 41–58.

Rose, L. C., & Gallup. A. M. (2003, September). The 35th annual Phi Delta Kappa/Gallup Poll of the public's attitudes toward the public schools. *Phi Delta Kappan, 85,* 41–56.

Schneid, T. (1992). *The Americans with Disabilities Act: A practical guide for managers.* New York: Van Nostrand Reinhold.

Scriven, M. (1980, October). *Teacher personnel policies: Equity, validity, and productivity.* Paper presented at the Midwest Policy Seminar, St. Louis. (ERIC Document Reproduction Service No. ED 206741).

Sovereign, K. (1999). *Personnel law.* Upper Saddle River, NJ: Prentice Hall.

State v. *Project Principle,* 724 S. W.2d 387 (Tex. 1987).

Thorne, J. (1996). *A concise guide to successful employment practices* (2nd ed.). Chicago: CCH, Inc.

Tyler, R. (1985). Conditions for effective learning. In M. Fantini & R. Sinclair (Eds.), *Education in school and nonschool settings* (pp. 203–229). Chicago: University of Chicago Press.

Valente, W. (1980). *Law in the schools.* Columbus, OH: Merrill.

Ware v. *Morgan County School District,* 748 P.2d 1295 (Colo. 1988).

Wake County Public School System. (2002). *Board Policy 3430. Reduction in Force: Certified Employees.* Available online: http://www.wcpss.net/policy-files/series/policies/3430-bp.html

Wright v. *Superintending School Committee,* 331 A.2d 640 (Me. 1976).

Wygant v. *Jackson Board of Education,* 476 U.S. 267 (1986).

York v. *Board of School Commissioners of Mobile County,* 460 So.2d 857 (Ala. 1984).

Zirkel, P., & Bargerstock, C. (1981, January). Reduction-in-force. *A Legal Memorandum,* pp. 1–8.

CASE STUDIES

Case Study I

Dr. Donna Mobley is Director of Human Resources in the district, and although it is only February, she has been asked by the Superintendent, Dr. Howard Brubaker, to begin planning for the next school year. The superintendent has raised two specific issues that he has asked Dr. Mobley to address. He wants her thoughts on how to recruit more minority teachers in view of the fact that enrollment in the district's schools is approaching 40 percent minority and only about 12 percent of the teachers are minorities. Dr. Mobley is aware also that the district has a poor record of retaining minority teachers. Of those hired within the past five years, only about 30 percent remain with the district, compared with a five-year retention rate of more than 50 percent for white teachers.

The second issue about which the superintendent has expressed concern is related to No Child Left Behind. That legislation requires that all teachers employed by the district be "highly qualified." Dr. Brubaker asked two questions about this issue: How many teachers in the district do not meet the definition of highly qualified, and what action should the district take with regard to this problem?

QUESTIONS FOR CASE I

1. If you were helping Dr. Mobley prepare a plan to recruit minority teachers for the district, what specific actions would you recommend be taken?
2. If you were charged with identifying the factors that contribute to the high attrition rate among minority teachers, how would you go about carrying out research to find answers to that question? Be specific in your answer.
3. What is a "highly qualified" teacher, according to NCLB? What actions can the district take to retain teachers who are effective in the classroom but do not currently meet the definition of highly qualified?

Case Study II

The assistant superintendent for instruction, Dr. Helen Adams, met with you, the director of human resources for the district, to discuss the opening of a new elementary school in the district. When the new school opens, approximately 200 students will move from three other elementary schools to the new school, Hinson Elementary. Dr. Adams has asked you to develop a plan for transferring teachers from the schools that are losing students to the new school. She wants to avoid disruption of instructional programs.

One of the schools affected by the opening of the new school is Beacon Elementary, in which student performance has recently improved after a long struggle that included replacing two principals. The current principal brought in several new teachers who helped the school raise its test scores. Dr. Adams is concerned that if some or all of these teachers should choose to leave Beacon, the school will slip back.

The board's policy on teacher transfers reads as follows:

TEACHER TRANSFERS

When teacher transfers within the district are made necessary by enrollment changes or opening or closing of schools, teachers from school(s) that are losing teachers will be given priority for reassignment to a school of their choice, when possible.

QUESTIONS FOR CASE II

1. Dr. Adams has asked you to prepare a plan for reviewing and approving teachers' requests to transfer. Explain what guidelines you would adopt for this process and tell how you propose to review and approve the transfer requests.
2. Will you give the principal of the receiving school the final decision to accept or reject a teacher requesting a transfer to that school? Who should have the final say concerning whether a teacher's request to transfer is approved?
3. How much weight would you give to seniority in weighing teachers' requests to transfer? Would a teacher with more seniority be given preference over one with less seniority? Why or why not?

Case Study III

Dale Sheppard, principal of Midland Elementary School, is in his second year in the job and has asked for a conference with you, Assistant Superintendent for Human Resources, to discuss a problem teacher in his school. The teacher, Ms. Williams, teaches third grade and has been at the school for five years. She received tenure after three years at the school although she had been evaluated by a previous principal as needing improvement in classroom management skills and lesson preparation. Mr. Sheppard reports that she is still deficient in these areas. He also tells you that some parents have complained that they have not been able to schedule conferences with Ms. Williams to discuss their children's progress in her class. He said that one parent told him that Ms. Williams has a second job at a discount store and for that reason was not able to stay after school to meet with the parent. Mr. Sheppard asks for your advice on how to proceed in working with Ms. Williams.

QUESTIONS FOR CASE III

1. Do this teacher's deficiencies justify a decision to dismiss her? Why do you think she may have been granted tenure even though the principal of the school at that time had identified deficiencies in her performance? Since this teacher is tenured, what procedures should be followed if a decision should be made to dismiss her?

2. How would you design a professional growth plan for Ms. Williams to help her with lesson planning and classroom management? Since these two problems are probably related, explain how you would design a plan that would enable the teacher to improve in both areas simultaneously?

3. What specific advice would you give Mr. Sheppard with regard to Ms. Williams' failure to meet with parents to discuss their children's progress in school?

Case Study IV

Three employees have met with you, the director of human resource services for the district, with a request to be paid for overtime work they have performed for the school district over the past three years.

Wanda Martin is cheerleading coach at Township High School, a job that requires her to spend time after school selecting team members and planning and directing team practice sessions. She also attends 8–10 football and basketball games each year. She receives no pay for serving as cheerleading coach but does receive an extra free period during the school day.

David Wallin is coach of the girls' soccer team at Township High, a job that requires extensive work after school during the soccer season. Wallin estimates that team practice requires about three hours each afternoon during the 8-week soccer season, except on afternoons when the team has a game. On those days he puts in about two hours coaching. When the team makes the regional playoffs, as happened this year, Wallin spends additional time preparing for and coaching playoff games. He receives a $500 coaching stipend but contends that is not adequate compensation for the time he spends on this activity.

Sarah Murphy is secretary at Elk River Middle School, and she is responsible for contacting substitute teachers for the school, although that task is not part of her job description. Arranging for substitutes requires Ms. Murphy to spend from 15 minutes to an hour and a half a day on the telephone trying to locate substitute teachers to fill in for teachers who are ill. The job is most demanding during December through February, when many people must miss work because of colds and flu.

QUESTIONS FOR CASE IV

1. How will you respond to the employees who requested overtime pay? Would you give the same answer to each?
2. What provisions of the Fair Labor Standards Act are relevant to the issue of overtime pay? According to this legislation, should these employees have received overtime pay?
3. Some people argue that jobs such as cheerleading coach are "volunteer" activities and that allowing a coach a free period recognizes the coach's dedication but is not meant to be payment for the work. Do you agree with that statement? In your opinion, is the free period adequate compensation for this job?

Case Study V

The teachers' union is pressing for a provision in the new contract that would allow employees who are laid off from their jobs to "bump" employees with less seniority. The present contract is silent on the issue. Since the district's enrollment has dropped each of the last two years, union leaders are concerned that layoffs may be necessary in the near future. So far no layoffs have been needed since normal attrition has taken up the slack.

QUESTIONS FOR CASE V

1. Assume that you are the chair of either the board's bargaining team or the union team. Prepare a statement presenting the board's or the union's position on the proposal. Give reasons why you think the proposal to allow more senior employees to "bump" those with less seniority is or is not a good idea.
2. One of the board's concerns regarding the union's proposal is that it would allow a teacher with more seniority to "bump" a less senior teacher and take a position teaching a subject that he or she has not taught in recent years, if ever. What conditions would you add to the union's proposal in order to prevent this from happening?
3. How would you word the statement that the board wants to include in the union's proposal to give district administrators power to review and approve "bumping," using as a criterion the best interests of the school district?

Case Study VI

It has been discovered that a male teacher who was hired this year to teach fifth grade in an elementary school in the district was arrested two years earlier in another state for driving under the influence. The case was dismissed because the arresting officer left the force before the teacher went on trial. There is no evidence that the teacher has ever been arrested or convicted for any other crime. On the affidavit he completed at the time he was hired, the teacher indicated that that he had never been dismissed from a job for an illegal or moral offense and that he had never been convicted of a crime. He did not answer a question asking if he had been accused of any offenses, including drug or alcohol abuse.

The principal of the school reports that the teacher is well-liked by both students and parents and that his students are making good progress. The principal recommends that the teacher be asked to resubmit the affidavit but that he not be dismissed from his position.

QUESTIONS FOR CASE VI

1. As director of human resources for the district, you have been asked by the superintendent to make a recommendation on this case. Do you concur with the principal's suggestion to retain the teacher? Why or why not?
2. If the teacher had actually been convicted of DUI and that fact had only now come to light, would your recommendation at this time be different? Why would you change (or not change) your recommendation? If you would change it, what would you recommend?
3. The superintendent has asked whether tighter control is needed in conducting background checks of previous arrests and convictions of new hires. What actions would you recommend to improve the process of conducting background checks for new hires?

INDEX